CONNECT FEATURES

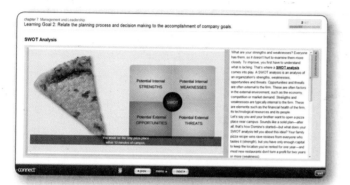

Interactive Presentations

Interactive Presentations cover each chapter's core learning objectives with narrated, animated presentations that pause frequently to check for comprehension. Interactive Presentations harness the full power of technology to appeal to all learning styles. Interactive Presentations are a great way to improve online or hybrid sections, but also extend the learning opportunity for traditional classes, such as in facilitating a "flipped classroom."

Interactive Applications

Interactive Applications offer a variety of automatically graded exercises that require students to **apply** key concepts. Whether the assignment includes a *click and drag*, *video case*, or *decision generator*, these applications provide instant feedback and progress tracking for students and detailed results for the instructor.

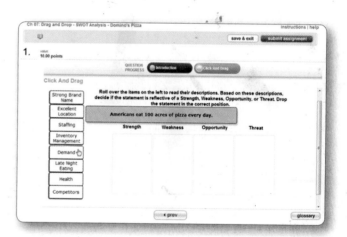

POWERFUL REPORTING

Connect generates comprehensive reports and graphs that provide instructors with an instant view of the performance of individual students, a specific section, or multiple sections. Since all content is mapped to learning objectives, Connect reporting is ideal for accreditation or other administrative documentation.

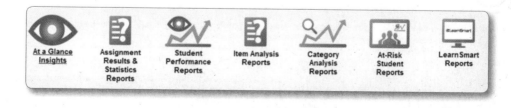

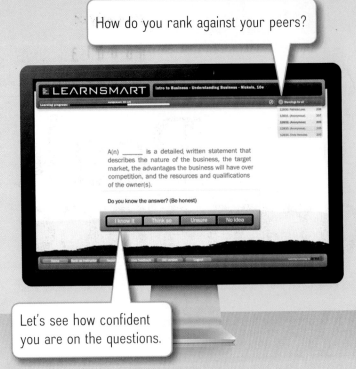

How do you rank against your peers?

Let's see how confident you are on the questions.

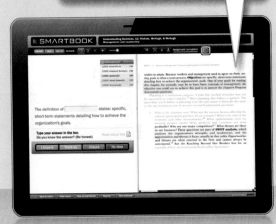

What you know (green) and what you still need to review (yellow), based on your answers.

COMPARE AND CHOOSE WHAT'S RIGHT FOR YOU

	BOOK	LEARNSMART	ASSIGNMENTS	
Mc Graw Hill connect plus+	✓	✓	✓	LearnSmart, assignments, and SmartBook—all in one digital product for maximum savings!
Mc Graw Hill connect plus+ Looseleaf	✓	✓	✓	Pop the pages into your own binder or carry just the pages you need.
Mc Graw Hill connect plus+ Bound Book	✓	✓	✓	The #1 Student Choice!
Mc Graw Hill SMARTBOOK™ Access Code	✓	✓		The first and only book that adapts to you!
Mc Graw Hill LEARNSMART™ ADVANTAGE Access Code		✓		The smartest way to get from a B to an A.
CourseSmart eBook	✓			Save some green and some trees!
Mc Graw Hill Education create™	✓	✓	✓	Check with your instructor about a custom option for your course.

> Buy directly from the source at www.ShopMcGraw-Hill.com.

Peak Performance

ninth edition **SUCCESS IN COLLEGE AND BEYOND**

Sharon K. Ferrett, Ph.D.
Humboldt State University

McGraw Hill Education

Dedication

To the memory of my parents, Albert Lawrence Ferrett and Velma Mary Hollenbeck Ferrett, for setting the highest standards and their seamless expression of love.

To my husband, Sam, and my daughters, Jennifer Katherine and Sarah Angela, and my grandchildren, Emily and Caden, for making it all worthwhile.

—Sharon K. Ferrett

PEAK PERFORMANCE: SUCCESS IN COLLEGE AND BEYOND, NINTH EDITION
Published by McGraw-Hill Education, 2 Penn Plaza, New York, NY 10121. Copyright © 2015 by McGraw-Hill Education. All rights reserved. Printed in the United States of America. Previous editions © 2012, 2010, and 2008. No part of this publication may be reproduced or distributed in any form or by any means, or stored in a database or retrieval system, without the prior written consent of McGraw-Hill Education, including, but not limited to, in any network or other electronic storage or transmission, or broadcast for distance learning.

Some ancillaries, including electronic and print components, may not be available to customers outside the United States.

This book is printed on acid-free paper.

1 2 3 4 5 6 7 8 9 0 RMN/RMN 1 0 9 8 7 6 5 4

ISBN 978-0-07-352248-7 (student edition)
MHID 0-07-352248-1 (student edition)

ISBN 978-1-259-17407-0 (annotated instructor's edition)
MHID 1-259-17407-7 (annotated instructor's edition)

Senior Vice President, Products & Markets: *Kurt L. Strand*
Vice President, Content Production & Technology Services: *Kimberly Meriwether David*
Director: *Scott Davidson*
Executive Director of Development: *Ann Torbert*
Development Editor: *Alaina Tucker*
Digital Development Editor II: *Kevin White*
Executive Marketing Manager: *Keari Green*
Marketing Specialist: *Lindsay Pawlik*

Director, Content Production: *Terri Schiesl*
Content Project Manager: *Kristin Bradley*
Buyer: *Nicole Baumgartner*
Design: *Matthew Baldwin*
Cover Image: © *Getty Images/ Philip and Karen Smith*
Content Licensing Specialist: *Brenda Rolwes*
Typeface: *11/14 Minion*
Compositor: *Laserwords Private Limited*
Printer: *R. R. Donnelley*

All credits appearing on page or at the end of the book are considered to be an extension of the copyright page.

The Internet addresses listed in the text were accurate at the time of publication. The inclusion of a website does not indicate an endorsement by the authors or McGraw-Hill Education, and McGraw-Hill Education does not guarantee the accuracy of the information presented at these sites.

www.mhhe.com

Brief Table of Contents

v

Table of Contents

> **PART TWO**
> # Basic Skills and Strategies

5   Listen and Take Effective Notes   147

6   Actively Read   175

7 Improve Your Memory Skills 213

8 Excel at Taking Tests 241

9 Express Yourself in Writing and Speech **271**

PART THREE
Application

10 Become a Critical Thinker and Creative Problem Solver **301**

11 Create a Healthy Mind, Body, and Spirit 335

12 Build Supportive and Diverse Relationships 371

The 9th Edition

Peak Performance: Success in College and Beyond continues to lead the way in showing students how to:

- **Learn how they learn best—and incorporate new ways to learn**
- **Maximize their available resources and seek out new opportunities**
- **Relate what they are exploring now to future success on the job**
- **Strive to become the best individuals they can be**

The ninth edition of Peak Performance provides students with common sense strategies for excelling in school and life. From the unique **Take 3** feature, which encourages making smart use of even small segments of time, to tips on "How to Say No" to avoid the stress of stretching your time too thin, to "Getting the Most Out of a Class Lecture" that helps students focus during a variety of challenging lecture situations, *Peak Performance* delivers the essential tools for managing time and resources. Students are provided with ample opportunities to apply and enhance critical thinking skills through **Think Fast** case studies, in-text questions and activities, and a wide variety of end-of-chapter **Worksheets**.

New Features

Along with key strategies and skills related to both college and career success, the ninth edition also includes a wealth of new material in the following areas of special importance to today's college student:

- *Technology:* From selfies to respecting others' online privacy, this edition is updated to reflect the latest digital tools and social media. TWW (Texting While Walking), getting the most out of your smartphone, taking online courses, using apps and tablets, rising cell phone thefts, and documenting digital sources are just a few of the topics discussed in this edition.

- *Visual Learning:* Many of today's traditional-aged students have had the opportunity to combine all ways of learning, but especially visual aspects. This new edition includes a number of new illustrations that present both new and existing material in a visual format that is more effective in reinforcing core content and skills presented in the text.

- *Hot topics, new guidelines and legislation, and updated statistics:* A hallmark of *Peak Performance* is the inclusion of the latest topics college students are interested in and need to be aware of. Some critical new topics include the mounting student loan debt—which is second only to housing debt—recent legislation and descriptions of various aid options, and a visual activity walking the reader through the reality of paying back student loans. Other critical topics include the prevalence of HPV and available vaccinations; texting and distracted driving injuries; changes in credit and debit card use; current alcohol, smoking, and drug (legal and illegal) use and abuse facts; and the latest MyPlate and national recommendations, for optimal diet and physical activity.

Sampling of New and Revised Topics

CHAPTER 1: BE A LIFELONG LEARNER

- New illustration highlights the characteristics of Peak Performers.
- Revised mission statement questions guide the reader in developing a focused and personal statement of lifelong goals.
- PEN 1.4: Multiple Intelligences includes new questions connecting to the student's mission statement.
- The Four-Temperament Profile includes new major and career opportunities.
- Current coursework is presented in the Adult Learning Cycle.
- Updated profile on Blake Mycoskie, author of *Start Something That Matters*, includes TOMS' venture into eyewear and World Sight Day.

CHAPTER 2: EXPAND YOUR EMOTIONAL INTELLIGENCE

- Revised Figure 2.1 personalizes responsibilities.
- New illustration highlights the differences between a positive and negative attitude.
- Motivational strategies mention the importance of commitment.
- New Figure 2.4 indicates annual earnings and employment opportunities based on education.
- New image of Boston Marathon bombings survivor relays the connection between resilience and survivors of recent catastrophic events.
- "Hardiness" is included in the discussion on resilience.

CHAPTER 3: MANAGE YOUR TIME

- PEN 3.3: Looking Ahead: Your Goals reflects new mission statement questions from Chapter 1.
- Revised Figure 3.1 more concisely shows how to use a planner.

- Updated Figure 3.2: Smartphone 101 shows how to use a smartphone to help manage time.
- New illustration questions "Am I a Procrastinator?"
- Peak Progress 3.4 Online Learning reflects current procedures.

CHAPTER 4: MAXIMIZE YOUR RESOURCES

- New illustration provides questions to ask your academic advisor.
- Health Center discussion includes a note about health insurance and changing health care laws.
- New image and discussion of TWW (Texting While Walking) and cell phone safety warn the reader of injury and theft concerns.
- Peak Progress 4.2: Staying Safe includes "call a ride" services.
- The discussion of school catalog and online resources has been updated.
- New illustration gives tips for commuting students.
- Latest statistics on financial debt, including student loans, are provided.
- A completely rewritten discussion of Financial Assistance, FAFSA, and new Figure 4.1: Student Loan Payback focus on not only securing aid but also preparing to pay off student loan debt.
- Table and terminology related to financial aid sources have been updated.
- Latest statistics on credit card use, including results of the 2009 Credit Card Responsibility and Disclosure Act, are provided.
- Revised Figure 4.2: The Power of Compound Interest highlights the importance of long-term saving.
- Mention of increased debit card use and watching your balance is included.
- New Peak Performer Profile on Eric Greitens and The Mission Continues discusses issues and resources related to military veterans and their families.

CHAPTER 5: LISTEN AND TAKE EFFECTIVE NOTES

- Terminology reflects current digital devices.
- Note-taking samples were revised for clarity.

CHAPTER 6: ACTIVELY READ

- New illustration highlights essential reading tasks.
- Definition of "inferences" added.
- Peak Progress 6.2: Reading for Different Courses includes how to read trade and professional preparation books.
- Peak Progress 6.5: Digital Material reflects the latest technology, including use of tablets, e-books, and social media sites.
- Mention of avoiding use of inappropriate expletives is added to vocabulary discussion.
- Updated Peak Progress 6.6: Look It Up! Using a Dictionary shows how to navigate both print and online dictionaries.
- New illustration provides tips on accurately completing forms.

CHAPTER 7: IMPROVE YOUR MEMORY SKILLS

- Revised Peak Progress 7.2: Short-Term and Long-Term Memory and Figure 7.1 relate the latest technology to personal memory.
- New illustration highlights how to use note cards effectively.
- New cartoon jokingly reinforces how to not remember names.
- New illustration queries the reader on his or her commitment to improving memory by providing strategies.

CHAPTER 8: EXCEL AT TAKING TESTS

- Revised illustration highlights key test-taking skills.
- New Figure 8.2: Reasons for Incorrect Test Answers gives examples of common problems.
- The importance of checking word count parameters when completing essay tests is mentioned.
- The dangers of abusing Adderall (ADHD medications) for studying and test preparation is discussed.

CHAPTER 9: EXPRESS YOURSELF IN WRITING AND SPEECH

- Revised discussion of key elements to write down when taking notes, either digitally or on note cards, uses research example of caffeine addiction and highly caffeinated drinks to show how to record information from various sources.
- New bullet point reinforces adhering to word count, paragraph, or page parameters when writing papers.
- New Figure 9.3: Overcoming Writer's Block offers tips on overcoming writer's block.
- Peak Progress 9.4: Writing Citations includes current digital sources.
- Discussion on using the library and popular sources for historical speeches has been updated.

CHAPTER 10: BECOME A CRITICAL THINKER AND CREATIVE PROBLEM SOLVER

- New Figure 10.2: Critical Thinking Qualities highlights the attributes of a critical thinker.
- New image emphasizes that good ideas can happen anywhere.

CHAPTER 11: CREATE A HEALTHY MIND, BODY, AND SPIRIT

- Revised Figure 11.1: Cancer Caution Signs lists the most common signs of cancer.
- New discussion on the importance of fiber offers good dietary sources.
- New discussion of "diet foods" includes 100-calorie packs and the latest research on diet soft drinks.
- New discussion and illustration of USDA MyPlate food guide plan mentions SuperTracker online diet analysis resource.
- New DASH diet plan combats hypertension.
- Revised physical activity section includes the latest national guidelines.
- New illustration lists signs of burnout from stress.
- New illustration describes how to practice deep relaxation.
- Latest statistics on alcohol use and abuse and smoking are listed.
- Discussion of prescription and OTC abuse includes mention of Adderall.
- New image of last text by college student Alexander Heit before fatally crashing his car reinforces the hazards of texting while driving.

- Data on anxiety disorders and increase in mental health drug use is included.
- New illustration lists common symptoms of depression.
- New illustration lists warning signs of suicide.
- New discussion of human papillomavirus (HPV) provides vaccination information.
- Updated statistics on AIDS and HIV are included.

CHAPTER 12: BUILD SUPPORTIVE AND DIVERSE RELATIONSHIPS

- New photo highlights the importance of body language.
- New illustration offers tips on becoming more assertive.
- The importance of forgiveness appears in the conflict discussion.
- Respecting others' privacy by not posting photos online without permission is mentioned.
- Revised Figure 12.2: Understanding the Meaning explains stereotypes, prejudice, and discrimination.
- New illustration looks at the makeup of the Earth's population.
- Online "oversharing" is the topic of a new Tech for Success tip.

CHAPTER 13: DEVELOP POSITIVE HABITS

- Revised Figure 13.2: Peak Habits lists the 10 habits of a Peak Performer.
- New photo asks if you are a half-glass-empty or half-glass-full person.
- Revised Figure 13.3: Courage to Overcome highlights examples of great people who overcame tremendous obstacles.
- Reformatted Career Development Portfolio: Planning for Your Career provides a more comprehensive guide.

CHAPTER 14: EXPLORE MAJORS AND CAREERS

- "Interests" section offers new career options.
- Revised and reorganized discussion of portfolio development also reflects digital portfolios.
- Visual examples of portfolio elements are updated throughout the chapter.
- Revised Figure 14.3: Sample Introduction Page better reflects personal goals.

- Revised Figure 14.5: Sample Mission Statement includes more specific goals.
- Scanning and creating pdfs of recommendation letters is mentioned.
- Annotating the bibliography with personal insights is suggested.
- New photo highlights the importance of shaking hands in an interview.
- Turning off digital devices during interviews is discussed.
- Discussion of the interview thank-you reflects e-mail follow-up.
- PEN 14.4: Assessment Is Lifelong is revised to match earlier discussion of skills and competencies and provide more opportunity for reflection.

Ancillaries

Get Connect + Student Success. Get Results.

CONNECT PLUS+

McGraw-Hill Connect Plus+ Student Success is a digital teaching and learning environment that gives students the means to better connect with their coursework, with their instructors, and with the important concepts that they will need to know for success now and in the future. With Connect Student Success, instructors can deliver assignments, quizzes and tests easily online. Students can practice important skills at their own pace and on their own schedule.

LEARNSMART

LearnSmart maximizes productivity and efficiency in learning by identifying the most important learning objectives for each student to master at a given point in time. LearnSmart also knows when students are likely to forget specific information and it brings that content back so students can advance the knowledge from their short-term to long-term memory. Data driven reports highlight the concepts individual students—or the entire class are struggling with. LearnSmart is proven to improve academic performance—including higher retention rates and better grades.

SMARTBOOK

SmartBook is the first and only adaptive reading experience. Powered by LearnSmart's proven adaptive technology, SmartBook identifies and highlights the most important learning objectives for each student to master at a given point in time. SmartBook also knows when students are likely to forget specific information and it brings that content back so students can advance the knowledge from their short-term to long-term memory. Data driven reports highlight the concepts individual students - or the entire class are struggling with.

ANNOTATED INSTRUCTOR'S EDITION

(978-1-25917407-1) The AIE contains the full text of the student edition of the text, along with instructional strategies that reinforce and enhance the core concepts. Notes and tips in the margin provide topics for discussion, teaching tips for hands-on and group activities, and suggestions for further reading.

INSTRUCTOR RESOURCES (WWW.MHHE.COM/FERRETT9E)

Located on the Online Learning Center, these extensive resources include chapter goals and outlines, teaching tips, additional activities, and essay exercises. Also included are unique resource guides that give instructors and administrators the tools to retain students and maximize the success of the course, using topics and principles that last a lifetime. Resources include:

- Instructor Manual
- Retention Kit, containing:
  - Facilitator's Guide
  - Tools for Time Management
  - Establishing Peer Support Groups
  - Developing a Career Portfolio
  - Involving the Faculty Strategy
  - Capitalizing on Your School's Graduates
- Course Planning Guide
- Sample Syllabi
- PowerPoints
- Testbank—includes matching, multiple choice, true/false, and short answer questions

CUSTOMIZE YOUR TEXT

Peak Performance can be customized to suit your needs. The text can be abbreviated for shorter courses and can be expanded to include school schedules, campus maps, additional essays, activities, or exercises, along with other materials specific to your curriculum or situation. However you want to customize, we can make it happen, easily. McGraw-Hill can deliver a book that perfectly meets your needs. Contact your McGraw-Hill sales representative for more information or:

United States: 1-800-338-3987

Canada: 1-866-270-5118

E-mail: FYE@mcgraw-hill.com

Thank You

We would like to thank the many instructors whose insightful comments and suggestions provided us with inspiration and the ideas that were incorporated into this new edition:

Reviews

Barbara Blackstone	University of Maine at Presque Isle
Dudley Chancey	Oklahoma Christian University
Norman Crumpacker	Mount Olive College
Laura Ringer	Newberry College
Carol Decker	Tennessee Wesleyan College
Kina Lara	San Jacinto College South
Tanya Stanley	San Jacinto College
Belinda Manard	Kent State University at Stark
Sherri Singer	Alamance Community College
Deborah Olson-Dean	North Central Michigan College
Gina Garber	Austin Peay State University
Richard Fabri	Husson University
Becky Samberg	Housatonic Community College
Curtis Sandberg	Berea College
Nicole Griffith-Green	Ashland Community & Technical College
Dr. Kristi Snuggs	Edgecombe Community College
Carolyn Camfield	Oklahoma Panhandle State University
Tara Cosco	Glenville State College
Carol Martinson	Polk State
Charity Ikerd Travis	Somerset Community College
Ruth Hoffman	University of Illinois
Richard Garnett	Marshall University
Miriam Moore	Lord Fairfax Community College
Denise Baldwin	University of Jamestown
Julie Hunt	Belmont University
Amy Hassenpflug	Liberty University
Dean Bortz	Columbus State Community College
Car Kenner	St. Cloud State University
Tora Johnson	University of Maine at Machias
Jeff Rankinen	Pennsylvania College of Technology
Julie Bennety	Central Methodist University

Acknowledgements

Patricia White	Danville Community College
Nikita Anderson	University of Baltimore
Skip Carey	Monmouth University
Michael Dixon	Angelo State
Elizabeth S. Kennedy	Florida Atlantic University
Christopher Thompson	Loyola University Maryland
Linda Kardos	Georgian Court University
Dianne Aitken	Schoolcraft College
Amanda Mosley	York Technical College
Laura J. Helbig	Mineral Area College
Jane Johnson	Central Michigan University
Cora Dzubak, Ph.D.	Penn State York
Andrew Webster	Belmont University
Darin LaMar Baskin	Houston Community College
Linda B. Wright	Western Piedmont Community College
Shelly Ratliff	Glenville State College
Ann C. Hall	Ohio Dominican University
Kaye Young	Jamestown Community College
Joseph Hayes	Southern Union State Community College
Yvonne M. Mitkos	Southern Illinois university Edwardsville
Linda Girouard	Brescia University
Teresa Houston	East Central Community College
Debra Starcher Johnson	Glenville State College
Sandra Soto-Caban	Muskingum University
Liz Moseley	Cleveland State Community College
Christopher Tripler	Endicott College
Rachel Hoover	Frostburg State University
Kay Cobb	University of Arkansas at Cossatot
Jeff Bolles	University of North Carolina at Pembroke
Amanda Bond	Georgia Military College
Catherine Heath	Victoria College
Patrick Peyer	Rock Valley College
Andrea Conway	Houstonic Community College
Alisa Agozzino	Ohio Northern University
Joseph Kornoski	Montgomery County Community College
Claudia Bryan	Wallace Community College
Virginia Watkins	Texas A&M International University
Kim Childress	Eastern New Mexico University—Roswell
Mark Smith	Temple College
Eva Menefee	Lansing Community College
Ross Bandics	Northampton Community College
Chad Brooks	Austin Peay State University
Conchita C. Hickey	Texas A&M International University
Billie Anderson	Tyler Junior College
Kay Adkins	Ozarka College
Becky Osborne	Parkland College
Kathie L. Wentworth, M.Ed.	Trine University
Shawndus Gregory	Phillips Community College
Susan Underwood	Arkansas Tech University
Jalika Rivera Waugh, Ph.D	Saint Leo University
Ryck Hale	Iowa Lakes Community College
Melanie Marine	University of Wisconsin—Oshkosh
Leah Lidbury	University of Wisconsin—Oshkosh
Mike Wood	Missouri State University
Carla Garrett	San Jacinto College
Nancy Sleger	Middlesex Community College
Tonya Greene	Wake Technical Community College
Dr. Elisah B. Lewis	University of Miami School of Business
Robyn Linde	Rhode Island College
Diane Taylor	Tarleton State University
Cheyanne Lewis	Blue Ridge Community and Technical College
Megan Osterbur	Xavier University of Louisiana
James Wallace	Indiana University Northwest
Maria LeBaron	Randolph Community College
Keith Ramsdell	Lourdes University
Kelly Moor	Idaho State University
Kathryn Jarvis	Auburn University
Joel Krochalk	Lake Superior College
Karen Smith	East Carolina University
Chandra Massner	University of Pikeville
Mike Hoffshire	University Of New Orleans
Billy Wesson	Jackson State Community College
Liza Brenner	Glenville State College
Dr. Priscilla T. Robinson	Hinds Community College-UT
Kristi Concannon	King's College
Jodi P. Coffman	Santa Ana College
Judith Lynch	Kansas State University
Daniel Rodriguez	Palo Alto College
Liese A. Hull	University of Michigan
Kim Thomas	Polk State College
Virginia B. Sparks	Edgecombe Community College
Terry Bridger	Prince George's Community College

Dewayne Dickens	Tulsa Community College
Michelle Yager	Western Illinois University
Shane Y. Williamson	Lindenwood University
Michael Starkey	University of Rhode Island
J. Lesko-Bishop	Rose State College
Jon Meeuwenberg	Muskegon Community College
Melissa Johnson	Hazard Community & Technical College
C. Miskovich	Randolph Community College
Mary Carstens	Wayne State College
Grace Palculict	South Arkansas Community College
Bev Greenfeig	University of Maryland
Nancy Michael	Columbia College Chicago
Erika Deiters	Moraine Valley Community College
Ileka Leaks	Limestone College
Christopher Fields	Franklin University
Brandi Baros	Pennsylvania State University—Shenango
Ken Weese	El Paso Community College
Linda Wheeler	Jackson State University
Sharon C. Melton	Hinds Community College
Chris Kazanjian	El Paso Community College
Kim Wagemester	Kirkwood Community College
Nari Kovalski	Atlantic Cape Community College
Gretchen Starks-Martin	College of St. Benedict & St. Cloud State University
Stephen Coates-White	South Seattle Comunity College
Cathy Hall	Indiana University Northwest
Susam Epps	East Tennessee State University
F. Janelle Hannah-Jefferson	Jackson State University
Cecile Arquette	Bradley University
Nancy Lilly	Central Alabama Community College
David Roos	Dixie State University
William McCormick	University of Central Oklahoma
Sue Maxam	Pace University
Tracy Ethridge	Tri-County Technical College
Dr. Reyes Ortega	Sierra College
Susan Sies	Carroll Community College
Leigh Smith	Lamar Institute of Technology
Mary Silva	Modesto Junior College
Donna Wood	Holmes Community College
Gretchen Haskett	Newberry College
Debbi Farrelly	El Paso Community College
Miriam Foll	Florida State College at Jacksonville
Paul DeLaLuz	Lee University
Mirjana Brockett	Georgia Institute of Technology
Mari Miller Burns	Iowa Lakes Community College
David Hall	Clarendon College
Kimberly Britt	Horry Georgetown Technical College
Buck Tilton	Central Wyoming College
Dr. Roxie A. James	Kean University
Ashleigh Lewis	Tyler Junior College
Kathleen Hoffman	Anoka Ramsey Community College—Cambridge Campus
J. Andrew Monahan	Suffolk County Community College
Shane Armstrong	Marymount California University
LuAnn Walton	San Juan College
Katrina Daytner	Western Illinois University
Adrian Rodriguez	Portland Community College
Kirsten Miller	Columbia College
Geneva Baxter	Spelman College
Sheer Ash	San Jacinto College
Sara Henson	Central Oregon Community College
Darla Rocha	San Jacinto College
Debra Ellerbrook	Concordia University Wisconsin
Adolfo Nava	El Paso Community College
Anthony Westphal	Shasta College
Barbara J. Masten	Lourdes University
Shannon Maude	Blue Mountain Community College
Barbara J. Masten	Lourdes University
Mary Ann Ray	Temple College
Kimberly Dasch-Yee	Holy Family University
David Trimble	El Paso Community College
Susan Selman	Patrick Henry Community College
Nicki Michalski	Lamar University
Donna Hanley	Kentucky Wesleyan College
Stephen Van Horn	Muskingum University
Beverly Hixon	Houston Community College
Bruce A. Wehler	Pennsylvania College of Technology
Hilary Billman	Northern Michigan University
Jonathan Villers	Alderson Broaddus University
Lynn M. Fowler	Cosumnes River College
Rico Gazal	Glenville State College
Marcia Laskey	Cardinal Stritch University
Cheryl Spector	California State University, Northridge
Christopher Lau	Hutchinson Community College
Gail Malone	South Plains College
Elias Dominguez	Fullerton College
Vincent Fitzgerald	Notre Dame de Namur University
Jayne Nightingale	Rhode Island College
Annette Sisson	Belmont University

Kathie Erdman Becker	South Dakota State University
Kendra Hill	South Dakota State University
Jennifer Parrack-Rogers	Blue Ridge Community College
Virginia Wade, Ed.D.	Marymount Calfornia Univeristy
Dixie Elise Hickman	American InterContinental University
Gail Tudor	Husson University
Wayne Smith	Community Colleges of Spokane
R. Lee Carter	William Peace University
Pam Nussbaumer	Anne Arundel Community College
Eric Belokon	Miami-Dade College
Karen O'Donnell	Finger Lakes Community College
Jean Raniseski, Ph.D.	Alvin Community College
Sandra Berryhill	Triton College
John Paul Manriquez	El Paso Community College
Pamela Bilton Beard	Houston Community College—Southwest
Janet Florez	Cuesta College
Holly Seirup	Hofstra University
Susan Wilson	Portland Community College
James K. Goode	Austin Peay State University
Walter Tucker	Miami Dade College—North Campus
Andrea Smith	Florida Gateway College
Aubrey Moncrieffe Jr.	Housatonic Community College
Susan Bossa	Quincy College
Kathy Daily	Tulsa Community College Southeast Campus
Anita Leibowitz	Suffolk County Community College
Dr. Steve Holcombe	North Greenville University
Stephanie Huskey	Tennessee Wesleyan College
Sarah Sherrill	West Kentucky Community & Technical College
Carol Billing	College of Western Idaho
Heather Mayernik	Macomb Community College
Joanna Reed	Sussex County Community College
Robert Melendez	Irvine Valley College
Jennifer Garcia	Saint Leo University
Jennifer Treadway	Blue Ridge Community College
Marian Teachey	South Piedmont Community College
Cindy Sledge	San Jacinto College - South
Lourdes Rassi, Ph.D	Miami-Dade College
Dr. Arlene Trolman	Adelphi University
Keri Keckley	Crowder College
Desiree Fields-Jobling	Brookline College
Agostine Trevino	Temple College

MaryJo Slater	Community College of Beaver County
Beth Shanholtzer	Lord Fairfax Community College
Cheryl Ziehl	Cuesta College
David Housel	Houston Community College
Sandra Sego	American International College
Joseph Selvaggio	Three Rivers Community College
Michael Abernethy	Indiana University Southeast
Jean Buckley-Lockhart	LaGuardia Community College
Jane M. McGinn, Ph. D	Southern Connecticut State University
Christine M ViPond	Lord Fairfax Community College
Ami Massengill	Nashville State Community College - Cookeville Campus
Kevin Ploeger	University of Cincinnati
Keith Bunting	Randolph Community College
Laura Skinner	Wayne Community College
Mary Lee Vance	Purdue University Calumet
Dr. Hanadi Saleh	Miami-Dade College
Judith Shultz	Fond du Lac Tribal and Community College
Bertha Barraza	Mt. San Jacinto Community College
Patricia Twaddle M.Ed.	Moberly Area Community College
Misty Engelbrecht	Rose State College
Scott Empric	Housatonic Community College
Tim Littell	Wright State University
Kerry Fitts	Delgado Community College
Judith Isonhood	Hinds Community College
Michael Kuryla	State University of New York—Broome
Bryan Barker	Western Illinois University
Jerry Riehl	University of Tennessee
Eunice Walker	Southern Arkansas University
Therese M. Crary	Highland Community College
Pauline Clark	West Valley College
Christopher Old	Sierra College
Lisa Marie Kerr	Auburn University at Montgomery
Remona Hammonds	Miami-Dade College West Campus
Sarah Strout	Dominican College

Also, I would like to gratefully acknowledge the contributions of the McGraw-Hill editorial staff—specifically, Vicki Malinee, for her considerable effort, suggestions, ideas, and insights.

—Sharon K. Ferrett

SCANS: Secretary's Commission on Achieving Necessary Skills

Competency Chart

Competencies and Foundations	Peak Performance Chapters That Address SCANS Competencies
Resources: Identifies, Organizes, Plans, and Allocates Resources	
• Managing time	Chapter 3, Take 3
• Managing money	Chapter 4
• Managing space	Chapters 3, 13
• Managing people	Chapters 2, 12
• Managing materials	Chapters 3, 4, 5, 6, 9
• Managing facilities	Chapters 4, 5, 9, 11
Information: Acquires and Uses Information	
• Acquiring information	Chapters 4, 5, 6, 9
• Evaluating information	Chapters 7, 8, 9
• Organizing and maintaining information	Chapters 3, 4, 7, 8, 9, 10, Take 3
• Using computer to process	Chapters 4, 9
Systems: Understands Complex Interrelationships	
• Understanding systems	All chapters
• Designing systems	Chapters 5, 6
• Monitoring systems	Chapters 3, 5, 6, 11
• Correcting systems	Chapters 3, 4, 5, 10
Interpersonal Skills: Works with Others	
• Positive attitudes	Chapters 2, 12, 13
• Self-control	Chapters 2, 12, 13
• Goal setting	Chapters 1, 2, 3
• Teamwork	Chapters 2, 12, 13
• Responsibility	Chapters 2, 12, 13
• Stress management	Chapter 11
Technology: Works with a Variety of Technologies	
• Selecting technology	Chapters 9, 14, Tech for Success
• Applying technology	Chapters 4, 9, 14, Tech for Success
• Maintaining technology	Chapters 9, 14
• Solving problems	Chapters 9, 10
• Staying current in technology	Chapters 4, 9, 14

Source: United States Department of Labor, 1992.

SCANS: Secretary's Commission on Achieving Necessary Skills *(concluded)*

Competencies and Foundations	Peak Performance Chapters That Address SCANS Competencies
Personal Qualities	
• Responsibility, character, integrity, positive habits, self-management, self-esteem, sociability	Chapters 2, 12, 13
Basic Skills	
• Reading—locates, understands, and interprets written information in prose and in documents, such as manuals, graphs, and schedules	Chapters 6, 9
• Writing—communicates thoughts, ideas, information, and messages in writing and creates documents, such as letters, directions, manuals, reports, graphs, and flowcharts	Chapter 9
• Arithmetic/mathematics—performs basic computations and approaches practical problems by choosing appropriately from a variety of mathematical techniques	Chapter 10
• Listening—receives, attends to, interprets, and responds to verbal messages and other cues	Chapters 5, 12
Thinking Skills	
• Creative thinking—generates new ideas	Chapter 10, Personal Evaluation Notebooks, Think Fast
• Decision making—specifies goals and constraints, generates alternatives, considers risks, and evaluates and chooses best alternative	Chapter 10, Case Study, Personal Evaluation Notebooks, Think Fast
• Listening—receives, attends to, interprets, and responds to verbal messages and other cues	Chapters 5, 12
• Seeing things in the mind's eye—organizes and processes symbols, pictures, graphs, objects, and other information	All chapters, with a strong emphasis in Chapter 10
• Knowing how to learn—uses efficient learning techniques to acquire and apply new knowledge and skills	Chapter 1
• Reasoning—discovers a rule or principle underlying the relationship between two or more objects and applies it when solving a problem	Chapter 10

Dear Student

Many of my students have told me I'm like a cheerleader, rooting them on to success. I know they all have what it takes to succeed, even when they have their own doubts. Why? Because I've been there, too. As I stepped onto the beautiful University of Michigan campus, I questioned whether I belonged. My small farming community seemed far away and I felt out of place. Many students had come from fancy prep schools and wealthy families. I had gone to a one-room schoolhouse and then to a tiny high school in the thumb of Michigan. I was putting myself through college with part-time jobs and baby-sitting in exchange for room and board. *Would I be able to make it here?*

Even though I was afraid, I was confident and determined. My experiences as a farm kid made me a hard worker, and I knew that no amount of effort was too great to achieve the goal of graduating from college. I was incredibly grateful for the opportunity to go to college, and I wanted to make my parents proud because they never had the choices that I had. I visualized myself as a college graduate and held that image firmly in my mind when I was discouraged.

After I graduated with honors, I earned a teaching credential and taught for a year in the same one-room schoolhouse that I (and my father) attended. I saved enough money to travel to Europe and return to school to earn a master's degree and Ph.D. I would have never dreamed of being a college professor and an administrator when I was in high school, but, at only 24 years old, I accepted a dean position at Delta College, a large community college in Michigan. A few years later, I moved to California as Dean of Continuing Education at Humboldt State University. As a professor and an academic advisor, I developed a new program in student success. That project launched this book and became my life's work.

Throughout this book, we talk about the attributes of a "peak performer" and attempt to define success—in school, career, and life. However, in the end, *you* have to define success for yourself. Only you can determine what drives you, what makes you happy, and what will become your own life's work.

If I could give you only three pieces of advice as you journey to find your passion in life, they would be

1. **Keep it simple.** We want to do and be everything for everyone. However, success comes from a clear focus on what you value most. Don't complicate your life with unnecessary distractions, and continually take small steps to get where you want to be.

2. **Realize you are smarter than you think.** Intelligence is not defined by a score on a test but rather by how you use all your experiences, abilities, resources, and opportunities to improve your situation and find what fulfills you. Don't ever believe anyone who says you can't accomplish something for lack of skill, talent, or lot in life. You can.

3. **Be your own best friend.** Too often we dwell on the inconveniences in life rather than being grateful for the fortunes and opportunities we do have. Whenever you find yourself creating excuses, blaming others, or feeling down or hopeless, be your own cheerleader and resolve that you can—and will—succeed.

And when you need a little help developing your own "cheer" along the way, please drop me an e-mail at **sharonferrett@gmail.com.** *I believe in you!*

—**Sharon K. Ferrett**

Getting Started

Congratulations! You are about to start or restart an amazing journey of opportunity, growth, and adventure. You may be at this point in your life for a number of reasons: You may be furthering your education right after high school; you may be focusing on a specific career or trade and want to acquire the appropriate skills or certification; or you may be returning to school after years in the workforce, needing additional skills or just looking for a change.

Whatever your reasons, this is an opportunity for you to learn new things, meet new people, acquire new skills, and better equip yourself both professionally and personally for the years ahead. This book is designed to get you started on that journey by helping you (1) learn how you learn best—and incorporate new ways to learn; (2) maximize available resources and seek out new opportunities; (3) relate what you are exploring now to future success on the job; and (4) strive to become the best person you can be.

Now that you have your book in hand, you are ready to get started. Or are you really ready? What else should you be aware of at this point? You may have already attended a basic orientation session where you learned about school and community resources and program requirements. Going through orientation, meeting with your advisor, and reviewing your catalog will help you get oriented. Additionally, this quick review is designed to outline the essentials that you will want to know, so that you not only survive but also make your first year a

success. **Peak Progress 1** provides a handy checklist for the essential tasks you need to consider and accomplish the first week of school. Add to this list any tasks that are unique to your situation or school.

Peak Progress

Tasks to Accomplish the First Week of School

- Attend orientation and meet with an advisor. Ask questions and determine available resources. (See **Peak Progress 2** for questions to ask.)
- Register and pay fees on time.
- Set up an e-mail account and check it daily.
- Check deadlines and procedures. *Never* just quit going to class.
- Buy books and keep receipts. Establish a record-keeping system.
- Find out the location of classrooms, parking, and school resources.

- Know expectations and requirements. Get a syllabus for each class. E-mail instructors for clarification.
- Create an organized study area. Post instructors' names, office locations, and hours, as well as important deadlines.
- Form study teams and exchange e-mails and phone numbers. Get to know instructors and other students.
- Explore resources, such as the library, learning skills center, health center, and advising center.
- Go to all classes on time and sit in the front row.

Why Are You Here?

College success begins with determining your goals and mapping out a plan. A good place to start is to reflect on why you are in college and what is expected of you. You will be more motivated if you clarify your interests and values concerning college. You will read in Chapter 2 the reasons students don't graduate from college, including juggling multiple responsibilities, having poor study skills and habits, and lacking preparation, motivation, and effort. College is a commitment of many precious resources you can't afford to waste—time, money, and mental energies. Consider the following statements and your reasons for being in college, and share this in your study team or with students you meet the first few weeks of class:

- I value education and want to be a well-educated person.
- I want to get a good job that leads to a well-paying career.
- I want to learn new ideas and skills and grow personally and professionally.
- I want to get away from home and be independent.

- I want to make new friends.
- I want to have new experiences and stretch myself.
- I want to fulfill my goal of being a college-educated person.

Jot down what you want from college and why you're motivated to get it.

_____
_____
_____
_____

List four values that are most important to you and how college will help you achieve them.

1. _____
   _____
2. _____
   _____
3. _____
   _____
4. _____
   _____

What You Need to Know and Should Not Be Afraid to Ask

You don't want to learn the hard way that you need one more class to graduate, only to find it's offered only once a year (and you just missed it). Make your time with your advisor productive by getting answers to important questions that will help you map out your coursework. **Peak Progress 2** provides a handy checklist of common questions to get you started.

What Do You Need to Do to Graduate?

You will be more motivated and confident if you understand graduation requirements. Requirements vary among schools. Don't rely on the advice of friends. Go to orientation and meet with your advisor early and often. Check out the catalog and make certain you know what is required to graduate. Fill in the following:

GRADUATION REQUIREMENTS

- Number of units required:
- General education requirements:
- Curriculum requirements:
- Residency at the school:
- Departmental major requirements:
- Cumulative GPA required:
- Other requirements, such as special writing tests and classes:

How to Register for Classes

Find out if you have an access code and the earliest date you can register. Meet with your advisor, carefully select classes, and review general education and major requirements. Add electives that keep you active and interested. Make certain that you understand why you are taking each class, and check with your advisor that it is meeting certain requirements.

Many colleges have a purge date and, if you miss the deadline to pay your fees, your class schedule is canceled. You may not be able to get into classes and may have to pay a late fee.

Know the Grading System

Learn the minimum grade point average (GPA) that you need to maintain good standing. If your GPA falls below 2.0, you may be placed on academic probation. The GPA is calculated according to the number of credit hours each course represents and your grade in the course. In the traditional system, $A = 4$ points, $B = 3$ points, $C = 2$ points, $D = 1$ point, and $F = 0$ points (your school may have a different system, so ask to be sure). To calculate your GPA, first determine your total number of points. Following is an example:

Course	Grade Achieved	Number of Credit Hours	Points
Political Science	C	2	$2 \times 2 = 4$
Psychology	B	3	$3 \times 3 = 9$
English	A	3	$4 \times 3 = 12$
Personal Finance	A	1	$4 \times 1 = 4$
TOTAL		9	29

Then, to arrive at your GPA, you must divide your total points by your total number of credit hours:

GPA = total points divided by total number of credit hours

Thus, in this example,

GPA = 29 divided by 9 = 3.22

Monitor your progress and meet with your instructors often, but especially at midterm and before final exams. Ask what you can do to improve your grade.

Adding or Dropping Classes

Ask about the deadlines for adding and dropping classes. This is generally done in the first few weeks of classes. A withdrawal after the deadline could result in a failing grade. Also make certain before you drop the class that

- You will not fall below the required units for financial aid.

The Most Common Questions Students Ask Advisors

1. What classes do I need to take for general education?
2. Can a course satisfy both a general education and a major requirement?
3. Can I take general elective (GE) courses for Credit/No Credit if I also want to count them for my major?
4. How can I remove an *F* grade from my record?
5. What is the deadline for dropping courses?
6. Can I drop a course after the deadline?
7. What is an "educational leave"?
8. What is the difference between a withdrawal and a drop?
9. Do I need to take any placement tests?
10. Are there other graduation requirements, such as a writing exam?
11. Where do I find out about financial aid?
12. Is there a particular order in which I should take certain courses?
13. Are there courses in which I must earn a *C*– or better?
14. How do I change my major?
15. Which of my transfer courses will count?
16. What is the minimum residency requirement for a bachelor's degree?
17. Is there a GPA requirement for the major?
18. Is there a tutoring program available?
19. If I go on exchange, how do I make sure that courses I take at another university will apply toward my degree here?
20. What is a major contract, and when should I get one?
21. When do I need to apply for graduation?
22. How do I apply for graduation?
23. What is a degree check?
24. What is the policy for incomplete grades?
25. Can I take major courses at another school and transfer them here?
26. As a nonresident, how can I establish residency in this state?
27. How do I petition to substitute a class?
28. Once I complete my major, are there other graduation requirements?
29. What is academic probation?
30. Is there any employment assistance available?
31. Is there a mentor program available in my major department?
32. Are there any internships or community service opportunities related to my major?

- You will not fall below the required units for playing sports.
- If required, the class is offered again before you plan to graduate.
- You don't need the class or units to meet graduation requirements.
- You are meeting important deadlines.
- You talk with the instructor first.
- You talk with your advisor.

Never simply walk away from your classes. The instructor will not drop you, nor will you be dropped automatically if you stop going to class at any time during the semester. It is your responsibility to follow-up and complete required forms.

An Incomplete Grade

If you miss class due to illness or an emergency, you may be able to take an incomplete if you can't finish a project or miss a test. Check out this option with your instructor before you drop a class. Sign a written agreement to finish the work at a specific time and stay in touch with the instructor through e-mail and phone.

Withdrawing or Taking a Leave of Absence

Some students withdraw because they don't have the money, they can't take time off from work, they lack child care, or they are having difficulty in classes. Before you drop out of college, talk with your advisor and see if you can get the support and motivation to succeed. If you want to take a leave to travel, want to explore other schools, are ill, or just need to take a break, make certain that you take a leave of absence for a semester, a year, or longer. Taking a leave means that you do not have to reapply for admission, and generally you fall under the same category as when you entered school.

Transferring

Before you transfer to another school, know the requirements, which courses are transferable, and if there is a residency requirement. If you plan to transfer from a 2-year school to a 4-year school, your advisor will help you clarify the requirements.

Expectations of Instructors

Most instructors will hand out a syllabus that outlines their expectations for the class. Understand and clarify those expectations and the course requirements. **Worksheet 1** on page xxxiv is a convenient guide to complete when checking your progress with your instructor.

The Best Strategies for Success in School

In this text, we will focus on a number of strategies that will help you determine and achieve your goals. **The Best Strategies for Success in School** provides a comprehensive list of the proven strategies you will find woven throughout this text. Apply these to your efforts in school now and through your course of study. You will find that not only are they key to your progress in school, but also they will help you develop skills, behaviors, and habits that are directly related to success on the job and in life in general.

The Best Strategies for Success in School

1. **Attend every class.** Going to every class engages you with the subject, the instructor, and other students. Think of the tuition you are paying and what it costs to cut a class.

2. **Be an active participant.** Show that you are engaged and interested by being on time, sitting in front, participating, asking questions, and being alert.

3. **Go to class prepared.** Preview all reading assignments. Highlight key ideas and main concepts, and put question marks next to anything you don't understand.

4. **Write a summary.** After you preview the chapter, close the book and write a short summary. Go back and fill in with more details. Do this after each reading.

5. **Know your instructors.** Choose the best instructors, call them by their preferred names and titles, e-mail them, and visit them during office hours. Arrive early for class and get to know them better.

6. **Know expectations.** Read the syllabus for each course and clarify the expectations and requirements, such as tests, papers, extra credit, and attendance.

7. **Join a study team.** You will learn more by studying with others than by reading alone. Make up tests, give summaries, and teach others.

8. **Organize your study space.** Create a quiet space, with a place for school documents, books, catalogs, a dictionary, a computer, notes, pens, and a calendar. Eliminate distractions by closing the door, and focus on the task at hand.

9. **Map out your day, week, and semester.** Write down all assignments, upcoming tests, meetings, daily goals, and priorities on your calendar. Review your calendar and goals each day. Do not socialize until your top priorities are completed.

10. **Get help early.** Know and use all available campus resources. Go to the learning center, counseling center, and health center; get a tutor; and talk with your advisor and instructors about concerns. Get help at the first sign of trouble.

11. **Give school your best effort.** Commit yourself to being extra disciplined the first 3 weeks—buy your textbooks early; take them to class; get to class early; keep up on your reading; start your projects, papers, and speeches early; and make school a top priority.

12. **Use note cards.** Jot down formulas and key words. Carry them with you and review them during waiting time and right before class.

13. **Review often.** Review and fill in notes immediately after class and again within 24 hours. Active reading, note taking, and reviewing are the steps that improve recall.

14. **Study everywhere.** Review your note cards before class, while you wait for class to begin, while waiting in line, before bed, and so on. Studying for short periods of time is more effective than cramming late at night.

15. **Summarize out loud.** Summarize chapters and class notes out loud to your study team. This is an excellent way to learn.

(continued)

The Best Strategies for Success in School

16. **Organize material.** You cannot remember information if it isn't organized. Logical notes help you understand and remember. Use a mind map for outlining key facts and supporting material.

17. **Dig out information.** Focus on main ideas, key words, and overall understanding. Make questions out of chapter headings, review chapter questions, and always read summaries.

18. **Look for associations.** Improve memory by connecting patterns and by linking concepts and relationships. Define, describe, compare, classify, and contrast concepts.

19. **Ask questions.** What is the obvious? What needs to be determined? How can you illustrate the concept? What information is the same and what is different? How does the lecture relate to the textbook?

20. **Pretest yourself.** This will serve as practice and reduces anxiety. This is most effective in your study team.

21. **Study when you are most alert.** Know your energy level and learning preference. Maximize reviewing during daytime hours.

22. **Turn in all assignments on time.** Give yourself an extra few days to review papers and practice speeches.

23. **Make learning physical.** Read difficult textbooks out loud and standing up. Draw pictures, write on a chalkboard, and use visuals. Tape lectures and go on field trips. Integrate learning styles.

24. **Review first drafts with your instructor.** Ask for suggestions and follow them to the letter.

25. **Pay attention to neatness.** Focus on details and turn in all assignments on time. Use your study team to read and exchange term papers. Proofread several times.

26. **Practice!** Nothing beats effort. Practice speeches until you are comfortable and confident, and visualize yourself being successful.

27. **Recite and explain.** Pretend that you are the instructor and recite main concepts. What questions would you put on a test? Give a summary to others in your study group. Make up sample test questions in your group.

28. **Take responsibility.** Don't make excuses about missing class or assignments or about earning failing grades. Be honest and take responsibility for your choices and mistakes and learn from them.

29. **Ask for feedback.** When you receive a grade, be reflective and ask questions: "What have I learned from this?" "How did I prepare for this?" "How can I improve this grade?" "Did I put in enough effort?" Based on what you learn, what new goals will you set for yourself?

30. **Negotiate for a better grade before grades are sent in.** Find out how you are doing at midterm and ask what you can do to raise your grade. Offer to do extra projects or retake tests.

31. **Always do extra credit.** Raise your grade by doing more than is required or *expected*. Immerse yourself in the subject, and find meaning and understanding.

(continued)

The Best Strategies for Success in School

32. **Take responsibility for your education.** You can do well in a class even if your instructor is boring or insensitive. Ask yourself what you can do to make the class more effective (study team, tutoring, active participation). Be flexible and adapt to your instructor's teaching style.

33. **Develop positive qualities.** Think about the personal qualities that you need most to overcome obstacles, and work on developing them each day.

34. **Stay healthy.** You cannot do well in school or in life if you are ill. Invest time in exercising, eating healthy, and getting enough sleep, and avoid alcohol, cigarettes, and drugs.

35. **Dispute negative thinking.** Replace it with positive, realistic, helpful self-talk, and focus on your successes. Don't be a perfectionist. Reward yourself when you make small steps toward achieving goals.

36. **Organize your life.** Hang up your keys in the same place, file important material, and establish routines that make your life less stressful.

37. **Break down projects.** Overcome procrastination by breaking overwhelming projects into manageable chunks. Choose a topic, do a rough draft, write a summary, preview a chapter, do a mind map, and organize the tools you need (notes, books, outline).

38. **Make school your top priority.** Working too many hours can cut into study time. Learn to balance school, your social life, and work, so that you're effective.

39. **Meet with your advisor to review goals and progress.** Ask questions about requirements, and don't drop and add classes without checking on the consequences. Develop a good relationship with your advisor and your instructors.

40. **Be persistent.** Whenever you get discouraged, just keep following positive habits and strategies and you will succeed. Success comes in small, consistent steps. Be patient and keep plugging away.

41. **Spend less than you make.** Don't go into debt for new clothes, a car, CDs, gifts, travel, or other things you can do without. Education is the best investment you can make in future happiness and job success. Learn to save.

42. **Use critical thinking, and think about the consequences of your decisions.** Don't be impulsive about money, sex, smoking, or drugs. Don't start a family until you are emotionally and financially secure. Practice impulse control by imagining how you would feel after making certain choices.

43. **Don't get addicted.** Addictions are a tragic waste of time. Ask yourself if you've ever known anyone whose life was better for being addicted. Do you know anyone whose life has been destroyed by alcohol and other drugs? This one decision will affect your life forever.

44. **Know who you are and what you want.** Visit the career center and talk with a career counselor about your interests, values, goals, strengths, personality, learning style, and career possibilities. Respect your style and set up conditions that create results.

(continued)

The Best Strategies for Success in School *(concluded)*

45. **Use creative problem solving.** Think about what went right and what went wrong this semester. What could you have done that would have helped you be more successful? What are new goals you want to set for next semester? What are some creative ways to overcome obstacles? How can you solve problems instead of letting them persist?

46. **Contribute.** Look for opportunities to contribute your time and talents. What could you do outside of class that would complement your education and serve others?

47. **Take advantage of your texts' resources.** Many textbooks have accompanying websites, DVDs, and study materials designed to help you succeed in class. Visit this book's website at **www.mhhe.com/ferrett9e.**

48. **Respect yourself and others.** Be supportive, tolerant, and respectful. Look for ways to learn about other cultures and different views and ways to expand your friendships. Surround yourself with people who are positive and successful, who value learning, and who support and respect you and your goals.

49. **Focus on gratitude.** Look at the abundance in your life—your health, family, friends, and opportunities. You have so much going for you to help you succeed.

50. **Just do it.** Newton's first law of motion says that things in motion tend to stay in motion, so get started and keep working on your goals!

Progress Assessment

Course: _____

Instructor: _____

Office: _____   Office hours: _____

Phone: _____   E-mail: _____

1. How am I doing in this class?

_____

_____

_____

2. What grades have you recorded for me thus far?

_____

_____

_____

3. Are there any adjustments that I should make?

_____

_____

_____

4. Am I missing any assignments?

_____

_____

_____

5. Do you have any suggestions as to how I can improve my performance or excel in your class?

_____

_____

_____

Be a Lifelong Learner

LEARNING OUTCOMES

In this chapter, you will learn to

1.1 List the characteristics of a peak performer

1.2 Identify self-management techniques for academic, job, and personal achievement

1.3 Create a personal mission statement

1.4 Identify skills and competencies for school and job success

1.5 Integrate learning styles and personality types

1.6 Apply the Adult Learning Cycle

SELF-MANAGEMENT

> *It's the first day of class and I'm already overwhelmed. How will I manage all this?*

Are you feeling like this? Are you afraid you will never achieve your goals, or do you even know what your goals are? Instead of focusing on negative feelings, channel your energies into positive results and envision yourself being successful. In this chapter, you will learn about "self-management" and many tools—such as self-assessment, critical thinking, visualization, and reflection—you can use to become a success in all facets of life.

JOURNAL ENTRY What are you hoping to gain from your college experience? How does earning a college degree help you both personally and professionally? Consider answering the question "Why am I here?" Is your answer part of a bigger life plan? In **Worksheet 1.1** on page 38, take a stab at answering those questions. Think about the obstacles you may have faced to get to this point and what you did to overcome them. In this chapter, you'll discover that successful, lifelong learning begins with learning about yourself.

1

Learning is a lifelong journey. People who are successful—peak performers—are on this journey. We are constantly faced with many types of changes—economic, technological, societal, and so on. These changes require us to continually learn new skills in school, on the job, and throughout life. You will meet these challenges through your study and learning strategies, in your methods of performing work-related tasks, and even in the way you view your personal life and lifestyle.

Lately, you may have been asking yourself, "Who am I?" "Why am I in school?" "What course of study should I take?" "What kind of job do I want?" or "What should I do with my life?" These are all important questions. Some you may have already answered—and some of those answers may change by tomorrow, next week, or next year. And that's OK. This is all part of a continual process—of learning about yourself and what you want out of life.

As you journey on the road to becoming a peak performer, this book will show you methods that will help you master self-management, learn critical skills, set goals, and achieve success. One of the first steps is self-assessment. Self-assessment requires seeing yourself objectively. This helps you determine where you are now and where you want to go. Then, by assessing how you learn—including your learning and personality styles—you will discover how to maximize your learning potential.

The many exercises, journal entries, and portfolio worksheets throughout this text support one of its major themes—that success in school and success in your career are definitely connected! The skills, competencies, and behaviors you learn and practice today will guide your marketability and flexibility throughout your career, and will promote success in your personal life.

What Is a "Peak Performer"?

Peak performers come from all lifestyles, ages, cultures, and genders. Some are famous, such as many of the people profiled in this book. However, anyone can become a peak performer by setting goals and developing appropriate attitudes and behaviors to achieve desired outcomes. Peak performers excel by focusing on results. They know how to change their negative thoughts into positive, realistic affirmations. They focus on their long-term goals and know how to break down goals into daily action steps. They are not perfect or successful overnight. They learn to face the fear of making mistakes and work through them. They use the whole of their intelligence and abilities.

Every day, thousands of individuals quietly overcome incredible setbacks, climb over huge obstacles, and reach within themselves to find inner strength. They are successful because they know they possess the personal power to produce results and find passion in what they contribute to life. They are masters, not victims, of life's situations. They control the quality of their lives. In short, they are their own best friend.

Copyright © 2015 The McGraw-Hill Companies

Peak Performers

Take responsibility for their actions, behaviors, and decisions

Know their learning styles and preferences and how to maximize their learning

Identify and acknowledge their strengths and weaknesses

Take risks and move beyond secure comfort zones

Use critical thinking to solve problems creatively

Make sound judgments and decisions

Remain confident and resilient when faced with doubt and fear

Are motivated to overcome barriers

Seek out and utilize available resources

Continually acquire new skills and competencies

Take small, consistent steps that lead to long-term goals

Build supportive relationships

Are effective at time management and self-management

Self-Management: The Key to Reaching Your Peak

What is a primary strength of every peak performer? A positive attitude! Peak performers have a positive attitude toward their studies, their work, and virtually everything they do. This fundamental inclination to view life as a series of opportunities is a key to their success. Does this describe how you approach each day? Check your attitude by completing **Personal Evaluation Notebook 1.1** on page 4.

Anyone can develop the attitude of a peak performer, and it is not even difficult. It simply involves restructuring thought patterns. Instead of dwelling on problems, create options and alternatives to keep you on track. Redirecting your thought patterns in this way will give you more drive and make every task seem more meaningful and less daunting.

A positive attitude is one of the many components of **self-management**. Are you responsible for your own success? Do you believe you can control your own destiny? Think of self-management as a toolkit filled with many techniques and skills you can use to keep you focused, overcome obstacles, and help you succeed.

Along with a positive attitude (which we will discuss further in Chapter 2), some very important techniques in this toolkit are self-assessment, critical thinking, visualization, and reflection.

Personal Evaluation Notebook

Am I a Positive Person?

Having a positive attitude is key to effective self-management. Most people believe they are generally positive but often are not truly aware of their negative self-talk or behavior. Answer the following questions to determine your overall outlook. After you have answered the questions, ask a friend, co-worker, or family member to answer the questions about you. Were your answers the same?

	Mostly True	Sometimes True	Rarely True
I tend to look for the good in everyone.	_____	_____	_____
I look for the positive in each situation.	_____	_____	_____
I do not take offense easily.	_____	_____	_____
I welcome constructive criticism and use it to improve.	_____	_____	_____
I am not easily irritated.	_____	_____	_____
I am not easily discouraged.	_____	_____	_____
I do not take everything personally.	_____	_____	_____
I take responsibility and face problems, even when it is not comfortable.	_____	_____	_____
I don't dwell on personal mistakes.	_____	_____	_____
I don't look for perfection in myself.	_____	_____	_____
I don't look for perfection in others.	_____	_____	_____
I do not depend on others to make me happy.	_____	_____	_____
I can forgive and move on.	_____	_____	_____
I do not become overly involved or disturbed by others' problems.	_____	_____	_____
I do not make snap judgments about people.	_____	_____	_____
I praise others for their accomplishments.	_____	_____	_____
I don't start conversations with something negative.	_____	_____	_____
I view mistakes as learning experiences.	_____	_____	_____
I know if Plan A doesn't work, Plan B will.	_____	_____	_____
I look forward to—not worry about—what tomorrow will bring.	_____	_____	_____

Self-Assessment

One of the first steps in becoming a peak performer is **self-assessment**. Out of self-assessment comes recognition of the need to learn new tasks and subjects, relate well with others, set goals, manage time and stress, and create a balanced, productive life. Self-assessment requires facing the truth and seeing yourself objectively. It isn't easy to admit you procrastinate or lack certain skills. Even when talking about your strengths, you may feel embarrassed. However, honest self-assessment is the foundation for making positive changes.

Self-assessment can help you

- Understand how you learn best
- Work with your strengths and natural preferences
- Balance and integrate your preferred learning style with other styles
- Use critical thinking and reasoning to make sound decisions
- Determine your interests and what you value
- Change ineffective patterns of thinking and behaving
- Create a positive and motivated state of mind
- Work more effectively with diverse groups of people
- Handle stress and conflict
- Earn better grades
- Determine and capitalize on your strengths
- Recognize irrational and negative thoughts and behavior
- Most important, focus on self-management and develop strategies that maximize your energies and resources

The world is full of people who believe that, if only the other person would change, everything would be fine. This book is not for them. Change is possible if you take responsibility for your thoughts and behaviors and are willing to practice new ways of thinking and behaving.

Self-assessment is very important for job success. Keep a portfolio of your awards, performance reviews, and training program certificates, as well as the projects you have completed. Assess your expectations in terms of the results achieved, and set goals for improvement. At the end of each chapter, you will find a Career Development Portfolio worksheet, which will help you relate your current activities to future job success. This portfolio will furnish you with a lifelong assessment tool for learning where you are and where you want to go and a place for documenting your results. This portfolio of skills and competencies will become your guide for remaining marketable and flexible throughout your career. Chapter 14 further explores how to develop an effective portfolio and prepare for your future career.

Critical Thinking Skills

Throughout this book, you will be asked to apply critical thinking skills to college courses and life situations. **Critical thinking** is a logical, rational, systematic thought process that is necessary in understanding, analyzing, and evaluating information in order to solve a problem or situation. Self-management involves using your critical thinking skills to make the best decisions and solve problems.

Using critical thinking helps you

- Suspend judgment until you have gathered facts and reflected on them
- Look for evidence that supports or contradicts your initial assumptions, opinions, and beliefs
- Adjust your opinions as new information and facts are known
- Ask questions, look for proof, and examine the problem closely
- Reject incorrect or irrelevant information
- Consider the source of the information
- Recognize and dispute irrational thinking

Because critical thinking determines the quality of the decisions you make, it is an important theme throughout this book. Chapter 10 is devoted to honing your critical thinking skills and practicing creative problem solving. You use your critical thinking skills every day—from analyzing and determining your learning styles to communicating effectively with family members, classmates, and co-workers.

Make sure to complete the exercises and activities throughout this book, including the **Personal Evaluation Notebook** exercises and the end-of-chapter **Worksheets.** **Think Fast** case studies throughout the text highlight that we are constantly making decisions that often have many repercussions—both positive and not-so-positive. Work through these to enhance your critical thinking skills.

Visualization and Affirmations

Visualization and affirmations are powerful self-management tools that help you focus on positive action and outcomes. **Visualization** is using your imagination to see your goals clearly and to envision yourself successfully engaging in new, positive behavior. **Affirmations** are the positive self-talk—the internal dialogue—you carry on with yourself. Affirmations counter self-defeating patterns of thought with more positive, hopeful, and realistic thoughts and feelings.

Using visualization and affirmations can help you relax, boost your confidence, change your habits, and perform better on exams, in speeches, or in sports. You can use them to rehearse for an upcoming event and practice coping with obstacles.

Through self-management, you demonstrate that you are not a victim or passive spectator; you are responsible for your self-talk, images, thoughts, and behaviors. When you observe and dispute negative thoughts and replace them with positive, and realistic thoughts, images, and behaviors, you are practicing critical thinking and creativity. You are taking charge of your life, focusing on what you can change, and working toward your goals.

You can practice visualization anytime and anywhere. For example, between classes, find a quiet place and close your eyes. It helps to use relaxation techniques, such as taking several deep breaths and seeing yourself calm, centered, and focused on your goals. This is especially effective when your mind starts to chatter and you feel overwhelmed, discouraged, or stressed. See yourself achieving your goals. Say to yourself, "I feel calm and centered. I am taking action to meet my goals. I will use all available resources to be successful."

Reflection

Another important self-management tool is **reflection**. To reflect is to think about something in a purposeful way, with the intention of making connections, exploring options, and creating new meaning. Sometimes the process causes us to reconsider our previous knowledge and explore new alternatives and ideas.

Don't confuse reflection with daydreaming. Reflection is conscious, focused, purposeful—not simply letting your mind wander. When you reflect, you direct your thoughts and use imagination. Think of your mind as an ultra-powerful database. To reflect on a new experience is to search through this vast mental database to discover—or create—relationships between experiences: new and old, new and new, old and old. As you reorganize countless experiences stored in your mental database, it becomes more complex, more sophisticated, and ultimately more useful. This ongoing reorganization is a key component of your intellectual development; it integrates critical thinking, creative problem solving, and visualization.

A convenient way to reflect is simply to record your thoughts, such as in a journal. In this text is ample opportunity to practice reflection and critical thinking, including a **Journal Entry** exercise at the beginning of each chapter and a follow-up **Worksheet** at the end of each chapter.

Throughout the text, we'll explore additional self-management techniques that focus on certain aspects of your schoolwork, employment, and personal life. **Peak Progress 1.1** explores the ABC Method of Self-Management, a unique process to

> **"** It's not the load that breaks you down, it's the way you carry it. **"**
>
> LOU HOLTZ
> *College football coach*

Peak Progress   1.1

The ABC Method of Self-Management

Earlier in this chapter, you answered some questions to determine if you approach everyday life with a positive attitude. Researchers believe that positive, optimistic thinking improves your skills for coping with challenges, which may also benefit your overall health and minimize the effects of stress.

What does "negative thinking" mean? If you are negative, you may tend to

- Filter out and eliminate all the good things that happen and focus on one bad thing
- Blame yourself (or someone else) automatically when something bad happens
- Anticipate the very worst that could happen
- See things as only good or bad—there's no middle ground
- Criticize yourself—either aloud or internally—in a way you would never do to someone else
- Waste time complaining, criticizing, reliving, and making up excuses—rather than creating solutions and moving on

The good news is that anyone can become a positive thinker. First, you need to become aware of patterns of defeating thoughts that are keeping you from achieving your goals. Then you can challenge and dispute these negative and irrational thoughts.

Clear thinking will lead to positive emotions. Let's say you have to give a speech in a class and speaking in public has caused you anxiety in the past. You might be saying to yourself, "I am terrified. I just hate getting up in front of people. I just can't do this." These negative beliefs and irrational thoughts can cause severe anxiety and are not based on clear thinking. You can direct your thoughts with positive statements that will dispel anxiety: "Public speaking is a skill that can be learned with practice and effort. I will not crumble from criticism and, even if I don't do well, I can learn with practice and from constructive feedback. I will explore all the resources available to help me and I'll do well in this class."

Self-management can be as easy as ABC. These simple steps help you manage your thoughts, feelings, and behaviors, so that you can create the results you want.

(continued)

The ABC Method of Self-Management *(concluded)*

A = **Actual event:** State the actual situation that affected your emotions.

B = **Beliefs:** Describe your thoughts and beliefs about the situation that created these emotions and behavior.

C = **Challenge:** Dispute the negative thoughts and replace them with accurate and positive statements.

Let's use another example. When you read the quote on page 1 of this chapter, you might have felt the same way—overwhelmed. You are in a new situation, with many new expectations. Let's apply the ABC Method to focus your energies on developing a positive outcome. For example, you might say,

A = **Actual event:** "It's the first day of class and I have a mountain of reading and lecture notes to go over."

B = **Beliefs:** "What if I fail? What if I can't keep it all straight—learning styles, personalities, temperaments? These other people are probably a lot smarter than me. Maybe I should drop out."

C = **Challenge:** "Going to college is a big change, but I have handled new and stressful situations before. I know how to overcome feeling overwhelmed by breaking big jobs into small tasks. I know I'm talented and smart in many ways. Going to college is a good investment in my future, and I want to graduate. I've handled transitions in the past, and I can handle these changes, too."

When you challenge negative thoughts and replace them with positive thinking, you feel energized, and your thoughts spiral upward: "I'm excited about discovering my learning and personality styles and how I can use them to my advantage. So many resources are available to me—my instructor, my classmates, the book's resources. I will get to know at least one person in each of my classes, and I will take a few minutes to explore at least one resource at school that can provide support. I see myself confident and energized and achieving my goals."

In the end-of-chapter **Worksheets** throughout this text, you will find opportunities to practice the ABC Method of Self-Management, as well as the self-management exercises at **www.mhhe.com/ferrett9e.**

---

help you work through difficult situations and achieve positive results. It uses skills such as critical thinking, visualization, and reflection to find positive outcomes.

Discover Your Purpose: A Personal Mission Statement

At the beginning of the chapter, you were asked to write about why you're in school and how it relates to your life plan. In the Getting Started section, you also explored many reasons you are attending college, such as to learn new skills, get a well-paying job, and make new friends. (If you haven't read the Getting Started, now is the perfect time.) Thinking about the answers to these and related questions gets you started on writing your mission statement.

A **mission statement** looks at the big picture of your life, from which your goals and priorities will flow. This written statement (which can be one or more sentences) focuses on the contributions you want to make based on your values, philosophy, and principles. When you have a sense of purpose and direction, you will be more focused, and your life will have more meaning.

In one sense, you are looking at the end result of your life. What do you want to be remembered for? What legacy do you want to leave? What—and who—do you think will be most important to you?

Here is one example of a mission statement: "I want to thrive in a health care career that allows me to use my creativity, grow in knowledge from mentors and colleagues, advance into leadership positions, make a positive impact on my profession, and provide an effective balance with personal interests, including having a family, traveling, and participating in my community."

Think about how a college education will help you fulfill your mission in life. If you have chosen a profession (for example, nursing or teaching), you may want to include the aspects of the career that interested you (such as helping others achieve healthy lifestyles or educating and nurturing young children). It does not need to be lengthy and detailed, but it should reflect your individuality. Focusing on your mission statement will help you overcome obstacles that will challenge you.

To write your mission statement, begin by answering these (or similar) questions:

1. What do I value most in life? (List those things.)

2. What nouns and/or adjectives best describe me? (such as designer, traveler, parent, compassionate, dependable)

3. Which verbs best describe what I like to do? (such as create, explore, write)

4. What is my life's purpose? Or, if I could help make one change in this world, what would it be?

5. What legacy do I want to leave? Or, how do I want others to think of me and my accomplishments?

[handwritten note: 10 EC points on Mid Mod]

Now, considering the answers to those questions, draft a personal mission statement.

My mission statement:

In Chapter 2, we'll discuss how to use goals for motivation. Then, in Chapter 3, we'll explore how your mission statement and personal goals guide you to use your time effectively. You will also review your mission statement at the end of this text. Over the years, review and update your mission statement as you change and grow personally and professionally.

Skills for School and Job Success

What does it take to succeed in a job? Based on feedback from employers, the Secretary's Commission on Achieving Necessary Skills (SCANS; **Figure 1.1**) lists the skills and competencies that are necessary for job as well as academic success. Rate your skills by using honesty and critical thinking to complete **Personal Evaluation Notebook 1.2** on pages 11 and 12.

Discover Your Learning Style

Everyone processes information differently and there is no single right way to learn, but knowing your preferred learning style can increase your effectiveness in school or at work; enhance your self-esteem; and help you to reduce frustration, focus on your strengths, and integrate various styles.

Figure 1.1
Peak Performance Competency Wheel

SCANS recommends these skills and competencies for job success. *Which of these skills have you been acquiring?*

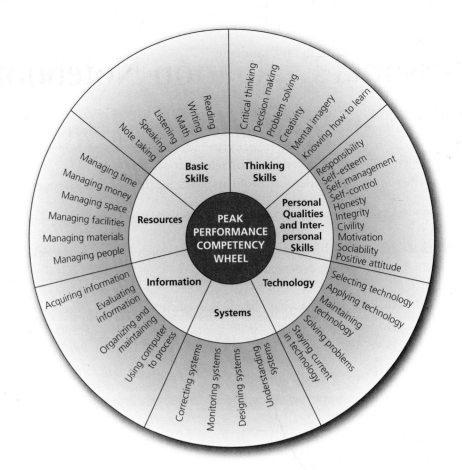

Integrate Both Sides of the Brain

Do you use both sides of your brain? "I use my whole brain!" you might answer—and, indeed, you do. However, you have a preference for using the left or right side of the brain for many mental and physical functions. In the 1960s, Dr. Roger Sperry and his colleagues discovered that the left and right sides of the brain specialize in different modes of thinking and perception. Dominant brain function may play a significant role in how you learn.

The brain has two systems by which it classifies information. One is linguistic and factual (left brain), and one is visual and intuitive (right brain). Although they are interconnected, one system is usually more dominant. For example, if you are left-brain dominant, you may like facts and order, think in a concrete manner, and use a logical, detailed thought process. If you are right-brain dominant, you are more inclined to use an intuitive and insightful approach to solving problems and processing new information. You are more comfortable with feelings and hunches and like to think abstractly and intuitively. **Figure 1.2** lists left-brain or right-brain dominant traits on page 13.

Although you may favor one side of your brain, the key is to use all your brain power and integrate a variety of learning styles (which we'll explore next). Doing this enhances learning, memory, and recall.

Are You a Reader, Listener, or Doer?

Your brain allows you to experience the world through your senses. One way to explore how you learn best is to ask yourself if you are a reader, listener, or doer. Do

Personal Evaluation Notebook

Peak Performance Self-Assessment Test

Assess your skills and behaviors on a scale of 1 to 5 by placing a check mark. Examples are given for each. Review your answers to discover your strongest and weakest areas.

Area	Excellent 5	4	OK 3	2	Poor 1
1. Reading (e.g., comprehending; summarizing key points; reading for pleasure)	___	___	___	___	___
2. Writing (e.g., using correct grammar; presenting information clearly and concisely; documenting accurately)	___	___	___	___	___
3. Speaking (e.g., expressing main points in an interesting manner; controlling anxiety)	___	___	___	___	___
4. Mathematics (e.g., understanding basic principles and formulas; showing work)	___	___	___	___	___
5. Listening and note taking (e.g., staying focused and attentive; recording key points)	___	___	___	___	___
6. Critical thinking and reasoning (e.g., assessing facts; making decisions; linking material)	___	___	___	___	___
7. Creative problem solving (e.g., developing options; weighing alternatives)	___	___	___	___	___
8. Positive visualization (e.g., creating mental images to support goals)	___	___	___	___	___
9. Knowing how you learn (e.g., recognizing preferred learning style; integrating all styles)	___	___	___	___	___
10. Honesty and integrity (e.g., doing the right thing; telling the truth; presenting original work)	___	___	___	___	___
11. Positive attitude and motivation (e.g., being optimistic; identifying personal motivators; establishing goals)	___	___	___	___	___
12. Responsibility (e.g., keeping commitments; not blaming others)	___	___	___	___	___
13. Flexibility/ability to adapt to change (e.g., being open to new ideas; seeing the big picture)	___	___	___	___	___

(continued)

Personal Evaluation Notebook

Peak Performance Self-Assessment Test *(concluded)*

Area	Excellent 5	4	OK 3	2	Poor 1
14. Self-management and emotional control (e.g., taking ownership of thoughts and behaviors)	____	____	____	____	____
15. Self-esteem and confidence (e.g., focusing on strengths; maintaining a positive self-image)	____	____	____	____	____
16. Time management (e.g., setting priorities; planning; accomplishing tasks)	____	____	____	____	____
17. Money management (e.g., budgeting; minimizing debt; saving)	____	____	____	____	____
18. Management and leadership of people (e.g., inspiring; communicating; delegating; training)	____	____	____	____	____
19. Interpersonal and communication skills (e.g., building rapport; listening; being an effective team member)	____	____	____	____	____
20. Ability to work well with culturally diverse groups (e.g., respecting and celebrating differences)	____	____	____	____	____
21. Organization and evaluation of information (e.g., identifying key points and ideas; summarizing; documenting)	____	____	____	____	____
22. Understanding technology (e.g., using essential programs; troubleshooting basic problems)	____	____	____	____	____
23. Commitment and effort (e.g., being persistent; working consistently toward goals)	____	____	____	____	____

you get more information from reading and seeing, talking and listening, or doing? Of course, you do all these things, but your learning strength, or preferred style, may be in one of these areas. For example, you may organize information visually, favoring right-brain activities. Although such classifications may oversimplify complex brain activity, the goal is to help you be more aware of your natural tendencies and habits and how you can use these preferences and learn new ways to enhance your success.

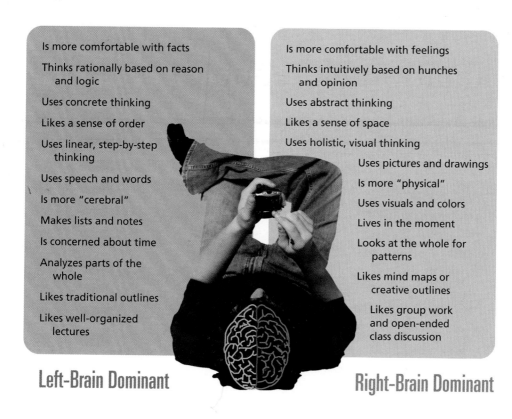

Left-Brain Dominant	Right-Brain Dominant
Is more comfortable with facts	Is more comfortable with feelings
Thinks rationally based on reason and logic	Thinks intuitively based on hunches and opinion
Uses concrete thinking	Uses abstract thinking
Likes a sense of order	Likes a sense of space
Uses linear, step-by-step thinking	Uses holistic, visual thinking
Uses speech and words	Uses pictures and drawings
Is more "cerebral"	Is more "physical"
Makes lists and notes	Uses visuals and colors
Is concerned about time	Lives in the moment
Analyzes parts of the whole	Looks at the whole for patterns
Likes traditional outlines	Likes mind maps or creative outlines
Likes well-organized lectures	Likes group work and open-ended class discussion

Figure 1.2
Left-Brain versus Right-Brain Traits

Put a check mark next to the descriptions that apply to you. *Would you consider yourself more of a left-brain dominant person or a right-brain dominant person?*

A person who learns better by reading possesses a visual learning style. Someone who learns better by listening is considered an auditory learner. A kinesthetic learner learns by touch and physical activity. **Personal Evaluation Notebook 1.3** on pages 14 and 15 has a Learning Style Inventory that will help you discover your learning style.

VISUAL LEARNERS

Visual learners prefer to see information and read material. They learn most effectively with pictures, graphs, illustrations, diagrams, time lines, photos, and pie charts. They like to contemplate concepts, reflect, and summarize information in writing. They might use arrows, pictures, and bullets to highlight points. Visual learners are often holistic in that they see pictures in their minds that create feelings and emotion. They often use visual descriptions in their speech, such as "It is clear . . . ," "Picture this . . . ," or "See what I mean?" Visual learners tend to

- Be right-brain dominant
- Remember what they see better than what they hear
- Prefer to have written directions they can read
- Learn better when someone shows them rather than tells them
- Like to read, highlight, and take notes
- Keep a list of things to do when planning the week
- Gesture frequently while talking and watch facial expressions
- Like to read for pleasure and to learn

● **Visual Careers**
Visual learners may enjoy being an interior designer, a drafter, a journalist, or a graphic artist. *Are you interested in any of these careers?*

Personal Evaluation Notebook  1.3

Learning Style Inventory

Determine your learning preference. Complete each sentence by checking a, b, or c. No answer is correct or better than another.

1. I learn best when I
   _____ a. see information.
   _____ b. hear information.
   _____ c. have hands-on experience.

2. I like
   _____ a. pictures and illustrations.
   _____ b. listening to recordings and stories.
   _____ c. working with people and going on field trips.

3. For pleasure and relaxation, I love to
   _____ a. read.
   _____ b. listen to music.
   _____ c. garden or play sports.

4. I tend to be
   _____ a. contemplative.
   _____ b. talkative.
   _____ c. a doer.

5. To remember my student ID, I need to
   _____ a. look at my ID card over and over.
   _____ b. say it out loud several times.
   _____ c. write it down several times.

6. In a classroom, I learn best when
   _____ a. I have a good textbook, visual aids, and written information.
   _____ b. the instructor is interesting and clear.
   _____ c. I am involved in doing activities.

7. When I study for a test, I
   _____ a. read my notes and write a summary.
   _____ b. review my notes aloud and talk to others.
   _____ c. like to study in a group and use models and charts.

8. I have
   _____ a. a strong fashion sense and pay attention to visual details.
   _____ b. fun telling stories and jokes.
   _____ c. a great time building things and being active.

(continued)

Personal Evaluation Notebook

Learning Style Inventory *(concluded)*

9. I often

_____ **a.** remember faces but not names.

_____ **b.** remember names but not faces.

_____ **c.** remember events but not names or faces.

10. I remember best

_____ **a.** when I read instructions and use visual images to remember.

_____ **b.** when I listen to instructions and use rhyming words to remember.

_____ **c.** with hands-on activities and trial and error.

11. When I give directions, I might say,

_____ **a.** "Turn right at the yellow house and left when you see the large oak tree."

_____ **b.** "Turn right. Go three blocks. Turn left onto Buttermilk Lane."

_____ **c.** "Follow me," after giving directions by using gestures.

12. When driving in a new city, I prefer to

_____ **a.** use a map and find my own way.

_____ **b.** stop and get directions from someone.

_____ **c.** drive around and figure it out by myself.

Score: Count the number of check marks for all your choices:

Total a choices _____ (visual learning style)

Total b choices _____ (auditory learning style)

Total c choices _____ (kinesthetic learning style)

The highest total indicates your dominant learning style. If you are a combination, that's good. It means you are integrating styles already.

AUDITORY LEARNERS

Auditory learners prefer to rely on their hearing sense. They may like music and prefer to listen to information, as in lectures. They like to talk, recite, and summarize information aloud. Auditory learners may create rhymes out of words and play music that helps them concentrate. When they take study breaks, they listen to music or chat with a friend. They are usually good listeners but are easily distracted by noise. They often use auditory descriptions when communicating, such as "This rings true . . . ," "It's clear as a bell . . . ," or "Do you hear what you're saying?"

Auditory learners tend to

- Be left-brain dominant
- Remember what they hear better than what they see

- Prefer to listen to instructions
- Like lectures organized in a logical sequence
- Like to listen to music and talk on the telephone
- Plan the week by talking it through with someone
- Use rhyming words to remember
- Learn best when they hear an assignment as well as see it

Auditory learners may enjoy being a disc jockey, trial lawyer, counselor, or musician.

KINESTHETIC LEARNERS

Kinesthetic learners are usually well coordinated, like to touch things, and learn best by doing. They like to collect samples, write out information, and spend time outdoors. They like to connect abstract material to something concrete. They are good at hands-on tasks. They often use phrases such as "I am getting a handle on . . . ," "I have a gut feeling that . . . ," and "I get a sense that . . ."

Kinesthetic learners tend to

- Be right-brain dominant
- Create an experience
- Use hands-on activities
- Build things and put things together
- Use models and physical activity
- Write down information
- Apply information to real-life situations
- Draw, doodle, use games and puzzles, and play computer games
- Take field trips and collect samples
- Relate abstract information to something concrete

Kinesthetic learners may enjoy being a chef, a surgeon, a medical technician, a nurse, an automobile mechanic, an electrician, an engineer, a forest ranger, a police officer, or a dancer.

Redefining Intelligence: Other Learning Styles

Because each of us has a unique set of abilities, perceptions, needs, and ways of processing information, learning styles vary widely. Besides visual, auditory, and kinesthetic learning styles, there are other, more specific styles, and some people have more than one learning style.

Plus, intelligence has been redefined. We used to think of it as measured by an IQ test. Many schools measure and reward linguistic and logical/mathematical modes of intelligence; however, Thomas Armstrong, author of *7 Kinds of Smart: Identifying and Developing Your Many Intelligences,* and Howard Gardner, who wrote *Frames of Mind: The Theory of Multiple Intelligences,* illustrated that we all possess many

● **Know How You Learn**
Everyone has his or her own way of learning. *What type of learning style do you think best suits this person?*

different intelligences. (See **Personal Evaluation Notebook 1.4** on page 18, which includes a number of traits associated with each "intelligence.")

1. **Verbal/linguistic.** Some people are **word smart.** They have verbal/linguistic intelligence and like to read, talk, and write information. They have the ability to argue, persuade, entertain, and teach with words. Many become journalists, writers, or lawyers. **To learn best:** Talk, read, or write about it.

2. **Logical/mathematical.** Some people are **logic smart.** They have logical/mathematical intelligence and like numbers, puzzles, and logic. They have the ability to reason, solve problems, create hypotheses, think in terms of cause and effect, and explore patterns and relationships. Many become scientists, accountants, or computer programmers. **To learn best:** Conceptualize, quantify, or think critically about it.

3. **Spatial.** Some people are **picture smart.** They have spatial intelligence and like to draw, sketch, and visualize information. They have the ability to perceive in three-dimensional space and re-create various aspects of the visual world. Many become architects, photographers, artists, or engineers. **To learn best:** Draw, sketch, or visualize it.

4. **Musical.** Some people are **music smart.** They have rhythm and melody intelligence. They have the ability to appreciate, perceive, and produce rhythms and to keep time to music. Many become composers, singers, or instrumentalists. **To learn best:** Sing, record, mix, or rap, or play music.

5. **Bodily/kinesthetic.** Some people are **body smart.** They have physical and kinesthetic intelligence. They have the ability to understand and control their bodies; they have tactile sensitivity, like movement, and handle objects skillfully. Many become dancers, carpenters, physical education teachers, or coaches and enjoy physical activities and sports. **To learn best:** Build a model, dance, use note cards, or do hands-on activities.

6. **Environmental.** Some people are **outdoor smart.** They have environmental intelligence. They are good at measuring, charting, and observing plants and animals. They like to keep journals, collect and classify, and participate in outdoor activities. Many become park and forest rangers, surveyors, gardeners, landscape architects, outdoor guides, wildlife experts, or environmentalists. **To learn best:** Go on field trips, collect samples, go for walks, and apply what you are learning to real life.

7. **Intrapersonal.** Some people are **self smart.** They have intrapersonal (inner) intelligence. They have the ability to be contemplative, self-disciplined, and introspective. They like to work alone and pursue their own interests. Many become writers, counselors, theologians, or self-employed businesspeople. **To learn best:** Relate information to your feelings or personal experiences or find inner expression.

8. **Interpersonal.** Some people are **people smart.** They have interpersonal intelligence. They like to talk and work with people, join groups, and solve problems as part of a team. They have the ability to work with and

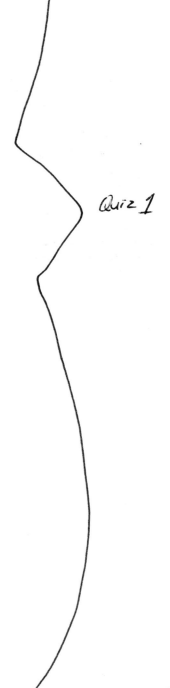

Quiz 1

Personal Evaluation Notebook

Multiple Intelligences

Put a check mark on the line next to the statement that is most often true for you.
Consider what interests you or what you believe you are good at doing.

Ch1 Quiz

Verbal/ Linguistic	Logical/ Mathematical	Spatial	Musical	Bodily/ Kinesthetic	Environmental	Intrapersonal	Interpersonal
"Word Smart"	"Logic Smart"	"Picture Smart"	"Music Smart"	"Body Smart"	"Outdoor Smart"	"Self Smart"	"People Smart"
I like to —Tell stories —Read —Talk and express myself clearly —Persuade, argue, or negotiate —Teach or discuss topics with others —Write	I like to —Use logic to solve problems —Explore mathematics —Explore science —Observe and question how things work —Figure out how to fix things —Use logic to solve problems	I like to —Draw or sketch —Visualize —Add color —Build models —Create illustrations —Use space and spatial relationships	I like to —Use rhythms —Respond to music —Sing —Recognize and remember melodies and chords —Use songs to help me remember —Relax with music	I like to —Experience physical movement —Act things out —Use note cards and models to learn —Work with others —Touch and feel material —Be active and enjoy sports	I like to —Be outdoors —Camp and hike —Work in the earth —Collect samples —Take field trips —Appreciate nature	I like to —Be independent and work on my own —Reflect on ideas —Read and contemplate new thoughts —Go off and think through a situation alone —Be self-disciplined and set individual goals —Use personal experiences and inner expression	I like to —Inspire and lead others —Learn through discussions —Work with a group of people —"Read" other people —Hear another person's point of view —Be compassionate and helpful

Multiple Intelligences

Your goal is to try new strategies and create learning opportunities in line with each category. *What are some strategies you could easily incorporate? Also, do some of these descriptions appear in your personal mission statement?*

For more information, see

Frames of Mind: The Theory of Multiple Intelligences, 3rd ed., by Howard Gardner, Basic Books, 2011.

Their Own Way: Discovering and Encouraging Your Child's Multiple Intelligences by Thomas Armstrong, Tarcher/Putnam, 2000.

understand people, as well as to perceive and be responsive to the moods, intentions, and desires of other people. Many become mediators, negotiators, social directors, social workers, motivational speakers, or teachers. **To learn best:** Join a group, get a study partner, or follow or start a blog.

● **Learning Styles**
There is no one best way to learn. *How do you think you can develop and integrate different learning styles?*

Discover Your Personality Type

Your learning style is often associated with your personality type—your "temperament." The concepts of learning styles, personality, and temperament are not new. Early writings from ancient Greece, India, the Middle East, and China addressed various temperaments and personality types. The ancient Greek founder of modern medicine, Hippocrates, identified four basic body types and a personality type associated with each body type. Several personality typing systems grew out of this ancient view of body/mind typing.

Carl Jung's Typology System

In 1921, psychologist Carl Jung proposed in his book *Psychological Types* that people are fundamentally different but also fundamentally alike. He identified three main attitudes/psychological functions, each with two types of personalities:

● **Understanding Personality Types**
Psychologists have developed a variety of categories to identify how people function best. *What personality type or types might apply to this person?*

1. *How people relate to the external or internal world.* **Extroverts** are energized and recharged by people, tending to be outgoing and social. They tend to be optimistic and are often uncomfortable with being alone. **Introverts** enjoy solitude and reflection, preferring the world of ideas and thoughts. They tend to have a small but close set of friends and are more prone to self-doubt.

2. *How people perceive and gather information.* **Sensors** learn best from their senses and feel comfortable with facts and concrete data. They like to organize information systematically. **Intuitives** feel more comfortable with theories, abstraction, imagination, and speculation. They respond to their intuition and rely on hunches and nonverbal perceptions.

3. *How people prefer to make decisions.* **Thinkers** like to analyze problems with facts, rational logic, and

analysis. They tend to be unemotional and use a systematic evaluation of data and facts for problem solving. **Feelers** are sensitive to the concerns and feelings of others, value harmony, and dislike creating conflict.

Jung suggested that differences and similarities among people can be understood by combining these types. Although people are not exclusively one of these types, he maintained that they have basic preferences or tendencies.

The Myers-Briggs Type Indicator

Jung's work inspired Katherine Briggs and her daughter, Isabel Briggs Myers, to design a personality test, called the Myers-Briggs Type Indicator (MBTI), which has become the most widely used typological instrument. They added a fourth attitude /psychological function (judgment/perception), which they felt was implied in Jung's writings, focusing on *how people live*. **Judgers** prefer orderly, planned, structured learning and working environments. They like control and closure. **Perceivers** prefer flexibility and spontaneity and like to allow life to unfold. Thus, with the four attitudes/ psychological functions (extroverts vs. introverts, sensors vs. intuitives, thinkers vs. feelers, and judgers vs. perceivers), the MBTI provides 16 possible personality combinations. Although we may have all 8 preferences, 1 in each pair tends to be more developed. (See **Figure 1.3**, which lists many characteristics of extroverts, introverts, sensors, intuitives, thinkers, feelers, judgers, and perceivers.)

Connect Learning Styles and Personality Types: The Four-Temperament Profile

You now are aware of your preferred learning styles and have a sense of your personality type. How are these connected? How can you use this information to improve your learning skills and participate in productive group and team situations?

The Four-Temperament Profile demonstrates how learning styles and personality types are interrelated. **Personal Evaluation Notebook 1.5** on page 22 includes questions that will help you determine your dominant temperament.

The following descriptions elaborate on the four temperaments in Personal Evaluation Notebook 1.5. Which is your dominant temperament: analyzer, creator, supporter, or director? Did the answer surprise you? Keep in mind that inventories provide only clues. People change over time and react differently in different situations. However, use this knowledge to discover your strengths and become a well-rounded, balanced learner and team contributor. Peak performers know not only their dominant style but also the way to integrate other styles when appropriate.

Analyzers

Analyzers tend to be logical, thoughtful, loyal, exact, dedicated, steady, and organized. They like following direction and work at a steady pace. The key word for analyzers is *thinking*. (See **Figure 1.4** on page 24.)

> **Strengths:** Creating concepts and models and thinking things through
> **Goal:** To gain intellectual recognition; analyzers are knowledge seekers

Figure 1.3
Characteristics of Personality Types

This chart reflects information influenced by psychologists Carl Jung and Myers and Briggs. *How can understanding your personality help you succeed in school and life?*

~~Thinkers (T)~~ Thinkers	vs.	~~Feelers (F)~~ Feelers	Sensors (S)	vs.	Intuitives (iN)
Gregarious		Quiet	Practical		Speculative
Active, talkative		Reflective	Experience		Use hunches
Speak, then think		Think, then speak	See details		See the big picture
Outgoing, social		Fewer, closer friends	Sequential, work steadily		Work in burst of energy
Energized by people		Energized by self	Feet on the ground		Head in the clouds
Like to speak		Like to read	Concrete		Abstract
Like variety and action		Like quiet for concentration	Realistic		See possibilities
Interested in results		Interested in ideas	Sensible and hardworking		Imaginative and inspired
Do not mind interruptions		Dislike interruptions	Good and precise work		Dislike precise work

↑ Extroverts (E)	vs.	↑ Introverts (I)	Judgers (J)	vs.	Perceivers (P)
Analytical		Harmonious	Decisive		Tentative
Objective		Subjective	Closure		Open-minded
Impersonal		Personal	Plan ahead		Flexible
Factual		Sympathetic	Urgency		Open time frame
Want fairness		Want recognition	Organized		Spontaneous
Detached		Involved	Deliberate		Go with the flow
Rule		Circumstances	Set goals		Let life unfold
Things, not people		People, not things	Meet deadlines		Procrastinate
Lineal		Whole	Just the facts		Interested and curious

Source: *Please Understand Me II* by Dr. David Keirsey © 1998, Prometheus Nemesis Book Company, PO Box 2748, Del Mar, CA 92014.

Classroom style: Analyzers relate to instructors who are organized, know their facts, and present information logically and precisely. They dislike the ambiguity of subjects that lack right or wrong answers. They tend to be left-brained and seem more concerned with facts, abstract ideas, and concepts than with people.

Learning style: Analyzers often perceive information abstractly and process it reflectively. They learn best by observing and thinking through ideas. They like models, lectures, textbooks, and solitary work. They like to examine how things work. They evaluate and come to a precise conclusion.

(continued on page 24)

Personal Evaluation Notebook

The Four-Temperament Profile

The following statements indicate your preferences in working with others, making decisions, and learning new information. Read each statement, with its four possible choices. Mark 4 next to the choice MOST like you, 3 next to the choice ALMOST ALWAYS like you, 2 next to the choice SOMEWHAT like you, and 1 next to the choice LEAST like you.

1. I learn best when I
   _____ **a.** rely on logical thinking and facts.
   _____ **b.** am personally involved.
   _____ **c.** can look for new patterns through trial and error.
   _____ **d.** use hands-on activities and practical applications.

2. When I'm at my best, I'm described as
   _____ **a.** dependable, accurate, logical, and objective.
   _____ **b.** understanding, loyal, cooperative, and harmonious.
   _____ **c.** imaginative, flexible, open-minded, and creative.
   _____ **d.** confident, assertive, practical, and results-oriented.

3. I respond best to instructors and bosses who
   _____ **a.** are factual and to the point.
   _____ **b.** show appreciation and are friendly.
   _____ **c.** encourage creativity and flexibility.
   _____ **d.** expect me to be involved, be active, and get results.

4. When working in a group, I tend to value
   _____ **a.** objectivity and correctness.
   _____ **b.** consensus and harmony.
   _____ **c.** originality and risk taking.
   _____ **d.** efficiency and results.

5. I am most comfortable with people who are
   _____ **a.** informed, serious, and accurate.
   _____ **b.** supportive, appreciative, and friendly.
   _____ **c.** creative, unique, and idealistic.
   _____ **d.** productive, realistic, and dependable.

6. Generally, I am
   _____ **a.** methodical, efficient, trustworthy, and accurate.
   _____ **b.** cooperative, genuine, gentle, and modest.
   _____ **c.** high-spirited, spontaneous, easily bored, and dramatic.
   _____ **d.** straightforward, conservative, responsible, and decisive.

(continued)

Personal Evaluation Notebook  1.5

The Four-Temperament Profile (concluded)

7. When making a decision, I'm generally concerned with
   _____ a. collecting information and facts to determine the right solution.
   _____ b. finding the solution that pleases others and myself.
   _____ c. brainstorming creative solutions that feel right.
   _____ d. quickly choosing the most practical and realistic solution.

8. You could describe me in one word as
   _____ a. analytical.
   _____ b. caring.
   _____ c. innovative.
   _____ d. productive.

9. I excel at
   _____ a. reaching accurate and logical conclusions.
   _____ b. being cooperative and respecting people's feelings.
   _____ c. finding hidden connections and creative outcomes.
   _____ d. making realistic, practical, and timely decisions.

10. When learning at school or on the job, I enjoy
   _____ a. gathering facts and technical information and being objective.
   _____ b. making personal connections, being supportive, and working in groups.
   _____ c. exploring new possibilities, tackling creative tasks, and being flexible.
   _____ d. producing results, solving problems, and making decisions.

Score: To determine your style, mark the choices you made in each column below. Then add the column totals. Highest number in

- Column a, you are an analyzer
- Column b, you are a supporter
- Column c, you are a creator
- Column d, you are a director

	Choice a	Choice b	Choice c	Choice d
1.	_____	_____	_____	_____
2.	_____	_____	_____	_____
3.	_____	_____	_____	_____
4.	_____	_____	_____	_____
5.	_____	_____	_____	_____
6.	_____	_____	_____	_____
7.	_____	_____	_____	_____
8.	_____	_____	_____	_____
9.	_____	_____	_____	_____
10.	_____	_____	_____	_____
Total	_____	_____	_____	_____
	Analyzer	**Supporter**	**Creator**	**Director**

Figure 1.4
Profile of an Analyzer

Analyzers want things done right. Their favorite question is "What?" *Do you recognize any analyzer traits in yourself?*

Effective Traits	Ineffective Traits	Possible Majors	Possible Careers	How to Relate to Analyzers
Objective	Too cautious	Accounting	Computer programmer	Be factual
Logical	Abrupt	Bookkeeping	Accountant	Be logical
Thorough	Unemotional	Mathematics	Drafter	Be formal and thorough
Precise	Aloof	Computer science	Electrician	Be organized, detached, and calm
Detail-oriented	Indecisive	Drafting	Engineer	Be accurate and use critical thinking
Disciplined	Unimaginative	Electronics	Auto mechanic	State facts briefly and concisely
		Automotive	Librarian	

Supporters

People who are supporters tend to be cooperative, honest, sensitive, warm, and understanding. They relate well to others. They value harmony and are informal, approachable, and tactful. In business, they are concerned with the feelings and values of others. The key word for supporters is *feeling*. (See **Figure 1.5.**)

Strengths: Clarifying values, creating harmony, and being a loyal team player
Goal: To create harmony, meaning, and cooperation; they are identity seekers
Classroom style: Supporters tend to learn best when they like an instructor and feel accepted and respected. They are easily hurt by criticism. They like to integrate course concepts with their own experiences. They relate to instructors who are warm and sociable, tell interesting stories, use visuals, and are approachable. They learn best by listening, sharing ideas and feelings, and working in teams.

Figure 1.5
Profile of a Supporter

Supporters want things done harmoniously and want to be personally involved. Their favorite question is "Why?" *Do you recognize any supporter traits in yourself?*

Effective Traits	Ineffective Traits	Possible Majors	Possible Careers	How to Relate to Supporters
Understanding	Overly compliant	Counseling or therapy	Elementary teacher	Be positive
Gentle	Passive	Social work	Physical therapist	Be sincere and build trust
Loyal	Slow to act	Family and consumer science	Social worker	Listen actively
Cooperative	Naive	Nursing	Psychologist	Focus on people
Diplomatic	Unprofessional	Medical assisting	Counselor	Focus on personal values
Appreciative	Can be overly sensitive	Physical therapy	Nurse	Create a comfortable, relaxed climate
		Education	Medical assistant	Create an experience they can relate to

Effective Traits	Ineffective Traits	Possible Majors	Possible Careers	How to Relate to Creators
Imaginative	Unrealistic	Art	Writer	Be enthusiastic
Creative	Unreliable	English	Event planner	Be involved
Visionary	Inconsistent	Music	Travel agent	Be flexible
Idealistic	Hasty	Design	Hotel manager	Be accepting of change
Enthusiastic	Impulsive	Hospitality	Graphic artist	Focus on creative ideas
Innovative	Impatient	Marketing/Advertising	Musician	Talk about dreams and possibilities
	Fragmented	Theater	Composer	
		Communications	Journalist	
			Drama teacher	
			Florist	
			Costume designer	

Figure 1.6
Profile of a Creator

Creators want things done with a sense of drama and style. Their favorite question is "What if?" *Do you recognize any creator traits in yourself?*

Learning style: Supporters perceive information through intuition and process it reflectively. They like to deal with their feelings. They prefer learning information that has personal meaning, and they are patient and likeable. They are insightful; they are imaginative thinkers and need to be personally involved.

Creators

Creators are innovative, flexible, spontaneous, creative, and idealistic. They are risk takers; they love drama, style, and imaginative design. They like fresh ideas and are passionate about their work. The key word for creators is *experience*. (See **Figure 1.6.**)

Strengths: Creating visions that inspire people
Goal: To make things happen by turning ideas into action; they are experience seekers
Classroom style: Creators learn best in innovative and active classrooms. They relate to instructors who have a passion for their work; who are challenging, imaginative, and flexible; and who present interesting ideas and make the topic exciting.
Learning style: Creators learn by doing and being involved in active experiments. They perceive information concretely and process it actively. They like games, role-playing, stories, plays, music, illustrations, drawings, and other visual stimuli. They ask questions and enjoy acting on ideas. They are usually good public speakers. They are future-oriented and good at seeing whole systems.

Directors

Directors are dependable, self-directed, conscientious, efficient, decisive, and results-oriented. They like to be the leader of groups and respond to other people's ideas when they are logical and reasonable. Their strength is in the practical

Figure 1.7
Profile of a Director

Directors want to produce results in a practical manner. Their favorite question is "How?" *Do you recognize any director traits in yourself?*

Effective Traits	Ineffective Traits	Possible Majors	Possible Careers	How to Relate to Directors
Confident	Aggressive	Law enforcement	Lawyer	Set deadlines
Assertive	Pushy	Construction	Police officer	Be responsible for your actions
Active	Insistent	Engineering	Detective	Focus on results and achievements
Decisive	Overpowering	Carpentry	Consultant	Do not try to take control
Forceful	Dominating	Business/Management	Banker	Do not make excuses
Effective leader		Forestry	Park ranger	Communicate schedule changes
Results-oriented			Sales Representative	
			Administrator for outdoor recreation	

application of ideas. Because of this ability, they can excel in a variety of careers, such as law enforcement, banking, and legal professions. The key word for directors is *results*. (See **Figure 1.7**.)

> **Strengths:** Integrating theory with practical solutions
> **Goal:** To find practical solutions to problems; they are security seekers
> **Classroom style:** Directors relate to instructors who are organized, clear, to the point, punctual, and results-oriented. They prefer field trips and hands-on activities.
> **Learning style:** Directors learn by hands-on, direct experience. They learn best by practical application. They work hard to get things done.

Integrate Styles to Maximize Learning

Just as there is no best way to learn, there is no one instrument, assessment, or inventory that can categorize how you learn best. There are many theories about learning styles, and none of them should be regarded as air-tight explanations. Any learning style assessment or theory is, at best, a guide.

The assessment instruments discussed in this text have been adapted from various sources and are based on many years of research. They are simple, yet they provide valuable strategies for determining how you learn, process information, and relate to others. They also provide clues for possible college majors and careers that fit your personality and style. Ask your instructor or learning center if there are certain assessments they recommend.

Use these inventories as a guide, not a restriction. All learning styles are connected, and we use all of them, depending on the situation, task, and people involved. Develop positive strategies based on your natural talents and abilities, and expand your effectiveness by integrating all learning styles.

Psychologist William James believed that people use less than 5 percent of their potential. Think of what you can accomplish if you work in alignment with your natural preferences and integrate various learning styles and techniques. The Peak

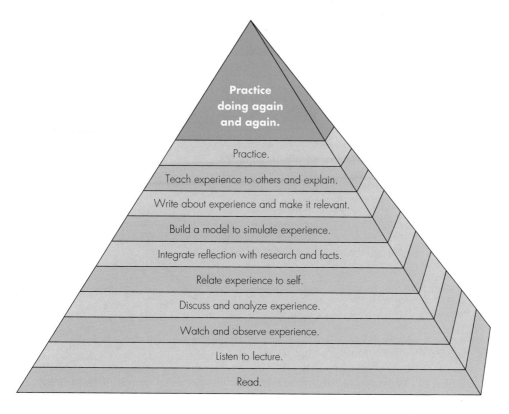

Figure 1.8
**Peak Performance
Learning Pyramid**

Maximize your effectiveness by integrating various learning styles and skills as you move up the pyramid. *What additional skills and learning styles would enhance your learning ability?*

Performance Learning Pyramid in **Figure 1.8** illustrates how you can maximize your effectiveness by integrating learning styles and moving up from passive to active, engaged learning. Now that you have assessed how you learn best—as well as new ways to learn—let's explore how learning is a never-ending cycle.

The Adult Learning Cycle

David Kolb, a professor at Case Western Reserve University, developed an inventory that categorizes learners based on how they process information:

1. Concrete experience: learn by feeling and personal experience
2. Reflective observation: learn by observing and reflecting
3. Abstract conceptualization: learn by thinking and gathering information
4. Active experimentation: learn by doing and hands-on activities

Kolb's theory about learning styles is similar to Carl Jung's four attitudes/psychological functions (feeling, intuition, thinking, and sensation). The crux of Kolb's theory is that you learn by practice, repetition, and recognition. Thus, do it, do it again, and then do it again.

The following Adult Learning Cycle is an adaptation of both Kolb's and Jung's theories. It includes a fifth stage (teach) and illustrates how the stages are complementary to one another. (See **Figure 1.9**.)

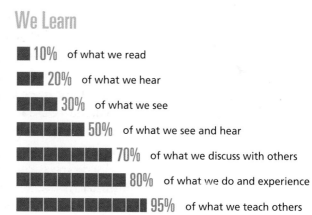

We Learn

10% of what we read
20% of what we hear
30% of what we see
50% of what we see and hear
70% of what we discuss with others
80% of what we do and experience
95% of what we teach others

Figure 1.9
The Adult Learning Cycle

The key to learning is practice and repetition. *Why is "Teach" an essential, unique step?*

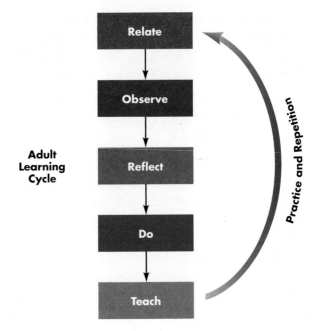

1. **RELATE. Why do I want to learn this?** What personal meaning and interest does this have for me? I learn by feeling, having personal experiences, and talking with others.

2. **OBSERVE. How does this work?** I learn by watching, listening, and experiencing.

3. **REFLECT. What does this mean?** I learn by thinking, gathering information, and reflecting.

4. **DO. What can I do with this?** I learn by doing, finding practical applications, and defining procedures.

5. **TEACH. How can I relay this information to others?** I learn by demonstrating and explaining, as well as by acknowledging and rewarding positive outcomes.

Depending on your learning style, the information to be learned, and the situation, you may find yourself starting the cycle at different stages. *The key to learning is practice and repetition.* As you repeat the stages, meaning and recall are strengthened. To make learning long-lasting, you need to find ways to make it meaningful and physical. For example, let's say you are taking a web design class:

1. **RELATE personal meaning, interests, and relevance.** Why do you want to take this class? What are the benefits to you, your coursework, and your career? How does this relate to what you already know, such as other areas of programming and design? Which new skills will translate well to other courses and interests, such as setting up a website for a new club you joined?

2. **OBSERVE your instructor and watch other people.** Listen and ask questions. Talk, read, write, or blog about your experiences. What is new and different? Jot down instructions; sketch possible layouts. Find music to illustrate ideas or use background music as you learn. Experience doing a task as your instructor or a friend helps you.

3. **REFLECT on problems critically and sequentially.** Which tasks are difficult to learn or remember? Test new ways of doing things. Ask people when you get stuck. Find new ways to solve problems. Relate what you know to new information. Review instructions when you are stumped.

4. **DO it and learn by trial and error.** Jump in and try new tasks. Learning web design is a great example of hands-on learning. Find new applications.

5. **TEACH it to others.** Demonstrate to someone else what you have learned. Answer questions and ask for feedback.

Then return to Stage 1 and reaffirm the benefits of learning this valuable new skill.

You can adapt the Adult Learning Cycle to fit your preference, but you will be most effective if you integrate all the learning styles and make learning physical and meaningful.

In each chapter, we will explore practical examples of the Adult Learning Cycle. For example, in Chapter 12, the Adult Learning Cycle will be applied to effective communication and how you can enhance your communication skills.

Overcome Obstacles

On your journey to success, you will run into stumbling blocks (or even big boulders). Maintain a positive attitude and make sure you are using your self-management tools.

Adjust Your Learning Style to Your Instructor's Teaching Style

Just as we all have different learning styles, your instructors will have a variety of teaching styles. Rather than resisting, find ways to adapt. Maximize the ways you learn best and incorporate other techniques. For example, if you prefer a highly structured lecture, focusing on facts and taking notes, you may feel uncomfortable in a student-centered course where ideas and class discussion are key and you work in small groups with little structure. The following strategies may help you succeed in this type of course:

- Ask questions and clarify expectations.
- Be flexible and try new approaches.
- Be an active participant in class and go to every class.
- Get to know other students and form study teams.
- Be interested in other points of view.
- See exercises and class discussions as learning opportunities.
- Visit your instructor during office hours and ask what you can do to improve.
- Do any extra-credit projects that are offered.
- Try looking at the whole of a concept before breaking it into parts.
- If the instructor jumps around a lot in a lecture or digresses, ask for main points.
- Find or ask for the theme or key points of each class.
- Focus on the learning process, not just the final product.

> **WORDS TO SUCCEED**
>
> **"I have not failed. I've just found 10,000 ways that won't work."**
>
> THOMAS EDISON
> *Inventor*

Jenna is a medical technician student who excels in her science and math courses, but she's struggling in sociology, where her instructor likes to teach in small groups, asks a lot of open-ended questions, and has a very informal classroom style.

- What assumptions can you make about how her science and math classes may be taught?
- What are most likely Jenna's preferred learning styles?
- How can Jenna adjust her learning to adapt to her sociology class?

Let's say you prefer warm relationships and a nonstructured class. You find yourself in a traditional, content-centered, straight lecture class with few visuals or class discussion. Here are a few suggestions for adapting:

- Read the syllabus and know expectations.
- Listen attentively and take detailed notes.
- Clarify the weight of each test, paper, or project.
- Make certain you know and meet each deadline.
- Focus on the lecture and avoid talking to others during class.
- Work in a study team, discuss lecture concepts, and predict test questions.
- Ask for examples from the instructor and study team.
- Take advantage of the logical sequence of material and take notes accordingly.
- Add color, supporting examples, and drawings to your notes.
- Connect lectures to drawings, photographs, and diagrams in the textbook.
- Ask the instructor for visuals that help illustrate the points made in class.
- Have your questions ready when talking to your instructor during office hours.
- Use analytical thinking and focus on facts and logic.
- Be precise in definitions and descriptions.

If absolutely necessary, you can drop the class and sign up for a class with an instructor who has a teaching style that matches your learning style. However, in the workplace you will interact with people who have a variety of personality types and learning styles, so it's important for you to learn coping and adapting skills now.

Make It Simple

The "M" word: **multitasking.** In our high-speed world of fast food, multimedia, and instant gratification, it's no wonder that we think we can do it all at once. Cell phone commercials boast of being able not only to chat about dinner plans but also to search the Internet for the best local sushi restaurant and make a reservation—all with your friend still on the line.

Enhanced productivity? Maybe, but many would argue that "multitasking" really means you aren't doing anything very well because you're trying to do too many things at the same time. Layering task upon task only complicates our hectic lives even more. However, few would disagree that we have more demands on our time and have to figure out the best way to accomplish as much as possible.

Rather than lumping tasks together, focus on one thing at a time for a short period of time. For example, take only three minutes right now and review what you've just read about learning styles and your instructors. Jot down each one's name and how you would characterize his or her teaching. Put an asterisk by those whose teaching style is a little more challenging for you. Write down three specific strategies you want to try during the next class. Make it simple by trying just a few techniques now to find out what works for you.

Use a watch, clock, phone—whatever is handy—to time yourself. You will be surprised how much you can accomplish in just short intervals of time. We often procrastinate or complain that there's "not enough time." If you keep to the mindset that small chunks of time make a big difference, you may discover that you can do it all—or at least most of it!

In Chapter 3, we'll tackle time management in more detail, but focusing your time and efforts and finding what works for you are essential to every topic in this book and everything you do, in both school and life. This book provides a litany of proven strategies, but it's up to you to find out what works—and to stick with it!

TAKING CHARGE

Summary

In this chapter, I learned to

- **Strive to become a peak performer.** Peak performers come from all walks of life, maximize their abilities and resources, and focus on positive results.

- **Practice self-management.** I know I am responsible for my own success, and there are self-management techniques and behaviors I can practice that will make me successful.

- **Self-assess.** Assessing and objectively seeing myself will help me recognize my need to learn new skills, relate more effectively with others, set goals, manage time and stress, and create a balanced and productive life.

- **Use my critical thinking skills.** Critical thinking is a logical, rational, and systematic thought process I can use to think through a problem or situation to make sound choices and good decisions.

- **Visualize success.** Visualization is a self-management tool I can use to see myself being successful. I will also use affirmations (positive self-talk) to focus on what's important.

- **Reflect on information.** I will think about how experiences are related and what I can learn from them, including keeping a journal to record my thoughts.

- **Create a personal mission statement.** Drafting a mission statement will help me determine my values and interests and focus on my long-term goals.

- **Make connections between skills for school and job success.** The Secretary's Commission on Achieving Necessary Skills (SCANS) outlines skills and competencies that are critical to success in school as well as in the job market.

- **Determine my learning style.** Knowing my preferred learning style, such as visual, auditory, or kinesthetic, tells me how I learn best and how to incorporate features of other learning styles in order to maximize my learning opportunities.

- **Explore various personality types.** Although personality typing has been around for centuries, Jung identified extroverts vs. introverts, sensors vs. intuitives, and thinkers vs. feelers. Myers and Briggs added judgers and perceivers and developed the Myers-Briggs Type Indicator.

- **Create teams by using the Four-Temperament Profile.** People tend to have the characteristics of an Analyzer, Supporter, Creator, or Director. Knowing how to work with others' traits and strengths helps to build an effective team.

- **Integrate learning styles and personality types.** Once I understand my learning style(s) and personality type(s), I can incorporate features of other styles to maximize my learning. Although I tend to be either left-brain dominant (linguistic) or right-brain dominant (visual), the goal is to use all my brain power to learn new skills and information.

- **Apply the Adult Learning Cycle.** This five-step process (relate, observe, reflect, do, and teach) demonstrates that learning comes from repetition, practice, and recall.

- **Adjust to my instructor's teaching style.** If my learning style is different from my instructor's teaching style, I will try new strategies to maximize my learning in that class.

- **Make it simple by focusing my time.** Rather than trying to tackle everything at once, I can accomplish much more by focusing my efforts in short intervals of time and finding strategies that work for me.

Performance Strategies

Following are the top 10 strategies for becoming a lifelong learner.

- Strive to become a peak performer in all aspects of your life.
- Practice self-management to create the results you want.
- Use critical thinking, reflection, and honesty in self-assessment.
- Practice visualization and state affirmations that focus on positive outcomes.
- Create a personal mission statement.
- Make the connection between school and job success.
- Discover your learning and personality styles.
- Integrate all learning styles.
- Apply the Adult Learning Cycle to maximize your learning.
- Make it simple by focusing on one task or strategy at a time.

Tech for Success

Take advantage of the text's website at **www.mhhe.com/ferrett9e** for additional study aids, useful forms, and convenient and applicable resources.

- **Electronic journal.** Sometimes critical thinking is easier when you write down your responses. Keeping an electronic reflection and self-assessment journal allows for easy updating and gathering of information, which can be pulled into your career portfolio later.
- **Mission statement business cards.** To keep yourself motivated and focused, print your mission statement on business cards, carry them with you, and share them with family and friends. You can order them relatively inexpensively online, or chip in with another student or your study group and buy prescored printer paper, or simply print on a heavier paper stock and cut the cards apart.
- **Online self-assessments.** A number of online assessments can help you determine the best careers to fit your personality. Talk with your instructor, as your school may already have some available in your career center, such as the Learning and Study Strategies Inventory (LASSI).

Study Team Notes

Career *in* focus

Louis Parker
ACCOUNTANT AND FINANCIAL PLANNER

Related Majors: Accounting, Business Administration, Economics, Finance

Setting Business Goals

Louis Parker is a certified public accountant (CPA) and financial planner. In 2004, he started his own business, Parker Inc., by offering accounting services. Louis prepares taxes, financial reports, and payroll, and he does bookkeeping for individuals and small businesses. He employs three full-time and one part-time assistant but needs five full-time workers to help during peak tax season (January–April).

To get feedback on his services, Louis occasionally does a survey of his clients. The survey shows whether his clients are getting the services they want at prices they believe are reasonable. Louis uses the results of the survey to set goals and plan for the future.

One of Louis's goals is to continually increase business, as Louis believes that, without marketing and growth, his business will decline. Louis has used telemarketing services and social media to help him initiate contact with prospective clients.

A few years ago, Louis decided to add financial planning because his clients were continually asking for his advice in financial areas. Financial planners help clients attain financial goals, such as retirement or a college education for their children. Louis was able to get certified in financial planning. Because he is affiliated with a financial services organization, he sometimes helps clients invest in the stock market, mainly in mutual funds. Currently, financial planning is only 10 percent of his business, but Louis's goal is to eventually increase that amount to 30 percent.

CRITICAL THINKING How might a survey of his clients help Louis assess his personal strengths and weaknesses? What strategies should he put in place to follow up on client feedback? How can he incorporate the feedback into his long-term goals?

Peak Performer

PROFILE

Blake Mycoskie

In just his thirties, Blake Mycoskie has already had an "amazing race" of a life. He started his first business (a campus laundry service) while attending college at Southern Methodist University. The business was successful and, after selling it, Blake continued to create successful businesses—five altogether. It was after competing on the CBS primetime show *The Amazing Race*, however, that Mycoskie realized his true passion. He returned to all of the countries he had raced through on the show and was struck by the extreme poverty of Argentina. He decided then that he needed to do something to help.

In May 2006, Mycoskie used the skills and experiences he had acquired creating and owning a company and took a risk by doing something he had no knowledge of: making shoes. TOMS: Shoes for Tomorrow was created, a shoe company which promised that for every pair of shoes purchased, TOMS would give a pair to a child in need. His initial pledge of 250 shoes to children in Argentina quickly outpaced his expectations, and on that first Shoe Drop, TOMS gave 10,000 pairs of new shoes to children Mycoskie had met on previous visits. By 2010, TOMS had given more than 600,000 pairs of new shoes to children in need around the world. In 2011, TOMS branched into eyewear and pledged the same kind of support to improve vision throughout the world.

In 2011, Mycoskie authored *Start Something That Matters*, a best-seller that highlights the importance of social entrepreneurship. Mycoskie has said that his

favorite quote is by Gandhi: "Be the change you wish to see in the world." By thinking critically about his different areas of knowledge and passions, Mycoskie was truly able to understand how he could effect the change he wanted to see in the world.

PERFORMANCE THINKING How did Blake Mycoskie use the principles discussed in this chapter to create TOMS? Would the company have been as successful if Mycoskie had been unable to make the initial connection between his skills and his developing passion and new mission in life?

CHECK IT OUT TOMS "One Day Without Shoes" movement asks people from all over the world to do one thing together: walk barefoot for a day. You can find out more about this, World Sight Day, and other company events that support their "One for One" mission at **www.toms.com/our-movement**. Read some of the "Notes from the Field" stories posted on the website. Which one most affected you? How are online movements such as this capable of making people better understand the difficulties faced by other people in the world?

Starting Today

At least one strategy I learned in this chapter that I plan to try right away is

_____

_____

_____

What changes must I make in order for this strategy to be most effective?

_____

_____

_____

Review Questions

Based on what you have learned in this chapter, write your answers to the following questions:

1. What is a peak performer? List at least three potential characteristics.

_____

_____

2. Define visualization and how and when you can practice this self-management tool.

_____

_____

3. Explain the differences among the three types of learners (visual, auditory, kinesthetic).

_____

_____

4. Why is it important to know your learning style and personality type?

_____

_____

5. Why is it important to determine your instructor's teaching style as well as your own learning style?

_____

_____

To test your understanding of the chapter's concepts, complete the chapter quiz at **www.mhhe.com/ferrett9e**.

Making a Commitment

In the Classroom

Eric Silver is a freshman in college. He doesn't know what major to choose and isn't even sure if he wants to continue going to college. At times, he feels like he's just doing this for his parents. In high school, he never settled on a favorite subject, though he did briefly consider becoming a private investigator after reading a detective novel. His peers seem more committed to college and have better study habits. Eric prefers a hands-on approach to learning, and he finds it difficult to concentrate while studying or listening to a lecture. However, he enjoys the outdoors and is creative. Once he gets involved in a project he finds interesting, he is very committed.

1. What strategies from this chapter would be most useful to help Eric understand himself better and gain a sense of commitment?

   _____

   _____

2. What would you suggest to Eric to help him find direction?

   _____

   _____

In the Workplace

Eric has taken a job as a law enforcement officer. He feels more comfortable in this job than he did in school because he knows he performs best when actively learning. He enjoys teamwork and the exchange of ideas with his co-workers. Eric also realizes that, in order to advance in his work, he needs to continue his education. He is concerned about balancing his work, school, and family life. He does admit that he did not excel in subjects he was less interested in. Eric never learned effective study habits but realizes that he must be disciplined when returning to college.

3. What suggestions would you give Eric to help him do better in school?

   _____

   _____

4. Under what category of learning style does Eric fall, and what are the ineffective traits of this style that he needs to work on most?

   _____

   _____

Applying the ABC Method of Self-Management

In the Journal Entry on page 1, you were asked to think about what you are hoping to gain from your college experience. How does earning a college degree help you both personally and professionally? Essentially, "Why are you here?" On the lines provided, indicate your answers to those questions.

_____

_____

_____

Think about the obstacles you may have faced to get to this point and what you did to overcome them. State at least one of those obstacles:

_____

_____

_____

Now apply the ABC method to one of the obstacles.

A = Actual event:

_____

_____

B = Beliefs:

_____

_____

C = Challenge:

_____

_____

Did you use this or a similar thought process when you first encountered the obstacle? Was the obstacle not really as big as it first seemed?

PRACTICE SELF-MANAGEMENT

For more examples of learning how to manage difficult situations, see the "Self-Management Workbook" section of the Online Learning Center website at **www.mhhe.com/ferrett9e.**

REVIEW AND APPLICATIONS | CHAPTER 1

My Learning Style, Personality Types, and Temperament

LEARNING STYLES

I am a(n) (circle one):

Visual learner   Auditory learner   Kinesthetic learner

The following learning habits make me most like this learning style:

What features of the two other learning styles should I incorporate to make me a well-rounded learner?

PERSONALITY TYPES

I am a(n) (circle one from each pair):

Extrovert or introvert   Sensor or intuitive   Thinker or feeler   Judger or perceiver

The following characteristics make me most like these personality types:

How can I incorporate positive features of the opposite personality types?

TEMPERAMENTS

I am a(n) (circle one):

Analyzer   Supporter   Creator   Director

The following characteristics make me most like this temperament:

What positive behaviors/traits can I incorporate from the other three temperaments?

REVIEW AND APPLICATIONS | CHAPTER 1

Creating the Ideal Team

In school and at work, you will often be a member of a project team. In most cases, you do not have the opportunity to select your team members but, instead, need to learn how to maximize each other's strengths.

Pretend, however, that you have the opportunity to select a four-person team to tackle an assignment. Now that you know your preferences, indicate the characteristics of three potential teammates who would be complementary. Indicate why you think each person would be an asset to the team.

PERSON #1

Learning style:

Personality type:

Temperament:

What this person will add to the team:

PERSON #2

Learning style:

Personality type:

Temperament:

What this person will add to the team:

PERSON #3

Learning style:

Personality type:

Temperament:

What this person will add to the team:

AND ME

What I add to the team:

REVIEW AND APPLICATIONS | CHAPTER 1

Applying the Four-Temperament Profile

You've explored your temperament and discovered your preferred learning style and personality type. Apply this knowledge by associating with people who have various styles, and find ways to relate to and work more effectively with different people.

For example, let's say that you are assigned to a five-person team that will present a serious public health issue to your personal health class. You are a supporter type, and you find yourself having a conflict with Joe, a director type. You are in your first meeting, and Joe is ready to choose a topic for the group project, even though one team member is absent.

Apply the ABC Method of Self-Management to focus your energies on building rapport and understanding:

A = Actual event: "Joe wants to choose a topic for the group project, even though one person isn't here to voice her opinion."

B = Beliefs: "I think we are not taking the time to be sensitive to the needs of all the team members. Everyone should be present before we make a decision. Joe is trying to take control of the group and is just impatient. I'm worried that the absent group member will not like the decision or may be hurt that she wasn't involved. I resent being rushed and worry that conflict will result. Maybe this person will even quit the group."

C = Challenge: "What is the worst thing that could happen if we choose a topic today? We can always refocus later if we find this topic doesn't fit our goals. Chances are, the absent member would agree with the topic in question, anyhow. Joe is probably not impatient—he just wants to make a decision and get us moving. I'm glad our group is made up of different strengths and personalities. Our team members have complementary strengths and respect and work well with each other. I know that Joe will keep us moving forward and will be sensitive to my concerns that we listen to each other and respect each other's feelings."

Are you experiencing a similar situation or conflict in your school, work, or personal life? If so, use the ABC Method to visualize a positive solution:

A = Actual event:

_____

_____

B = Beliefs:

_____

_____

C = Challenge:

_____

_____

Autobiography

The purpose of this exercise is to look back and assess how you learned skills and competencies. Write down the turning points, major events, and significant experiences of your life. This autobiography, or chronological record, will note events that helped you make decisions, set goals, or discover something about yourself. Record both negative and positive experiences and what you learned from them. Add this page to your Career Development Portfolio—for example,

Year/Event	Learned Experience
2001 Moved to Michigan.	Learned to make new friends and be flexible.
2003 First job baby-sitting.	Learned responsibility and critical thinking.
2005 Grandmother became ill.	Helped with care. Learned dependability, compassion.

Year/Event	Learned Experience

REVIEW AND APPLICATIONS | CHAPTER 1

Expand Your Emotional Intelligence

LEARNING OUTCOMES

In this chapter, you will learn to

2.1 Describe emotional intelligence and the key personal qualities

2.2 Explain the importance of good character, including integrity, civility, and ethics

2.3 Demonstrate responsibility, self-management, and self-control

2.4 Define self-esteem and confidence

2.5 Incorporate a positive attitude and motivation

2.6 List the benefits of a higher education

SELF-MANAGEMENT

"On my commute to class, a car cut me off. I was furious and yelled at the driver. I was fuming and distracted during classes, and later I blew up at a co-worker. This just ruined my entire day. How can I handle my angry feelings in a more constructive way?"

Have you ever had a similar experience? Are you easily offended by what others do or say? Have you said things in anger that have caused a rift in a relationship? In this chapter, you will learn how to control your emotions and create a positive and resourceful state of mind.

JOURNAL ENTRY In **Worksheet 2.1** on page 70, describe a time when you were angry and lost control of your emotions. How did you feel? How did others react to your outburst? What would you do differently? Visualize yourself calm and in control, and realize you have a choice in how you interpret events.

There is a tendency to define intelligence as a score on an IQ test or the SAT or as school grades. Educators trying to predict who will succeed in college have found that high school grades, achievement test scores, and ability are only part of the picture. Emotional intelligence and maturity have more effect on school and job success than traditional scholastic measures. In fact, research has indicated that persistence and perseverance are major predictors of college success. A landmark study by the American College Test (ACT) indicated that the primary reasons for first-year students' dropping out of college were not academic but, rather, emotional difficulties, such as feelings of inadequacy, depression, loneliness, and a lack of motivation or purpose.

Employers list a positive attitude, motivation, honesty, the ability to get along with others, and the willingness to learn as more important to job success than a college degree or specific skills. In Chapter 1, you learned that SCANS identifies many personal qualities as important competencies for success in the workplace. These qualities and competencies are also essential for building and maintaining strong, healthy relationships throughout life. Essential personal qualities should be viewed as a foundation on which to build skills, experience, and knowledge.

In this chapter, you will learn the importance of emotional intelligence and why character is so important for school and job success. You will also develop personal strategies for maintaining a positive attitude and becoming self-motivated. You may realize that you are smarter than you think. You are smarter than your test scores or grades. Success in your personal life, school, and career depends more on a positive attitude, motivation, responsibility, self-control, and effort than on inborn abilities or a high IQ. Peak performers use the whole of their intelligence.

Emotional Intelligence and Maturity

Emotional intelligence is the ability to understand and manage yourself and relate effectively to others. **Maturity** is the ability to control your impulses, think beyond the moment, and consider how your words and actions affect yourself and others before you act. People who have developed a set of traits that adds to their maturity level increase their sense of well-being, get along better with others, and enhance their school, job, and life success.

Emotional maturity contributes to competent behavior, problem-solving ability, socially appropriate behavior, and good communication. Being unaware of or unable to control emotions often accompanies restlessness, a short attention span, negativism, impatience, impulsiveness, and distractibility. Clearly, having emotional intelligence distinguishes peak performers from mediocre ones. Becoming more emotionally mature involves three stages:

1. Self-awareness—tuning in to yourself
2. Empathy—tuning in to others
3. Change—tuning in to results

In Chapter 1, you explored strategies to increase your self-awareness and tune in to yourself. You assessed your skills and personal qualities in the Peak Performance Self-Assessment Test on page 11. By learning personality types, you also began to tune in to others as well. The central theme of this book is that you can use self-management to begin changing your thoughts, images, and behaviors to produce the results you want in every aspect of your life. Enhancing your emotional intelligence and focusing on positive personal qualities are key to achieving those results.

Character First: Integrity, Civility, and Ethics

Good **character** is an essential personal quality for true success. A person of good character has a core set of principles that most of us accept as constant and relatively noncontroversial. These principles include fairness, honesty, respect, responsibility, caring, trustworthiness, and citizenship. Surveys of business leaders indicate that dishonesty, lying, and lack of respect are top reasons for on-the-job difficulties. If an employer believes an employee lacks integrity, all of that person's positive qualities—from skill and experience to productivity and intelligence—are meaningless. Employers usually list honesty or good character as an essential personal quality, followed by the ability to relate to and get along with others.

Following The Golden Rule (treating others as we want to be treated) is a simple way to weave integrity and civility into our everyday lives. The word **integrity** comes from the Latin word *integre,* meaning "wholeness." Integrity is the integration of your principles and actions. In a sense, people who have integrity "walk the talk" by consistently living up to their highest principles. Integrity is not adherence to a rigid code but, rather, an ongoing commitment to being consistent, caring, and true to doing what is right—and the courage to do it even when it is difficult.

Civility is a set of tools for treating others with respect, kindness, and good manners, or etiquette. It also includes the sacrifices we make each day so that we live together peacefully. Civility (like integrity) requires **empathy**—understanding of and compassion for others. You can practice civility in your classes by being on time, turning off your cell phone, staying for the entire class, and listening to the instructor and other students when they speak.

Ethics are the principles of conduct that govern a group or society. Because a company's reputation is its most important asset, most organizations have a written code of ethics that describes how people are expected to behave. It is your responsibility to know and understand the code of ethics at your place of employment and at school. Look on your school's website for statements regarding academic integrity, honesty, cheating, and plagiarism. **Cheating** is using or providing unauthorized help in test taking or on projects. One form of cheating is **plagiarism**, which means presenting someone else's ideas as if they were your own. The consequences of unethical behavior could result in an *F* grade, suspension, expulsion, or firing from a job. You always have the choice of telling the truth and being responsible for your own work. (We'll discuss plagiarism versus paraphrasing in Chapter 9 and the importance of giving credit and citing sources.)

> **❝** Character is like a tree and reputation like its shadow. The shadow is what we think of it; the tree is the real thing. **❞**
>
> ABRAHAM LINCOLN
> *U.S. president*

● **Be a "Class Act"**
These may seem like harmless acts, but they are clear examples of disrespect—for your instructor, your classmates, and your education. *How would an employer respond to this behavior on the job?*

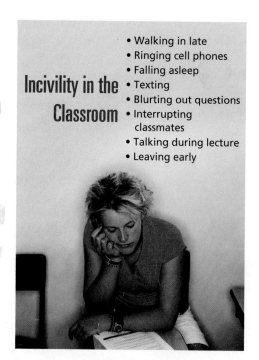

Incivility in the Classroom

- Walking in late
- Ringing cell phones
- Falling asleep
- Texting
- Blurting out questions
- Interrupting classmates
- Talking during lecture
- Leaving early

Devon's midterm exam will determine 50 percent of his final grade. He's been so busy at home and his part-time job that he skipped class and study group all last week. He's afraid of bombing the exam, and someone he met in the cafeteria tells him he can buy a copy of the test.

- If he buys it, what are the repercussions if he gets caught?
- What are potential repercussions if he *doesn't* get caught?
- What would you do to prepare for the exam?

THINK FAST

"The measure of a man's character is what he would do if he knew he never would be found out.**"**

THOMAS MACAULAY
British writer and politician

Every day, you run into situations that test your character. **Personal Evaluation Notebook 2.1** includes questions and situations to get you thinking about your experiences. While completing this exercise, consider the personal qualities that make you smarter than you think you are, such as positive attitude, motivation, dependability, and honesty—for example, "I was raised on a farm in Michigan. What personal quality makes me smarter than my IQ or test scores?" If you answer "hard work," you're right. That one personal quality—putting in extra effort—has helped many people be more successful in life.

Personal qualities, especially honesty, are very important when you are think of hiring someone to work for a business you own. A candidate sends in an outstanding resumè. She has a college degree, experience, and a great personality, and she is positive and motivated, but you find out she stole from her last employer. No matter how bright or talented someone is, you don't want a dishonest person working for you. Complete **Personal Evaluation Notebook 2.2** on page 48 to see what qualities you would look for in a potential employee and which of those qualities you possess.

There is no universal code of ethics, and many questions about ethical issues do not have clear-cut answers. For example, taking money out of a cash drawer is clearly dishonest, but what about coming in late to work, padding your expense account, or using someone else's words without giving credit? You will be faced with situations in your personal, school, and business lives that will force you to make decisions that will be viewed as either ethical or unethical. Sometimes it is not easy. You will have to call on your own personal code of ethics. When defining your code and subsequent actions, you may find the following questions helpful:

- Is this action against the law?
- Is this action against company policy or code of behavior?
- How would this situation read if reported on the front page of the newspaper?
- How would you explain this to your mother? To your child?
- What might be the negative consequences?
- Are you causing unnecessary harm to someone?
- If unsure, have you asked a trusted associate outside of the situation?
- Are you treating others as you would want to be treated?

Remember, unethical behavior rarely goes unnoticed!

Responsibility

Peak performers take responsibility for their thoughts, state of mind, and behavior. They don't blame others for their problems but, rather, use their energy to solve them. They are persistent and patient and exert a consistently high effort to achieve their goals. When they say they are going to do something, they keep their commitment. People can depend on them.

Personal Evaluation Notebook

2.1

Character and Ethics

Integrity and honesty are essential qualities. It is important for you to assess and develop them as you would any skill. Use critical thinking to answer these questions.

1. What is the most difficult ethical dilemma you have faced in your life?

   _____

   _____

2. Do you have a code of ethics that helps guide you when making decisions? Explain.

   _____

   _____

3. Who have you known that is a role model for displaying integrity and honesty?

   _____

   _____

4. Do you have a code of ethics at your college? Where did you find it? (Hint: Check your school's website or ask the dean of students.)

   _____

   _____

Examples of being responsible include showing up on time and prepared for class, work, meetings, study teams, and so on. Responsible people own up to their mistakes and do what they can to correct them. The model in **Figure 2.1** on page 48 illustrates many important, interrelated personal responsibilities. Other personal qualities related to responsibility include perseverance, punctuality, concentration, attention to details, follow-through, high standards, and respect for others.

Peak performers realize they are responsible for their attitudes and actions and know they have the power to change. They have an **internal locus of control**, meaning they believe that they have control over their lives and that their rewards or failures are a result of their behavior, choices, or character. People with an **external locus of control** credit outside influences, such as fate, luck, or other people, with their success or failure. They are impulsive about immediate pleasures and easily swayed by the influences of others, and they often have a negative attitude and an inability to cope effectively with change, conflict, and frustration.

Learning to adjust to frustration and discouragement can take many forms. Some people withdraw or become critical, cynical, shy, sarcastic, or unmotivated. Blame, excuses, justification, and criticism of others are devices for those who cannot accept personal responsibility. Acknowledge your feelings and attitudes. Decide if they support your goals; if they do not, adopt a state of mind and actions that do.

Personal Evaluation Notebook  2.2

Skills and Personal Qualities

1. Jot down the skills, personal qualities, and habits you are learning and demonstrating in each of your classes.

Skills	Personal Qualities	Habits
_____	_____	_____
_____	_____	_____
_____	_____	_____

2. Pretend you own a business. List the skills and personal qualities you would want in your employees. *Which answers also appear in your lists above?*

Type of business: _____

Employees' Skills	Employees' Personal Qualities
_____	_____
_____	_____
_____	_____

Figure 2.1
Personal Responsibilities

What you do or don't do in one area of life can affect other areas of your life and other people. *What one area of personal responsibility would you improve?*

Forming positive habits

My health and energy

Managing time and stress

Keeping my agreements

My feelings and actions

Setting goals

Managing money

Learning study and job skills

Major and career planning

Knowing what resources are available

Paying back student loans

My decisions and choices

Personal and professional relationships

Assessing my skills

Asking for help

I am responsible for

Being responsible creates a sense of integrity and a feeling of self-worth. For example, if you owe someone money or have a student loan, take responsibility for repaying the debt on schedule or make new arrangements with the lender. Not repaying can result in years of guilt and embarrassment, as well as a poor credit rating. It is important to your self-worth to know you are a person who keeps commitments and assumes responsibility.

Self-Control

If anger were a disease, there would be an epidemic in this country. Road rage, spousal and child abuse, and a lack of civility are just a few examples. Emotionally mature people know how to control their thoughts and behaviors and how to resolve conflict. Conflict is an inevitable part of school and work, but it can be resolved in a positive way. Try these tips for redirecting and transforming your anger:

1. **Calm down.** Step back from the situation and take a deep breath. Take the drama out of the situation and observe what is happening, what behavior is triggering angry emotions, and what options you have in responding appropriately and positively. If you lash out verbally, you may cause serious harm to your relationship. You cannot take back words once they are spoken. Resist the urge to overreact.

2. **Clarify and define.** Determine exactly with whom or what you are angry and why. What specific behavior in the other person is causing your anger or frustration? Determine whose problem it is. For example, your instructor may have an annoying tone and style of lecturing. If a behavior annoys only you, perhaps it is something you alone need to address.

3. **Listen with empathy and respect.** Empathy includes the ability to listen, understand, and respond to the feelings and needs of others. Take the tension out of the conflict by really listening and understanding the other person's point of view. Communicate that you have heard and understood by restating the other person's position.

4. **Use "I" statements.** Take ownership of your feelings. Using "I" statements—direct messages you deliver in a calm tone with supportive body language—can diffuse anger. Instead of blaming another person, express how a situation affects you. For example, you can say, "Carlos, when I hear you clicking your pen and tapping it on the desk, I'm distracted from studying." This is usually received better than saying, "Carlos, you're so rude and inconsiderate. You're driving me nuts with that pen!"

5. **Focus on one problem.** Don't rattle off every annoying behavior you can think of. Let's continue with the previous example: "In addition to clicking your pen, Carlos, I don't like how you leave your dishes in the sink, drop your towels in the bathroom, and make that annoying little sound when you eat." Work to resolve only one behavior or conflict at a time.

6. **Focus on win–win solutions.** How can you both win? Restate the problem and jot down as many different creative solutions as you can both agree on.

Don't let anger and conflict create more stress in your life and take a physical and emotional toll. You can learn to step back automatically from explosive situations and control them, rather than let your emotions control you. **Peak Progress 2.1** explores how you can use the Adult Learning Cycle to manage your emotions.

Self-Esteem and Confidence

Self-esteem is how you feel about yourself. People with positive self-esteem have the confidence that allows them to be more open to new experiences and accepting of different people. They tend to be more optimistic. They are more willing to share their feelings and ideas with others and are willing to tolerate differences in others. Because they have a sense of self-worth, they do not feel a need to put down or discriminate against others.

Confidence can develop from

- Focusing on your strengths and positive qualities and finding ways to bolster them. Be yourself and don't compare yourself with others.
- Learning to be resilient and bouncing back after disappointments and setbacks. Don't dwell on mistakes or limitations. Accept them, learn from them, and move on with your life.
- Using affirmations and visualizations to replace negative thoughts and images.
- Taking responsibility for your life instead of blaming others. You cannot control other people's behavior, but you have control over your own thoughts, emotions, words, and behavior.
- Learning skills that give you opportunities and confidence in your abilities. It is not enough to feel good about yourself; you must also be able to do what is

Peak Progress   2.1

Applying the Adult Learning Cycle to Self-Control

The Adult Learning Cycle can help you increase your emotional intelligence. For example, you may have felt the same anger and frustration mentioned in the Self-Management exercise on the first page of this chapter. Maybe it happened when you lost your keys, had three papers due, or felt so overwhelmed with responsibilities that you developed a negative attitude.

1. **RELATE. Why do I want to learn this?** What personal meaning and interest does controlling my anger have for me? Has it been a challenge? Has it hurt important relationships in my personal life or at school or work? How will controlling my anger help me in those situations?

2. **OBSERVE. How does this work?** I can learn a lot about anger management by watching, listening, and engaging in trial and error. Whom do I consider an emotionally mature person? Whom do I respect because of his or her patience, understanding, and

ability to deal with stressful events? When I observe the problems other people have, how do they exhibit their emotional maturity in general and anger specifically?

3. **REFLECT. What does this mean?** Test new ways of behaving, and break old patterns. Explore creative ways to solve problems instead of getting angry. Look into anger management strategies, and reflect on what works and doesn't work.

4. **DO. What can I do with this?** Learn by doing and finding practical applications for anger management. Practice the steps outlined on page 49. Apply the ABC Method of Self-Management to situations to determine positive outcomes.

5. **TEACH. Whom can I share this with?** Talk with others and share experiences. Model by example.

Now return to Stage 1 and realize your accomplishment in taking steps to control your anger better.

required to demonstrate that you are competent, honest, and responsible. The more skills and personal qualities you acquire, the more confident you will feel.

- Focusing on giving, not receiving, and make others feel valued and appreciated. You will increase your self-esteem when you make a contribution.

- Surrounding yourself with confident and kind people who feel good about themselves and make you feel good about yourself.

If you want to change your outer world and experiences for the better, you must begin by looking at your thoughts, feelings, and beliefs about yourself. Assess your self-esteem at the end of the chapter in **Worksheet 2.3** on page 72.

A Positive Attitude and Personal Motivation

There is an old story about three men working on a project in a large city in France. A curious tourist asks them, "What are you three working on?" The first man says, "I'm hauling rocks." The second man says, "I'm laying a wall." The third man says with pride, "I'm building a cathedral." The third man has a vision of the whole system. When college and work seem as tedious as hauling rocks, focus on the big picture.

Your attitude, possibly more than any other factor, influences the outcome of a task. **Motivation** is the inner drive that moves you to action. Even when you are discouraged or face setbacks, motivation can help you keep on track. You may have skills, experience, intelligence, and talent, but you will accomplish little if you are not motivated to direct your energies toward specific goals.

A positive attitude results in enthusiasm, vitality, optimism, and a zest for living. When you have a positive attitude, you are more likely to be on time, alert in meetings and class, and able to work well even on an unpleasant assignment. A negative attitude can drain you of enthusiasm and energy. It can result in absenteeism, tardiness, and impaired mental and physical health.

> **" It is better to light a candle than curse the darkness. "**
> ELEANOR ROOSEVELT
> *U.S. first lady and political leader*

A Positive Attitude Encourages:

- Higher productivity
- An openness to learning at school and on the job
- School and job satisfaction
- Creativity in solving problems and finding solutions
- The ability to work with diverse groups of people
- Enthusiasm and a "can do" outlook
- Confidence and higher self-esteem
- The ability to channel stress and increase energy
- A sense of purpose and direction

A Negative Attitude Makes You:

- Feel like a victim and helpless to make a change
- Focus on the worst that can happen in a situation
- Blame external circumstances for your attitude
- Focus on the negative in people and situations
- Believe adversity will last forever
- Be angry and blame other people

Take 3 minutes right now and make a list of all the positives in your life:
- What opportunities do you have that your parents or grandparents didn't?
- Who is there to support you when you need help?
- Who or what on the list makes you the happiest?

What else can you do in 3 minutes?
- Write down anything negative that happened today, the outcome, and how it could be addressed the next time.
- Close your eyes, breathe deeply, and meditate to relieve the day's stressors.
- Make a list of commitments you must keep tomorrow.

As discussed in Chapter 1, peak performers display a positive attitude even when faced with adversity. Having a positive attitude is more than simply seeing the glass as half full—it's a way of life.

How Needs and Desires Influence Attitudes and Motivation

One of the deepest needs in life is to become all that you can be by using all of your intelligence and potential. Abraham Maslow, a well-known psychologist, developed the theory of a hierarchy of needs. According to his theory, there are five levels of universal needs. **Figure 2.2** illustrates these levels, moving from the lower-order needs—physiological and safety and security needs—to the higher-order needs—the needs for self-esteem and self-actualization. Your lower-order needs must be met first before you can satisfy your higher-order needs. For example, participating in hobbies that foster your self-respect is difficult if you don't have enough money for food and rent. For some people, the lower-order needs include a sense of order, power, or independence. The higher levels, which address social and self-esteem factors, include the need for companionship, respect, and a sense of belonging.

As your lower-order needs are satisfied and cease to motivate you, you begin to direct your attention to the higher-order needs for motivation. As you go up the

Figure 2.2
Maslow's Hierarchy of Needs

Maslow's theory states that most people need to satisfy the universal basic needs before considering the higher-order needs. *Which level of needs is motivating you right now?*

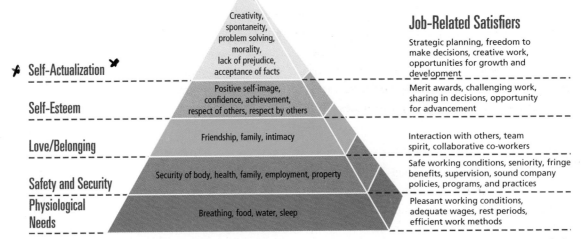

Source: "Hierarchy of Needs" from *Motivation and Personality*, 3rd ed., by Abraham H. Maslow. Revised by Robert Frager, James Fadiman, Cynthia McReynolds, and Ruth Cox. Copyright 1954, © 1987 by Harper & Row, Publishers, Inc. Copyright © 1970 by Abraham H. Maslow. Reprinted by permission of HarperCollins, Inc.

Personal Evaluation Notebook

2.3

Needs, Motivation, and Commitment

1. What needs motivate you at this time?

_____

_____

2. What do you think will motivate you in 20 years?

_____

_____

3. Complete this sentence in your own words: "For me to be more motivated, I need . . ."

_____

_____

4. Describe a time in your life when you were committed to something—such as a goal, a project, an event, or a relationship—that was important to you.

_____

_____

5. Regarding your answer to Question 4, what kept you motivated?

_____

_____

ladder of higher-order needs, you'll find that you're learning for the joy of new ideas and the confidence that comes from learning new skills. You have more energy and focus for defining and pursuing your dreams and goals. You want to discover and develop your full potential. You not only love learning new ideas but also value emotional maturity, character, and integrity. You are well on the path to self-actualization. According to Maslow, self-actualizing people embrace the realities of the world rather than deny or avoid them. They are creative problem solvers who make the most of their unique abilities to strive to be the best they can be. Complete **Personal Evaluation Notebook 2.3** to assess what motivates you.

The Motivation Cycle

The motivation cycle in **Figure 2.3** on page 54 amplifies what you learned in Chapter 1 about the power of visualization. It illustrates how your self-esteem influences what you say to yourself, which in turn influences your physical reactions—breathing, muscular tension, and posture. These physical reactions influence your behavior—both your verbal and your nonverbal responses. Your emotions, body, and mind are interrelated—if you change one part, you change the whole system.

Figure 2.3
The Motivation Cycle

Your emotions, body, and mind respond to what you say to yourself. *What positive message can you send to yourself?*

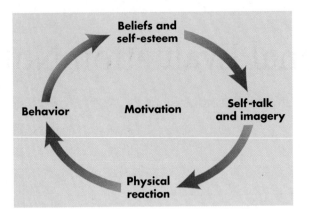

Motivational Strategies

Keeping yourself motivated isn't always easy when you're feeling pressures from school, work, and family. However, you can use these motivational strategies:

1. **Act as if you are motivated.** Your attitude influences your behavior, and behavior influences attitude. The key is to first make a personal commitment to remaining positive and motivated.

   For example, pretend you are performing in a movie. Your character is a positive, motivated student. How do you enter the room? Are you smiling? What are your breathing, posture, and muscle tension like? What kinds of gestures and facial expressions do you use to create this character? What kinds of friends does this person enjoy being with? If you develop positive study and work habits and do them consistently, even when you don't feel like it, you'll be successful, and this will create a positive state of mind.

2. **Use affirmations.** Any discussion of motivation must include your self-talk, what you say to yourself throughout the day. Once you start paying attention to your self-talk, you may be amazed at how much of it is negative. Countless thoughts, images, and phrases go through your brain daily almost unnoticed, but they have a tremendous influence on your mood and attitude. The first step, then, is to replace negative self-talk with affirmations (positive self-talk). For example, don't say, "I won't waste my time today." Instead, affirm, "I am setting goals and priorities and achieving the results I want. I have plenty of energy to accomplish all that I choose to do, and I feel good when I'm organized and centered." Complete **Personal Evaluation Notebook 2.4** to determine if your self-talk needs to become more positive.

3. **Use visualization.** If you imagine yourself behaving in certain ways, that behavior will become real. For example, businessman Calvin Payne knows the power of visualization. Before he graduated from college, he bought his graduation cap and gown and kept them in his room. He visualized himself crossing the stage in his gown to accept his diploma. This visual goal helped him when he suffered setbacks, frustration, and disappointments. He graduated with honors and now incorporates visualization techniques in his career.

Personal Evaluation Notebook

2.4

Self-Talk and Affirmations

Listen to your self-talk for a few days. Jot down the negative thoughts you say to yourself. For example, when you first wake up, do you say, "I don't want to go to class today"?

Do your thoughts and self-talk focus on lack of time, lack of money, or other problems? Observe when you are positive. How does this change your state of mind and your physical sense of well-being? List examples of your negative self-talk and positive affirmations:

Negative Self-Talk	Positive Affirmations
1. _____	1. _____
2. _____	2. _____
3. _____	3. _____

Most right-brain dominant people are visual and use imagery a great deal. They can see scenes in detail when they read or daydream. In fact, their imagery is like a movie of themselves, with scenes of how they will react in certain situations, or a replay of what has occurred in the past. These images are rich in detail, expansive, and ongoing. Left-brain dominant people tend to use imagery less, but using imagery is a technique that can be learned.

4. **Use goals as motivational tools.** Just as an athlete visualizes crossing the finish line, you can visualize your final goal. Working toward your goal can be a great motivator; however, you first must know what your goal is. **Peak Progress 2.2** on page 56 will help you distinguish desires from goals and long-term goals from short-term goals.

   Besides visualizing goals peak performers often write them down. Try keeping yours in your wallet, taping them on your bathroom mirror, or putting them on yellow sticky notes around your computer screen. Without a specific goal, it's not easy to find the motivation, effort, and focus required to go to classes and complete assignments. Make certain your goals are realistic. Achieving excellence doesn't mean attaining perfection or working compulsively toward impossible goals. Trying to be a perfectionist sets you up for frustration, which can decrease your motivation, lower productivity, increase stress, and lead to failure.

5. **Understand expectations.** You will be more motivated to succeed if you understand what is expected of you in each class. Most instructors hand out a syllabus on the first day. Read it carefully and keep a copy in your class notebook. Review the syllabus with a study partner and clarify expectations with your instructor. Meet with your academic advisor to review general college and graduation requirements. You will find that what is expected of

Setting Goals

As the Cheshire cat said to Alice: "If you don't know where you are going, any road will take you there." The key, then, is to figure out where you are going, and then you can determine the best way to get there. Goal setting will help you do that. But goals provide more than direction and a clear vision for the future. When appropriately understood and applied, they are very effective motivators.

It is helpful first to distinguish between goals and desires. Identifying what you want out of life (that is, creating your mission statement, as discussed in Chapter 1) is certainly an important step in developing effective goals, but the goals themselves are not mere desires; rather, they are specific, measurable prescriptions for action. For example, if you want to be financially secure, you should start by identifying the actions that will help you fulfill that desire. Knowing that financial security is tied to education, you might make college graduation your first long-term goal. However, be careful how you construct this goal. "My goal is to have a college degree" is passive and vague. "I will earn my Bachelor of Science degree in computer technology from State University by June 2017" prescribes a clear course of action that you can break down into sequences of short-term goals, which then can be broken down into manageable daily tasks.

Your long-term goal always comes first. Sometimes when people are uncomfortable with long-term commitment, they try to address short-term goals first. Do not fall into this trap. Short-term goals are merely steps toward achieving the long-term goal, so they cannot even exist by themselves. To understand this better, imagine driving to an unfamiliar city and then trying to use a road map without having first determined where you are going. It cannot be done. You must know where you are going before you can plan your route (as illustrated in the accompanying figure).

When defining your goals, remember:

- Desires and wishes are not goals.
- Goals prescribe action.
- Effective goals are specific.
- Goal setting always begins with a long-term goal.
- Short-term goals are the steps in achieving the long-term goal.
- Daily tasks are the many specific actions that fulfill short-term goals. In Chapter 3, we will explore using your goals to plan how to use your time effectively.

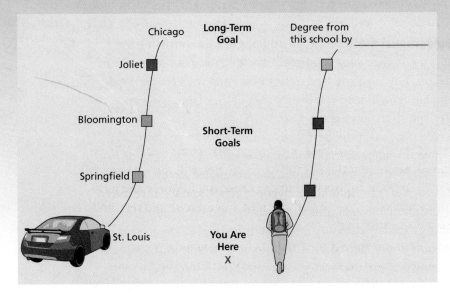

Goal Setting

Setting goals is like planning a trip—first you need to know your destination (long-term goal). Then you determine the best route to get there, including the milestones along the way (short-term goals). *If your long-term goal is to obtain your college degree, write in some of the short-term goals you need to accomplish (such as completing coursework, consulting with advisors and instructors, obtaining financial resources, and completing internships).*

Peak Progress

Differences between High School and College

Entering college brings a new level of responsibility and expectations as compared to your previous educational experiences, mimicking what is expected on the job as well as managing your personal life. For example, in college, you are expected to

- Have more responsibilities and budget your time and money
- Express your opinions logically, not just give facts
- Motivate yourself
- Handle more freedom and independence
- Attend larger classes that meet for longer periods but less often
- Be responsible for knowing procedures and graduation requirements

- Write and read more than you have before
- Think critically and logically
- Receive less feedback and be tested less often but more comprehensively
- Use several textbooks and supplemental readings
- Complete more work and turn in higher-quality work
- Interact with people of different values, cultures, interests, and religions
- Learn to be tolerant and respectful of diversity
- Encounter new ideas and critique those ideas in a thoughtful way
- Get involved in the community, school clubs, volunteer work, and internships related to your major

---

you in college—from personal responsibility to independent thinking—is likely to be much more intense than your previous educational experiences. (See **Peak Progress 2.3.**)

6. **Study in teams.** Success in the business world relies on teamwork—the sharing of skills, knowledge, confidence, and decision-making abilities. Teamwork aims for *synergy,* meaning the whole (the team's output) is greater than the sum of the parts (each member's abilities). Working as a team in school you can

- Teach each other material and outline main points.
- Read and edit each other's reports.
- Develop sample quizzes and test each other.
- Learn to get along with and value different people. (We will explore healthy relationships in more detail in Chapter 12.)

7. **Stay physically and mentally healthy.** It is difficult to motivate yourself if you don't feel well physically or emotionally. If you are ill, you will miss classes, fall behind in studying, or both. Falling behind can cause you to worry and feel stressed. Talk out your problems, eat well, get plenty of exercise and rest, and create a balance of work and play.

8. **Learn to reframe.** You don't have control over many situations or the actions of others, but you do have control over your responses. **Reframing** is choosing to see a situation in a new way. For example, to pay for school, Joan works at a fast-food restaurant. She could have chosen to see this negatively. Instead, she has reframed the situation to focus on learning essential job skills. She is learning to be positive, dependable, hardworking, service-oriented, flexible, and tolerant.

9. **Reward yourself.** The simplest tasks can become discouraging without rewards for progress and completion. Set up a system of appropriate rewards for finishing projects. For an easier task, the reward might be a snack or a

phone call to a friend. For a larger project, the reward might be going out to dinner or a movie. What rewards would motivate you?

10. **Make learning relevant.** Your coursework will be more motivating if you understand how the knowledge you gain and new skills you learn will relate to your career performance. You may be attending college just because you love to learn and meet new people. However, it's more likely that you are enrolled to acquire or enhance your knowledge and skills, increasing your marketability in the workforce.

The Benefits of Higher Education

As just mentioned, you will be more motivated in your schoolwork—and more likely to graduate and excel—if you understand how attending college benefits you today and in the future.

HIGHER EDUCATION ENCOURAGES CRITICAL THINKING

Many years ago, being an educated person meant having a liberal arts education. *Liberal* comes from the Latin root word *liber,* which means "to free." A broad education is designed to free people to think and understand themselves and the world around them. The liberal arts include such areas as the arts, humanities, social sciences, mathematics, and natural sciences. Classes in philosophy, history, language, art, and geography focus on how people think, behave, and express themselves. The liberal arts integrate many disciplines and provide a foundation for professional programs, such as criminal justice, journalism, computer systems, business, medicine, and law.

Technology is no longer a separate field of study from liberal arts but is an important tool for everyone. Employers want professionals who are creative problem solvers, have good critical thinking skills, can communicate and work well with others, can adapt to change, and understand our complex technical and social world. Liberal arts classes can help make a skilled professional a truly educated professional who integrates and understands history, culture, self, and the world.

HIGHER EDUCATION IS A SMART FINANCIAL INVESTMENT

As mentioned earlier, you will be more motivated to put in long hours of studying when you feel the goal is worth it. With rising costs everywhere—including higher education—and fluctuating job opportunities, some wonder if college is worth the investment. Statistics show it is. College graduates earn an average of well over $800,000 more in a lifetime than do high school graduates. (See **Figure 2.4.**) Although graduating from college or a career school won't guarantee you a job in your chosen field, it can pay off with more career opportunities, better salaries, more benefits, more job promotions, increased workplace flexibility, better workplace conditions, and greater job satisfaction. Many college career centers are committed to helping their students find employment.

Also, various reports from the U.S. Department of Labor indicate that people who attend at least 2 years of college tend to be more disciplined, have more self-confidence, make better decisions, and be more willing to adapt to change and learn new skills. They often have more hobbies and leisure activities, are more involved in their communities, and live longer, healthier lives.

Figure 2.4
Annual Earnings and Employment Opportunities Based on Education

Statistically, the level of your education is directly related to your potential employment and income. *What other advantages, besides a good job and income, do you think education offers?*

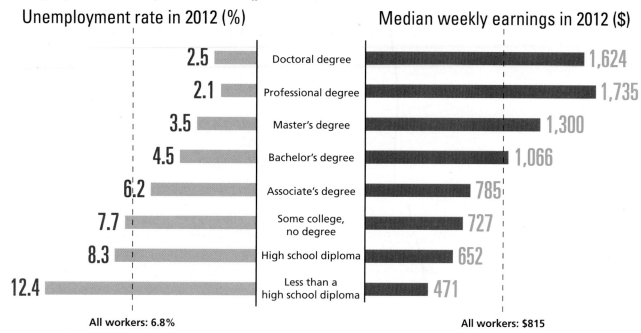

Source: Bureau of Labor Statistics, Current Population Survey.

HIGHER EDUCATION PREPARES YOU FOR LIFE ON THE JOB

What you learn in school today correlates directly with finding and keeping a job, as well as succeeding in a chosen career. As you go through school, think about how the skills, personal qualities, and habits you are learning and demonstrating in class are related to job and life success. **Peak Progress 2.4** on page 60 lists skills and qualities you are learning, practicing, and enhancing in your coursework and indicates how you will use them on the job.

As you develop your time- and stress-management skills, which we will explore in more detail later in this text, your habits in school and on the job will improve. Time management helps you show up for class on time and be prepared every day, leading to better grades. Punctuality in school will carry over to punctuality for work. Stress management may help you get along better with your roommates, instructors, or co-workers. Learning how to succeed in the school or college system can serve as a model for working effectively in organizational systems. Do you think you are maximizing your strengths, skills, and personal qualities? See **Peak Progress 2.5** on page 61 to determine what kind of student/worker you are and what you need to do to improve.

Overcome Obstacles

Don't Get Discouraged

Even peak performers sometimes feel discouraged and need help climbing out of life's valleys. To create and maintain a positive state of mind and learn self-management, you cannot just read a book, attend a lecture, or use a few strategies for a day or two.

Peak Progress

Skills for School and Career

Skills	School Application	Career Application
Motivation	Attending class, being prepared and participating, submitting quality work on time	Performing exceptional work, striving to become proficient at necessary skills
Critical thinking	Solving case studies, equations, essays	Solving work problems, improving employee relations, responding to market changes
Creativity	Conducting experiments, developing term papers	Creating work solutions, developing products, launching sales campaigns
Time management	Scheduling studying, prepping for exams, completing papers and projects	Prioritizing workflow, hitting deadlines, product launches
Financial management	Paying fees and expenses, personal budgeting and saving, repaying student loans	Developing and managing departmental budgets, projecting growth and profits
Writing	Writing papers, speeches, essay exams, e-mails, blogs	Writing reports, e-mails, product descriptions, promotional material
Public speaking	Giving classroom speeches, presenting research, participating in class discussions	Delivering product presentations, leading and participating in meetings
Test taking	Taking quizzes and exams, applying for advanced degrees	Receiving performance reviews, certification and licensure exams
Research	Finding, evaluating, and citing information	Linking processes to results, testing new products
Learning	Learning new content to fulfill major, maximizing learning styles	Learning new job skills, adapting to changes in technology
Systems	Understanding college rules, procedures, deadlines, expectations, resources	Understanding company rules, policies, reporting procedures
Technology	Using technology for papers, team projects, research, testing, course management	Using technology for developing reports, communicating, managing systems

● **Being Strong**

We've seen numerous examples of resilience in the aftermath of events such as Hurricane Sandy, the Boston Marathon bombings, and devasting tornadoes. *What characteristics make people persevere through such tragic losses?*

Peak Progress

What Kind of Student/Worker Are You?

A peak performer or an *A* student

- Is alert, actively involved, and eager to learn
- Consistently does more than required
- Consistently shows initiative and enthusiasm
- Is positive and engaged
- Can solve problems and make sound decisions
- Is dependable, prompt, neat, accurate, and thorough
- Attends work/class every day and is on time and prepared

A good worker or a *B* student

- Frequently does more than is required
- Is usually attentive, positive, and enthusiastic
- Completes most work accurately, neatly, and thoroughly
- Often uses critical thinking to solve problems and make decisions
- Attends work/class almost every day and is usually on time and prepared

An average worker or a *C* student

- Completes the tasks that are required
- Shows a willingness to follow instructions and learn
- Is generally involved, dependable, enthusiastic, and positive
- Provides work that is mostly thorough, accurate, and prompt
- Misses some work/classes

A problem worker or a *D* student

- Usually does the minimum of what is required
- Has irregular attendance, is often late, or is distracted
- Lacks a positive attitude or the ability to work well with others
- Often misunderstands assignments and deadlines
- Lacks thoroughness
- Misses many days of work/classes

An unacceptable worker or an *F* student

- Does not do the work that is required
- Is inattentive, bored, negative, and uninvolved
- Is undependable and turns in work that is incorrect and incomplete
- Misses a significant amount of work/class time

It takes time and effort. Everyone gets off course now and then, but the key is to realize that setbacks are part of life. You have to become **resilient**—adapt to difficult or challenging life experiences and overcome adversity, bounce back, and thrive under pressure. Demonstrating **hardiness** (a combination of commitment, control, and challenge) will give you the courage and motivation to turn rough patches into opportunities for personal growth.

“I've missed more than 9,000 shots in my career. I've lost almost 300 games. 26 times, I've been trusted to take the game winning shot and missed. I've failed over and over and over again in my life. And that is why I succeed.**”**

MICHAEL JORDAN
Professional basketball player

Figure 2.5 shows reasons students have given for dropping out of college. Many of these seem out of the student's control, but many may simply be excuses for not finding a way to persevere. For example, not all classes will be exhilarating and indeed may seem boring at times—but is that a reason to give up? If you think, "I'll be more motivated as soon as I graduate and get a real job," you may never develop the necessary qualities and skills to achieve that. Starting today, you should

- Commit to being motivated and positive.
- Focus on your successes and accomplishments.
- Surround yourself with positive, supportive, and encouraging friends.
- Tell yourself, "This is a setback, not a failure."
- Learn self-control and self-management strategies.
- Make certain you are physically renewed; get more rest, exercise more, and every day do something you love.
- Replace negative and limiting thoughts and self-talk with affirmations and positive visualization.
- Collect short stories about people who were discouraged, received negative messages, and bounced back.

Create Positive Mind Shifts

Your beliefs and expectations about yourself can either limit or expand your success. Other people's expectations of you may cause you to redefine who you think you are and what you think you can achieve. You may start to believe what you tell yourself or hear from others again and again, which may limit your thinking.

Figure 2.5
Reasons Students Do Not Graduate.

Juggling the demands of work and school is a major reason why students drop out of college. Besides the reasons cited in this survey, students also struggle with poor study habits, managing their social time, and taking responsibility for their education—including asking for help. *Which "reasons" in the survey are you facing and how are you coping in order to achieve your goals?*

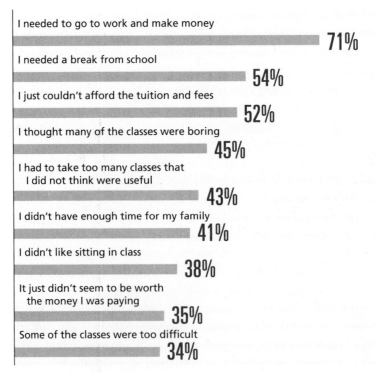

I needed to go to work and make money **71%**
I needed a break from school **54%**
I just couldn't afford the tuition and fees **52%**
I thought many of the classes were boring **45%**
I had to take too many classes that I did not think were useful **43%**
I didn't have enough time for my family **41%**
I didn't like sitting in class **38%**
It just didn't seem to be worth the money I was paying **35%**
Some of the classes were too difficult **34%**

Source: Jean Johnson and Jon Rochkind with Amber N. Ott and Samantha DuPont, "With Their Whole Lives Ahead of Them: Myths and Realities About Why So Many Students Fail to Finish College." A Public Agenda Report for The Bill & Melinda Gates Foundation, December 20, 2009. Reprinted with permission.

For example, Steve comes from a long line of lumber mill workers. Although they have lived for generations in a college town, his family has never had anything to do with the college. Steve was expected to go to work at the mill right after high school. He never thought about other options. However, during his senior year in high school, he attended Career Day. He met instructors and students from the local college who were friendly and encouraging. His world opened up, and he saw opportunities he had never considered. Steve experienced a major mind shift. Although he had to overcome a lack of support at home, he is now a successful college student with a bright future.

College is an ideal time to develop your natural creativity and explore new ways of thinking. Try the following:

1. **Create a support system.** Without support and role models, you may question whether you can succeed. First-generation college students, women in technical programs, and men in nursing programs may feel uncomfortable and question whether they belong. Cultural minorities, veterans, and physically challenged or returning students may feel out of place. Some students may be told that they are not college material. You can find encouragement with a support system of positive, accepting people. Join a variety of clubs. Make friends with diverse groups of students, instructors, and community leaders.

2. **Reprogram your mind.** Affirmations and visualization can create a self-fulfilling prophecy. If you think of yourself as a success and are willing to put in the effort, you will succeed. Focus on your successes and accomplishments, and overcome limitations. For example, if you need to take a remedial math class, take it and don't label yourself as "dumb" or "math-impaired." Instead, focus on how improved your math skills will be.

3. **Use critical thinking.** Question limiting labels and beliefs. Where did they come from, and are they accurate?

4. **Use creative thinking.** Ask yourself, "What if?" Explore creative ways of achieving your goals. Find out how you learn best, and adopt positive habits.

5. **Take responsibility.** You are responsible for your thoughts, beliefs, and actions. You can question, think, and explore. You can achieve almost anything you dream.

6. **Learn new skills.** Focus on your strengths, but be willing to learn new skills and competencies continually. Feeling competent is empowering.

7. **Use the whole of your intelligence.** You definitely are smarter than you think you are. Use all your experiences and personal qualities to achieve your goals. Develop responsibility, self-control, dependability, sociability, character, manners, and all the other qualities necessary for school, job, and life success.

TAKING CHARGE

Summary

In this chapter, I learned to

- **Use the whole of my intelligence.** Developing emotional maturity and strong personal qualities is just as, if not more, important to my future success as learning new skills and information. Essential personal qualities include character, responsibility, self-management and self-control, self-esteem, confidence, attitude, and motivation.

- **Focus on character first.** Strong leaders have an equally strong set of values. Having personal integrity gives me the courage to do the right thing, even when it is difficult. I display civility and empathy by interacting with family, friends, and colleagues with respect, kindness, good manners, empathy, and compassion. It's important for me to have a personal code of ethics that I follow in all facets of my life.

- **Take responsibility for my thoughts, actions, and behaviors.** I don't blame others for my setbacks, and I focus my energy on positive solutions. Others can depend on me to keep my commitments.

- **Manage and control my emotions, anger, and negative thoughts.** Conflict is an inevitable part of life, but it can be resolved in a positive way. Steps I can follow to redirect my negative thoughts and anger are (1) calm down; (2) clarify and define; (3) listen with empathy and respect; (4) use "I" statements; (5) focus on one problem; and (6) focus on win-win solutions.

- **Develop self-esteem and confidence.** Through self-assessment, I understand my strengths and will continue to learn new skills and competencies that will build my confidence.

- **Maintain a positive attitude and keep myself motivated.** A positive attitude is essential for achieving success; it influences the outcome of a task more than any other factor. Motivation is the inner drive that moves me to action. Working toward goals increases my motivation. Maslow's hierarchy of needs shows that I can fulfill my higher needs for self-esteem and self-actualization only when I have fulfilled my more basic needs first. The motivation cycle further demonstrates how affirmations, visualization, and self-talk affect my physical responses and behavior.

- **Realize the benefits of higher education.** Higher education has its roots in the liberal arts. Liberal arts classes can help make me a truly educated professional by providing an integration and understanding of history, culture, ourselves, and our world. My pursuit of a higher education should pay off with more career opportunities, a higher salary, more benefits, more job promotions, increased workplace flexibility, better workplace conditions, and greater job satisfaction. I will become more prepared for life on the job.

- **Overcome the barriers to staying positive and motivated.** Discouragement is the number one barrier to motivation. Setbacks will occur, but I am resilient by focusing on my successes and accomplishments, surrounding myself with supportive and encouraging people, keeping physically renewed, and replacing negative self-talk with positive affirmations and visualization.

- **Create positive mind shifts.** My beliefs and perceptions must be realistic. If they aren't, I must refocus my expectations in order to achieve my goals. I should not allow my beliefs to limit my potential, and I will use critical thinking techniques to expand my mind and comfort zone.

Performance Strategies

Following are the top 10 strategies for expanding your emotional intelligence and personal qualities:

- Cultivate character and integrity.
- Create a personal code of ethics.
- Take responsibility for your thoughts, actions, and behaviors.
- Practice self-control.
- Develop positive self-esteem and confidence.
- Determine personal motivators.
- Use goals as motivational tools.
- Reward yourself for making progress, and strive for excellence, not perfection.
- Become resilient to bounce back from setbacks.
- Create positive mind shifts.

Tech for Success

Take advantage of the text's web site at **www.mhhe.com/ferrett9e** for additional study aids, useful forms, and convenient and applicable resources.

- **Ethics information on the Web.** Search for articles on ethics, business etiquette, and codes of ethics. Check out different businesses, the military, government agencies, and colleges to find out if each has a code of ethics. Print some samples and bring them to class. What do the codes of ethics have in common?

- **Online discussion groups.** When you are interested in a topic or goal, it's very motivating to interact with others who share your interests. Join a discussion group and share your knowledge, wisdom, and setbacks with others. You will learn their stories and strategies in return.

- **Goal-setting examples.** Although your goals should be personal, sometimes it helps to see how others have crafted theirs. This may inspire you to realize that setting goals isn't difficult—it just takes thinking critically about what you want out of life. A number of resources on the Web provide goal-setting ideas on everything from becoming more financially responsible to learning a second language.

Study Team Notes

Positive Attitudes at Work

As a sales representative for a large medical company, Jacqui Williams sells equipment, such as X-ray and electrocardiograph (EKG) machines, to hospitals nationwide. Her job requires travel to prospective clients, where she meets with buyers to show her products and demonstrate their installation and use. Because Jacqui cannot take the large machines with her, she relies on printed materials and her iPad, from which she can point out new aspects of the machines she sells. The sales process usually takes several months and requires more than one trip to the prospective client.

Jacqui works on commission, being paid only when she makes a sale. Because she travels frequently, Jacqui must be able to work independently without a lot of supervision. For this reason, being personally motivated is a strong requirement for her position. Jacqui has found that what motivates her most is believing in the products she sells. Jacqui keeps up on the latest in her field by reading technical information and keeping track of the competition. She sets sales goals and then rewards herself with a short vacation.

Because personal relations with buyers are so important, Jacqui is careful about her appearance. While traveling, she keeps a positive mindset through affirmations, and she gets up early to eat a healthy breakfast and exercise in the hotel gym. She uses integrity by presenting accurate information and giving her best advice, even if it means not making a sale. Her clients describe Jacqui as positive and helpful, someone whom they look forward to seeing and whose advice they trust.

Jacqui Williams
SALES REPRESENTATIVE

Related Majors: Business, Marketing, Public Relations

CRITICAL THINKING In what way does having integrity, good character, and a code of ethics enhance a sales representative's business?

Peak Performer

PROFILE

Christiane Amanpour

"Amanpour is coming. Is something bad going to happen to us?"* That's how CNN's Chief International Correspondent, Christiane Amanpour, says she's often greeted. Whether she appreciates the grim humor or not, Amanpour knows that her name and face have become linked in people's minds with war, famine, and death. But she has earned the respect of journalists and viewers around the world with her gutsy reporting from war-ravaged regions, such as Afghanistan, Iran, Israel, Pakistan, Somalia, Rwanda, and the Balkans.

Amanpour launched her career at CNN as an assistant on the international assignment desk in 1983, when some observers mockingly referred to the fledgling network as "Chicken Noodle News." "I arrived at CNN with a suitcase, my bicycle, and about 100 dollars,"* she recalls. Less than a decade later, Amanpour was covering Iraq's invasion of Kuwait, the U.S. combat operation in Somalia, and the breakup of the Soviet Union as these events unfolded.

Amanpour's globe trotting began early. Born in London, Amanpour soon moved with her family to Tehran, where her father was an Iranian airline executive. Her family fled the country and returned to England during the Islamic Revolution of 1979. After high school, Amanpour studied journalism at the University of Rhode Island. She took a job after college as an electronics graphic designer at a radio station in Providence. She worked at a second radio station as a reporter, an anchor, and a producer before joining CNN.[†]

"I thought that CNN would be my ticket to see the world and be at the center of history—on someone else's dime,"* she says, noting that she's logged more time at the front than most military units. Fear, she admits, is as much a part of her daily life as it is for the soldiers whose activities she chronicles: "I have spent almost every working day [since becoming a war correspondent] living in a state of repressed fear."*

Amanpour worries about the changes that have transformed the television news industry in recent years, as competition for ratings and profits has heated up.

But Amanpour remains optimistic. "If we the storytellers give up, then the bad guys certainly will win," she says. "Remember the movie *Field of Dreams* when the voice said 'Build it and they will come'? Well, somehow that dumb statement has always stuck in my mind. And I always say, 'If you tell a compelling story, they will watch.'"*

PERFORMANCE THINKING Christiane Amanpour demonstrates courage, integrity, and commitment. In what ways do you speak out for freedom, justice, and equality?

CHECK IT OUT The Committee to Protect Journalists indicates that 70 journalists were killed in 2012 because of their work. Visit **www.cpj.org** to see what's being done to safeguard the lives of journalists in the world's hotspots. Use the search field to find the manual "Journalist Security Guide" to see what precautions journalists themselves must take in high-risk situations.

*AIDA International, 2000 Murrow Awards Ceremony Speech, September 13, 2000. www.aidainternational.nl.
[†]CNN Anchors and Reporters: Christiane Amanpour. **www.cnn.com/CNN/anchors_reporters/amanpour.Christiane.html.**

Starting Today

At least one strategy I learned in this chapter that I plan to try right away is

_____

_____

_____

What changes must I make in order for this strategy to be most effective?

_____

_____

_____

Review Questions

Based on what you have learned in this chapter, write your answers to the following questions:

1. What personal qualities are essential to success in school and work?

_____

_____

2. Give an example of a short-term goal versus a long-term goal.

_____

_____

3. List at least five motivational strategies.

_____

_____

4. Explain how affirmations and visualization affect the motivational cycle.

_____

_____

5. Explain what a mind shift is.

_____

_____

To test your understanding of the chapter's concepts, complete the chapter quiz at **www.mhhe.com/ferrett9e.**

Getting Motivated

In the Classroom

Carol Rubino is a drafting and design major at a community college. To pay her expenses, she needs to work several hours a week. She is very organized and responsible with her school and work obligations. Most of her peers would describe Carol as motivated because she attends every class, is punctual, and works hard in school and at work. Throughout high school, Carol participated in extracurricular activities but never really enjoyed them. She likes college but questions if she'll be able to find a job in her field when she graduates. As a result, Carol sometimes feels as if she is just wasting time and money.

1. What strategies in this chapter can help Carol find a strong sense of purpose and motivation?

_____

_____

2. What would you recommend to Carol for creating a more resourceful and positive attitude?

_____

_____

In the Workplace

Carol is now a draftsperson for a small industrial equipment company. She has been with the company for 10 years. Carol is a valuable employee because she is competent and well liked. Carol has a supportive family, is healthy, and travels frequently. Although she enjoys her job, Carol feels bored with the mundane routine. She wants to feel more motivated and excited on the job, as well as in her personal life.

3. What strategies in this chapter can help Carol become more enthusiastic about work or find new interest in her personal life?

_____

_____

4. What would you suggest to Carol to help her get motivated?

_____

_____

REVIEW AND APPLICATIONS | CHAPTER 2

Applying the ABC Method of Self-Management

In the Journal Entry on page 43, you were asked to describe a time when you were angry and lost control of your emotions. Describe that event here and indicate how others reacted to your actions.

_____

_____

_____

_____

_____

Now apply the ABC method to the situation and visualize a situation under control:

A = Actual event:

_____

_____

B = Beliefs:

_____

_____

C = Challenge:

_____

_____

While completing this exercise, were you surprised by the amount of time you spend on negative thoughts?

PRACTICE SELF-MANAGEMENT

For more examples of learning how to manage difficult situations, see the "Self-Management Workbook" section of the Online Learning Center website at **www.mhhe.com/ferrett9e**.

My Reinforcement Contract

Use this example as a guide; then fill in the following contract for one or all of the courses you are taking this term.

Name *Sara Jones*

Course *General Accounting*   Date *September 2014*

If I *study for 6 hours each week in this class and attend all lectures and labs*

Then I will *be better prepared for the midterm and final exams.*

I agree to *learn new skills, choose positive thoughts and attitudes, and try out new behaviors.*

I most want to accomplish *an "A" in this course to qualify for advanced accounting courses.*

The barriers to overcome are *my poor math skills.*

The resources I can use are *my study group and the Tutoring Center.*

I will reward myself for meeting my goals by *going out to dinner with some friends.*

The consequences for not achieving the results I want will be *to reevaluate my major.*

REINFORCEMENT CONTRACT

Name _____

Course _____ Date _____

If I _____

Then I will _____

I agree to _____

_____

I most want to accomplish _____

The barriers to overcome are _____

The resources I can use are _____

I will reward myself for meeting my goals by _____

The consequences for not achieving the results I want will be _____

Self-Esteem Inventory

Do this simple inventory to assess your self-esteem. Circle the number of points that reflects your true feelings.

4 = all the time

3 = most of the time

2 = some of the time

1 = none of the time

1. I like myself and I am a worthwhile person.	4	3	2	1
2. I have many positive qualities.	4	3	2	1
3. Other people generally like me and I have a sense of belonging.	4	3	2	1
4. I feel confident and know I can handle most situations.	4	3	2	1
5. I am competent and good at many things.	4	3	2	1
6. I have emotional control and I am respectful of others.	4	3	2	1
7. I am a person of integrity and character.	4	3	2	1
8. I respect the kind of person I am.	4	3	2	1
9. I am capable and willing to learn new skills.	4	3	2	1
10. Although I want to improve and grow, I am happy with myself.	4	3	2	1
11. I take responsibility for my thoughts, beliefs, and behavior.	4	3	2	1
12. I am empathetic and interested in others and the world around me.	4	3	2	1
Total points	___	___	___	___

Add up your points. A high score (36 and above) indicates high self-esteem. If you have a high sense of self-esteem, you see yourself in a positive light. If your self-esteem is low (below 24), you may have less confidence to deal with problems in college or on the job. If you scored at the lower end, list some strategies you can implement that may help boost your self-esteem:

Learning Styles and Motivation

You will feel more motivated and positive when you align your efforts with your learning and personality styles. Review your preference and style and think of the factors that help motivate you.

For example, *auditory learners* may be more motivated when they listen to their favorite inspirational music and say affirmations. *Visual learners* may be more motivated when they surround themselves with pictures and practice visualizing themselves as motivated and positive. *Kinesthetic learners* may be more motivated when they work on activities, dance, hike, jog, and work with others. (See pages 10–16 for the complete discussion.)

Analyzers may be more motivated when they think, reflect, and organize information into sequential steps. *Supporters* may be more motivated when they work in a group and make information meaningful. *Creators* may be more motivated when they observe, make active experiments, and build models. *Directors* may be more motivated when they clearly define procedures and make practical applications. (See pages 20–26 for the complete discussion.)

List the ways you can motivate yourself that are compatible with your learning style and personality type:

1. _____
   _____
   _____

2. _____
   _____
   _____
   _____

3. _____
   _____
   _____

4. _____
   _____
   _____

5. _____
   _____
   _____

6. _____
   _____
   _____

REVIEW AND APPLICATIONS | CHAPTER 2

Assessment of Personal Qualities

Category	Assessment	Y/N	Example
Emotional intelligence	Do I value and practice essential personal qualities?		
Character	Do I value and practice being a person of character and integrity?		
Civility	Do I treat others with respect and courtesy?		
Ethics	Do I have a code of ethics?		
Responsibility	Do I take responsibility for my thoughts and behavior?		
Self-control	Do I have self-control and know how to manage anger?		
Self-esteem	Do I have a realistic and positive sense of myself?		
Positive attitude	Do I strive to be positive and upbeat?		
Motivation	Do I create the inner drive and determination to achieve my goals?		
Self-actualization	Am I committed to growing and realizing my full potential?		
Visualization	Do I use visualization as a powerful tool for change and growth?		
Affirmation	Do I dispute and replace negative self-talk with affirmations?		
Critical thinking	Do I use critical thinking to challenge my beliefs and see new possibilities?		

The area I most want to improve is:

Strategies I will use to improve are:

Manage Your Time

LEARNING OUTCOMES

In this chapter, you will learn to

3.1 Determine how you use your time and how you *should* use your time.

3.2 Use personal goals to identify priorities

3.3 List time-management strategies

3.4 Work in alignment with your learning style

3.5 Overcome procrastination

3.6 Handle interruptions

3.7 Juggle family, school, and job commitments

SELF-MANAGEMENT

It's 7:30 a.m., I'm late for class, and I can't find my keys. It always seems like there's too little time and too much to do. I feel as if I have no control over my life. How can I manage my time and get organized?

Have you ever had a similar experience? Do you find yourself spending hours looking for things? Do you get angry at yourself and others because you feel frustrated and unorganized? In this chapter, you will learn how to take control of your time and your life and focus on priorities. Visualize yourself going through the day organized and centered. You have a clear vision of your goals and priorities, and you work steadily until tasks are finished. Feel the sense of accomplishment and completion. You are in charge of your time and your life.

JOURNAL ENTRY In **Worksheet 3.1** on page 104, describe a time or situation when you felt overwhelmed by too much to do and too little time. What were the consequences?

Focus on PRIORITIES,
not *tasks*.

In this chapter, we look at time management with a positive attitude. Instead of controlling, suppressing, or constricting your freedom, time management enables you to achieve the things you really want and frees up time to enjoy life. Peak performers use a systematic approach that allows them to

- Organize projects and achieve results
- Accomplish goals and priorities
- Be effective, not just efficient
- Avoid crises
- Remain calm and productive
- Feel a sense of accomplishment

Everyone has the same amount of time: 24 hours a day. You can't save or steal time. When it's gone, it's gone. However, you can learn to invest it wisely. This chapter will help you learn how to get control of your life by managing your time wisely and choosing to spend it on your main goals. You will discover that there is always time to do what you really want to do. Too many people waste time doing things that should be done quickly (if at all) and ignoring their long-term goals.

As you go through this chapter, think about what you want to achieve and how you can use your time skillfully to perform at your peak level. This chapter will help you become effective, not just efficient. You are efficient when you do things faster. You are effective when you do the right things in the right way. As a wise time manager, you can avoid feeling overwhelmed and falling behind in school, at work, or in your personal life. Whether you are an 18-year-old living on campus or a 45-year-old juggling school, family, and work, the principles in this chapter can help you manage your time and your life.

Use Time Effectively

Time management is much more than focusing on minutes, hours, and days. Your attitude, energy level, and ability to concentrate have a major impact on how well you manage time. Clearly evaluate situations that may have spun out of control because you procrastinated or failed to plan and how these situations may have affected other people. Others suffer when you are late for class, miss a study group meeting, or don't do your share of a team project.

Let's look at two important questions concerning your present use of time. The answers will help you develop a plan that will fine-tune your organizational and time-management skills—ultimately leading you to become an efficient peak performer.

1. Where does your time go? (Where are you spending your time and energy?)
2. Where should your time go?

Where Does Your Time Go?

You can divide time into three types: committed time, maintenance time, and discretionary time.

- **Committed time.** Committed time is devoted to school, labs, studying, work, commuting, family, and other activities involving the immediate and long-term goals you have committed to accomplishing. Your committed time reflects what is important to your career, health, relationships, and personal growth—what you value most.

- **Maintenance time.** Maintenance time is the time you spend "maintaining" yourself. Activities such as eating, sleeping, grooming (showering, styling your hair, cleaning your contact lenses, getting dressed, etc.), cooking, cleaning/laundry, shopping, and bill paying use up your maintenance time.

- **Discretionary time.** The time that is yours to use as you please is discretionary time. Although this is your "free" time, you should spend it on the most important things in your life, such as relationships with family and friends; service to the community; intellectual development; and activities that give you joy and relaxation and that contribute to your physical, mental, and spiritual well-being. These should tie in with your long-term goals of being healthy, feeling centered and peaceful, and having loving relationships.

● **Where does fitness "fit"?**

Daily exercise can be considered committed time if it's part of your overall life plan to remain healthy. Some would consider it maintenance, and others would place it under discretionary activities. *Where would you record it?*

As you consider where your time goes, notice whether you are using most of the day for commitments. A good place to start is with an assessment of how you spend your time and energy. Complete **Personal Evaluation Notebook 3.1** on page 78 (or use the weekly planner in **Worksheet 3.7** on page 110) to track how you use your time. The far right column asks you to indicate your energy level during the day: Do you feel focused and alert, or are you distracted or tired? Many people have certain hours during the day when they are most productive.

After you have recorded your activities, review your Time Log to determine how much time you are devoting to daily tasks, such as studying, commuting, and socializing. Complete **Personal Evaluation Notebook 3.2** on page 79 and tally how much time you currently spend on various activities (and add others from your Time Log). Determining where you are currently spending your time will help you figure out the best way to use your time to achieve important goals. Even if you are juggling school, work, and family and feel you have no discretionary time, this will help you use what little discretionary time you do have to be most effective.

Where Should Your Time Go?

The first rule of time management is to make a commitment to what you want to accomplish—in other words, to set goals. As discussed in Chapter 2, goals are not vague wishes or far-away dreams. They are specific, measurable, observable, and realistic. A goal is a target that motivates you and directs your efforts. Goal setting is

Personal Evaluation Notebook

Time Log

Fill in this Time Log to chart your activities throughout the day. Identify activities as committed (C), maintenance (M), or discretionary (D). Also determine your energy level throughout the day as high (H), medium (M), or low (L). Use **Worksheet 3.7** on page 110 to chart your activities for more than 1 day to see patterns in how you spend your time.

Time	Activity	Type C/M/D	Energy H/M/L
12:00–1:00 a.m.			
1:00–2:00			
2:00–3:00			
3:00–4:00			
4:00–5:00			
5:00–6:00			
6:00–7:00			
7:00–8:00			
8:00–9:00			
9:00–10:00			
10:00–11:00			
11:00–12:00 (noon)			
12:00–1:00 p.m.			
1:00–2:00			
2:00–3:00			
3:00–4:00			
4:00–5:00			
5:00–6:00			
6:00–7:00			
7:00–8:00			
8:00–9:00			
9:00–10:00			
10:00–11:00			
11:00–12:00 (midnight)			

Personal Evaluation Notebook   3.3

Ahead: Your Goals *(concluded)*

SHORT-TERM GOALS (ACCOMPLISH THIS YEAR)

goals you want to accomplish in the next year. Consider your answers to these questions:

- What is the major goal for which I am striving this year?
- How does this goal relate to my life's mission or purpose?
- Is this goal in conflict with any other goal?
- What hurdles must I overcome to reach my goal?
- What resources, help, and support will I need to overcome these hurdles?
- What specific actions are necessary to complete my goal?

E. SEMESTER GOALS

List goals you want to accomplish this semester—for example,

- I will preview chapters for 10 minutes before each lecture.
- I will go to all of my classes on time.
- I will jog for 30 minutes each day.

Be sure to include these goals in your daily and monthly planners. Consistently accomplishing these goals is the key to achieving your bigger goals.

Urgent priorities are pressing, deadline-driven projects or activities, such as dropping a class, paying your fees, and turning in papers. They directly affect your top goals and priorities, and not completing them on schedule can require even more time to fix the problem. For example, if you don't meet the deadline for adding classes, you have to pay additional fees or may not get into the class. Not paying for classes on time could result in having all your classes dropped.

Important priorities are essential activities that support your long-term goals and create the results you want—not just for today but also for future success. These activities and commitments include attending every class, creating study teams, completing homework, forming healthy relationships, planning, and exercising regularly. People who spend time daily on important items prevent crises. For example, if you build a personal fitness routine into every day, you will increase your energy, health, and overall sense of well-being and prevent medical problems that result from inactivity and weight gain. Long-term priorities must be built into your daily activities.

Ongoing activities require continual attention and may be urgent, but they may not be important. For example, as you go through your e-mail, open mail, and answer phone calls, some messages will be urgent (needing an immediate response) but not important for your long-term goals. These activities require continual attention and follow-up and should be managed to prevent future problems. Jot down whom you need to see or call. Follow up with deadlines and determine if these activities support your top goals. For example, maybe you were pressured to join a club or

> **"**Ordinary people merely think how they shall spend their time; a man of talent tries to use it.**"**
> ARTHUR SCHOPENHAUER
> *German philosopher*

WORDS TO SUCCEED

community group that has been taking a lot of time. You may need to say, "This is a worthwhile project and I appreciate being invited to attend, but I cannot participate at this time." Ask yourself if this activity meets your highest priority at this time.

Trivial activities make up all the daily stuff of life, and many are major time wasters. These unimportant activities can be fun, such as chatting online, going to parties, shopping, and watching TV. They can also be annoying, such as dealing with junk mail—both real and virtual. The key is to stay focused on your important, top-priority items and schedule a certain amount of time for trivial activities. For example, because checking Facebook, Twitter, or e-mail, or texting friends can quickly eat up your discretionary time, limit these activities to just a few times each day after major tasks are done. You want a balanced life and need to socialize with friends, but sometimes a phone call or quick visit can turn into an hour-long gossip session. If this happens too often, you will not accomplish your important goals.

Setting priorities helps you focus on immediate goals. These essential, small steps lead you to your big goals. Your awareness of where your time goes becomes a continual habit of assessing, planning, and choosing tasks in the order of their importance, and this leads to success.

Ask yourself these questions: Do I have a sense of purpose and direction? Are my goals clearly defined? Are any in conflict with each other? Are they flexible enough to be modified as needed? Do I forget to write priorities in my planner? Do I daydream too much and have a problem with concentration? Do I invest time in high-priority tasks? Do I attend to small details that pay off in a big way? Refer to **Peak Progress 3.1** to see if the 80/20 rule applies to you.

Peak Progress   3.1

Investing Your Time in High-Priority Items: The 80/20 Rule

Whether you are a student, an executive, or an entry-level worker, your effectiveness will increase if you focus on top priorities. According to the 80/20 rule (the Pareto Principle), 80 percent of the results flow out of 20 percent of the activities—for example,

- Eighty percent of the interruptions come from 20 percent of the people.
- Eighty percent of the clothes you wear come from 20 percent of your wardrobe.
- Eighty percent of your phone calls come from 20 percent of the people you know.
- Eighty percent of a company's sales may come from 20 percent of its total customers.

A look at your time wasters may reveal that you are spending too much time on low-priority activities and short-changing your top priorities. Wasting time on low-priority activities is a major reason for not accomplishing major tasks.

To produce results, focus on what is important—for example,

- Twenty percent more effort can result in an 80 percent better paper or speech.
- Twenty percent more time being involved and prepared in classes could produce 80 percent better results.
- Twenty percent more time developing positive relationships could reduce conflicts by 80 percent.
- Twenty percent more time taking care of yourself— getting enough sleep, eating healthy, exercising, and controlling stress—can result in 80 percent more effectiveness.

The 80/20 rule is just a rule of thumb. The exact percentage may change based on the circumstance. However, it reminds you to spend your time on the activities that are really important and achieve the results you want.

Time-Management Strategies

Use the following strategies to improve your time-management skills and help you achieve your goals in a balanced and effective way.

1. **Keep a calendar.** An inexpensive, pocket-size calendar is easy to carry with you and handy for scheduling commitments, such as classes, labs, and work for the entire semester. This helps you see the big picture. Review your calendar each week and list top priorities, due dates, and important school, work, and family activities. Each day, review urgent priorities that must be done by a deadline, such as paying fees, dropping a class, or paying taxes. Schedule important activities that support your goals, such as classes, exercise, study teams, and deadlines for choosing a topic. Jot down people to see or call, such as your instructor or advisor, or activities, such as meetings or social events. Remember, the shortest pencil is better than the longest memory. For example, if your advisor gives you a code for registration, put it on your calendar at the date and time for your registration. Don't just write your code on your binder or toss it into your backpack. The worksheets at the end of this chapter include handy calendars to help you plan your week, month, and semester.

2. **Create a daily to-do list.** Some people like to write a to-do list for the next day, taking some time at the end of a day to review briefly what they want to focus on for the next day. Others like to write their list in the morning at breakfast or when they first get to school or work. *List the tasks you need to accomplish during the day and map them out on a daily calendar. Circle or place a number 1 by the most important priority to make sure it gets accomplished.* Make certain you build in time for family and friends. If you have children, plan special events. Bear in mind that the schedule should be flexible; you will want to allow for free time and unexpected events. Follow this schedule for 2 weeks and see how accurate it is. You can follow the format of the Time Log on page 78, or see **Worksheet 3.6** on page 109, which includes a planner for mapping out your daily to-do list. (See **Figure 3.1** on page 84 for tips on using a daily planner and to-do list and **Figure 3.2** on page 85 on using your cell phone to help manage your time.)

   Once you have written your list, do your urgent, top-priority items. Keep your commitments, such as attending every class, and don't do fun activities until the most important ones are done. When you see important items checked off, you'll be inspired. It's OK if you don't get to everything on your list. If tasks are left over, add them to your next to-do list if they are still important. Ask yourself, "What is the best use of my time right now?"

3. **Do the tough tasks first.** Start with your most difficult subjects, while you're fresh and alert. For instance, if you are avoiding your statistics homework because it is difficult, get up early and do it before your classes begin. Start projects when they're assigned.

4. **Break projects down into smaller tasks.** Begin by seeing the whole project or each chapter as part of a larger system. Then break it into manageable chunks. You may get discouraged if you face a large task, whether it's writing a major

> **"**Don't start your day until you have finished it on paper first.**"**
>
> JIM ROHN
> *Motivational speaker*

WORDS TO SUCCEED

Figure 3.1
How to Use a Planner

The best way to use a planner to manage your time is to make it an essential part of your day. Some time-management experts even recommend giving your planner a name and finding it a "home" (a place in plain sight where it should always be put at the end of the day). *What name would you give your planner and where would its "home" be?*

Determine which works better for you:
a weekly planner (shown here) or a daily planner that has slots for each hour of the day (see *Worksheet 3.6*).

Size matters:
- It should be a convenient size for carrying.
- Spaces should be big enough to write in legibly.

- Record all appointments, due, dates, and events.
- Schedule study sessions, exam prep.

March

Su	M	T	W	Th	F	Sa
		1	2	3	4	5	6
7	8	9	10	11	12	13
14	15	16	17	18	19	20
21	22	23	24	25	26	27
28	29	30	31

2013

22 Monday
New quarter begins
Dentist appt 2:45
Study team meeting @ 7:00

23 Tuesday
Proofread Biology paper
Guest lecturer series @ 6:30
Order Mom's b-day cake

24 Wednesday
Biology paper due 3:00
Write sample questions for test on April 1
Yoga class @ 6:00

25 Thursday
Lunch with Loren @ 12:15
Drop off donations at animal shelter after class

26 Friday
Financial aid forms due by 5:00!
Meet with advisor @ 11:00
Steven's soccer game @ 6:00

27 Saturday
Mom's b-day party 6:00
--pick up cake by 1:00

28 Sunday
Review notes for Biology test 12:00–2:00
Study team 7:00

To Do

Notes — Include a "great ideas" section for recording thoughts and inspirations.

Contacts — Add important contacts and information (phone numbers, e-mails, office hours).

- Write down priorities and tasks for the week.

Tips:
- Use only 1 planner for work, school, and personal.
- Record everything in it as soon as possible.
- Carry it all the time.
- Check it 3 times a day (such as breakfast, lunch, bedtime).

term paper or reading several chapters. Getting started is half the battle. Sometimes working for just 15 minutes before you go to bed can yield big results. For example, preview a chapter, outline the main ideas for your term paper, or write a summary at the end of a chapter. You will find inspiration in completing smaller tasks, and you will feel more in control.

Some students find a project board helpful for long-term projects, as shown in **Figure 3.3.** on page 86 Begin with today's date (or the start date),

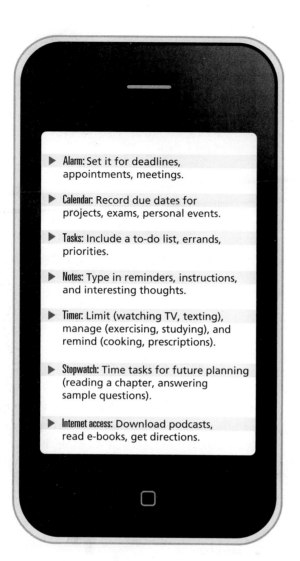

Figure 3.2
Smartphone 101

Use the features on your phone to help you manage your time. Almost every cell phone has these basic features. Many also include video conferencing and 3-way calling, so you can communicate on projects. And a voice recorder allows you to summarize lectures, notes, and ideas. *Which ones do you already use?*

Within the image:

▶ Alarm: Set it for deadlines, appointments, meetings.

▶ Calendar: Record due dates for projects, exams, personal events.

▶ Tasks: Include a to-do list, errands, priorities.

▶ Notes: Type in reminders, instructions, and interesting thoughts.

▶ Timer: Limit (watching TV, texting), manage (exercising, studying), and remind (cooking, prescriptions).

▶ Stopwatch: Time tasks for future planning (reading a chapter, answering sample questions).

▶ Internet access: Download podcasts, read e-books, get directions.

along with the due date, clearly indicated at the top. Your start date also should be realistic—and as soon as possible. Then separate the "board" into two columns: "Key Activities" and "Date Completed." In the date column, put today's date (or start date) at the top and the project's due date at the bottom. (Some prefer to reverse that, putting the due date at the top and working backwards. Use whichever process works best for you.) With these two dates set, begin in the activities column by listing in order the project-related tasks that need to be accomplished between the start and end dates. Go back to the date column and start plugging in optimal dates next to the tasks, working from beginning to end. You may find that the time you think you need for each task adds up to a schedule that extends beyond your due date—obviously, that's a problem. If so, revise your dates and create a new schedule that achieves your completion date. (Allow time for proofreading and potential setbacks, such as computer problems.)

5. **Consolidate similar tasks.** Grouping similar tasks can maximize your efforts. For example, if you need to make several calls, make them all at a specific time and reduce interruptions. Set aside a block of time to shop, pay bills, and run

Figure 3.3
Sample Project Board

Making a project board is an effective time-management strategy. You can plan your tasks from start to end, or some people prefer to work backwards—starting with the end date. *How can you incorporate your project board into your daily planner?*

Project: Term Paper for Business Class 110	
Today's date: January 23, 2014	Due date: April 23, 2014
Key Activities	**Date Completed**
Explore topics	January 23
Finalize topic	January 28
Mind map outline	February 4
Initial library research	February 8
General outline	February 22
Library research	March 5
Detailed library research	March 10
Detailed outline	March 15
First draft	March 27
Do additional research and spell-check	April 5
Proof second draft; revise	April 10
Prepare final draft and proof	April 15
Paper finished and turned in	April 23

● **Study Anywhere and Everywhere**
Use your time between classes and while waiting for appointments to study and prepare for class. *What is something you can always carry with you, so that you are prepared for down time?*

errands. Try to answer e-mails at designated times, rather than as each one comes in. Write a list of questions for your advisor, instructor, or study team. Make certain you know expectations, so that you don't have to repeat tasks.

6. **Study at your high-energy time.** Know your body rhythms and study your hardest subjects during your high-energy time. Review the Time Log to determine the time of day when you have the most energy, and complete **Personal Evaluation Notebook 3.4.** Guard against interruptions, and don't do mindless tasks or socialize during your peak energy period. For example, if your peak time is in the morning, don't waste time answering mail, cleaning, or doing other routine work. Use your high-energy time to do serious studying and work that requires thinking, writing, and completing projects. Use your low-energy time to do more physical work or easy reading or previewing of chapters.

7. **Study everywhere and anywhere.** Ideally, you should choose a regular study location with few distractions, such as the library. However, you should be prepared to study anywhere, as you never know when you might get some unexpected down time. Carry note cards with you to review formulas, dates, definitions, facts, and important data. Take class notes or a book with you to review during the 5 or 10 minutes of waiting between classes, for the bus, in line at the grocery store, or for appointments. Digitally record important material and lectures and listen to them while commuting, exercising, dressing, walking, or waiting for class to begin. Even if you plan well, you will occasionally get stuck in lines, but you can make the most of this time.

8. **Study in short segments throughout the day.** Studying in short segments is much more effective than studying in marathon

Personal Evaluation Notebook

 **3.4**

Your Daily Energy Levels

Keep track of your energy levels every day for a week or more. Revisit your Time Log on page 78 to determine your daily energy levels, so that you can become more aware of your patterns.

1. What time(s) of the day are your energy levels at their peak?

   _____

2. What time(s) of the day are your energy levels at their lowest?

   _____

3. What tasks do you want to focus on during your high-energy time?

   _____

4. What can you do to increase your energy at your low-energy time?

   _____

sessions. Your brain is much more receptive to recall when you review in short sessions at various times.

9. **Get organized.** Think of the time you waste looking for items (and the unnecessary stress it causes). Choose your clothes and pack your lunch the night before, put your keys on the same hook, place your backpack by the door, put your mail and assignments in the same space, and keep records of bills and important information in your file. Keep an academic file that includes your grades and transcripts, tests, papers, and projects. If you need to negotiate a grade, you will have the background support you will need. Make sure you save and back up any important work created on your computer and can easily retrieve it (to avoid losing hours of work).

10. **Be flexible, patient, and persistent.** Don't try to make too many changes at once, and don't get discouraged if a strategy doesn't work for you. You are striving for excellence, not perfection. Change certain aspects until a strategy fits your style. If it works, do it. If not, try something new. Give yourself at least 30 days to develop new habits. It often feels strange and uncomfortable to do any new task or vary your schedule of daily events. For example, you might discover that you have a habit of getting coffee every morning and spending an hour socializing with friends before your morning classes. Try changing this habit by doing it only once a week.

11. **Realize that you can't do it all (at least right now).** You may feel overwhelmed by too many demands and determine that some tasks are better done by others. This does not mean you can offload your responsibilities onto others, but focus on your important priorities and say no to activities that

Take 3 minutes to get organized to head out the door on time tomorrow:

- Where is the best place to put everything you'll need? Create a checklist of "must-have" items to refer to every night, if that helps.
- Is your phone charged? Are your keys, glasses, pens, and so on in your purse or backback?
- Which books, notepads, and assignments will you need for class tomorrow? Make as many piles as necessary if you'll be going back and forth to class during the day.

What else can you do in 3 minutes?

- Pack your lunch.
- Unload the dishwasher.
- Check your e-mails and respond to urgent ones.

Take 3

don't support your goals. Consider delegating certain tasks, joining a club later in the year, or participating in a fundraiser when you are on school break. Do social activities when your top-priority tasks are done.

Time Management and Your Learning Style

Many time-management strategies are designed for people with left-brain dominance. Left-brain dominant people like routine, structure, and deadlines. They tend to be **convergent** thinkers because they are good at looking at several unrelated items and bringing order to them. Right-brain dominant people like variety, flexibility, creativity, and innovation. They are usually **divergent** thinkers because they branch out from one idea to many. They are good at brainstorming because one idea leads to another. They are able to focus on the whole picture. However, they can also learn to break the global view of the whole project into steps, break each of these steps into activities, and schedule and organize activities around the big goal. If you are right-brain dominant, you should

- **Focus on a few tasks.** It is very important for right-brain dominant people to focus their efforts on one or two top-priority items instead of being scattered and distracted by busywork. Imagine putting on blinders and focusing on one step until it is completed, and then move on to the next step. This creates discipline.
- **Write it down.** A daily calendar is vital to making certain that your activities support your short- and long-term goals. Write down phone numbers, e-mail addresses, and office hours of instructors and study team members. Highlight in color any deadlines or top-priority activities. Besides a daily calendar, use a master calendar in your study area and allow for variety and change. Make certain you review both your daily calendar with to-do items and your master calendar before you go to bed at night, so that you see the big picture.
- **Use visuals.** Right-brain dominant people often like to use visuals. One creative way to brainstorm, plan, and put your vision into action is to use a mind map (see Chapter 5, page 155). Use visual cues and sticky notes. When you think of an activity that will help you meet your goal, write it down.
- **Integrate learning styles.** Visualize yourself completing a project, and create a vision board of your goals and dreams. Use auditory cues by recording yourself talking through ideas and project plans. Make your project physical by adapting a hands-on approach and working with others to complete your project. Ask yourself, "Is there a way to simplify this task?" Planning is important, even if you are a creative person. **Peak Progress 3.2** explores the process of learning to take control of your time.

❝You may delay, but time will not.**❞**

BENJAMIN FRANKLIN
Inventor, publisher, statesman

Peak Progress

Applying the Adult Learning Cycle to Taking Control of Your Time and Life

Applying the Adult Learning Cycle will help you establish goals and create a plan to meet them.

1. **RELATE. Why do I want to learn this?** Planning my time better and getting organized are essential for juggling the demands of school, work, and life. What are the areas where I need the most work?

2. **OBSERVE. How does this work?** I can learn a lot about time management by observing people who are on time, get their work done, work calmly and steadily, and seem to accomplish a lot in a short time. I'll also observe people who are unorganized, and often late, miss classes, and waste time blaming, complaining, and being overly involved in other people's lives. How do their problems relate to poor time management or self-management?

3. **REFLECT. What does this mean?** What strategies are working for me? What new strategies can I try? I will explore creative ways to solve problems rather than feeling overwhelmed.

4. **DO. What can I do with this?** Each day, I'll work on one area. For example, I'll choose one place to hang my keys and consistently put them there. If I find them on the table, I'll put them on the hook until it becomes a habit.

5. **TEACH. Whom can I share this with?** I'll share my tips and experiences with others and find out their strategies in return. I should continue to reward myself, at least mentally, for making positive changes.

Now return to Stage 1 and think about how it feels to be focused, instead of rushed, by managing your time and priorities.

Overcome Obstacles

Stop Procrastinating

Procrastination is deliberately putting off tasks, and most of us have been guilty of putting off doing what we know should be done. However, a continual pattern of delaying and avoiding is a major barrier to time management.

Complete **Personal Evaluation Notebook 3.5** on page 90 to determine if you procrastinate too much and, if so, why.

Self-assessment is often the key to understanding why you procrastinate and to developing strategies to help you control your life and create the results you want. Once you have identified what is holding you back, you can create solutions and apply them consistently until they are habits. To avoid procrastination, try the following strategies on the next page.

Am I a Procrastinator?

- I do what I enjoy rather than what should be done.
- I'm a perfectionist and can't work unless the outcome is the best it can be.
- I worry too much about details.
- I get overwhelmed by responsibilities.
- I'm too shy and avoid working with others.
- I'm embarrassed because I put it off for so long—so I'll just write it off.
- I get easily distracted.
- I blame others.
- I don't want to be told what to do.
- I work better under pressure.
- I lack the discipline to complete a task.

Personal Evaluation Notebook

Procrastination

1. What is something I should have accomplished by now but haven't?

2. Why did I procrastinate?

3. What are the consequences of my procrastination?

4. What kind of tasks do I put off?

5. When do I usually procrastinate?

6. Where do I procrastinate? Am I more effective in the library or at home?

7. How does my procrastination affect others in my life?

8. Who supports, or enables, my procrastination?

1. **Set daily priorities.** Be clear about your goals and the results you want to achieve and allow enough time to complete them. Use your to-do list to check off tasks as you complete them. This will give you a feeling of accomplishment.

2. **Break the project into small tasks.** A large project that seems overwhelming can encourage procrastination. Do something each day that brings you closer to your goal. Use a project board or write down steps and deadlines that are necessary to achieve success. For example, as soon as a paper is assigned, start that day to choose a topic, the next day do research, and so on until each step leads to an excellent paper.

3. **Gather everything you'll need to start your project.** Clear off a space, and prepare your notes and other materials. Reread the assignment, and clarify expectations with your instructor or study team. Having everything ready

creates a positive attitude and makes it easier to start the task. This strategy is effective whether you're doing a term paper or making cookies.

4. **Focus for short spurts.** We discussed in Chapter 1 how concentrating on one task for a short period of time is more effective and helps create a positive, can-do attitude, such as "I'm going to preview this chapter for 15 minutes with full concentration." This is more effective than telling yourself you're going to study for 2 or 3 hours, which creates a mindset that says, "This is too difficult." Seeing how fully you can concentrate in a short amount of time builds confidence and uses discipline instead of guilt and willpower. Before you go to bed or when you have a few minutes during the day, use the same strategy: "I'm just going to spend 10 minutes writing a rough draft for my English paper." Ask yourself if you can do one more thing to get you started the next day.

5. **Surround yourself with supportive people.** Ask for help from motivated friends, instructors, or your advisor, or visit the Learning Center for support. Sometimes talking out loud can help you clarify why you are avoiding a project. Study buddies or a study team can also help you stay on track. Just knowing that someone is counting on you to deliver may be enough to keep you from procrastinating.

6. **Tackle difficult tasks during your high-energy time.** Do what is important first, while you are at your peak energy level and concentration is easiest. Once you get a difficult or unpleasant task done, you will feel more energy. When your energy dips and you need a more physical, less mentally demanding task, return messages or tidy up your desk.

7. **Develop a positive attitude.** Negative emotions, such as anger, jealousy, worry, and resentment, can eat up hours of time and sap your energy. Instead, resolve to have a positive attitude and use affirmations. Think, "I get to work on my project today," instead of "I have to work on this project." Feel grateful that you have the opportunity to be in college. Resourceful and positive attitudes don't just happen; they are created.

8. **Reward yourself.** Focus on the sense of accomplishment you feel when you make small, steady steps and meet your deadlines. Reward yourself with a small treat or break when you complete activities and a bigger reward (such as a nice dinner or movie) when you complete a goal. Work first and play later.

9. **Don't expect perfection.** You learn any new task by making mistakes. For example, you become a better writer or speaker with practice. Don't wait or delay because you want perfection. Your paper is not the great American novel. It is better to do your best than to do nothing. You can polish later, but avoiding writing altogether is a major trap. Do what you can today to get started on the task at hand.

Chloe is always late. Her family, friends—everyone—continually tell her how frustrating it is that she keeps them waiting. She finally got the message when her best friend texted her that she was tired of her inconsideration and the group was leaving for a party without her. The rush she always felt from "making an entrance" was replaced with a feeling of abandonment and the realization that she had let others down.

- What negative characteristics are being demonstrated by someone who is habitually late?
- What problems does this create—in school, on the job, in personal situations?
- Give Chloe some specific strategies that might help her become more prompt and dependable.

Control Interruptions

Interruptions steal time. They cause you to stop projects, disrupt your thought pattern, divert your attention, and make it difficult to rebuild momentum. To avoid time wasters, take control by setting priorities everyday that will help you meet goals and reduce interruptions. Don't let endless activities, e-mail, texting, and other people control you. For instance, if a friend calls, set a timer for 10 minutes or postpone the call until later, after you have previewed an assigned chapter or outlined a speech. Let calls go to voicemail if you are studying, or tell the caller that you will call back in an hour. Combine socializing with exercising or eating lunch. If you watch a favorite program, turn the television off right after that show. The essence of time management is taking charge of your life and not allowing interruptions to control you. Complete **Personal Evaluation Notebook 3.6** to determine the sources of your interruptions. (Also see **Worksheet 3.3** on page 106 to identify your time wasters.)

Peak performers know how to effectively live and work with other people. Try these tips to help you reduce interruptions:

1. **Create an organized place to study.** A supportive, organized study space can help you reduce interruptions and keep you focused. Have all your study tools—pencils, pens, books, papers, files, notes, a calendar, a semester schedule, and study team and instructor names and phone numbers—in one place, so that you won't waste time looking for items you need. Keep only one project on your desk at a time, and file everything else away or put it on a shelf. If you have children, include a study area for them, close to yours, where they can work quietly with puzzles, crayons, or books. This will allow study time together and create a lifelong study pattern for them.

2. **Determine your optimal time to study.** When you are focused, you can study anywhere, anytime. However, to increase your effectiveness, do your serious studying when your energy level is at its peak.

3. **Create quiet time.** Discuss study needs and expectations with your roommates or family, and ask for an agreement. You might establish certain study hours or agree on a signal, such as closing your door or hanging a "Quiet" sign, to let each other know when you need quiet time.

4. **Study in the library.** If it is difficult to study at home, study in the library. Once you enter, your brain can turn to a serious study mode. Sitting in a quiet place and facing the wall can reduce interruptions and distractions. You can accomplish far more in less time, and then you can enjoy your friends and family.

5. **Do first things first.** You will feel more in control if you have a list of priorities every day. Knowing what you want and need to do makes it easier to say no to distractions. Make certain that these important goals include your health, taking time to exercise, eat right, and relax.

6. **Just say no.** Tell your roommates or family when an important test or project is due. If someone wants to talk or socialize when you need to study, say no. Set aside time each day to spend with your family or roommates, such as dinner, a walk, or a movie. They will understand your priorities when you

Personal Evaluation Notebook

3.6

Interruptions!

Keep a log of interruptions for a few days. List all the interruptions you experience and their origins. Some examples are friends, family, visitors, phone calls, and unexpected news. Also be aware of internally caused interruptions, such as procrastination, daydreaming, worry, negative thoughts, anger, and lack of concentration. Then think of possible solutions for handling the interruption the next time.

Interrupted By	Incident	Possible Solutions

include them in your plans. See **Peak Progress 3.3** on page 94 for additional tips on how to say no and still maintain a positive relationship.

Juggling Family, School, and Job

Many college students are juggling more than coursework and school activities. Many are spouses, partners, parents, caregivers (for both children and elderly relatives), and co-workers. Making the decision to attend college—or return to college—may have been difficult because of these commitments and responsibilities.

Having a family involves endless physical demands, including cleaning, cooking, chauffeuring to activities, helping with homework, and nonstop picking up. Anyone who lives with children knows how much time and energy they require. Children get sick, need attention, and just want you there sometimes for them.

The following strategies can help you succeed in school while juggling many roles:

1. **Be flexible.** Around children, certain kinds of studying are realistic, and other kinds are hopeless. Carry flash cards to use as you cook dinner or while supervising children's homework or playtime. Quiz yourself, preview chapters, skim summaries, review definitions, do a set number of problems, brainstorm ideas for a paper, outline a speech, review equations, sketch a drawing, or explain a chapter out loud. Save the work that requires deeper concentration for time alone.

2. **Communicate with your family.** Let family members know that earning a college degree is an important goal and you need their support and understanding. Use every bit of time to study before you go home. Once home, let them know when you need to study and set up a specific time.

Peak Progress

How to Say No

Some people have a hard time saying no. They are afraid they will hurt someone's feelings, send a message that they aren't interested, or miss an opportunity that may not come along again. But you can't say yes all the time and still accomplish all you need to. Following are some tips on how to say no, limit your time, and exit situations gracefully:

- **Check your to-do list:** "It doesn't fit with my schedule." It is easy to give in to the impulse to say yes to an invitation or a request from a friend or family member. However, you need to determine what priorities and commitments must be met first. You may find you have to decline the request.

- **Answer in a timely fashion:** "I can't do this right now." If you know you can't participate, let the other person know right away. Others will be more understanding if you let them know you have other commitments rather than waiting until the last minute to give a response (or no response at all).

- **Set a later date:** "I can't right now, but can we do this later?" Find another time that works better for everyone's schedule and record it in your planner.

- **Set a time limit:** "I need to leave by _____." If phone calls or lunch dates usually turn into hours of conversation, set a time limit upfront and make it known—and then stick to it.

- **Clarify expectations:** "How much time will this involve?" It's easy to get involved in something that turns out to be more time-consuming than planned. Sometimes that's unavoidable, but make sure you ask upfront what is expected.

- **Ask for alternate responsibilities:** "I can't do this, but is there something else I can do?" The original request may require too much time (such as planning a school event), but there may be a lesser role you could take (such as lining up the speaker, contacting a caterer, or handing out flyers).

- **Sleep on it before answering:** "Let me get back to you in a day." For bigger commitments, try to take a day or two to consider if the benefits of the new opportunity outweigh the time it will take to be involved. You don't want to disappoint others by committing to a project and then not following through.

- **Don't feel guilty:** "This is the best decision for me at this time." Once you say no, don't feel guilty or have regrets. You must focus on your priorities. Be firm and polite—not defensive or overly apologetic. And definitely do not make up false excuses, which could end up causing you more stress in the long run.

---

3. **Delegate and develop.** Clarify expectations, so that everyone contributes to the family. Even young children can learn to be important contributors to the family unit. Preschool children can help put away toys, set the table, and feel part of the team. Preteens can be responsible for cooking a simple meal one night a week and for doing their own laundry. When your children go to college, they will know how to cook, clean, do laundry, get up on time in the morning, and take responsibility for their lives. An important goal of being a good parent is to raise independent, capable, responsible adults.

4. **Find good day care.** Explore public and private day-care centers, preschools, family day-care homes, parent cooperatives, baby-sitting pools, other family members, and nannies. Line up at least two backup sources of day care.

5. **Prepare the night before.** Avoid the morning rush of getting everyone out the door. The night before, do tasks such as showering, packing lunches, and checking backpacks for keys, books, notes, and supplies. Good organization helps makes the rush hour a little less stressful.

6. **Use your school's resources.** Check out resources on campus through the reentry center. Set up study teams for all your classes. Make friends with other students who have children. (See Chapter 4 for more resources for returning students.)

7. **Communicate with your employer.** Communicate your goals to your employer, and point out how learning additional skills will make you a more valuable employee. Some companies offer tuition reimbursement programs or even allow time off to take a class.

8. **Look into online options.** See if any of your classes are offered online or at alternate times, including evenings and weekends. An online class may fit better with your schedule, but it requires just as much commitment as any other class—maybe even more. See **Peak Progress 3.4** on page 96 for tips on taking online courses.

9. **Increase your physical and emotional energy.** Focus on activities that relax you and help you recharge. Schedule time to meditate, walk, and read for pleasure. Exercise, dance, do yoga, get enough rest, and eat healthy foods. Keep a gratitude journal and remind yourself that you are blessed with a full and rewarding life.

10. **Create positive time.** Don't buy your children toys to replace spending time with them. You can enjoy each other as you study together, garden, take walks, read, play games, or watch a favorite television show. The activity is secondary to your uninterrupted presence. At bedtime, share your day, talk about dreams, read a story, and express your love and appreciation. Your children will remember and cherish this warm and special time forever, and so will you.

11. **Model successful behavior.** Returning to school sends an important message. It says learning, growing, and being able to juggle family, a job, and school are possible, worthwhile, and rewarding. It is important for children to see their parents setting personal and professional goals while knowing that the family is the center of their lives. You are modeling the importance of getting an education, setting goals, and achieving them.

12. **Balance your life.** Reflect on all areas of your life and the time you are investing in them. Decide if you are investing too much or too little in each area. Also, look at the roles you play in each area of your life. In the family area, you may be a wife, mother, daughter, and so on. In the work area, you may be a manager, a part-time worker, or an assistant. Accompanying each role in your life are certain goals. Some goals demand greater time than others, requiring trade–offs. For instance, you may have a big term paper due, so you trade off a family outing to accomplish this goal. Complete **Personal Evaluation Notebook 3.7** on age 97 to determine how you can achieve balance.

● **Balancing Your Life**
Balancing family with work sometimes requires making trade-offs to have a more fulfilling life. *What can you do to create a more balanced life?*

Online Learning

Taking classes online can be very appealing, especially if you're juggling other demands. Also, with some courses you may not have a choice—they are offered only online. Most strategies that apply to taking traditional, face-to-face courses apply to online courses; however, your time-management skills may be even more critical for success. If you are considering an online course, ask yourself the following questions:

- Do I like to work independently?
- Am I persistent and self-motivated?
- Am I comfortable e-mailing or phoning my instructor if I need help?
- Am I comfortable asking questions and following up if I need more clarification?
- Am I comfortable working online, including using basic software programs, submitting projects, testing, and collaborating via Skype or other services?

If you answered yes to most of these questions, an online course may be a good option for you. The following strategies will help you navigate online courses:

1. **Keep up on the coursework.** Think of it this way: What if you crammed a semester-long, face-to-face course, including all the reading, into 1 week? Many people try taking online courses that way, waiting until the last minute to do the work. Instead, you must treat your online course as you would any other class by building it into your schedule. List due dates for assignments, tests, and projects. Build in time to read (the textbook as well as online materials) and study.

2. **Know the technology required for the course.** Make certain you have all the necessary equipment and software, and work out any bugs. Verify passwords and access to course websites, chat rooms, and so on.

3. **Communicate with the instructor.** In an online environment, you miss the nonverbal cues often given in a traditional course, so effective communication is even more important. Clarify the expectations for the class, including reading assignments, exams, projects, and papers, as well as how to deliver finished work to the instructor. How will you know if items are received? Where will your grade be posted? Is there a set time for the class or a chat room? Learn

your instructor's office hours and the best time to respond by e-mail and phone. Ask for feedback from your instructor often, and keep track of your progress. Verify your grade with your instructor before grades are submitted. (See chapter 12 for tips on communicating online with instructors.)

4. **Communicate with other students.** Create online study teams to share notes, ask questions, and study for tests. If this is your first online course, knowing there are other students out there to work with can make it less daunting. You may find that others have had the same questions about content and key points, technology problems, and so on that you do, and they may have answers.

5. **Check the school's tips.** Read any tips and frequently asked questions your school has posted about how to succeed in online courses. Many of them may be specific to the needs of the institution and its instructors.

6. **Watch for announcements.** Know how the instructor or school will alert you to any changes in assignments, tests, and upcoming events and check for them each week.

7. **Print out essential information.** If possible, print the syllabus, project assignments, and key content information, so that you can quickly refer to it, especially when you do not have access to your computer. Annotate the material with questions you need to follow up on, possible test questions, and key points to remember.

8. **Sign in early.** If your course offers or requires participation in a chat room or message board, sign in early to make sure you are involved and can keep up on the discussion. Active participation may be a percentage of your total grade.

9. **Have a computer "Plan B."** To prepare for emergencies, locate computer labs on campus and ask a friend, roommate, or family member if you can use his or her computer if yours crashes. Create organized folders, and back up important material, such as assignments and papers.

10. **Don't cheat.** All rules of ethics and academic honesty apply to online courses just as they do to traditional courses. Your work and responses must be your own.

Personal Evaluation Notebook  3.7

Keeping Your Life Goals in Balance

Several life areas are listed on this chart. Write one goal you have for each major area. Explain how you can commit a certain amount of time to meeting that goal and still maintain overall balance.

Life Areas	Goals
1. Career (job, earning a living)	_____
2. Education	_____
3. Spirituality (your inner being, peace of mind)	_____
4. Relationships (your family, friends, associates)	_____
5. Health (weight, exercise, food, stress, personal care)	_____
6. Recreation (hobbies, sports, interests)	_____
7. Finance	_____
8. Home	_____
9. Community involvement and service	_____
10. Personal growth and renewal	_____
11. Other	_____

TAKING CHARGE

Summary

In this chapter, I learned to

- **Assess where my time goes.** Knowing where I am already spending my time is essential for time management. I assess how much time I (1) commit to school, work, and other activities; (2) spend maintaining myself and home; and (3) devote to discretionary time.

- **Determine where my time should go.** I set goals to determine what I want to accomplish. I identify my values and priorities and use them to write a mission statement. I evaluate my dreams as I write my long-term goals. I break down my tasks and goals by short-term, intermediate, and long-term.

- **Set priorities.** I know what I'd like to accomplish, what I should accomplish, and what is urgent and must be accomplished. I focus on urgent and important priorities, manage ongoing activities, and minimize my time on trivial activities.

- **Assess my energy level.** I know when my energy level is high and work on top-priority goals when I am alert and focused.

- **Break down projects.** I break a large project into manageable chunks. I make a project board, with deadlines for each assignment, and divide the assignment into realistic steps I can do each day. I consolidate similar tasks to maximize my efforts.

- **Study everywhere and anywhere.** I make the most of waiting time, commuting time, and time between classes. I know it is more effective to study in short segments throughout the day than to study late at night in a marathon session.

- **Get organized.** I will develop a habit of putting everything in its place and getting organized. Spending a few extra minutes organizing my space and schedule pays off later.

- **Integrate learning styles.** Left-brain dominant people tend to be convergent thinkers who like structure, whereas right-brain dominant people tend to be divergent thinkers who need more flexibility. Right-brain dominant thinkers can incorporate time-management techniques by focusing on top-priority tasks, writing down upcoming events, using visual cues, and integrating learning styles.

- **Overcome procrastination and interruptions.** By setting daily priorities, breaking large projects into manageable tasks, being positive, creating an organized place to study, and being disciplined, I can accomplish what needs to be done. I've learned to say no when necessary, and I reward myself after completing projects and finishing priorities.

- **Juggle family, school, and job responsibilities.** I communicate my educational goals to others in my life in order to establish expectations and create balance. I am flexible and creative with my time, focusing on schoolwork and involving others in the process.

Performance Strategies

Following are the top 10 strategies for time management:

- Focus on goals and priorities.
- Keep a calendar and create a to-do list.
- Break down projects and consolidate similar tasks.
- Study at the right time, in the right space, and in short segments.
- Study everywhere and anywhere.
- Get organized.
- Be flexible, patient, and persistent.
- Don't procrastinate.
- Manage interruptions.
- Create balance.

Tech for Success

Take advantage of the text's website at **www.mhhe.com/ferrett9e** for additional study aids, useful forms, and convenient and applicable resources.

- **Semester calendar.** It's unavoidable—most of your tests and class papers will occur around the same time. Start planning your semester now by mapping out the major events and daily tasks you'll need to accomplish. A number of planning options are available with this text (worksheets and downloadable forms), or access planners online at a variety of websites, such as **www.timeanddate.com**.

- **Management gurus.** Best-selling authors and popular writers and speakers—such as David Allen ("getting things done"), Merlin Mann ("43 folders"), and the late Stephen Covey ("habits of highly effective people")—have developed strategies, methods, and even humorous takes on overcoming obstacles to effective time management. Visit their websites for advice on becoming more productive: **www.davidco.com**; **www.43folders.com**; **www.stephencovey.com**.

- **A personal time-out.** It's easy to waste hours shopping online, watching YouTube videos, and perusing the latest "find" on auction sites, such as eBay. You may need to give yourself a time-out or, rather, a "time's up." Set a timer as you get online and commit to turning off the computer when the timer goes off. Use your discretionary time wisely.

Study Team Notes

Career *in* focus

Deborah Page
FOOD SCIENTIST

Related Majors: Agricultural Science, Chemistry, Microbiology, Nutrition

Focus on Tasks

Deborah Page is a food scientist for a large company in the food-processing industry. Her job is to develop new food products and ways to preserve or store foods. To do this, she engages in research and conducts tests and experiments, keeping in mind consumer demand for safety and convenience. Occasionally, she analyzes foods to determine levels of sugar, protein, vitamins, or fat.

Because her job is task-oriented, Deborah has a great deal of freedom in structuring her day. Her company allows flexible scheduling, so Deborah arrives at work at 9:30 a.m., after her children have left for school. She can work until 6:30 p.m. because her children are involved in after-school activities and her husband picks them up by 5 p.m.

Deborah finds that she does her best work in late mornings and early afternoons. She plans research and testing during those times. She schedules most calls during the first hour at work and uses the latter part of her day to organize tasks for the next day. Good planning helps her manage her time well and focus on her tasks at hand.

Deborah's job includes a fair amount of reading, which she often tackles at home in the evening. That allows her to leave work early if needed to take her children to appointments or attend their sports activities. Giving attention to her family and personal interests helps Deborah create a balanced life.

CRITICAL THINKING Why is it important for Deborah to organize her time wisely? What are some of the prioritization strategies she uses daily to manage her time? What are some strategies to help her balance her personal and career commitments with a healthy, fulfilling lifestyle? Explore ways for Deborah to find time for herself for personal renewal.

Peak Performer
PROFILE

Malcolm Gladwell

Referred to as a "pop sociologist," international best-selling author Malcolm Gladwell constantly analyzes the way we look at everyday events and concepts of time. By studying what we often think of as "ordinary," Gladwell looks at how these issues of time shape future success.

Gladwell's background is as varied as his way of thinking. His mother was born in Jamaica as a descendant of slaves and worked as a psychotherapist. His British father was a civil engineering professor at the University of Waterloo in Ontario, Canada. Gladwell was born in England and grew up in rural Ontario, graduating with a degree in history from the University of Toronto. In his distinguished career, he has been named one of *Time Magazine*'s 100 Most Influential People. He has worked as a staff writer for *The New Yorker* magazine since 1996.

In his book *Outliers: The Story of Success,* one of the major questions Gladwell explores is why some people, such as Bill Gates and the members of the Beatles, have become outrageously successful in their professions, whereas others have not. Gladwell formulates the hypothesis of the "10,000 Hour Rule." In this rule, he states that the key to success in any field or profession is largely due to practicing a task for a total of 10,000 hours (20 hours a week for 10 years). By making this long, extended time commitment (along with other factors), individuals can fully develop their innate abilities and succeed in their chosen field. (Recall how practice and repetition are key components of the Adult Learning Cycle discussed throughout this text.)

In *The Tipping Point: How Little Things Can Make a Big Difference,* Gladwell explores, among other things, how small actions can have a ripple effect and "spread like viruses do." He explores many historical and cultural situations in which actions by just a few rapidly lead to what he calls a "tipping point" of major change. (Similarly, the **Take 3** activities throughout this text reinforce how small, focused steps can accomplish more in the end.)

In *Blink: The Power of Thinking Without Thinking,* Gladwell studies our abilities to make snap decisions. In looking at short fragments of time, Gladwell reveals the benefits of expert judgment by citing examples of how certain experts have relied on their intuition rather than studied data. (Likewise, **Think Fast** activities throughout the text exercise your critical thinking abilities to quickly solve everyday issues.)

Gladwell's writings have been considered insightful as well as controversial. However, his perceptions of time and critical thinking and the connections he finds to success and other social phenomena have spurred lively debates on the best ways to utilize time and focus efforts.

PERFORMANCE THINKING Do you think it's true that it takes 10,000 hours to become proficient in a profession? How does this idea relate to your success in a class? Have you ever relied on your intuition to solve a problem? Did you arrive at the right answer for you?

CHECK IT OUT Experts explore different approaches to thinking in the popular TED video series (**www.ted.com/**). Named for an alliance among the areas of technology, entertainment, and design (though including many more disciplines today), these brief talks challenge the world's most inspired thinkers to give the "talk of their lives." More than 1,400 TEDTalks are available for free viewing online, including speakers such as Malcolm Gladwell, Al Gore, and Jane Goodall. How can watching these speeches affect the way you think?

Starting Today

At least one strategy I learned in this chapter that I plan to try right away is

_____

_____

_____

What changes must I make in order for this strategy to be most effective?

_____

_____

_____

Review Questions

Based on what you have learned in this chapter, write your answers to the following questions:

1. How does time management help you achieve your goals?

_____

_____

2. What is the difference between an "urgent" priority and an "important" priority?

_____

_____

3. Name at least five time-management strategies.

_____

_____

4. What can you do to avoid procrastination?

_____

_____

5. Why is it important to control interruptions?

_____

_____

To test your understanding of the chapter's concepts, complete the chapter quiz at **www.mhhe.com/ferrett9e.**

Juggling Family and School

In the Classroom

Laura Chen is a returning part-time student. She also works full-time and takes care of her family. Her husband says he supports her goal to become a dental hygienist but does little to help with taking care of the children or housework. Their children are 12 and 14 and have always depended on Laura to help them with their homework and drive them to their activities. Laura prides herself on being efficient at home, as well as being a loving mother and wife.

1. What can Laura do to get more control over her life?

_____

_____

2. What strategies in the chapter would be most helpful to Laura?

_____

_____

In the Workplace

Laura is now a dental hygienist. She has always had a busy schedule, but she expected to have more free time after she graduated. Instead, she is even busier than before. Her children are active in school, and she feels it is important to be involved in their activities and schoolwork. Laura also belongs to two community organizations, volunteers at the local hospital, and is active in her church. Recently, she has been late for meetings and has been rushing through her day. Because she knows her health is important, Laura has resumed her regular exercise program. Since graduation, she has had difficulty finding time for herself.

3. What strategies can help Laura gain control over her time and her life?

_____

_____

4. What areas of her life does she need to prioritize?

_____

_____

Applying the ABC Method of Self-Management

In the Journal Entry on page 75, you were asked to describe a situation when you were overwhelmed by too much to do and too little time. Describe that event here. What were the consequences?

_____

_____

_____

_____

Now apply the ABC Method and visualize a more organized situation:

A = Actual event:

_____

_____

_____

_____

B = Beliefs:

_____

_____

_____

_____

C = Challenge:

_____

_____

_____

_____

While completing this exercise, did you determine ways you can become more organized and efficient?

PRACTICE SELF-MANAGEMENT

For more examples of learning how to manage difficult situations, see the "Self-Management Workbook" section of the Online Learning Center website at **www.mhhe.com/ferrett9e.**

My Time-Management Habits

Complete the following statements with a Yes or No response.

	Yes	No
1. I do the easiest and most enjoyable task first.	_____	_____
2. I do my top-priority task at the time of day when my energy is the highest and I know I will perform best.	_____	_____
3. I use my time wisely by doing high-return activities—previewing chapters, proofreading papers.	_____	_____
4. Even though I find interruptions distracting, I put up with them.	_____	_____
5. I save trivial and mindless tasks for the time of day when my energy is low.	_____	_____
6. I don't worry about making lists. I don't like planning and prefer to be spontaneous and respond as events occur.	_____	_____
7. My work space is organized, and I have only one project on my desk at a time.	_____	_____
8. I set goals and review them each semester and each year.	_____	_____
9. My workspace is open, and I like to have people wander in and out.	_____	_____
10. My study team socializes first, and then we work.	_____	_____
11. I have a lot of wasted waiting time, but you can't study in small blocks of time.	_____	_____
12. I block out a certain amount of time each week for my top-priority and hardest classes.	_____	_____

SCORING

1. Add the number of Yes responses to questions 2, 3, 5, 7, 8, 12. _____
2. Add the number of No responses to questions 1, 4, 6, 9, 10, 11. _____
3. Add the two scores together. _____

The maximum score is 12. The higher the score, the more likely you are to be practicing good time management. Which areas do you need to improve?

REVIEW AND APPLICATIONS | CHAPTER 3

Time Wasters

Getting control of your time and life involves identifying time wasters and determining your peak energy level. It also involves identifying goals, setting priorities, and creating an action plan. Use critical thinking to answer the following questions.

1. What are the major activities and tasks that take up much of your time?

_____

_____

2. What activities cause you to waste time? Some common time wasters are
   - Socializing
   - Losing things and not organizing
   - Doing what you like to do first
   - Watching television
   - Complaining and whining
   - Being overly involved with other people's problems
   - Not writing down deadlines

_____

_____

3. What activities can you eliminate or reduce?

_____

_____

4. When is your high-energy time?

_____

_____

5. When do you study?

_____

_____

6. Look at your committed time. Does this block of time reflect your values and goals? Explain your answer.

_____

_____

7. Do you complete top-priority tasks first? If not, which tasks do you usually tackle first?

_____

_____

Practice Goal Setting

Determine a personal desire or want and plan out a strategy of long-term, short-term, and daily goals that help you achieve it.

Goal-Setting Steps	Examples	Your Turn . . .
Step 1 Plainly state your *desire* or *want*.	"I want to be financially secure."	
Step 2 Develop a long-term goal that will help you fulfill your stated *desire* or *want*.	"I will earn a Bachelor of Science degree in computer technology from State University by June 2011."	
Step 3 Develop short-term goals that will help you achieve the long-term goal.	"I will enroll in all the classes recommended by my academic advisor."	
	"I will earn at least a 3.5 GPA in all my classes."	
	"I will join a small study group."	
Step 4 Develop daily objectives that focus on achieving your short-term goals.	"I will set aside 2 hours of study for every 1 hour in class."	
	"I will make note cards to carry with me and review them when I'm waiting for class."	
	"I will review the day's lecture notes with my study team to make sure I didn't miss any important points."	

REVIEW AND APPLICATIONS | CHAPTER 3

Map Out Your Goals

Use this illustration as a visual guide for mapping out your goals. To get started, plug in your responses from **Personal Evaluation Notebook 3.3**.

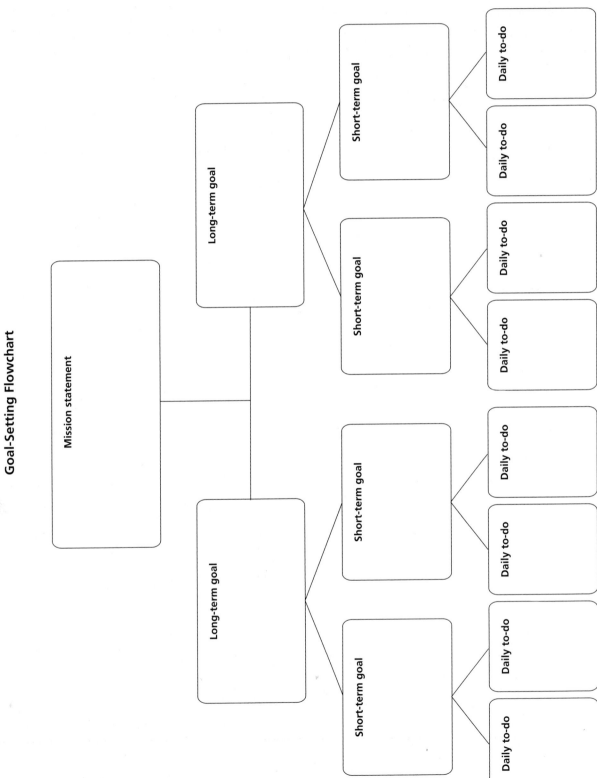

Goal-Setting Flowchart

Daily Prioritizer and Planner: Your To-Do List

Consider the 80/20 rule on page 82 as you use this form to prioritize your tasks and schedule your daily activities. On the left side, write down the tasks you want to accomplish during the day. Then enter those tasks in the "Activity" column, focusing on urgent and important tasks first. Also make sure you include your maintenance and committed activities. Check off your tasks on the left side once they are completed. At the end of the day, see what tasks did not get accomplished and, if need be, include them on tomorrow's to-do list.

	Time	Activity
Urgent	12:00–1:00 a.m.	
	1:00–2:00	
	2:00–3:00	
	3:00–4:00	
	4:00–5:00	
Important	5:00–6:00	
	6:00–7:00	
	7:00–8:00	
	8:00–9:00	
	9:00–10:00	
	10:00–11:00	
	11:00–12:00 p.m.	
Ongoing	12:00–1:00	
	1:00–2:00	
	2:00–3:00	
	3:00–4:00	
	4:00–5:00	
	5:00–6:00	
Trivial	6:00–7:00	
	7:00–8:00	
	8:00–9:00	
	9:00–10:00	
	10:00–11:00	
	11:00–12:00	

Weekly Planner

Week of _____/_____/_____

Time	Sunday Activity	Monday Activity	Tuesday Activity	Wednesday Activity	Thursday Activity	Friday Activity	Saturday Activity
12:00–1:00 a.m.							
1:00–2:00							
2:00–3:00							
3:00–4:00							
4:00–5:00							
5:00–6:00							
6:00–7:00							
7:00–8:00							
8:00–9:00							
9:00–10:00							
10:00–11:00							
11:00–12:00 p.m.							
12:00–1:00							
1:00–2:00							
2:00–3:00							
3:00–4:00							
4:00–5:00							
5:00–6:00							
6:00–7:00							
7:00–8:00							
8:00–9:00							
9:00–10:00							
10:00–11:00							
11:00–12:00							

Urgent	Important	Ongoing

Month/Semester Calendar

Plan your projects and activities for the school term.

Month of ___					

Appointment — **Date**

Test — **Date**

Project — **Due Date**

REVIEW AND APPLICATIONS | CHAPTER 3

Demonstrating Your Time-Management Skills

List all the factors involved in time management. Indicate how you would demonstrate them to employers. Add this page to your Career Development Portfolio.

Areas	Your Demonstration
Dependability	*Haven't missed a day of work in my job*
Reliability	
Effectiveness	
Efficiency	
Responsibility	
Positive attitude	
Persistence	
Ability to plan and set goals and priorities	
Visionary	
Ability to follow through	
High energy	
Ability to handle stress	
Ability to focus	
Respect for others' time	
Ability to overcome procrastination	
Reputation as a doer and self-starter	

Maximize Your Resources

LEARNING OUTCOMES

In this chapter, you will learn to

4.1 Identify your school's resources

4.2 List resources of interest to students with special concerns

4.3 Describe how to use the library and technology to your advantage

4.4 Manage your financial resources and save for the future

4.5 Explain how you are your greatest resource

SELF-MANAGEMENT

"Using a credit card is easy—in fact, much too easy. Before I knew it, I rang up thousands of dollars, and I can barely handle the minimum monthly payments. In addition to credit card debt, I have student loans to pay back. I feel like I'll be in debt forever."

Are you struggling with your finances or finding it hard to make ends meet? Have you ever bought things that you didn't need or spent too much on a luxury item that you really couldn't afford? In this chapter, you will learn how to find and use your school and local resources to help you succeed in every area of your life, including financial. You will learn how to manage money, get on a debt-free track, and find ways to participate in your school and community.

JOURNAL ENTRY In **Worksheet 4.1** on page 142, write about a time when you set a financial goal, such as buying a new car. How difficult was it to achieve? What sacrifices did you have to make?

Going to college is a big change. This is true whether you are going from high school to college, leaving home, commuting, returning, or starting college later in life. The strategies and information you learn throughout this book will help you cope with major life transitions, including the transition from college to career. The more information and support you have during a transition, the more easily you'll be able to adjust and thrive. In this chapter, we will look at ways of finding and using the resources available to you, including your inner resources, to adjust to change and meet your goals. A great deal of success in life depends on solving problems through decision making. This requires knowing what resources are available and having the good sense to use them.

When you enter college or a job, you are entering a new system and culture. It is your responsibility to understand how the system and culture work. This understanding includes knowing the system's rules, regulations, deadlines, procedures, requirements, and language. The culture is all the written and unwritten rules of any organization. It includes the work atmosphere and the way people treat each other. In a sense, you are learning how things are done and who best can solve specific problems. Knowing the system and culture reduces stress and anxiety. Many advisors say the top advice they would give students is to address problems as they occur and seek help when they need it.

● Check Out What's Available

Your school probably offers many resources to help you adjust, learn, and enjoy your college experience. *What are some resources you have already tapped into?*

Explore Your School's Resources

Many college graduates say they regret not having been more involved in school activities and not using the amazing resources available. Your college experience will be much more rewarding and successful if you take advantage of all the resources available to you. In fact, you can avoid many potentially big problems if you address situations as soon as they arise and know where to go for help.

You may have attended an orientation program, gone on a campus tour, and visited the bookstore and student center when you applied to or arrived at school. You may have picked up a student newspaper or map or looked at the schedule of classes. This is a good place to start. Walking around campus, finding your classrooms before classes begin, and locating your advisor's and instructors' offices can help you feel more comfortable and reduce the anxiety of the unknown. You will be amazed at the support services and resources available at most schools. The resources we'll explore in this chapter include

- People resources: advisors, faculty, classmates, and counselors

- Program resources: offices for special needs, areas of study, groups, clubs, and activities
- Online and information resources: catalogs, guides, and local news and events
- Financial resources: financial aid, credit agencies, financial planning services, and personal budgeting

Use the handy form on the inside back cover of this text to record the important information for a number of key resources. Also in the back of the text you will find an extensive list of resources that may be available at your school.

People Resources

The most important resources at school are the people with whom you work, study, and relate. Faculty, advisors, counselors, study team members, club members, sports teammates, guest speakers, administrators, and all the students with whom you connect and form relationships make up your campus community. These people will provide information, emotional support, and friendship—and they may even help you find a job! They want to see you succeed as much as you do. We'll discuss a few key contacts, and others will be discussed in the section "Program Resources."

ACADEMIC ADVISOR

One of your most important contacts at school will be your academic advisor. This person will help you navigate academic life. Your advisor will clarify procedures, answer other academic concerns or questions, create a major contract, and refer you to offices on campus that can best meet your needs. If you weren't already provided with this information, go to the departmental office and find out your advisor's name, office number, and posted office hours. It is best to make an appointment early in the semester and develop a good relationship. Do your part to be prepared, ask questions, and follow through on suggestions. However, if your personalities clash, check with the department about changing advisors. It is important to have an advisor who is accessible, takes time to listen, and will work closely with you to meet your academic goals. (Review **Peak Progress 2** in the Getting Started section for questions to ask your advisor. Also see Chapter 12, for more tips on communicating with advisors and instructors.)

INSTRUCTORS

Most instructors enjoy teaching and getting to know their students. At most universities and

Ask your advisor

General education and other requirements

Helpful suggestions concerning your academic program

If certain instructors are better suited to your learning style

Potential career opportunities within the major

The best sequence of classes and when certain courses are offered

Service learning and volunteer programs

Internships, co-ops, work study, and job placement programs

Requirements for your major and substitutions available

many colleges, faculty are also very involved in research, professional organizations, campus committees, community projects, and academic advising. It is important that you get to know your instructors and view them as a tremendous resource. Instructors are more supportive of students who attend class regularly, show responsibility, and are prepared and engaged in class.

MENTORS

A **mentor** is a person (such as a coach, an instructor, an employer, or a colleague) who is a role model, supports your goals, takes an interest in your professional and personal development, and helps you achieve, either directly through instruction or indirectly by example. A mentor can open doors for you. Check to see if your college has a formal mentoring program that connects students to faculty, staff, or more experienced students. Once you develop a supportive relationship, your instructor may be willing to serve as a mentor to help you make connections in your career.

PEERS

Your fellow students may be very involved in the learning community. They are active in orientation, campus tours, information and advising centers, clubs, and almost every service area on campus. Take the initiative to organize a study team or partner for each class; get to know your lab assistant, tutor, and peers in the academic advising center, clubs' offices, and so on. This is a great way to improve learning, get help, and build a network of relationships. See **Peak Progress 4.1** for tips on setting up an effective study group.

Networking, a term often used in business, simply means enriching yourself and your opportunities by building relationships with others. Not only is networking one of the best strategies for overcoming isolation and developing long-lasting relationships, but it will likely help you land a job and further your career. More than 60 percent of all jobs are found by networking—through friends, family, neighbors, co-workers, and acquaintances. At college, you have ample opportunity to build a diverse network of "who you know," including instructors, advisors, alumni, and peers. Stretch your comfort zone by getting to know people with backgrounds different from yours. (See **Worksheet 4.2** on page 143 for a handy guide.) Build a wide and diverse network at school by using these tips:

- **Get to know other students in class.** Introduce yourself and correctly write down the names of new acquaintances and try to pronounce them—ask for help if necessary. See who is interested in joining a study team.
- **Get to know students out of class.** Smile and say "hi" when you see them out of class, and take time to discuss lectures and assignments. Go to the student union, the library, and events at the multicultural and career center, and be friendly.
- **Get to know your instructors.** Throughout this book, you'll find tips for building supportive relationships with instructors. Get to know them and take an interest in their research and area of expertise.
- **Join clubs.** Almost every academic department has a club, and there are clubs where you can meet students who have similar interests, such as chess, skiing, religion, or music. Does your school offer any intramural sports you enjoy? If you can't find a club that interests you, consider starting one and see if other classmates are interested in participating.

Peak Progress

How to Form a Study Group

The old saying "Two heads are better than one" is never more true than when participating in a study group:

- Working in a study group gives you practice speaking in front of others and being an active part of a productive unit—skills that will be essential on the job.
- If someone is depending on your involvement, you are more likely to show up and come prepared. You may also become more organized, as others will get frustrated if you spend the time shuffling notes into order.
- When comparing notes, you will discover if you missed or misunderstood key points discussed in class or presented in the course materials.
- You are encouraged to explain things aloud to others (as in the "Teach" step in the Adult Learning Cycle). Speaking and listening to others can improve your ability to remember the information later, especially at test time.

Whether your instructor requires it or not, take advantage of the opportunity to buddy-up with classmates who are focused on excelling. But where do you start? First, notice which classmates arrive on time, stay focused, and ask thoughtful questions. Ask these individuals if they are interested in forming a study team, and exchange contact information.

Look for students whose learning styles complement each other (see Chapter 1 for learning styles). For example, one person may be great at taking notes, another at synopsizing the instructor's lecture, another at locating key information in the text, and another at formulating possible test questions. When you get to know each other better, you'll see each person's strength.

Determine a neutral place to meet and a consistent day and time (including starting and ending times) that accommodates everyone. An ideal study group should have no more than six members. Otherwise, maintaining focus and attendance will be a challenge.

The group should initially discuss the overall goals for the study group (such as talking through the reading assignment, comparing notes, preparing for exams, and working on a major project) and let each member comment on his or her strengths as well as weaknesses (such as "I'd like to take better notes in class"). This will encourage the members to function more as a team.

Then, keep the socializing to a minimum and focus on the group's goals. Ask questions when a point isn't clear. In the last few minutes of each meeting, develop a tentative agenda for the next get-together (such as reviewing a specific chapter or going over test results), so that each person is prepared to participate and brings the necessary materials.

If you are hesitant to line up a group yourself but see that another classmate is getting one together, politely ask to join and let that person know your strengths and what you will bring to the group. This also gives you practice selling yourself, which will better prepare you for job-hunting.

Participating in a study group can benefit anyone, especially older students who may feel out of place returning to school after an extended period. Many returning students bring practical, professional experience that offers a different perspective on the course material. It also gives nontraditional students a chance to connect more with the school and fellow classmates.

- **Work on campus.** A great way to meet people and earn extra money is to work on campus. Check out the career center for work study and student assistant jobs.
- **Perform.** Join the band, choir, jazz group, or chamber readers; perform in a play; or work in theater behind the scenes. Some campus groups serve the community by performing in local schools or reading in library story hours.
- **Join the school newspaper.** Write stories or work in the office, which will also help build your portfolio of work samples.
- **Join a political group.** Campus and community political groups are a great way to meet people, become better informed, and support a cause.

- **Attend campus events.** Go to lectures, political debates, sporting events, and the many rich cultural, musical, intellectual, and fun events that are offered.
- **Consider your living situation.** Depending on the availability and your personal situation, you may be interested in living in a learning community or housing sponsored by the Greek system.

Program Resources

Depending on the type of institution you attend, your school may have a variety of programs, departments, and offices that provide services and help, including services for specific needs. The people you meet in these offices can provide key information and help you find, evaluate, and use information of all kinds.

ADVISING CENTER

Most colleges have a central advising center to provide general education advising and answer questions about policies, procedures, graduation requirements, and deadlines. The center has **professional advisors** who work closely with other departments, such as admissions, records, registration, learning centers, exchange and study abroad programs, and the cashier's office. If you are coming from high school, you will want to verify that your advanced placement classes have been credited appropriately. If you are a transfer student, you need to know what upper-division and general education courses are required, what credits were transferred from your previous school, and whether they were accepted as general education or as electives.

While your academic advisor is responsible for helping you prepare a major contract and guide you through your major's requirements, at most schools an **evaluator** does a degree check to make certain you have met not only your major's requirements but also all the university requirements, such as general education, diversity and common ground requirements, credit and no credit guidelines, the institution's requirements, the required tests, and the number of college units. You may want to make an appointment once you have submitted your academic major contract and have applied for graduation (about three semesters before you graduate). You don't want to find out a month before graduation that you are short two units or have failed to meet a basic requirement.

ADMISSIONS, RECORDS, AND REGISTRATION

This office will have your transcripts, including information about grades, transfer credits, and the dropping or adding of classes. The registrar and staff can also assist you with graduation deadlines and requirements. You should keep your own copies of your transcripts, grades, grade changes, and other requirements.

LEARNING CENTERS

Many schools have a learning center or academic support services to help with academic problems and grade improvement. They offer workshops in test-taking skills; time management; reading skills; note taking; and math, vocabulary, and science study strategies. They may offer individual or group tutoring and study groups. They also do diagnostic testing to determine learning difficulties. If you are diagnosed with a learning disability, you may be eligible for additional time on tests, tutors, or other services. They often help students on probation by creating an academic success plan. Probation is a warning that you are doing substandard work—typically, a GPA below 2.0. If your GPA remains below 2.0 or falls to a certain level, you may be disqualified. Disqualification means being denied further school attendance until you are reinstated. Disqualified students may petition for reinstatement, usually through the office of admissions and records. Many resources are available to help you stay in school, avoid probation, and raise your GPA. Tutoring is often available for all students who want to improve their grades, not just for students on probation.

LIBRARY

The library is a rich source of books, periodicals (magazines and newspapers), encyclopedias, dictionaries, pamphlets, directories, and more. Libraries also offer many services besides the written and spoken word. They may vary in size and services, but they all have information, ideas, facts, and a mountain of treasures waiting to be explored. Librarians and media center staff are trained to find information about almost every subject. They can often order special materials from other libraries or direct you to other sources. Many libraries have electronic access to books and periodicals, and even more material is available via inter-library loans. Check out

- **The library's website.** Find out what the library offers and what research you can do from your own computer. (If access to materials is password protected, ask a librarian or an instructor for help.) Many libraries offer online tutorials and tips on evaluating information and citing material.
- **The catalog.** Look up the library's collection of print and online encyclopedias, biographies, and government works, as well as all the other available materials.
- **Searchable databases.** Find out what's available on CD-ROM and online. Ask about policies regarding use of the Internet on the library's computers.
- **DVDs, CDs, and digital recordings in the media center.** This is a wonderful way to access information, especially if you are a commuter student and want to listen to recordings on your commute or watch campus speakers or special events that you missed.
- **Reserves.** Many instructors put textbooks, supplemental readings, sample tests, and study aids on reserve.
- **Specialized libraries.** Specialized libraries may be available for your use, such as a medical or health sciences, law, journalism, or engineering library. Check the main library's website or ask a librarian.

CAREER CENTER

The career center is not just for seniors. If you're undecided about your major and want to explore options and find out how academic majors relate to careers, this center can help. The staff can also help you with **internships** and co-ops related to your major. These opportunities are very helpful for gaining experience and getting a job. Also, check out job placement services

> **❝** The library is the temple of learning, and learning has liberated more people than all the wars in history. **❞**
> CARL T. ROWAN
> *Journalist, author*

● Use the Library
Although you can do research online, your school may have an excellent library, which you should explore. *What assistance or resources can you get at the library that may be difficult to find online?*

for summer, part-time, or full-time employment. The career center may offer career counseling, job fairs, and interview and resumé workshops. Keep a copy of personal inventories, assessments, and possible majors and careers in your Career Development Portfolio.

HEALTH CENTER

If available, take advantage of free or low-cost medical services for illnesses, eating disorders, alcohol or drug problems, anxiety, stress, birth control, and sexually transmitted diseases. If you have a high fever, nausea, severe headache, or stiff neck, go immediately to the health center or, the emergency room because you might have meningitis or another serious illness. Make certain you have the necessary vaccinations, or a hold may be placed on your registration. Because of changing health care regulations, be aware of any health insurance restrictions and have your insurance card or information handy.

MEDIATION AND CONFLICT RESOLUTION

You may need assistance or advice in solving conflicts with instructors, roommates, neighbors, or your landlord. Check if your school has an ombudsperson, mediation services, or legal aid.

COUNSELING CENTER

Adjusting to the demands of college life can be challenging. Most campuses have professional counselors who are trained to help with personal problems, such as loneliness, shyness, eating disorders, addictions, depression, and relationship problems. They often offer group counseling and classes, as well as individual support. They also refer students to agencies for specific problems. Many counseling centers offer classes in study skills, time and stress management, and other topics to help students succeed.

STUDENT ACTIVITIES OFFICE

Working with other offices, student services provide many programs and activities, starting with an orientation program and campus tour. Sometimes these orientation programs are offered online for first-time, transfer, and reentry students. There are usually many activities for students to participate in, such as

- **Multicultural centers.** Support, classes, activities, and events are offered to celebrate diversity and provide support for racial and ethnic groups and the LGBT community. A women's center may offer classes and support for women.
- **International and exchange programs.** Your school may offer an exchange program, which is a great way to attend a different school without transferring. You stay enrolled at your own school but study for a term or a year at a designated school in this country or abroad. There may also be a center for international students.

Use **Personal Evaluation Notebook 4.1** on page 122 to record activities or clubs you want to check out, and determine which ones would fit in your weekly schedule.

SERVICE LEARNING

Many schools encourage students to incorporate service learning into their education. The emphasis is on students' contributing their time and talents to improve the

● **The Co-Curriculum**
Activities outside of the classroom are no longer considered "extra"—at least to employers looking for job candidates with real-life experiences. Find co-curricular activities that provide opportunities to meet new people and apply a variety of skills, such as communication, team-building, and leadership.

quality of the community and learn valuable job skills. Students often earn college credits and obtain valuable experience while integrating what they learn in classes into practical, on-the-job problem solving. Students also can create their own learning experiences through directed study and field experience. Some students tutor or work with the homeless, the elderly, or people with disabilities. (Learn more about incorporating service learning into your coursework in Chapter 14).

STUDENT UNION

Your school may have a student union or center, which may include a dining hall, a bookstore, lounges, a post office, ATMs, and bulletin boards for information on clubs and activities, student government, transportation, and off-campus housing. The bookstore sells textbooks, electronics, general interest books, and supplies.

RECREATIONAL CENTERS

If a recreation center is available on campus, you are probably already paying for access within your tuition costs. Check out classes, the pool, the weight room, and walking and running facilities. This is a great way to reduce stress and meet other students.

ALUMNI ASSOCIATION

Many schools have alumni associations and centers that offer benefits and services to both current and former students, including connecting students with graduates in related career fields.

SECURITY

Many schools have security or police departments, which provide information about safety, parking, traffic rules, and lost and found items. Some provide safe escort for night-class students, classes in self-defense, and information on alcohol and drugs. See **Peak Progress 4.2** on page 122 on personal safety issues.

● **Eyes Up**
Although cell phones can be a communication and safety necessity, related thefts and injuries are on the rise. Reported injuries from Texting While Walking (TWW) have quadrupled in 8 years. And more than 40% of robberies in major cities are of cell phones, often involving violent acts. *Is your phone password protected?*

Additional Online and Information Resources

Schools offer many resources on their website, such as the descriptions and schedule of classes, a phone and e-mail directory, links to departmental websites, and many financial transactions, such as financial aid applications, payment of fees, and bookstore purchases. You can register for classes, go through an orientation, and access your grades online. Many instructors distribute course materials, the syllabus, and assignments via e-mail or a course website. Online courses may include a blend of online instruction, websites, chat rooms, video conferencing, podcasts, and e-mail to ask questions and respond to lectures. See **Peak Progress 4.3** on page 123 for some tips on using technology to your advantage.

SCHOOL CATALOG

However you access resources—online or in print—the school catalog is a key resource, to review thoroughly. The catalog includes procedures, regulations, guidelines, academic areas, basic graduation requirements, and information on

Personal Evaluation Notebook

Activities and Clubs

Visit the student activities office or review your school's website to see what clubs or activities sound interesting. Look for activities that will increase your knowledge about your field of study, help you network and build business contacts, introduce you to people with similar interests, and give you a chance to enjoy your discretionary time, physically and emotionally.

1. Club/activity: _____ Day/time: _____
   Contact person: _____ Phone/e-mail: _____
   Meeting place: _____

2. Club/activity: _____ Day/time: _____
   Contact person: _____ Phone/e-mail: _____
   Meeting place: _____

3. Club/activity: _____ Day/time: _____
   Contact person: _____ Phone/e-mail: _____
   Meeting place: _____

4. Club/activity: _____ Day/time: _____
   Contact person: _____ Phone/e-mail: _____
   Meeting place: _____

Peak Progress

Staying Safe

The rigors of academic life can be stressful—even without the added pressure of the possibility of what, where, or when tragedy might occur. Knowing your surroundings is key to your safety in any situation, be it at school, home, work, the mall, or a parking lot. Know where the exits are—from the room and the building—and plan how you would react to and where you should go in an emergency, be it a violent threat or natural disaster.

Fortunately, school-associated homicides are very infrequent. The School-Associated Violent Death Study found that school-associated homicide rates decreased significantly from 1992 to 2006. Rarely does an individual just "snap." Rather, a series of behavior over time may lead to someone physically acting out. If you observe something that doesn't seem right, report it to a school counselor, official, professor, or mental health professional.

Most schools have implemented "e-lert" systems for contacting students regarding safety emergencies at school, via e-mail, phone, or text. Determine if you need to sign up to be alerted (and, if so, sign up within the first week of school or earlier if possible). Find out where at school you should go if an emergency does occur.

Many schools also offer "call a ride" services that are staffed by approved volunteer students who will drive you, and even your car, home from an evening out—usually for free and with no questions asked. Having a plan and using available resources such as these are the best safety practices.

most of the services offered at your school. Most school catalogs contain the following information:

- Welcome from the president and a general description of the school and area
- Mission of the college and information about accreditation
- Support services and main offices in the campus community
- Admissions information, including placement tests and estimated expenses
- Academic regulations, such as auditing of a course, credit/no credit, class level, academic standing, educational leave, drop/add, and withdrawal
- Fees and financial aid
- List of administrators, trustees, faculty, and staff
- Academic programs, minors, credentials, and graduate degrees
- Components of the degree, such as major, general education, institutions, diversity and common ground, and electives
- Course descriptions
- Expectations regarding academic honesty and plagiarism, discipline for dishonesty, class attendance, disruptive behavior, student responsibility, privacy act and access policy, grievance procedures, safety and security, substance abuse policy, and so on

Look up answers to questions before asking for help, and take responsibility for your own education. If someone gives you advice about a policy, ask where the rule

Peak Progress 4.3

Using Technology at School

You will no doubt use technology in your coursework, from researching papers to viewing simulations to submitting homework assignments online. However, don't overlook basic tasks and resources that you may need to follow-up on to make sure the technology is working for you:

- Thoroughly search the school's main website and periodically review it for recent postings.
- Register for a school e-mail account and check it often. You may decide to forward this e-mail account to another one, but make sure you look for messages daily as this is how your school and instructors will communicate with you.
- Investigate if your school offers online courses you may be interested in. (Remember, though, that taking online courses requires an even greater commitment because you will be responsible for keeping up with assignments and reading materials on your own.)

- Contact or visit the computer lab and ask about support, including available hours and any courses or workshops.
- Check to see if your school offers discounts on computers for students.
- Find out what and how technology will be used and required in your courses. Did your textbook come with a DVD or website that will be used? Does your course require a CPS (Classroom Performance System) device, and will you reuse it in future classes?
- Make sure you understand how to do quick searches on the Internet using search engines such as Yahoo!, Bing, and Google.
- Don't assume that everything you see on the Internet is true. Check out sources and think through opinions versus facts. If you are unsure about the reliability of the material you find on a website, ask your instructor.
- Respect copyrights and credit all sources.

Take 3 minutes to connect with your advisor:

- Do you know who your major advisor is? Call him or her, schedule an appointment, and record it in your planner.
- Jot down your major educational goals. (Refer to your responses earlier in this text.)
- Create a list of potential questions to ask during your visit. (Don't forget to check the "most common questions" box)

What else can you do in 3 minutes?

- Stop by the career center and inquire about upcoming internships.
- Visit the student activities office and ask for a list of clubs and programs.
- Search the school's website to see what study tips and library resources are available online.

Take 3

is covered in the catalog, so that you can review it. Look up academic areas. What fields of study interest you most or least? Which areas are so unusual you didn't even know they existed?

ORIENTATION GUIDE

Many colleges provide a student handbook or an orientation guide that familiarizes you with the school and basic requirements. If you attended an orientation program, keep your information packet. You may want to refer to planning guides and requirements before you register for next term's classes.

SCHEDULE OF CLASSES

Obtain a new schedule of classes each term. You will have not only a hard copy of classes to register for but also other up-to-date information, such as an exam schedule, deadlines, and a calendar of events. Most schools offer a schedule of classes online, but having a copy with you is helpful when you're planning and adjusting your schedule.

Students with Disabilities

Under the Americans with Disabilities Act, colleges are legally obligated to provide services and resources for students with disabilities, including physical disabilities, mental disabilities (such as depression, anxiety, or chronic illness), physical limitations (such as visual impairment), and learning disabilities (such as dyslexia or attention deficit hyperactivity disorder). Students should be informed about their rights and ask for assistance.

1. **Check out resources.** The first step is to see what is available at your school, such as a center for students with disabilities or a learning skills center. Special services may be provided by student services or counseling. The staff will inform you of services offered by the state and resources in the library. Some services to ask about include

   - Parking permits
   - Ramps and accessibility to buildings
   - Audio recordings and books in Braille
   - Extended time for test taking
   - Help in selecting courses, registering, and transcribing lectures
   - Lab course assistance
   - Availability of a Sign Language interpreter, note taker, and tutors

   A learning disability is a neurological disorder that can affect reading, writing, speaking, math abilities, and social skills. If you think you have persistent problems in these areas, you can contact the learning center or student health center for a referral to a licensed professional. Students whose learning disabilities are properly documented are entitled to certain accommodations. For more information, visit the National Center for Learning Disabilities at **www.ncld.org**.

2. **Meet with all of your instructors.** You are not asking for special favors or treatment but, rather, for alternatives for meeting your goals. You may want to sit in the front row, record lectures, take an oral test, or use a computer instead of writing assignments longhand, or you may need extra time taking a test.

3. **Meet with your advisor.** Discuss your concerns with your academic advisor or an advisor from the learning center. It is critical that you get help early, focus on your strengths, get organized, and map out a plan for success.

4. **Be assertive.** You have a right to services and to be treated with respect. Ask for what you need and want in clear, polite, and direct language. If you don't get results, go to the next administrative level.

5. **Be positive and focus on your goals.** Realize that, even though your mountain may be steeper, you have what it takes to adapt and succeed. Use the ABC Method of Self-Management to dispute negative thinking and visualize yourself succeeding.

Commuter Students

Commuters make up the largest number of college students. To get the most out of their college experience, commuter students (all students, for that matter) should get involved with school events and use available resources.

FOR COMMUTERS

1 Participate in school activities
Students who get involved are more likely to graduate and have a positive college experience.

2 Use on-site resources
Find the library, computer lab, and the best places to study.

3 Connect with others
Build relationships with students, instructors, advisors, and study groups.

4 Listen to recorded lectures
But don't let a podcast, music, or your thoughts distract you from driving safely.

5 Pack snacks
Bring your lunch and handy treats for long hours on campus.

6 Carry an emergency kit
If commuting by car, be prepared for accidents and weather emergencies.

7 Get support from your family
Make sure everyone understands your new responsibilities, expectations, and deadlines.
Delegate duties and ask for help and support.

Returning Students

If you are a returning or reentry student, you have lots of company. More than one-third of all students are over age 25, and many are well over 40. These students are sometimes referred to as **nontraditional students** (with a **traditional student** defined as 18 to 25 years old, usually going from high school directly to college). The number of nontraditional students is growing every year as more and more people return to school to complete or further their education. Some returning students are veterans or single parents, some work full-time, and almost all have other commitments and responsibilities. Returning students often do better than younger students because they have a sense of purpose, discipline, and years of experience to draw upon.

Schools are offering more and more services geared for the older, returning student, such as special orientation programs, support groups, on-campus child care, tutoring and resources for brushing-up on math or writing skills, credit for work or life experiences, and special classes. Other resources that are especially important for returning students include

- Adult reentry center
- Continuing education
- Distance learning office
- Veterans Affairs
- Office for credit for prior experience
- Women's center
- Counseling center
- Job placement center
- Information/referral services
- Financial aid office

No matter what your situation, take full advantage of all the resources available to help you succeed in school and all aspects of your life. See **Peak Progress 4.4** on community resources you should also explore.

Manage Your Financial Resources

In this section, we will analyze how to manage a very important resource—your money. Did you know the following facts?

- The average graduating senior of a public university has more than $26,600 in student loans. Thirteen percent owe more than $50,000. This is a 40 percent increase since 2002.
- The average college student has almost $800 in credit card debt.
- In 2012, there were more than 1.2 million personal bankruptcy filings in the United States.
- The average college student spends about $600 on alcohol each year.

If you want to be above average at handling your finances, you must plan ahead by establishing a budget, researching financial assistance, limiting (and eliminating) your credit card debt, protecting your identity, and saving for the future.

Keep a Budget

The first step in handling your finances is to write a budget. Calculate how much you earn and how much you spend. Write a short-term monthly budget, one for

Peak Progress

4.4

Explore Your Community's Resources

As a college student, you have a chance to get to know a city and make a contribution to the community. Even if you've always lived in the same city, you may not be aware of its rich resources and opportunities:

People Resources

- **Business professionals:** Connect with professionals in your field of study who can offer valuable information and advice, internships, scholarships, contacts, jobs, and career opportunities. Make contacts by volunteering your services or joining professional organizations. Many professional groups have student memberships.
- **Government officials:** Learn the names of your local political leaders, go to a city council meeting, or meet the mayor. Some city, county, and state governments have programs, internships, and fellowships for students. Do you know who your state senators and your state and local representatives are?
- **Political parties:** Political activity is one way to meet people, become informed about local issues, and contribute your organizational talents.

Program Resources

- **Chamber of Commerce:** The chamber of commerce has information about local attractions, special events, museums, hotels, restaurants, libraries, clubs, businesses and economic development, environmental and political issues, and organizations.
- **Clubs and organizations:** Many clubs, such as the Rotary, Lions, Elks, Soroptimist, and Kiwanis, offer scholarships. Clubs such as Toastmasters and the Sierra Club offer programs for people with specific interests. Big Brothers, Big Sisters, YWCA, YMCA, Girls Clubs, and Boys Clubs are always looking for suitable volunteers and lecturers, and they offer many free and low-cost services. (Note that most volunteer work with children requires completing a background check.)
- **Recreation centers:** Fitness centers, swimming pools, parks, and community education programs offer classes and locations to participate in enjoyable physical activity.
- **Health care:** Hospitals and health clinics may provide vaccinations, birth control, gynecological exams, and general health care at a reduced cost. Some may

sponsor support groups and offer classes on specific health conditions, CPR training, and diet and exercise for free or a nominal charge. Counselors and therapists can help with personal problems, such as depression, excessive shyness, or destructive behavior.
- **Houses of worship:** Great places to meet new friends, houses of worship hold social events, workshops, support groups, and conferences.
- **Job placement services:** Get career counseling, job listings, and help with interviewing skills and resumé writing.
- **Small Business Association (SBA):** Most cities have an SBA that provides free advice and essential contacts for those getting a business off the ground or are just considering the feasibility of starting a business.
- **Crisis centers:** Hot lines are usually available 24 hours a day for such crises as suicidal feelings, physical and/or emotional abuse, rape, AIDS, and severe depression.
- **Support groups:** Whatever your needs, there may be a support group to share your concerns and offer help.
- **Helping organizations:** The American Cancer Society, American Heart Association, Red Cross, Salvation Army, and animal protection agencies, such as the Humane Society and ASPCA, provide information, services, and help. These organizations always need volunteers.

Additional Online and Information Resources

- **City website:** Almost every community has a website that highlights local areas of interests, schools, housing, businesses, and upcoming events.
- **Local newspapers, magazines, and newsletters:** Many communities have publications describing the area, featuring local interest stories, and advertising community events and resources.
- **Libraries:** Apply for a library card at the city or county library and check out free resources, such as DVDs and music CDs, as well as special interest classes, seminars, and book clubs.
- **2-1-1:** The United Way offers a service in many communities that provides assistance and links you to related support agencies. Dial 2-1-1 or look online to see if this service is available in your area.

Copyright © 2015 The McGraw-Hill Companies

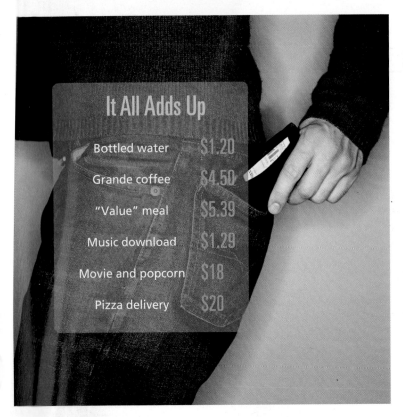

It All Adds Up

Bottled water	$1.20
Grande coffee	$4.50
"Value" meal	$5.39
Music download	$1.29
Movie and popcorn	$18
Pizza delivery	$20

the school term, and a long-term budget for a year or more. (See **Worksheet 4.4** on page 145 for samples.) You will then have a big picture of large expenses, such as tuition and will be able to monitor and modify your expenses each month. Your budget needs to include not only the big expenses, but also the "little" costs that quickly add up under the categories of "food" or "entertainment." Keep receipts, bills, canceled checks, and credit card statements in a file or box, in case you want to exchange your purchases or revise your budget for accuracy. Keep a file for taxes, and file applicable receipts. **Complete Personal Evaluation Notebook 4.2** to determine where you spend your money.

Research Financial Assistance

Student loan debt has tripled in the last decade, with 37 million students owing more than $1.1 trillion dollars. This exceeds credit card debt and is second only to housing costs. Because of this mounting debt and lack of realistic plans to pay it back, more than 13 percent of graduates are defaulting on their loans within three years. This results in damaged credit that will linger for years. Thus, in order for your financial plan to truly "aid" you, you must not only find the necessary dollars to complete your education, but also develop a plan to pay back any loans in a reasonable amount of time. The source of your loan (government or private), total amount, and other factors will determine the timeframe for your payback as well as the interest rate and how it accrues. Plus, government legislation is continually changing regarding student loan availability, interest rates, payback parameters, and debt forgiveness—all of which can be a confusing process to understand. However, before you incur debt, you need to calculate how much of your monthly income will need to be allocated toward your student loan (see **Figure 4.1**).

Although every school and state offers a variety of financial aid options, your search for assistance probably has (or will) included visiting the U.S. government's

Figure 4.1
Student Loan Payback

Go to **studentaid.ed.gov/ repay-loans/understand/ plans/standard/ comparison-calculator** (or search "repayment comparison calculator" on the home page) and scroll down to use the standard payback calculator. Plug in your anticipated loans to see what your monthly payback will be. *How much will you need to allocate each month for your student loan?*

Average student loan

$36,734 owed after graduation, including interest

$26,600 loan

$307 due each month for 10 years

Personal Evaluation Notebook

4.2

Money In/Money Out

The following chart will help you start planning your budget. Print out a copy of this chart at **www.mhhe.com/ferrett9e** and follow the instructions.

1. Monitor your spending for a month. To keep it simple, list money in and money out. Record everything, including earnings, food, travel, and school items. At the end of the month, total your monthly income and your monthly expenses. Put them in the appropriate categories. Subtract your total expenses from your total income. The money left is your monthly surplus. If you have a deficit, you will need to explore ways of increasing revenue or decreasing expenses. Following is a sample.

Date	Money In	Money Out
Jan. 2	$28.00 (edited paper)	
Jan. 3		$20.00 (dinner/movie)
		$50.00 (gas for car)
Jan. 4	$50.00 (house cleaning)	

2. How can you increase your earnings?

_____

_____

_____

3. How can you decrease your spending?

_____

_____

_____

4. List all the free or inexpensive entertainment available in your community. Discuss this list with your study team.

_____

_____

_____

_____

Use **Worksheet 4.4** on page 145 as a guide for planning your budget for the school term.

financial aid site at **studentaid.ed.gov**. Applying for FAFSA (Free Application for Federal Student Aid) required you to create a Personal Identification Number (PIN) and connected you with this site, which is the main portal for detailed information on federal financial assistance.

You will find on your search for financial aid that rarely do opportunities knock on your door—instead, you need to seek them out and apply. Meet with your school's financial aid officer periodically to find out about loans, grants, scholarships, and job opportunities. Discuss your personal situation and specific financial needs. Some sources of financial aid are included in the table on pages 131 and 132.

Avoid Credit Card Debt

When used wisely, credit cards are convenient and help establish a credit rating. Unfortunately, thousands of students fall into debt every year by using a credit card for everyday expenses without backup funds or a plan for repaying the balance. Besides having to pay the interest (usually from 10 to 18 percent), you can rack up additional charges by exceeding your credit limit or making payments late (which adds up fast if you use more than one card). The 2009 Credit Card Responsibility and Disclosure Act has made it more difficult for young adults to obtain credit cards because persons under 21 must have either an independent income or a co-signer. Although this has resulted in lower average debt for college students, unfortunately it has been replaced by student loan debt, as mentioned earlier.

Credit cards can be instrumental in establishing a good credit history, so it's important to pay off the balances as fast as possible. When you develop your monthly budget, don't just add the minimum balance that's due on each card because, interest will accrue for years. Suppose you have a credit card balance of $3,000 at a rate of 10 percent (which is at the very low end). Paying it off at $100 per month would take 3 years assuming you don't charge another dollar to the credit card. On your monthly statement, credit card companies are required to indicate how many months it will take you to pay off your balance based on making just the minimum payments. Take a look at your statement—how long will you be in debt if you pay only the minimum?

Protect Your Identity

Incidences of identify theft are increasing. Periodically check your account balances and always review your bank and credit card statements. If you handle your transactions online, carefully read the procedures on the bank's or company's website. Never respond to phone calls and e-mails asking for personal information, such as your Social Security number or bank account numbers, and do not post personal information on websites that can be viewed by persons you don't know or have only met online. Report any suspicious activity to your bank or credit card company immediately. You should also report any cases of suspected fraud to your state attorney general's office, and you can also contact the National Consumers League's Fraud Center for help at **www.fraud.org**.

By law, you are entitled to view your credit report for free every 12 months from each of the three consumer credit reporting companies (Equifax, Experian, and

Financial Aid Source	Description
Scholarships and Grants Financial aid awarded according to criteria as designated by donor	Scholarships and grants are awarded at most schools on the basis of academic achievement, athletics, music, art, or writing and usually do not have to be paid back. Look on your school (or department) scholarship page for scholarships offered through, or in cooperation with, your school. Many companies and organizations (such as the Rotary, Kiwanis, Lions, Elks, Soroptimist, and American Association of University Women) also offer scholarships, which fit a wide variety of interests and backgrounds. **For More Information** http://apps.collegeboard.com/cbsearch_ss/welcome.jsp www.fastweb.com www.princetonreview.com/scholarships-financial-aid.aspx
Pell Grants Need-based grants that do not have to be repaid	This is the largest student aid program financed by the federal government. Students will need to complete the FAFSA before being considered for these grants. Filing for the FAFSA is free and can be done online. **For More Information** www2.ed.gov/programs/fpg/index.html www.fafsa.ed.gov studentaid.ed.gov/types/grants-scholarships/pell
Loans Payment for school from government (or other lender) which must be repaid, usually with interest	The extent of your financial need and status (undergraduate, graduate student, or parent) determines your eligibility for Perkins, Direct Subsidized or Unsubsidized, or PLUS loans offered by the federal government. Interest rates and repayment terms vary. **For More Information** studentaid.ed.gov/types/loans www.simpletuition.com/esl/glossary_full
Work Study Aid program that allows students to work on-campus or at an approved off-campus organization to earn money to pay for college expenses	Individual colleges administer these federal funds to students participating in the Federal Work-Study (FWS) program. While on-campus, workers normally work for the school; off-campus workers may be able to work for local nonprofit organizations or in a job relevant to their course of study. Student employment, or work study, is an excellent way to earn money and gain valuable experience while still in school. **For More Information** studentaid.ed.gov/types/work-study
Veterans' Programs Financial support and housing provided to military veterans and their dependents	Bills such as the Post-9/11 GI Bill and the Montgomery GI Bill provide financial assistance for the cost of tuition (including undergraduate, graduate, and vocational/technical training), housing, and books to eligible veterans. Scholarships and financial assistance are also available for veterans, military personnel, and their children. **For More Information** www.studentaid.ed.gov/types/grants-scholarships/military www.gibill.va.gov

(continued)

Financial Aid Source	Description
Programs for Native American Students Aid from federal or private institutions provided to Native American students	Native American students can find financial aid from the U.S. Bureau of Indian Education or many private donors and organizations, including the American Indian College Fund. **For More Information** www.bie.edu/ParentsStudents/Grants/index.htm www.indianeducation.spps.org/College_Tuition_Waivers_for_Native_American_Students.html Contact your financial aid office or search online for aid programs designed for specific cultural or ethnic groups.

Other Sources

Loans, assistance programs, and aid programs may be available if you have special needs, such as visual impairments, hearing problems, or speech difficulties; are unemployed; or have a deceased parent. Search the Internet by using key words such as *college scholarship* or *college loans* to find available programs. While there are many valuable financial aid resources on the Internet, some websites are not reliable. Be especially wary of any websites that ask for money or unsecured personal information.

Trans Union). Check your credit report for accuracy by accessing it at **www.annual creditreport.com.** You do not need to sign up for additional services in order to access your credit report (although you may have to pay to view your credit score, which is optional). Be wary of look-alike sites that may charge you for your report.

Save for the Future

Getting in the habit of saving money is hard for many people. The U.S. Department of Commerce reports that most Americans save less than a penny for every $10 earned. And 35 percent of people under age 35 have less than $500 in the bank, leaving little cushion for unexpected expenses, such as car repairs or medical costs. However, there are ways to build your savings for a sound financial future. If you were to save and invest just $1 every day—the price of a small soft drink at a fast-food restaurant—you could have $90,000 in the bank at your retirement. For a traditional-aged college student, $25,000 today earning 8 percent interest will equal $800,000 at retirement. **Figure 4.2** shows how saving early—even for a shorter period of time—pays off later. (See **Peak Progress 4.5** for applications to the Adult Learning Cycle.)

There are many ways you can cut expenses and build your savings:

1. **Pay yourself first.** If you get a paycheck, determine a percentage of your income to go directly into a savings account, your company's 401k plan, an Individual Retirement Account (IRA), or a similar investment. If your employer offers direct deposit, see if you can split it between your checking and savings accounts, so that saving is automatic. When creating your budget, add an expense entitled "me" and set a dollar amount. Unfortunately, "me" is the easiest bill not to pay—but in the end it is the most important.

2. **Shop wisely.** Research expensive purchases, such as a car, furniture, or a laptop. Take into account warranties, payment options and interest, delivery expenses, features, and what you will be using it for, and ask yourself if it is

	TONYA	BEN
Invests $1,000 per year beginning: (About $84 per month in a tax-deferred retirement plan)	age 21	age 34
Stopped last contribution	age 31	age 65
Number of years contributing	10 years	31 years
Retirement	age 65	age 65
Total invested	$10,000	$31,000
Total investment value at retirement (based on 8% annual return, compounded monthly)	$249,000	$136,000

Figure 4.2
The Power of Compound *Interest*

There is a huge benefit to saving early. *Can you figure out how much Tonya would have had if she had not stopped after 10 years but continued investing until age 65? (The answer is on page 137.)*

a necessity. A big screen TV may be nice to have, but you shouldn't buy it if it's beyond your means. For everyday items, refer to a list when you shop, and don't buy on impulse or just because something is on sale.

3. **Pay cash.** Limit credit card use to emergencies or special items, such as airline tickets. You will be tempted to buy more with credit, and it may be more difficult to monitor how much you spend. The same is true for debit cards; twice as many college students have debit cards than credit cards because they are easier to obtain. Keep a tally on your withdrawals, but also limit the amount of cash you carry or keep in your home. You will be less tempted to spend if money isn't readily available.

Peak Progress
4.5

Applying the Adult Learning Cycle to Managing Financial Resources

1. **RELATE. Why do I want to learn this?** I know if I start a habit of wise spending, successful saving, and investing now, it will pay off later. I want to stay debt-free and maintain a good credit rating.

2. **OBSERVE. How does this work?** Who do I know that appears to be in good financial shape? What can I learn from resources such as investment websites and money counselors? What online tools can I explore to determine what my goals should be?

3. **REFLECT. What does this mean?** Where can I further limit my expenses? I'll keep track of my progress and see what strategies work for me.

4. **DO. What can I do with this?** I will practice reducing my spending every chance I get. Each day, I'll work on one area. For example, I'll pack my lunch, rather than buying it on the run.

5. **TEACH. Whom can I share this with?** I'll ask others for tips and share my progress with a financial counselor.

Make a commitment to paying your obligations on time. Investing in a wise financial plan today will pay off with big dividends later.

Luis recently moved into an unfurnished apartment. He has been contributing to his company's 401k and putting money aside each month into a savings account. As a draftsman for a small architectural firm, he's concerned that his job might be eliminated if more building projects don't come in soon—but he's also really tired of sitting on boxes.

- Should Luis stop contributing to his 401k and/or savings account in order to furnish his apartment?
- What are some creative ways Luis could explore to furnish his apartment more economically?
- What else can Luis do now (educationally, financially, socially) that will help him if his job gets cut?

4. **Inventory your everyday expenses.** Just as you plan your monthly budget and write down anticipated expenses, jot down the many expenses you dole out each day (see your spending record from **Personal Evaluation Notebook 4.2**). Pack your lunch rather than eating out; make your coffee at home; buy in bulk and take your water bottle and snacks rather than stopping at a convenience store (and often paying twice the amount).

5. **Pay bills and taxes on time.** Almost every credit card and utility bill incurs a late fee (on top of any interest) when not paid on time. The fee may be a percentage of the balance or a flat fee, which can be substantial (often $25 or more for credit cards). Besides adding up quickly, late fees can hurt your credit rating.

6. **Avoid payday loans.** Too many people opt for fast cash by borrowing against their next paycheck—and often end up extending the loan period or paying late because they don't have the funds on time. These types of loans have excessively high interest rates. For example, if you borrow $100 with the intention of paying it off when your check comes in 2 weeks, you may incur an immediate $20 interest fee—that's a 520 percent annual percentage rate (APR). If you ask for an extension and incur a $25 late fee on top of the interest, the APR goes up to 1,170 percent.

7. **Use public transportation, if possible.** Many cities have public transportation. Biking or walking when you can is cheaper, gives you exercise, and is better for the environment. A car can be expensive, and the purchase price is only the initial cost. Also consider the cost of insurance, sales and personal property taxes, annual inspections and license plate renewal, maintenance, gasoline, and parking.

8. **Stay healthy.** Illness is costly in terms of time, energy, missed classes, and medical bills. Eat healthy, get exercise and rest, and avoiding harmful substances. Not only is cigarette smoking expensive (a pack-a-day habit averages more than $31 per week), but smokers are sick more often than nonsmokers, pay higher health insurance premiums, and have more difficulty getting roommates and even employment.

9. **Look for free opportunities.** Take advantage of free concerts in the park, check out DVDs from the library, sign up for free birthday specials or frequent buyer cards, and visit your city's website to download discount coupons for local attractions. You may be surprised what you'll find with just a little bit of research.

10. **Conserve energy.** To save money on utilities, turn down the heat, turn off lights and switch to energy-efficient lightbulbs, unplug unused appliances, take quick showers, and turn the water off while you brush your teeth.

11. **Get a job.** You may need to earn money while going to school, but don't work long hours and neglect your education. Check with the career center for a list of on- and off-campus jobs.

12. **Exchange room and board for work.** Some students exchange room and board for lawn care, child care, or housecleaning. Because rent is expensive, an exchange situation can save you thousands of dollars over a few years.

13. **Spend less than you earn.** It's as simple as that. Write a budget and be absolutely firm about sticking to it. Once you have a habit of living within your means, you will reap the rewards of confidence and control.

Get Financial Help If You're in Trouble

If you are having financial problems and your credit rating might be in jeopardy, get help.

1. **Admit that you have a problem.** Denial only makes the problem worse. There are some warning signs that you may be in financial trouble. If you experience two or more of these signs, you need to take action:

- You make only the minimum monthly payments on credit cards.
- You struggle to make even the minimum monthly payments.
- The total balance on your credit cards increases every month.
- You miss loan payments or often pay late.
- You use savings to pay for necessities, such as food and utilities.
- You receive second or third payment-due notices from creditors.
- You borrow money to pay off old debts.
- You exceed the credit limits on your credit cards.
- You've been denied credit because of a bad credit bureau report.

2. **Get professional help.** Contact the local chamber of commerce and ask if your community has a consumer credit agency that helps with credit counseling. When you meet with a counselor, take all your financial information, including your budget, assets, bills, resources, loans, and any other requested items. Local branches of the Consumer Credit Counseling Service (CCCS) provide debt counseling for families and individuals, and they charge only a small fee when they supervise a debt-repayment plan. Other private and public organizations, such as universities, credit unions, the military, and state and federal housing authorities, also provide financial counseling for a little or no charge.

● Communicate About Your Finances

If your financial obligations are shared by a spouse or partner, be aware of each other's spending habits. *How can financial problems affect a relationship?*

You Are a Great Resource!

Your most important resource is yourself. You already possess the power to change your life; you just need to claim it and use it consistently. In college, you are surrounded by people and resources that can help you succeed—that's why they are there. But it's up to you to be resourceful and take advantage of these opportunities. Don't sit back and wait for them to come to you (chances are, they won't). "I didn't know." "Why didn't someone tell me?" "If I had only known, I would have . . ."—these statements are too easy to say in hindsight. A proactive person who asks questions, does a little research, and follows through on opportunities will achieve success.

> **"** Few men during their lifetime come anywhere near exhausting the resources dwelling within them. There are deep wells of strength that are never used. **"**
>
> REAR ADMIRAL RICHARD E. BYRD
> *Polar explorer*

WORDS TO SUCCEED

TAKING CHARGE

Summary

In this chapter I learned to

- **Explore and understand the college system.** It is important to understand the rules, regulations, deadlines, policies, procedures, requirements, and resources for help at my school.

- **Seek out people resources.** I appreciate the faculty, advisors, administrators, and study team members, as well as all the students and relationships that make up the campus community. I explore and build networks with all the people who provide information, help, and support. I meet with instructors and my advisor often to review and clarify my expectations and progress. I understand that having a mentor for guidance, knowledge, and advice is essential to my personal and academic growth as a person and my field of study.

- **Use program and online resources.** I explore various programs that offer help, support, and opportunities, such as the advising center, the career development center, counseling, the tutoring and learning center, exchange programs, the job placement office, clubs, campus events, and other activities. I spend time in the library, exploring books, magazines, and newspapers. I visit the bookstore and computer labs, read through the catalog, look at school material, and read the school newspaper. I explore service learning opportunities and resources available for my special needs, such as the adult reentry center and transferring student, legal aid, and veterans programs. As a commuting student, I check out carpooling boards and look for programs that can help me be more involved in campus activities.

- **Use technology to my advantage.** I determine how technology will be used in my courses and what opportunities and resources my school provides.

- **Explore community resources.** I go to city meetings and become familiar with community leaders and projects. I look into internships and part-time jobs. I check out the community's website and local publications to become familiar with local topics and opportunities for service, resources and special support groups, and agencies offering counseling and health services.

- **Manage my money.** I take full responsibility for my finances. I know how to make and stick to a budget, save money, and spend less than I earn. I limit my credit card use, watch for identity theft, and seek help managing my money when necessary.

- **Explore financial resources.** I explore scholarships and grants, loans, work study, and special assistance programs. I also explore campus jobs and student assistance programs.

- **Realize that I am my greatest resource.** I know I am capable of making the most of my opportunities and must be proactive, diligent, and resourceful in order to succeed.

Performance Strategies

Following are the top 10 tips for maximizing your resources:

- Explore all available resources.
- Join clubs and activities and widen your circle of friends.
- Investigate one new campus resource each week.
- Get involved and volunteer at school and in the community.
- Seek help at the first sign of academic, financial, health, or emotional trouble.

- Know where your money goes.
- Establish a budget—and stick to it.
- Use a credit card for convenience only and don't go into debt for unnecessary items.
- Protect your identity from fraud.
- Look for creative ways to reduce spending and save money.

Tech for Success

Take advantage of the text's website at **www.mhhe.com/ferrett9e** for additional study aids, useful forms, and convenient and applicable resources.

- **Websites and textbooks.** Many textbooks have accompanying websites that provide additional resources and study tools, such as online study guides, lab manuals, resources for research projects, and materials to study for certification exams. Many of these websites are free, usually when you have bought your textbook new. If you

aren't sure if your textbook has an accompanying website, read the book's preface (usually listed under "Ancillaries," "Supplements," or "Resources"), ask your instructor, or visit the publisher's website.

- **Bill paying online.** Most financial institutions offer a service that lets you pay your bills through their website. Would this feature help you keep up with your financial obligations?

Study Team Notes

Answer to Figure 4.2 (page 133): $385,506

Benefits of Community Resources

Donna Washington works as a social worker at an elementary school. School social workers help students, teachers, and parents cope with problems. Their work involves guidance and counseling regarding challenging issues in the classroom, as well as in the home. They diagnose behavior problems and advise teachers on how to deal with difficult students. They work with families to improve attendance and help working parents find after-school child care. They also help recent immigrants and students with disabilities adjust to the classroom.

A long list of community resources helps Donna provide appropriate referrals. She arranges services for children in need, such as counseling or testing. Other services on her list include legal aid societies, crisis hot lines, immigrant resource centers, and tutoring. Donna has developed her list over a 20-year career span and remains in touch with key community leaders to keep her list up-to-date.

Donna chose to be a school social worker because of a strong desire to make a difference in the lives of children. She possesses all the qualities that make her an excellent social worker: She is responsible, emotionally stable, warm and caring, and able to relate to a wide variety of clients, and she can work independently. Because of budget cuts, agencies in her district are understaffed, and Donna struggles with a huge caseload. Although she finds the work emotionally draining at times, Donna finds tremendous satisfaction when she sees the lives of her students improve due to her care.

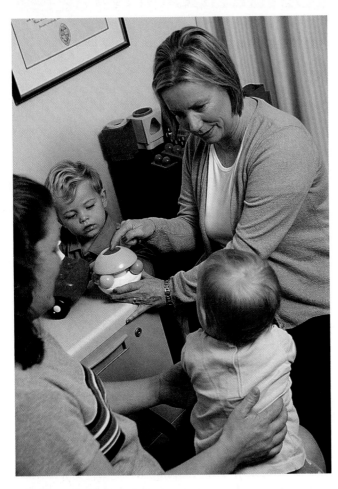

Donna Washington
SCHOOL SOCIAL WORKER

Related Majors: Social Work, Psychology, Sociology

CRITICAL THINKING What qualities make a good social worker? Why?

Peak Performer
PROFILE

Eric Greitens

It's not a charity. It's a challenge. That's the motto of The Mission Continues, founded by Navy SEAL officer Eric Greitens. The group's goal is to help post-9/11 veterans transition from military service by redeploying them on new missions at home. Greitens formulated the plan for The Mission Continues after visiting wounded colleagues. "Every single one of them said he wanted to find a way to continue to serve. They needed to know that when they came home, we saw them as vital."[1]

Returning veterans may face special challenges that affect their health and well-being after their service and combat has ended. According to the Department of Veteran's Affairs, veterans who served in the wars in Iraq or Afghanistan have a much higher rate of dying in vehicle crashes at home which in part can be attributed to post-traumatic stress disorder, which increases aggressive driving.

Sometimes, the violence of war also comes home, with veterans committing higher rates of spousal and child abuse and some turning to alcohol and drug use to deal with the trauma of war. Also, a U.S. military veteran commits suicide, on average, every 65 minutes. A study of veteran suicides from 1999 to 2010 showed that 22 vets were dying every day. More active duty soldiers die from suicide than combat.

Starting a new career after leaving military duty can also be a challenge. An estimated 250,000 recent veterans are searching for jobs. Many vets face the additional challenge of rehabilitating and finding employment after a serious life-altering injury.

These statistics prove that it's critical for returning veterans to find and utilize resources that will help them apply core skills they acquired in the military, such as team building, dependability, strategic critical thinking, and leadership. They also need support to help them adjust to home and family life after serving in tense, unpredictable combat situations.

Programs such as The Mission Continues are vital resources for giving veterans a sense of purpose, assimilating their skills and leadership abilities into the community, and helping them make personal and professional connections. This is a "win–win" for everyone—returning veterans needing to transition their life purpose, and welcoming communities needing their skills and abilities to tackle any challenge presented them. With The Mission Continues, Greitens, a Rhodes scholar and best-selling author, has used his vast education and military experience to continue his mission of providing opportunities for today's veteran.

PERFORMANCE THINKING Do you know anyone struggling with the aftereffects of military service? What resources does your college offer that help returning veterans further their education and participate in school and community affairs?

CHECK IT OUT The Mission Continues is one of many organizations focused on issues related to active and returning military personnel. Go to **www.missioncontinues.org** to see what volunteer opportunities are in your area. Think of local "missions" that would benefit from the services of returning veterans.

[1] Tony Perry, "To Ease Veterans' Return to Civilian Life, Program Offers Purpose, *Los Angeles Times,* February 18, 2013, http://articles.latimes.com/2013/feb/18/local/la-me-veterans-mission-20130218.

Starting Today

At least one strategy I learned in this chapter that I plan to try right away is

_____

_____

_____

What changes must I make in order for this strategy to be most effective?

_____

_____

_____

Review Questions

Based on what you have learned in this chapter, write your answers to the following questions:

1. What are some of the benefits of participating in a study group?

_____

_____

2. What type of school programs would you contact to find a full- or part-time job while attending school?

_____

_____

3. Name two college financial resources cited in this chapter that you would like to investigate, and explain why.

_____

_____

4. How can staying healthy help you financially?

_____

_____

5. What is your most important resource? Why?

_____

_____

To test your understanding of the chapter's concepts, complete the chapter quiz at **www.mhhe.com/ferrett9e.**

Using Resources

In the Classroom

Lorraine Peterson is a returning student at a 2-year business school. She also works part-time selling cosmetics at a retail store and would like to advance to a managerial position. She was away from school for several years. During that time, she started a family and is now eager to become involved in school and its activities. On returning to school, she happily discovered other returning students. Several of them get together for coffee on a regular basis. Lorraine is especially interested in international students and global business opportunities. She also wants to learn more about available computer services, guest speakers, marketing associations, and scholarships.

1. What suggestions do you have for Lorraine about involvement in campus and community events?

_____

_____

2. How can she find out about scholarships and explore all the resources that would increase her success as a returning student?

_____

_____

In the Workplace

Lorraine has been a salesperson for several years with a large cosmetics firm. She recently was promoted to a district sales manager position. Part of her job is to offer motivational seminars on the benefits of working for her company. She wants to point out the opportunities and resources available to employees, such as training programs, support groups, demonstrations, sales meetings, and conferences. The company also sponsors scholarships and community events. An elaborate incentive system offers bonuses and awards for increased sales.

3. How can Lorraine publicize these resources to her sales staff?

_____

_____

4. What strategies in this chapter would help her communicate the importance of contributing time and talents to the community and the company?

_____

_____

Applying the ABC Method of Self-Management

In the Journal Entry on page 115, you were asked to write about a time when you set a financial goal. How difficult was it to achieve? What sacrifices did you have to make?

_____

_____

Now think of a financial goal you may consider in the next few years and apply the ABC Method to work through the obstacles and create a plan for achieving that goal as well.

A = Actual event:

_____

_____

B = Beliefs:

_____

_____

C = Challenge:

_____

_____

Visualize yourself planning and saving money for investing in your goals. You feel confident about yourself, because you have learned to manage your money and your goals. See yourself feeling prosperous as you consider other aspects of wealth, such as being healthy, having supportive family and friends, having opportunities, and being surrounded by many college and community resources.

PRACTICE SELF-MANAGEMENT

For more examples of learning how to manage difficult situations, see the "Self-Management Workbook" section of the Online Learning Center website at **www.mhhe.com/ferrett9e**.

Networking

Using your contacts is especially important when looking for a job. Write information about your network of people on the following form. You can copy this worksheet form to extend your list of contacts.

Name_____ **How I met/know this person** _____

Company _____ Position _____

Phone _____ E-mail _____

Type of work _____

Name _____ **How I met/know this person** _____

Company _____ Position _____

Phone _____ E-mail _____

Type of work _____

Name _____ **How I met/know this person** _____

Company _____ Position _____

Phone _____ E-mail _____

Type of work _____

Name _____ **How I met/know this person** _____

Company _____ Position _____

Phone _____ E-mail _____

Type of work _____

REVIEW AND APPLICATIONS | CHAPTER 4

Community Resources

Research and list the various resources your community has to offer. Make a point to visit at least a few of them, and place a check mark by those you have visited. You can copy this worksheet form to extend your list of resources.

CHECK

_____   Resource _____   Website _____

Service offered _____

_____

Contact person _____   Title/Position _____

Phone _____   E-mail _____

_____   Resource _____   Website _____

Service offered _____

_____

Contact person _____   Title/Position _____

Phone _____   E-mail _____

_____   Resource _____   Website _____

Service offered _____

_____

Contact person _____   Title/Position _____

Phone _____   E-mail _____

_____   Resource _____   Website _____

Service offered _____

_____

Contact person _____   Title/Position _____

Phone _____   E-mail _____

_____   Resource _____   Website _____

Service offered _____

_____

Contact person _____   Title/Position _____

Phone _____   E-mail _____

Monthly Budget

Creating a budget is the first step to financial success. Complete the following list and review it every month to keep track of your expenses. Many of the expenses will vary per month or will be paid periodically rather than monthly. Include monthly estimates in your budget in order to plan ahead. Modify the list to fit your needs.

Monthly Expense	Projected Cost	Actual Cost	Annual Cost
Savings account			
Housing (mortgage, rent)			
Utilities (gas, electric, water, sewer)			
Phone			
Internet/cable			
Transportation (bus, metro, car loan, taxes)			
Gasoline			
Insurance (including homeowner's, renter's, car)			
Health care (including health insurance, co-pays, prescriptions)			
Credit card(s)			
Food			
Household items			
Clothing (including laundry)			
Entertainment			
Tuition (including fees)			
Books and supplies			
Student loan			
Other			
Other			
Other			
Other			
TOTAL			
Financial Resources	**Projected Income**	**Actual Income**	**Annual Income**
Employment (include full- and part-time, work study, contract work)			
Loan(s)			
Savings			
Parental contribution			
Other			
Other			
TOTAL			

REVIEW AND APPLICATIONS | CHAPTER 4

Managing Resources

Exploring your personal resources and abilities is important for your career development. Answer the following questions, and relate your community participation to your leadership skills. Add this page to your Career Development Portfolio.

1. Describe your ability to manage resources. What are your strengths in managing time, money, and information and in determining what resources are available to solve various problems?

_____

_____

_____

_____

2. Indicate how you would demonstrate to an employer that you have made a contribution to your school or community.

_____

_____

_____

_____

3. Indicate how you would demonstrate to an employer that you know how to explore and manage resources.

_____

_____

_____

_____

4. Indicate how you would demonstrate to an employer that you have learned leadership skills.

_____

_____

_____

_____

Listen and Take Effective Notes

LEARNING OUTCOMES

In this chapter, you will learn to

5.1 List effective listening strategies

5.2 Describe the various note-taking systems

5.3 Explain effective note-taking strategies

5.4 Refine and use your notes

SELF-MANAGEMENT

"I am having trouble staying focused and alert in my afternoon class. The instructor speaks in a monotone and I can hardly follow his lecture. How can I listen more effectively and take better notes?"

Have you had a similar experience? Have you left a class feeling frustrated because you couldn't stay focused and your notes were unreadable? In this chapter, you will learn how to be an attentive listener and take clear and organized notes.

JOURNAL ENTRY In **Worksheet 5.1** on page 170, describe a time when you had difficulty making sense out of a lecture and staying alert. Are there certain classes in which it is harder for you to listen attentively?

Attending lectures or meetings, listening, taking notes, and gathering information are a daily part of school and work. However, few people give much thought to the process of selecting, organizing, and recording information. Attentive listening and note taking are not just tools for school. They are essential job skills. Throughout your career, you will process and record information. Technology has dramatically expanded the volume of accessible information, but it has also compounded the number of distractions you may face. The career professional who can stay focused and can organize and summarize information will be valuable. This chapter addresses the fine points of attentive listening and note taking.

Listening to the Message: Attentive Listening Strategies

Before you can be an effective note taker, you must become an effective listener. Most people think of themselves as good listeners. However, listening is more than ordinary hearing. **Attentive listening** means being fully focused with the intent to understand the speaker. It is a consuming activity that requires physical and mental attention, energy, concentration, and discipline. It also requires respect, empathy, genuine interest, and the desire to understand. Researchers say we spend about 80 percent or more of our time communicating; of that time, almost half—45 to 50 percent—is spent listening, yet few of us have been trained to listen.

Not only is listening fundamental to taking good classroom notes, but it is also directly related to how well you do in college, in your career, and in relationships. Students are expected to listen attentively to lectures, to other student presentations, and in small-group and class discussions. Career professionals attend meetings, follow directions, work with customers, take notes from professional journals and lectures, and give and receive feedback. Many organizations have developed training programs to improve their employees' listening and communication habits.

Apply the following attentive listening strategies for building effective relationships at school, at work, and in the rest of your life.

Prepare to Listen

1. **Be willing to listen.** The first place to start is with your intention. You must want to be a better listener and realize that listening is an active process. Is your intention to learn and understand the other person? Or is your intention to prove how smart you are and how wrong the other person is? The best listening strategies in the world won't help if you are unwilling to listen and understand another's viewpoint. Prepare mentally by creating a positive attitude.

WORDS TO SUCCEED

"I only wish I could find an institute that teaches people how to listen. After all, a good manager needs to listen as much as he needs to talk. . . . Real communication goes in both directions."

LEE IACOCCA
Author, former chairman of Chrysler Corporation

2. **Be open to new ideas.** Many people resist change, new ideas, or different beliefs. This resistance gets in the way of actively listening and learning. It is easy to misinterpret a message's meaning if you are defensive, judgmental, bored, or upset. Be open to different points of view and styles of lecturing. With practice and discipline, you can create interest in any subject.

3. **Position yourself to listen.** In the classroom, this may mean taking a chair in the front or finding a location where you feel comfortable and able to focus on the message and create a more personal relationship with the speaker.

4. **Reduce distractions.** Avoid sitting next to a friend or someone who likes to talk or is distracting. Take a sweater if it is cold in the classroom or sit by an open window if it is warm. Carry a bottle of water with you to drink when your energy starts to lag. Don't do other activities (texting, doing math homework, making a to-do list, and so on).

5. **Show you are listening.** Attentive listening requires high energy. Sit up, keep your spine straight, and uncross your legs. Maintain eye contact and lean slightly forward. Your body language is important—whether you are in a chair or engaged in a dialogue with others.

Stay Attentive

1. **Be quiet.** The fundamental rule of listening is to be quiet while the speaker is talking. Don't interrupt or talk to classmates. The listener's role is to understand and comprehend. The speaker's role is to make the message clear and comprehensible. Don't confuse the two roles.

2. **Stay focused.** Everyone's mind wanders at times during a long lecture, but being mentally preoccupied is a major barrier to effective listening. It's up to you to focus your attention, concentrate on the subject, and bring your mind back to the present.

3. **Show empathy, respect, and genuine interest.** Focus on understanding the speaker's message and viewpoint. Look for common views and ways in which you are alike.

4. **Observe the speaker.** Watch for verbal and nonverbal clues about what information is important. If your instructor uses repetition, becomes more animated, or writes information on the board, it is probably important. PowerPoint presentations or handouts may include important diagrams, lists, drawings, facts, or definitions. Pay attention to words and phrases that signal important information or transitions, such as "One important factor is . . ."

5. **Predict and ask questions.** Keep yourself alert by predicting and asking yourself questions. What are the main points? How does the example clarify the material you read prior to class? What test questions could be asked about the main points? Pretend you are in a private conversation, and ask your instructor to elaborate, give examples, or explain certain points.

6. **Integrate learning styles and use all your senses.** If you are primarily an *auditory* learner, consider recording lectures (be sure to ask the instructor first). Record yourself reading your book notes aloud and play it back

several times. If you are primarily a *visual* learner, the more you see, the better you remember. Visualize what your instructor is talking about, and supplement your lecture notes with drawings, illustrations, and pictures. If you are a *kinesthetic* learner, write as you listen, draw diagrams or pictures, rephrase what you hear in your own words, and take special note of material on the board, screen, and handouts. Shift body position, so that you're comfortable.

7. **Postpone judgment.** Don't judge the speaker or the person's message based on clothes, reputation, voice, or teaching style. Listen with an open and curious mind and focus on the message, the course content, and your performance. Talk in private if you disagree, but do not embarrass or unnecessarily challenge the person in front of others. Of course, you should use critical thinking, but be respectful and open to new ideas.

Review What You Have Heard

1. **Paraphrase.** Clarify the speaker's message. After a conversation, paraphrase what you think the speaker said to you—for example, "Professor Keys, it is my understanding that the paper should be four to five pages long, is due on Friday, and should include supporting documentation. Is that correct?" Show that you understand the speaker by reflecting and paraphrasing: "Jan, do I understand that you feel you are doing more than your share of cleaning the apartment?" After a lecture, write a summary of the key points and main ideas. It is even more effective if you compare notes and summarize with your study team.

2. **Assess.** Evaluate how effective your listening skills are for recall, test taking, and studying with your study group. Reflect on conflicts, misunderstandings, and others' reactions to you. Notice nonverbal cues. If there is a misunderstanding, assess your part. Did you jump to conclusions or misunderstand nonverbal clues? Did you fail to clarify the message or to follow up? When there is a misunderstanding or something is missing, ask simple, direct questions with the intent to understand.

3. **Practice with awareness.** Changing old habits takes time. Choose one problem you want to work on. For example, do you continue to interrupt? Think about how you feel when that happens to you, and make a commitment to change. It won't happen overnight, but with consistent practice you can learn to stop annoying habits and improve your listening skills.

Peak Progress 5.1 explores how you can become a more attentive listener by applying the Adult Learning Cycle. Then, **Personal Evaluation Notebook 5.1** on page 152 asks you to think critically about your listening skills and how you can improve them.

Recording the Message

Now that you are prepared and have sharpened your listening and observation skills, let's look at how to outline your notes, so that you can organize material. **Note taking** is more than simply writing down words. It is a way to order and arrange

Peak Progress

Applying the Adult Learning Cycle to Becoming an Attentive Listener

Learning to be an attentive listener and take good notes requires time and effort.

1. **RELATE. Why do I want to learn this?** How will being an attentive listener help me in school, work, and life? How would I rate my listening skills now? What areas do I need to improve?

2. **OBSERVE. How does this work?** I can learn a lot about attentive listening by watching others. I'll observe people who are good listeners and take good notes. I'll also observe people who are not good listeners. Do their poor listening skills cause other problems for them?

3. **REFLECT. What does this mean?** I will gather information about listening and note taking and

determine the best strategies for me to apply. What works and what doesn't? I'll explore creative ways to listen and take notes.

4. **DO. What can I do with this?** I will commit to being a more attentive listener. I'll find opportunities to try my new listening skills. Each day, I'll focus on one area and work on it. For example, I'll choose one class in which I'm having trouble listening and experiment with new strategies.

5. **TEACH. Whom can I share this with?** I'll talk with others and share my tips and experiences. I'll demonstrate and teach others the methods I've learned.

Now return to Stage 1 and think about how it feels to learn the valuable skill of attentive listening.

---

thoughts and materials to help you remember information. You can use either a formal or an informal outline (see **Peak Progress 5.2** on page 153). The point of all note-taking systems is to distinguish between major and minor points and to add order to material. Let's start with one of the most widely used and effective systems—the Cornell System of Note Taking.

The Cornell System of Note Taking

← left Brain person

The Cornell System of Note Taking was developed in the 1950s by Walter Pauk at Cornell University. It is effective for integrating text and lecture notes. Start with a sheet of standard loose-leaf paper and label it with the class, date, and title of the lecture. Divide your notepaper into three sections ("Notes," "Cues," and "Summary") by drawing a vertical line about 2 inches from the left-hand margin; then draw a horizontal line below that. (See **Figure 5.1** on page 154.)

Notes. The right side is the largest section. Record information from class lectures in whatever format works best for you. You can use a formal system with standard Roman numerals or an informal system of indentation to distinguish between major and minor points and meaningful facts.

Cues. Then use the left side to jot down cues, main ideas, phrases, key words, or clarifications. List any pertinent examples or sample test questions from the lecture or the book. Try to pose questions that are answered by your notes. When you review, cover up the right side (the "Notes" section) and try to answer the questions you have written.

Summary. On the bottom of the page, include a "Summary" section. This is an effective way to summarize each class session in your own words. Fill in with details from the book, and elaborate after discussions with your study team or instructor.

Personal Evaluation Notebook

Attentive Listening

Use critical thinking to answer the following questions.

1. Do you go to class prepared and in a positive and receptive state of mind? Write down one tip you would be willing to try to improve your listening.

_____

_____

_____

2. Jot down the name of a person you consider to be a good listener. Consider your feelings toward this person. Attentive listening shows respect and caring. Does that describe this person?

_____

_____

_____

3. Write a list of daily situations that require attentive listening, such as talking to your child about his day at school, listening to your partner's views on politics, and meeting with a community group to plan a fundraising event. What listening strategies would increase your attention and responsiveness in the situations you listed?

_____

_____

_____

The Cornell System is a great tool for reviewing and comparing notes for lectures and books. (In Chapter 6, we'll look further at taking notes while reading.) Notes can be taken sequentially to preserve the order decided upon by the lecturer. It is an effective method for study teams because you can compare class notes, review summaries, and use the sample test questions on the left. One student can recite his or her notes on the right while another uses the cues on the left for possible test questions and examples. Each can recite his or her class and chapter summaries. Many people who are left-brain dominant prefer the logical, sequential, step-by-step Cornell System.

Mind Maps

A **mind map** (or "think link") is a visual, holistic form of note taking (see **Figure 5.2** and **Figure 5.3** on pages 155 and 156 for two examples). The advantage is that you can

Formal (Traditional) versus Informal (Creative) Outlines

Your learning style, or whether you are left-brain or right-brain dominant, can affect what outline style works for you. Left-brain dominant people tend to like a traditional outline that uses a logical, step-by-step, sequential pattern of thought and focuses on words and order. **Formal outlines** may use Roman numerals and capital letters to outline headings, main topics, and points, then list supporting points with lowercase letters and numbers. This system requires consistency. For example, the rules require at least two headings on the same level; if you have IA, you should also have IB. If you have IIIA1, you must also have IIIA2.

Some students find that formal outlines are too time-consuming and restrictive for classroom lectures.

However, they like using an outline because it organizes ideas and illustrates major points and supporting ideas. They prefer a free-form, or **informal, outline**. This system shows headings, main points, and supporting examples and associations, but it uses a more flexible system of dashes, bullets, numbers, and/or indenting—whatever works for the note taker. Many students find an informal method easier for in-class note taking because it lets them focus on main ideas and supporting examples instead of worrying about rules.

Following are examples of formal (top) and informal (bottom) outlines.

Formal (Traditional) Outline

Example 1:

Topic: Note Taking

Jana Rosa
April 9, 2014

Effective Strategies for Taking Notes

I. The traditional outline for note taking
   A. Advantages
      1. Occupies your attention totally
      2. Organizes ideas as well as records them
   B. Disadvantages
      1. Too structured for right-brain dominant person
      2. Time-consuming

II. The mapping system for note taking
   A. Advantages
      1. Presents a creative and visual model
      2. Can start anywhere on the page
   B. Disadvantages
      1. Too busy for a left-brain dominant person
      2. Too unorganized for a left-brain dominant person

Informal (Creative) Outline

Example 2:

NOTE TAKING

Jana Rosa
April 9, 2014

1. Summarize
2. Organize —— Traditional
                — Mind map
                — Cornell
3. Visualize and illustrate
4. Shorthand
5. Notebook
6. One side of paper
7. Write down blackboard notes
8. Review
   —10 minutes
   —24 hours
   —Weekly

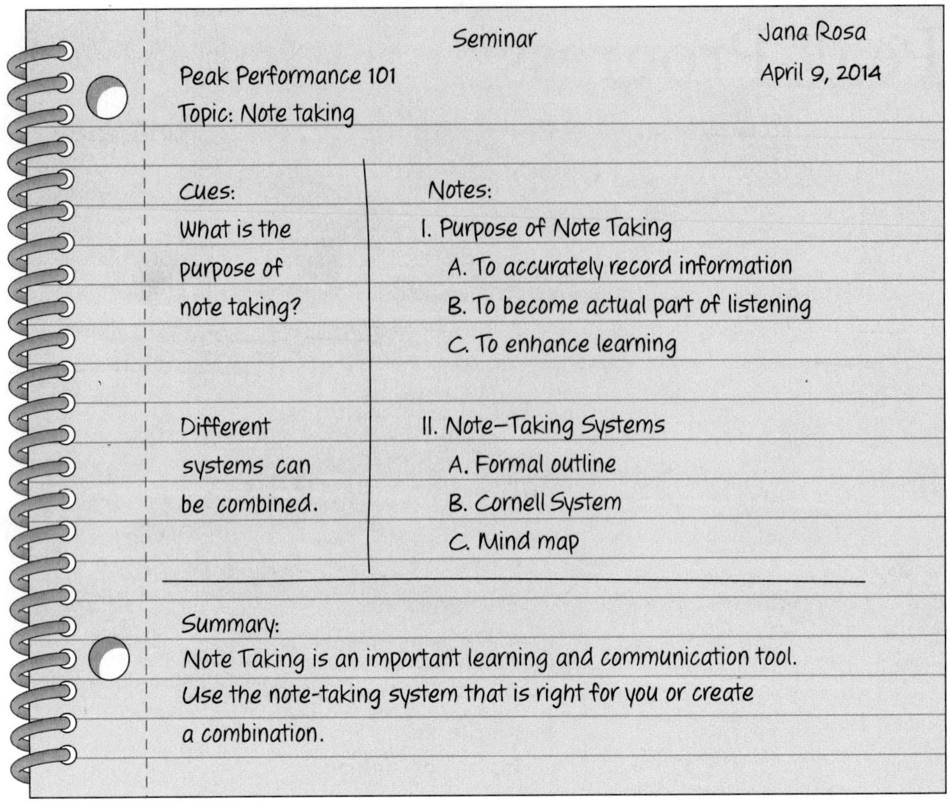

Figure 5.1
The Cornell System

This method integrates text and lecture notes and includes a summary section. *Which personality type might prefer the Cornell System?*

```
                            Seminar                  Jana Rosa
    Peak Performance 101                             April 9, 2014
    Topic: Note taking

    Cues:                   Notes:
    What is the             I. Purpose of Note Taking
    purpose of                  A. To accurately record information
    note taking?                B. To become actual part of listening
                                C. To enhance learning

    Different               II. Note–Taking Systems
    systems can                 A. Formal outline
    be combined.                B. Cornell System
                                C. Mind map

    Summary:
    Note Taking is an important learning and communication tool.
    Use the note-taking system that is right for you or create
    a combination.
```

see the big picture, including connections to the main idea. Mapping starts from the main idea, placed in the center of a page, and branches out with subtopics through associations and patterns. You may find that mapping increases your comprehension, creativity, and recall. Mind maps can be useful in brainstorming ideas for speeches or papers, serving as a framework for recalling topics, or helping you review. The method is less useful during class lectures because it has no sequential order.

Because right-brain dominant learners like creative, visual patterns, mind mapping may work for them. A left-brain dominant student may be uncomfortable mapping because the outline is not sequential, following the instructor's train of thought is difficult, there is little space for corrections or additions, and the notes must be shortened to key words and only one page. You could use a mind map to illustrate an entire chapter and a traditional outline for daily notes.

In certain classes, you will study several different topics that have the same patterns. For example, you may study different cultures, and the categories or patterns are the same for each culture. See **Worksheet 6.7** for a blank mind map template, which you can use or adapt for many situations.

Combination Note-Taking Systems

Because no two people take notes in the same way, you will want to experiment with several note-taking systems or a combination of systems. Effective note takers vary their strategies, depending on the material covered. These strategies include highlighting main ideas, organizing key points, comparing and contrasting relationships, and looking for patterns. Effective note takers listen, organize, record, and review. **Figure 5.4** on page 157 shows a combination note-taking system, using

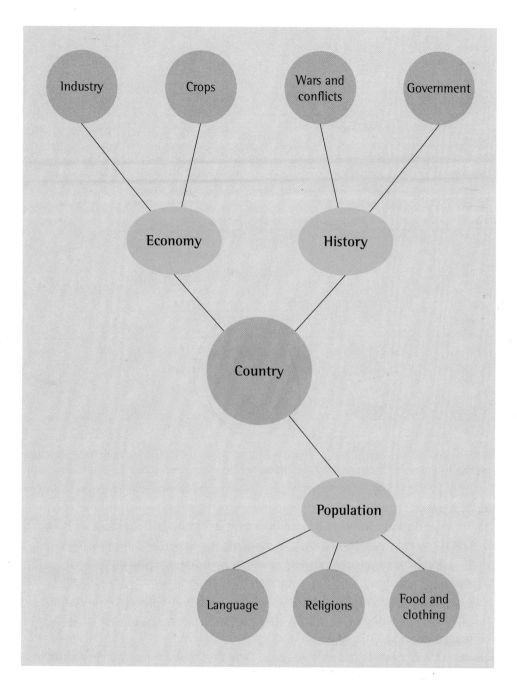

Figure 5.2
Sample Mind Map
This template can be adapted for many subjects. *In which of your courses would this format be useful for note taking?*

a formal outline, mind mapping, and the Cornell System. Find your own system that supports your learning style and helps you organize and recall information easily.

Note-Taking Strategies

The following strategies will help you make the most of the note-taking system you use. Review the strategies listed at the beginning of the chapter to prepare yourself mentally and physically for listening.

1. **Preview the material.** Can you imagine going to an important class without doing your homework or lacking pen and paper? Go to classes prepared, even

Figure 5.3
Another Sample Mind Map

This type of mind map uses branches to reveal concept connections and patterns. *Which mind map design do you prefer?*

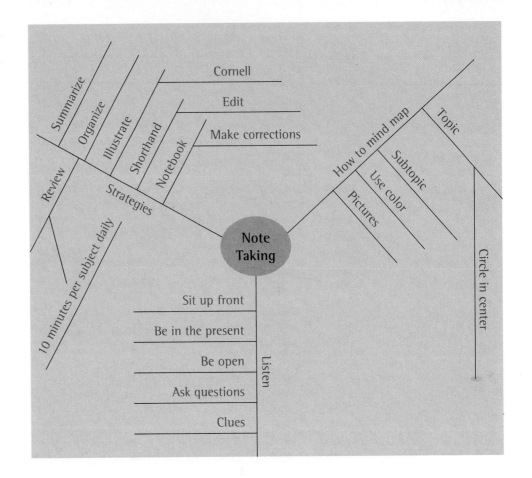

if you have only a few minutes to prepare the night before or right before class. Preview or skim textbook chapters for main ideas, general themes, and key concepts. Previewing is a simple strategy that enhances your note taking and learning. In a sense, you are priming your brain to process information efficiently and effectively. Also review previous notes and connect what you have learned to new ideas.

2. **Go to every class and be on time.** You cannot take effective notes if you are not there. Having someone else take notes for you is not the same as being in class. Of course, this doesn't mean "If I just show up, I should get an *A*." Walking in late for class indicates a similar attitude that class is not important to you, and it disrupts the instructor and other students. You have to invest in every class by showing up—on time—prepared, alert, and ready to participate.

3. **Sit up front.** You will be more alert and will see and hear better if you sit in the front of the class. You will also be more likely to ask questions and engage the instructor in eye contact. You will be less likely to talk with other students, text, or daydream. (See **Peak Progress 5.3** on page 159 for tips on getting the most out of your instructor's presentation.)

4. **Use all your senses.** Many people view note taking as an exclusively auditory activity. Actually, note taking is more effective if you integrate learning styles

Figure 5.4

Combination Note-Taking System

Note the various note-taking systems on the left, reflecting the lecture on the right. (The italicized words in the Lecture side denote inflection by the speaker.) *Which note-taking system do you prefer?*

Formal Outline

Jana Rosa
April 9, 2014

I. Selective Perception
  A. External
    1. Larger, brighter, louder
    2. Different
    3. Repetitive
    4. Contrast
  B. Internal
    1. Needs
      a. Hunger
      b. Fatigue
    2. Motives
      a. Food
      b. Lodging
      c. Entertainment

Mind Map

Activates senses: Louder, Brighter, Larger

External: Contrasts, Repetitive, Different

Selective Perception

Internal: Needs (Hunger, Fatigue, Food), Motives (Lodging, Entertainment)

Cornell Summary

Summary: Selective perception is the process by which information is selected for our attention. Both external and internal factors affect perception. External factors include stimuli that are larger, brighter, louder, unusual, unfamiliar, colorful, or intense. Internal factors include our motives and needs, such as hunger, anger, or attitude.

What is *Selective Perception?*

Selective perception is the *process by which certain events, objects, or information is selected for our attention*. Because of selection, we do not process the information required to make decisions or initiate behavior. Perception is selective. We all have the ability to tune out certain stimuli and focus on others or to shift our attention at will. We tend to hear and see what meets our *needs, interests, and motivation*. We fill in what is missing. We choose what we want to perceive and organize information into meaningful pictures. We block out some information and add to others. What are the factors that cause us to focus on and select certain events and ignore others? These factors fall into *two* categories: *external* and *internal*.

First let's look at *External Factors.*

External factors are *certain events* around us that determine whether we notice something or not. Many factors affect which objects will receive our attention and focus. Stimuli that activate our *senses* are noticed more (larger, brighter, louder). Anything that is out of the ordinary, colorful, or unfamiliar or that contrasts a background receives more attention. We notice what is *different* and incongruent (such as wearing shorts in church) and what is more *intense*. We also notice objects that are in motion and messages that are repetitive. The *more* information presented —or the frequency—the greater the chances that the information will be selected.

Marketing experts study these external factors and use them in advertisements. If a message is loud or bright, it increases the chance that it will be selected. We even use external factors in our daily life. For example, John is a public relations executive and wants to be noticed at his large company. He wears expensive suits and unusual, interesting ties. Even his office is decorated in a unique, colorful, yet professional style.

The second category is *Internal Factors.*

Several internal factors affect perception. What we focus on is affected by our current *motives or needs*. If you've ever attended a meeting close to lunchtime, you may have found yourself concentrating on the smells coming from a nearby restaurant. You tend to respond to stimuli that relate to your immediate needs (hunger or fatigue, for example). If you are driving down the highway and see a host of signs and billboards, you will notice the ones that are directed at your current motivational state, such as those for food, lodging, or entertainment.

and use all your senses. For example, if you are primarily a *kinesthetic* learner, you can make learning more physical by writing and rephrasing material, working with your study team or partner, collecting examples, creating stories and diagrams, using note cards, and standing when taking notes from your textbook. If you are primarily a *visual* learner, develop mental pictures and use your right-brain creativity. Draw and illustrate concepts. Practice visualizing images while the speaker is talking, form mental pictures of the topic, and associate the pictures with key words. Use colored pencils, cartoons, or any other illustrations that make the material come alive. Supplement your lecture notes with drawings, and take special note of

Selena loves to participate in her women's studies class—so much so that, by the end of the lecture, she has done more talking than note taking. Although she feels energized by the debates, she has little to refer to when reviewing for the weekly quizzes.

- How can Selena balance joining the discussions with taking good notes to refer to later?
- How does she know if she is listening attentively to her classmates?
- What could Selena do immediately after class to make sure she understands the main points?

material in PowerPoint presentations and handouts. If you are primarily an *auditory* learner, listen attentively and capitalize on this style of processing information. You might want to record lectures. Read your notes and recite aloud the main points of the lecture. Explain your notes to your study group, so that you can hear the material again.

5. **Make note taking active and physical.** Observe your body, how you hold your pen, and how your back feels against the chair. Sit up straight as slouching produces fatigue and signals the brain that this activity is not important.

6. **Link information.** Look for patterns that connect ideas as well as information that is different. Develop associations between what you are hearing for the first time and what you already know. When you link new knowledge to what you already know, you create lasting impressions. Ask yourself how this information relates to other classes or to your job.

7. **Reduce to the essential.** Don't make the mistake of trying to write down everything the instructor says. Notes are like blueprints: They represent a larger subject and highlight main details. Jot down only main points and key words. Add illustrations, statements, stories, introductions, and transitions that are important for depth, interest, and understanding. Devise a system for note taking that includes abbreviations and symbols. If you text, you may have already developed your own "shorthand vocabulary," which may be helpful when taking notes. See **Figure 5.5** on page 160 for common note-taking shortcuts.

8. **Organize your notes.** Use large, bold headlines for main ideas and large print for key words, important points, facts, places, and other supporting data. Write your name, the topic, and the date on each sheet of paper. Consider getting a binder for each class to organize notes, syllabi, handouts, tests, and summaries. Leave wide margins and plenty of space to make corrections, add notes, clarify, and summarize. If you crowd your words, the notes will be hard to understand. Keep all handouts you receive in class. Use a question mark if you do not understand something, so that you can ask about it later.

9. **Use note cards.** Use index cards to jot down key words, formulas, definitions, and other important information. Note cards and flash cards help you integrate all learning styles. Write down key words and main points, use them throughout the day, and review for tests.

10. **Expand on notes from others.** Many instructors lecture in conjunction with a PowerPoint presentation. Ask your instructor if the lecture outline is available as a handout, on a course website, or in a bookstore. Preview it before class, take a copy of the printout to class, and add notes and detail as the instructor talks. This is a handy note-taking tool that helps you follow the discussion, organize your notes, and read the text. If you missed class and borrowed notes from someone else, thoroughly review the notes, mark anything that is unclear and needs follow-up, and compare them with the textbook.

Getting the Most Out of a Class Lecture

In the classroom and in meetings you attend on the job, you will come across many styles of presenters, from dynamic and succinct to agonizingly vague and verbose. As discussed in Chapter 1, you can adjust your learning style to your instructor's teaching style, just as you would need to adjust your work style to that of your boss. But what if your instructor's style presents specific challenges to your learning? Following are some tips if your instructor

- **Talks too softly.** If you can't hear your instructor, first ask other students if they are having the same problem (to make sure it's not just your hearing). Then, try a seat in the front. If you still can't hear well, tell your instructor outside of class. Your instructor may not be aware it's a problem and may be able to adjust his or her speaking level or use a microphone.

- **Talks too fast.** If you find you can't keep up with your instructor as you take notes (or you are missing points), you might be a little slower jotting down notes than others and may have to speed it up. Focus on writing just key words. If you miss a section, leave a space in your notes with a notation (such as an asterisk or "missed") and ask another student or your study group about the missing material.

- **Is hard to understand because his or her native language is different from yours.** As our world becomes more globally connected, you will encounter instructors, colleagues, physicians, neighbors, and others with various native languages, cultures, and experiences. No matter what language you or your instructor is most accustomed to, you are both in the room for the same reason—to teach and learn the material. Thus, when you don't understand a point, ask questions and be persistent until you do understand.

- **Never allows time to ask questions.** Find out your instructor's e-mail or office hours and contact him or her directly with your questions.

- **Never addresses material from the text.** Some students get frustrated when they buy a text and then the instructor doesn't cover the same material during lecture. The instructor might be expecting you to read the text on your own and is using lecture time for other topics. If you have difficulty with any of the text material, ask the instructor if you should bring that up during or outside of class.

- **Only lectures, never writes on the board or uses PowerPoint.** Listen for verbal cues (such as a louder voice) and nonverbal cues (such as hand gestures) that suggest more important points to remember. Ask for examples that illustrate key points.

- **Puts a lot of content in the PowerPoint presentation.** PowerPoint presentations can be a visual way of organizing a lecture and showing key illustrations. But some instructors get carried away and try to put the whole lecture in a few slides. Rather than scrambling to write every word, ask the instructor if the presentation is available online. If so, bring a copy to class and take notes on it. Look at slide headings for key words or phrases as the instructor speaks.

- **Never follows the lecture outline or PowerPoint.** Not everyone stays on course when speaking, especially if questions or new topics sidetrack the discussion. Remember that the PowerPoint presentation is just a blueprint, and try to balance your notes with the key points from it and the instructor's discussion.

- **Seems to ramble and never gets to a point.** Some speakers are better than others. Here's where you have to be proactive and ask clarifying questions ("So what you are saying is _____, correct?"), and confer with fellow classmates to put the pieces together.

- **Uses too many personal anecdotes that may or may not be relevant.** Everyone loves to tell old "war stories," even though the relevance may be a stretch. However, this is a chance to connect personally with the instructor, and you may find you have similar experiences. Keep an open mind and resist the urge to ask, "Will this be on the test?"

In every situation, if you still have difficulties listening and taking notes, you should promptly and politely talk with your instructor. Only with feedback does a speaker improve his or her skills, which in turn benefits listeners.

Figure 5.5
Note-Taking Shortcuts

This chart lists some common symbols and abbreviations you can incorporate into your own note-taking system. *What is the essential element in taking effective notes?*

Symbol	Meaning	Abbreviation	Meaning
>	greater than; increase	i.e.	that is
<	less than; decrease	etc.	and so forth
?	question; unclear	lb.	pound
w/	with	assoc.	association
w/o	without	info	information
V or *	important ideas	e.g.	example
+	positive; benefit; pro(s); added; additional	p.	page
÷	negative; con(s); lost	pp.	multiple pages
X	times		
~	gaps in information		
→	leads to (e.g., motivation → success)		
∧	bridge of concepts; insert		
#	number; end		

11. **Use your electronic device.** Your instructor may allow you to take notes in class on a laptop, tablet, or other electronic device. This can be a convenient way to store, organize, review, and share notes after class. However, focusing on discussions, nonverbal cues, and visual illustrations may be difficult if you are looking at your keyboard or screen. If your power fails or you forget to save your work, you may have no back-up notes. Also, your classmates or instructor may be distracted by your typing. Consider taking lecture notes electronically only if it maximizes your learning. Another way you may be able to use it outside of the physical classroom is to download podcasts of lectures if the instructor makes them available. These offer a way to review lectures on your own. Use the same note-taking strategies, and follow up with your instructor if the main points are unclear.

Assess and Review Your Notes

Don't just file your notes away after class. Instead, reinforce your memory and understanding of the material by assessing and reviewing your notes. Research indicates that, even after only 1 hour, you will retain less than 50 percent of the lecture. (See **Figure 5.6.**) Thus, it's important to revisit your notes as soon as possible.

1. **Summarize in your own words.** When you finish taking text and lecture notes, summarize in your own words. You might write summaries on index cards. If you used the Cornell System, make sure you complete the summary section. Summarizing can be done quickly and can cover only main concepts. This one small action will greatly increase your comprehension and learning. It is even more effective when you read your summary out loud to others; teaching is a good way to learn.

2. **Edit and revise your notes.** Set aside a few minutes as soon as possible after the lecture to edit, fill in, or copy your notes. (If possible, avoid scheduling

Figure 5.6

Ebbinghaus's Forgetting Curve

German philosopher Hermann Ebbinghaus determined that after only 9 hours you remember about 36 percent of what you just learned. At 31 days, that amount drops to 21 percent. Thus, constant review is critical. *If you wait until midterm to review your lecture notes, how much will you remember from the first days of class?*

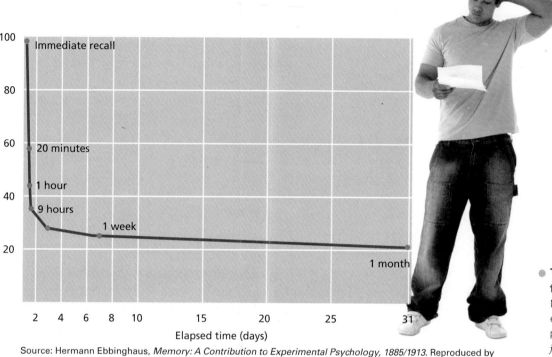

Source: Hermann Ebbinghaus, *Memory: A Contribution to Experimental Psychology, 1885/1913.* Reproduced by permission of Continuum, an imprint of Bloomsbury Publishing Plc.

● **Taking Notes on the Job**

Note taking is an essential skill in many professions. *What are some jobs or professions in which taking notes is a critical, daily task?*

classes back to back, so you can spend time with your notes right after class.) Underline what the instructor indicated is important. Clean up, expand, and rewrite messy or incomplete sections. Compare your notes with the material in the textbook. If you are unclear on a point, leave a space and mark it with a question mark or a colored highlighter. Ask for verification from other students or your instructor.

3. **Create a sample test.** Ask yourself what questions might be on a test and try to write a few sample test questions as if you were giving the exam. Note the correct answer and why it is correct (which may prove helpful later if there is an essay or short-answer exam).

4. **Use visual cues.** Consider drawing a mind map of your notes to display the main points and their connections. For math and science classes, creating flowcharts may help visually reinforce processes or systems.

5. **Review your notes.** Develop a review schedule that supports continual reviewing and reflects on material you have already learned. Think of how you can review your notes within the first hour, the first day, and each week. Add this to the daily planner you created in Chapter 3.

Take 3 minutes after class today to write a brief, one-paragraph summary:
- What were the main points of the lecture?
- What examples were given?
- What parts are unclear?

What else can you do in 3 minutes?
- Compare your summary to the chapter outline.
- Create test questions out of main topics.
- Make a list of discussion topics for your study group.

Take 3

There are many ways to work reviewing into your day:

- *Arrive at class early* and spend 5 minutes reviewing your notes from the previous class. Or review while the instructor passes out handouts or organizes the lecture.
- *Review right before you go to sleep* because your mind is receptive to new information at that time.
- *Compare notes with your study group members* to make sure you recorded and understood all the key points.

6. **Monitor and evaluate.** Periodically assess your note-taking system. Try different systems and strategies until you find the one that works best. Feedback from study group members, your instructor, and tests will help you assess how well your system is working. (See **Peak Progress 5.4** for note-taking tips for students who face special challenges.)

Overcome Obstacles

"Obstacles are those frightful things you see when you take your eyes off your goal."

HENRY FORD
Founder, Ford Motor Company

Some students do not realize the importance of note taking and doubt they will use this skill after they graduate from college. As a result, their notes are often disorganized, incomplete, illegible, and of little help in preparing for tests. However, effective note taking changes information you hear into information that is distinctly yours. You discard the unessential, highlight the essential, and organize information to give it meaning, relevance, and focus. Not only is mastering this process essential to improving your study skills, but it is a necessary job and life skill, whether you are learning how your job contributes to your company's objectives or listening to a presentation about employee health benefits. If you don't listen carefully and take complete, helpful notes (or any notes at all) you have nothing to fall back on if the results aren't what you expected.

Peak Progress

Taking Note of Special Challenges

For some students, note taking may be a more challenging skill. Students with learning disabilities often have more difficulty identifying the important information they should record. They often cannot write fast enough to keep up with the lecturer or decipher their notes after the lecture. Sitting through long lectures in which the instructor uses few visual cues (such as words or illustrations on the board or PowerPoint) can be especially tough, as visuals help students focus on important concepts and examples.

However, the act of taking notes has many benefits. Students with learning disabilities tend to be passive learners, and taking notes is one way to actively engage in the learning process. Note taking also encourages them to clarify confusing information and helps them recall it later.

The strategies discussed earlier in this chapter apply to all students. Also, the following tips may be helpful to those with specific challenges (although any student can benefit from trying them as well):

1. **Sit in the front of the room.** Although this is a good tip for any student, it's especially important for those who have trouble sitting or focusing for long periods of time. Put yourself where you are forced to pay attention and keep distractions, such as books and cell phones out of your hands.

2. **Use a binder instead of a traditional notebook.** This will help you keep everything organized, including lecture and reading notes, handouts, and assignments, and make studying for exams much easier. Write on loose-leaf paper, and three-hole punch everything.

3. **Put headings and dates at the top of all papers.** This makes them easier to identify and organize.

4. **Set up your paper in advance.** Create a note-taking form that helps you focus on the main points of the lecture. Include these items:
   - Today's topic
   - What you already know about the topic
   - Three to seven main points, with details of today's topic as they are being discussed (and then number each line)
   - A summary (quickly describe how the ideas are related)
   - New vocabulary or terms (write these terms in this section as they come up during class; repeat the previous sections as much as necessary)
   - The five main points of the lecture (describe each point)

5. **Cluster ideas as they are presented.** Write them with similar indentation or formatting, and separate clustered ideas by lines if that helps. Clustering information makes it easier to remember later.

6. **Leave space between notes.** Later, you can fill in comments, material you may have missed, or material from the text.

7. **Type your notes afterwards.** Typed notes are more legible to study from, and typing is an additional chance to think about the material and make sure you understand it.

8. **Clarify points with your instructor.** Students with learning disabilities often realize something is important to note after the instructor is well into the discussion, so they've already missed recording key points. Talk with your instructor outside of class and go over your notes together. Your instructor will appreciate that you are actively trying to improve your note-taking skills and may be able to provide additional tips related to his or her class.

TAKING CHARGE

Summary

In this chapter, I learned to

- **Listen attentively to the message.** Developing an interest in listening and making it meaningful to me are the first steps in becoming an attentive listener. I want to listen and am open to new information, new ideas, and different beliefs. My intent is to understand others and focus on the message.

- **Go to every class.** I know I must make a commitment to go to every class and form a relationship with my instructor and other students. I'm on time and sit in front, where I'm alert and aware. I sit up straight, maintain eye contact, and show I'm listening and involved with the speaker. I reduce distractions and focus on listening, not talking. I'm in the present and concentrate on the subject.

- **Observe my instructor and watch for verbal and nonverbal clues.** I watch for examples, words, and phrases that signal important information or transitions. I take note of handouts and visuals. I use critical thinking to postpone judgment. I focus on the message, not the presentation. I look beyond clothes, voice, teaching style, and reputation and focus on what the person is saying. Critical thinking helps me look for supporting information and facts and ask questions.

- **Prepare before class.** I preview chapters before class, so that I have a general idea of the chapter, and I make notes of questions to ask or concepts I want the instructor to give examples of or elaborate on. I do homework and use index cards to jot down and memorize key words, formulas, and definitions.

- **Focus on essential information.** I don't try to write down everything. I look for patterns, link information, and connect ideas in a way that makes sense and organizes the information. I leave space for corrections and additions and use marks, such as "?" for questions.

- **Integrate learning styles.** I not only use my preferred learning style but also integrate all styles. I make note taking active and physical. I draw illustrations, use outlines, supplement my notes with handouts, create models, and summarize out loud.

- **Get organized.** I know that information that is not organized is not remembered. I write the date and topic on each sheet and organize notes in a folder or binder.

- **Determine the note-taking style that works best for me.** A formal outline uses my left-brain, sequential side, while an informal outline helps me see connections and the big picture. The Cornell System of Note Taking is organized into three sections: "Notes," "Cues," and "Summary." A mind map is more visual and includes main points connected to supporting points or examples. I can combine elements of various note-taking systems to determine what works best for me.

- **Summarize in my own words when I am finished taking notes in class or from the text.** This action greatly improves my comprehension and learning. I compare this summary with the material in my book, review it with my study team, and fill in essential information. I note questions to ask my instructor or study group.

- **Review, monitor, and evaluate.** I review my notes for main ideas as soon as possible after class, within 24 hours. This increases my memory and helps me make sense of my notes. I edit and add to my notes. I evaluate my note-taking skills and look for ways to improve them.

Performance Strategies

Following are the top 10 strategies for attentive listening and effective note taking:

- Postpone judgment and be open to new ideas.
- Seek to understand and show respect to the speaker.
- Reduce distractions and be alert and focused.
- Maintain eye contact and look interested.
- Observe the speaker and listen for clues, examples, signal words, and phrases.
- Predict and ask questions to clarify main points.
- Look for information that is similar to what you already know and information that is different.
- Use a note-taking system that suits your learning style.
- Summarize in your own words and review often.
- Edit and revise while information is still fresh.

Tech for Success

Take advantage of the text's website at **www.mhhe.com/ferrett9e** for additional study aids, useful forms, and convenient and applicable resources.

- **Your instructor's visual presentation.** Many instructors lecture in conjunction with a PowerPoint presentation. Ask your instructor if the lecture outline is available as a handout, on a course website, or in a bookstore. Take a copy of the printout to class with you and add notes and detail as the instructor talks. This is a handy note-taking tool that helps you follow the discussion, organize your notes, and read the text.

- **Summarize on your computer.** Some people type faster than they write. It's important to summarize your notes as soon as possible after class to make sure you understand the main points. If that sounds like a daunting task, simply write incomplete sentences first and then flesh out the sentences. If you aren't sure if you really understand the main points of the lecture, consider e-mailing your recap to your instructor and ask him or her to review it. (This may also help your instructor determine if points presented in the lecture need clarification during the next class session.)

Study Team Notes

Listening in the Workplace

Danielle Sievert provides mental health care as an industrial-organizational psychologist for a *Fortune* 500 company. Most industrial-organizational psychologists hold master's degrees in psychology. Psychology is the study of human behavior and the mind and its applications to mental health. When most people think of psychologists, they think of clinicians in counseling centers or hospitals, but many large companies hire psychologists to tend to the needs of staff on all levels. Danielle and other industrial-organizational psychologists use psychology to improve quality of life and productivity in the workplace.

Danielle conducts applicant screenings to select employees who will work well within the company. She provides input on marketing research. She also helps solve human relations problems that occur in various departments. Danielle occasionally conducts individual sessions with employees who face problems within or outside the office. Danielle works a 9-to-5 schedule and is occasionally asked to work overtime. She is often interrupted to solve pressing problems.

Active listening is an important part of Danielle's job. Managers and other employees will ask for her help, she says, only when they sense that she is empathetic and wants to help. To hone her listening skills, Danielle asks questions to make sure she understands exactly what the person is saying. She also takes notes, either during or after a session. These skills help Danielle fulfill her role as a psychologist in the workplace.

Danielle Sievert
PSYCHOLOGIST

Related Majors: Psychology, Counseling

CRITICAL THINKING What kinds of problems might occur at the workplace that could be addressed by a firm's psychologist?

Peak Performer

PROFILE

Anna Sui

"What should I wear?" Many people ask this question almost daily. For international fashion and fragrance designer Anna Sui (pronounced *Swee*), the answer is simple: "Dress to have fun and feel great." Her first boutique, on Greene Street in Soho, New York, illustrated her attitude with a Victorian-inspired mix of purple walls, ornate clothing racks, glass lamps, and red floors.

To the second of three children and only daughter born to Chinese immigrants, the Detroit suburbs of the early 1960s were a long way from the fashion mecca of New York City. However, even then Sui seemed to be visualizing success. Whether designing tissue-paper dresses for her neighbor's toy soldiers or making her own clothes with coordinating fabric for shoes, Sui had flair.

After graduating from high school, Sui headed for the Big Apple. She eventually opened her own business after studying for 2 years at Parson's School of Design and working for years at various sportswear companies. Sui premiered her first runway show in 1991 and today has 300 stores in more than 30 countries.

To create her acclaimed designs, Sui takes note of the world around her. She continues to collect her "genius files"—clippings from pages of fashion magazines—to serve as inspiration. She listens to her clients, to music, to the street, and to her own instincts. Sui is quick to say

that, although her moderately priced clothes are popular with celebrities, they are also worn by her mother. It's not about age and money, she explains, but about the "spirit of the clothing." By listening actively and staying attuned to the world around her, Sui continues to influence trends and enchant with her designs.

PERFORMANCE THINKING For the career of your choice, how would attentive listening and note taking contribute to your success?

CHECK IT OUT Anna Sui's "genius files" have included people from a variety of creative professions, including photographers, illustrators, filmmakers, theater and movie actors, musicians, and, of course, fashion designers and trendsetters. She includes many of these people on her website at **www.annasui.com** (click on the Anna Sui Biography and then "Anna's Favorite Things"). Consider starting your own "genius file" of people and words that inspire you. Who would you include?

Starting Today

At least one strategy I learned in this chapter that I plan to try right away is

_____

_____

_____

What changes must I make in order for this strategy to be most effective?

_____

_____

_____

Review Questions

Based on what you have learned in this chapter, write your answers to the following questions:

1. What is attentive listening?

_____

_____

2. Why are listening and note-taking skills critical to job success?

_____

_____

3. Name two types of note-taking systems and describe how to use them.

_____

_____

4. Why is "Go to every class" an important note-taking strategy?

_____

_____

5. What should you do with your notes after attending class?

_____

_____

To test your understanding of the chapter's concepts, complete the chapter quiz at **www.mhhe.com/ferrett9e.**

Developing Attentive Listening Skills

In the Classroom

Roxanne Jackson is a fashion design student who works part-time at a retail clothing store. She is outgoing, enjoys being around people, and loves to talk and tell stories. However, Roxanne is a poor listener. In class, she is often too busy texting or talking with the person next to her to pay attention to class assignments. When she joins a study group, she starts off as popular but turns in assignments that are late and incorrect. Her study team members feel they spend too much time reminding Roxanne about class projects and expectations.

1. What strategies in this chapter can help Roxanne be a more effective listener?

_____

_____

2. What should she do to improve her relationship with others and stay on top of class expectations?

_____

_____

In the Workplace

Roxanne is now a buyer for a large department store. She enjoys working with people. She is a talented, responsible employee when she is actively aware and tuned in to others. People respond to her favorably and enjoy being around her. However, she is often too busy or preoccupied to listen attentively or take notes. She often forgets directions, misunderstands conversations, and interrupts others in her haste and enthusiasm.

3. What would you suggest to help Roxanne become a better listener?

_____

_____

4. What strategies in this chapter would help her become more aware, more sensitive to others, and able to record information more effectively?

_____

_____

Applying the ABC Method of Self-Management

In the Journal Entry on page 147, you were asked to describe a time when you had difficulty making sense out of a lecture and staying alert. Are there certain classes in which it is more challenging for you to be an attentive listener?

_____

_____

_____

Now apply the ABC Method to the situation and visualize yourself a more attentive listener:

A = Actual event:

_____

_____

_____

B = Beliefs:

_____

_____

_____

C = Challenge:

_____

_____

_____

Practice deep breathing, with your eyes closed, for just 1 minute. Imagine that you are calm, centered, and alert. See yourself enjoying your lectures, staying alert, and taking good notes.

PRACTICE SELF-MANAGEMENT

For more examples of learning how to manage difficult situations, see the "Self-Management Workbook" section of the Online Learning Center website at **www.mhhe.com/ferrett9e.**

Listening Self-Assessment

This simple assessment tool will give you an idea of your attentive listening skills. Read each statement. Then, check Yes or No as to whether these statements relate to you.

	Yes	No
1. My intention is to be an attentive and effective listener.	_____	_____
2. I concentrate on meaning, not on every word.	_____	_____
3. I focus on the speaker and use eye contact.	_____	_____
4. I am aware of emotions and nonverbal behavior.	_____	_____
5. I withhold judgment until I hear the entire message.	_____	_____
6. I am open to new information and ideas.	_____	_____
7. I seek to understand the speaker's point of view.	_____	_____
8. I do not interrupt, argue, or plan my response; I listen.	_____	_____
9. I am mentally and physically alert and attentive.	_____	_____
10. I paraphrase to clarify my understanding.	_____	_____
11. When I'm in class, I sit in the front, so that I can hear and see better.	_____	_____
12. I mentally ask questions and summarize main ideas.	_____	_____
13. I increase the value of my listening by previewing the textbook before class.	_____	_____
14. I adapt to the instructor's speaking and teaching style.	_____	_____
Total Responses:	_____	_____

If you checked Yes to 10 or more questions, you are well on your way to becoming an attentive, effective listener. If you did not, you have some work to do to improve those skills. Which areas are the most difficult for you?

Mind Map a Lecture

Create a mind map of one of your class lectures in the space provided here (see **Figure 5.2** on page 155 and **Figure 5.3** on page 156 for examples). Compare your mind maps with those drawn by other students in your class. Are there key points that you or other students missed? Did some include too much (or too little) detail?

Use the Cornell System of Note Taking

Take notes in one of your class lectures by using the Cornell System in the space provided here (see **Figure 5.1** on page 154 as a guide). Compare your notes with those from other students in your class. Are there key points that you or other students missed? Did some include too much (or too little) detail? Did you summarize your notes?

Cues:

Notes:

Summary:

REVIEW AND APPLICATIONS | CHAPTER 5

Listening and Note Taking in the Workplace

Write how you will demonstrate the listed listening and note-taking skills for future employers.

1. Finding meaning and interest in new information and projects

   _____

2. Showing interest and being prepared

   _____

3. Listening attentively

   _____

4. Observing and asking questions

   _____

5. Acquiring information

   _____

6. Thinking through issues

   _____

7. Organizing information and taking good notes

   _____

8. Staying alert and in the present

   _____

9. Being willing to test new strategies and learn new methods

   _____

10. Practicing attentive listening and note taking again and again

    _____

11. Teaching effective methods to others

    _____

Actively Read

LEARNING OUTCOMES

In this chapter, you will learn to

6.1 Describe active reading

6.2 Explain the Five-Part Reading System and SQ3R

6.3 Adopt active reading strategies

6.4 Build a better vocabulary

6.5 Manage language courses

6.6 Read technical material and manuals and complete forms

6.7 Address reading challenges

SELF-MANAGEMENT

"I usually love to read, but lately I feel like I'm on information overload. Sometimes I read several pages and realize I haven't understood a word I've read. What can I do to read more effectively and actually remember what I've read?"

Do you ever close a book and feel frustrated because you don't remember what you've just read? In this chapter, you will learn how to become an active reader and maximize your reading. You will visualize yourself reading quickly, comprehending, and recalling information. You will see yourself discovering new information, building on facts and concepts, developing memory skills, and feeling the joy of reading.

JOURNAL ENTRY Were you read to as a child? If so, use **Worksheet 6.1** on page 204 to describe a time when you enjoyed being read to by someone, such as a teacher, parent, or librarian. Why was the experience pleasurable? What types of books did you enjoy most? Did you have a favorite book or story? If you don't like to read, why? Are there specific obstacles that keep you from devoting more time to reading?

Some students complain about having a mountain of reading to finish each week. The challenge is not just the volume of reading required in college; you are also expected to comprehend, interpret, and evaluate what you read. **Comprehension** is the ability to understand the main ideas and details as they are written. **Interpreting** what you read means developing ideas of your own and being able to summarize the material in your own words. Interpretation requires several skills, such as noting the difference between fact and opinion, recognizing cause and effect, and drawing inferences and conclusions.

Because the amount of reading required in school can be enormous and demanding, it is easy to get discouraged and put it off until it piles up. However, as with any skill, it's important to keep a positive attitude that focuses on the benefits of improving your abilities. In this chapter, you will learn to create an effective reading system that helps you keep up with your reading assignments and increase your comprehension.

The Importance of Active Reading

When you were a child at home, you may have been told, "This is quiet time; go read a book," or "Curl up with a book and just relax." In school, your instructor may have said, "Read Chapters 1 through 5 for tomorrow's test," or "You didn't do well on the test because you didn't read the directions carefully." On the job, someone may have said to you, "I need your reactions to this report. Have them ready to discuss by this afternoon."

Whether you are reading for enjoyment, for a test, or for a project at work, to be an effective reader you must become actively involved with what you are reading. If you approach reading with a lack of interest or importance, you read only what's required and are less able to retain what you have read. **Retention** is the process by which you store information. If you think something is important, you will retain it.

"To read a writer is for me not merely to get an idea of what he says, but to go off with him, and travel in his company."

ANDREW GIDE
Author

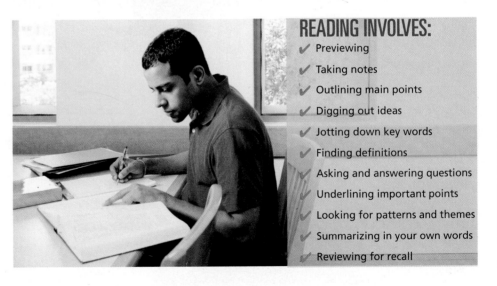

READING INVOLVES:

✔ Previewing
✔ Taking notes
✔ Outlining main points
✔ Digging out ideas
✔ Jotting down key words
✔ Finding definitions
✔ Asking and answering questions
✔ Underlining important points
✔ Looking for patterns and themes
✔ Summarizing in your own words
✔ Reviewing for recall

Reading Systems

Many factors affect your reading comprehension. Your skill level, vocabulary, ability to concentrate, and state of mind, as well as distractions, all affect what you comprehend and recall. There are a number of proven reading systems and, over the years, you may have developed a reading system that works best for you. Two helpful reading systems are the Five-Part Reading System and SQ3R.

The Five-Part Reading System

The Five-Part Reading System (see **Figure 6.1**) is similar to the Adult Learning Cycle, which is explored throughout this text (see **Peak Progress 6.1** on page 178). To remember the five parts, think of them as the five **P**s. As with many reading systems or strategies (and, in fact, many tasks in college), your first step is to prepare. Then you preview, predict questions, process information, and paraphrase and review.

1. **Prepare.** Prepare yourself mentally for reading by creating a positive, interested attitude. Look for ways to make the subject matter meaningful. Instead of telling yourself that the book is too hard or boring, say, "This book looks interesting because . . . ," or "The information in this book will be helpful because . . ." Clarify your purpose and how you will use the information. Think about what you already know about the subject. Prepare yourself physically by being rested, and read during high-energy times (refer to your Time Log in Personal Evaluation Notebook 3.1). Eliminate distractions by choosing a study area that encourages concentration. Experiment and make reading physical whenever possible. For example, take notes while reading, read while standing up, and read aloud.

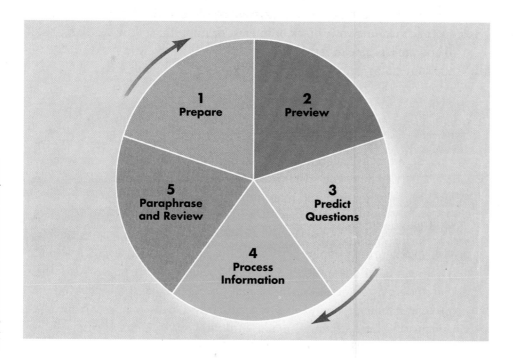

Figure 6.1
The Five-Part Reading System

This system can be useful for increasing your reading comprehension and recall. *In what ways is this system similar to your own reading system?*

Peak Progress

Applying the Adult Learning Cycle to Becoming a Better Reader

Becoming an active reader and learning to like reading take time, effort, and practice.

1. **RELATE. Why do I want to learn this?** Being an effective reader can help me get ahead in school, work, and life. Through reading, I continually learn and explore new ideas. I can also escape through fiction, relieving the stress of the day. What do I want to improve overall about my reading?

2. **OBSERVE. How does this work?** I can learn a lot about active reading by watching, listening, and trying new things. I'll observe people who are avid readers and who remember information. I will try new techniques and strategies for active reading and mark my improvement.

3. **REFLECT. What does this mean?** Which techniques work and which ones don't work for me? Can I find creative ways to make reading more enjoyable and effective?

4. **DO. What can I do with this?** I will make a commitment to be a more active reader. I'll find practical applications for practicing my new reading skills. Each day, I'll work on one area. For example, I'll choose one class in which I'm having trouble reading and experiment with new strategies.

5. **TEACH. Whom can I share this with?** I'll talk with others and share my tips and experiences. I'll demonstrate and describe the methods I've learned. I'll read more for pleasure and read to others when possible.

Remember, the more you go through the cycle, the more interest and meaning reading will have for you.

---

2. **Preview.** A quick survey of the chapter you are about to read will give you a general overview. Pay attention to the title, chapter headings, illustrations, and key terms. Look for main ideas connecting concepts, terms, and formulas. Gaining a general understanding of the assignment prepares you to read the material actively and understand the classroom lecture. When you have been exposed to a subject before, your brain is far more receptive to taking in more information, so jot down in the margins everything you can think of that you already know about the topic, even just a word or an image. Short preview sessions are effective, and you will be more motivated when you have set a goal and a time for completion.

3. **Predict questions.** Next, make questions out of chapter headings, section titles, and definitions. For example, if a section is titled "Groupthink," ask, "What is groupthink? What conditions are required for it to occur? What key word(s) define it? What are possible test questions?" Ask what, who, when, where, why, and how. You will make **inferences** (drawing conclusions based on previous information) and interpretations as you read. Which ones are based on your experiences or background? Which ones are logical and based on fact? The more questions you ask, the better prepared you will be to find answers. If there are sample questions at the end of the chapter, review them and tie them in with your other questions. Pretend you are talking with the author and jot down questions in the margin. Asking questions gets you more involved and focused, organizes information, and helps you prepare for tests. Create possible test questions on note cards and review them as you walk to

classes, eat, or wait in lines. Exchange questions with your study team or partner.

4. **Process information.** Outline, underline, and highlight key words, main ideas, definitions, facts, and important concepts. Look for supporting points, connections, and answers to the questions you have raised. Develop an outline, either a traditional outline or an informal one (such as a mind map), to help you organize the information. Integrate what you are reading into classroom lectures, notes, field trips, study group discussions, models, and graphs.

5. **Paraphrase and review.** Summarize in your own words and review. Recite your summary out loud right after class and again within 24 hours of previewing the chapter. Share it in your study group. Review several times until you understand the material and can explain it to someone else. This helps you integrate learning styles and remember the main points at the end of each major section. Review in your study group and take turns listening to each other's summary. Remember, the best way to learn is to teach. Carry your note cards, so that you can review questions and answers and can summarize often.

The SQ3R Reading System

The SQ3R Reading System is a five-step method that has helped many students improve their reading comprehension since it was developed by Professor Francis Robinson in 1941. It breaks reading down into manageable segments, so that you understand the material before proceeding to the next step.

1. **S = Survey.** Survey the material before reading it. Quickly peruse the contents, scan the main heads, look at illustrations and captions, and become familiar with the special features in each chapter. Surveying, or previewing, helps you see how the chapter is organized and supports the main concept. You get an overview of where the material is going.

2. **Q = Question.** Find the main points and begin to formulate questions. Developing questions helps you determine if you really understand the material. For example, here are some questions you can ask yourself as you read:
   - What is the main idea of this chapter?
   - What is the main idea of this section?
   - What are examples that support this main idea?
   - Who are the main people or what key events are discussed in this chapter?

● **Preview Your Reading**
You get the big picture by quickly scanning through a book, and you enhance your learning. *Besides identifying key concepts, what else should you look for when previewing?*

Take 3 minutes tonight to preview the next assigned chapter:

- What is the main topic? What are the subtopics?
- What do you already know about this topic? Have you studied it in a previous class?
- What do the supporting illustrations show? Are they clearly labeled?

What else can you do in 3 minutes?

- Preview the chapter's learning outcomes and formulate potential quiz questions.
- Check the syllabus for future reading assignments and schedule them in your planner.
- Time yourself reading the next chapter to see how many pages you read and if you can recall what the main points are.

- Why are they important?
- What are possible test questions?
- What points don't I understand?

3. **R = Read.** Actively read the material and search for answers to your questions. As you read, you will be asking more questions. Even when you read a novel, you will ask such questions as "What is the main theme of this novel? Who is this supporting character? Why did he turn up at this time in the novel? How does this character relate to the main characters? What are his motives?"

4. **R = Recite.** Recite the main ideas and key points in your words. After each section, stop and paraphrase what you have just read. Your summary should address the questions you developed for this section. Reciting promotes concentration, creates understanding, and helps raise more questions.

5. **R = Review.** Review the material carefully. Go back over your questions and make certain you have answered all of them. Review the chapter summary and then go back over each section. Jot down additional questions. Review and clarify questions with your study group or instructor.

The exercise in **Personal Evaluation Notebook 6.1** gives you an opportunity to try the SQ3R Reading System.

Reading Strategies

The Five-Part and SQ3R Reading Systems include strategies such as previewing the material and reciting or paraphrasing main concepts in your own words. You can also try the following overall reading strategies:

1. **Determine your purpose.** How will you use the information? Reading assignments vary in terms of difficulty and purpose. Some are technical and others require imagination. (See **Peak Progress 6.2** on page 183 for tips on reading in different disciplines.) Ask yourself, "Why am I reading this?" Whether you are reading for pleasure, previewing information, looking for background information, understanding ideas, finding facts, memorizing formulas and data, or analyzing a complex subject, you will want to know your purpose.

2. **Set reading goals.** You may be assigned many chapters to read each week, preferably before walking into a lecture. You do not want to wait until the day before exams to open your textbook. Pace your reading, not only to make sure you complete it but also to give yourself time to ask questions, be sure you understand the material, and review it—again and again if necessary. Just

(continued on page 183)

Personal Evaluation Notebook

Using the SQ3R Reading System

Follow the SQ3R Reading System on pages 179 and 180 as you read the following passages. Then complete the questions on the next page.

ORGANIZED INTERESTS: WHO ARE THEY?

Accomplishing broad yet shared goals is always easier when a number of people pitch in to help. Both joining with neighbors to clean up a community after a storm and banding together with friends to convince your college cafeteria to purchase "free trade" coffee are examples of cooperative action. Group activity is a hallmark of America's volunteer ethic. The same is true in politics. Organized groups are nearly always more effective in attaining common goals than individuals acting alone. The term **interest group** refers to those formally organized associations that seek to influence public policy. In America, it applies to a dizzying array of diverse organizations reflecting the broad spectrum of interests that make up our **pluralistic society.** They include corporations, labor unions, civil rights groups, professional and trade associations, and probably some of the groups with which you are associated as well.

Neighbors or Adversaries?

Theorists from Alexis de Tocqueville to Robert Putman have praised voluntary associations as training grounds for citizen involvement. De Tocqueville saw collective action as evidence of democracy at work. Putnam extols organized interests for creating social capital, the glue that binds the citizenry so they can achieve collective goals. Not all political theorists, however, share these views. In *The Federalist* No. 10, James Madison warned against factions—groups of individuals, "whether amounting to a majority or minority of the whole, who are united by some common impulse of passion, or of interest, adverse to the rights of other citizens, or to the permanent and aggregate interests of the community." Although opposed to factions, Madison felt that they could not be eliminated because they expressed the innately human drive for

self-interest. Instead, he argued, the government must dilute their influence by filtering their views through elected officials and submerging their interests in a sea of competing interests. Only by countering the ambition of such groups with the ambition of others, he believed, could government fashion the compromise necessary to accommodate interests common to all.

Distinctive Features

Like the political movements of the past that advanced causes such as abolition or civil rights, interest groups seek to use the power of government to protect their concerns. However, although political movements promote wide-ranging social change, interest groups are more narrowly focused on achieving success with regard to specific policies. Where the Women's Movement of the 1960s sought to change Americans' views about the role of women at home and in the workplace, interest groups like the National Organization for Women (NOW) focus on solving specific problems faced by women in a world that has already grown more accepting of the diverse roles women play.

Interest group causes may be purely economic, as in the case of a business seeking tax breaks or a union seeking negotiating clout; they may be ideological, as in the case of those favoring or opposing abortion rights. Some, known as **public interest groups,** advocate policies they believe promote the good of all Americans, not merely the economic or ideological interests of a few. Environmental groups such as the Sierra Club fall into this category. Some interest groups, such as trade associations and labor unions, have mass memberships; others represent institutions and have no individual membership at all. One example of the latter is the American Council on Education (ACE), a collective institution of higher education that promotes policies that benefit colleges and universities.

Source: Joseph Losco and Ralph Baker: *AM GOV 2009,* McGraw-Hill, 2009.

(continued)

Personal Evaluation Notebook

Using the SQ3R Reading System *(continued)*

S—Survey

1. What is the title of the selection?

   _____

2. What is the reading selection about?

   _____

3. What are the major topics?

   _____

4. List any boldface terms.

   _____

Q—Question

5. Write a question for the first heading.

   _____

6. Write a question for the second heading.

   _____

3 Rs

R—Read

Read the selection section by section.

R—Recite

Briefly summarize to yourself what you read. Then share your summary with a study team member.

R—Review

7. Can you recall the questions you had for each head?   Yes _____   No _____

8. Can you answer those questions?   Yes _____   No _____

Write your answers for each section head question on the following lines.

9. Head 1

   _____

10. Head 2

   _____

Peak Progress

Reading for Different Courses

Sometimes even successful students cringe at the thought of reading in disciplines they find difficult or uninteresting. If you find your textbook too difficult, you might ask your instructor for supplemental reading or check out other books or sources from the library to get a different view and approach. Also try the following tips for different reading assignments.

Literature: Make a list of key figures and characters. Think about their personalities and motives. See if you can predict what they will do next. Allow your imagination to expand through your senses; taste, smell, hear, and see each scene in your mind. What is the story's main point? What are supporting points? What is the author's intent?

History: Use an outline to organize material. You may want to create a time line and place dates and events as you read. Notice how events are related. Connect main people to key events. Relate past events to current events. Picture yourself living during the time period of the event and what your circumstances and beliefs might be.

Mathematics and science: When reading a math book, work out each problem on paper and take notes in the margin. Spend additional time reviewing graphs, tables, notations, formulas, and the visuals used to illustrate points and complex ideas. These are not just fillers; they are important tools you use to review and understand the concepts behind them. Ask questions when you review each visual, and write down formulas and concepts on note cards. Come up with concrete examples when you read about abstract and difficult concepts. (We will further explore critical

thinking and problem solving in math and science in Chapter 10.)

Psychology and sociology: Jot down major theories and summarize them in your own words. You will be asked how these theories relate to topics in other chapters. Use the margins to analyze research conclusions. Pay attention to how the research was conducted, such as sample size and the sponsors of the research. Look for biases and arguments. Was scientific evidence presented? Was the research study duplicated? Key terms and definitions are also important for building on additional information.

Anthropology: You may want to use a mind map to compare various cultures. For example, under the culture, you may look at religion, customs, food, and traditions. Ask yourself if the ideas apply to all people in all cultures or in all situations. Is the author's position based on observation, research, or assumptions? Is there a different way to look at these observations? What predictions follow these arguments?

Trade and technical: These courses tend to be very hands-on and the text materials will include background information, instructions, and key illustrations with multiple labels. As much as possible, read and re-read the material while working with the equipment to make sure you understand the process. Identify each component and its relevance. How does this information translate to working on the job? Working through the details with a study partner or reading aloud can help you see how all the pieces fit together.

---

as you map out the semester's exams, plan your reading assignments in your daily planner or calendar (see Chapter 3 for many handy forms). Be realistic as to how long it takes you to read a certain number of pages, especially for difficult courses. Check off reading assignments as you complete them, and rearrange priorities if need be. Schedule blocks of time to review reading assignments and prepare for exams.

3. **Concentrate.** Whether you are playing a sport, performing a dance, giving a speech, acting in a play, talking with a friend, or focusing on a difficult

book, being in the present is the key to concentration. Keep your reading goals in mind and concentrate on understanding main points as you prepare to read. Stay focused and alert by reading quickly and making it an active experience. If your mind wanders, become aware of your posture, thoughts, and surroundings and then gently bring your thoughts back to the task at hand.

4. **Create an outline.** Use a traditional or an informal outline to organize the main points. (See Chapter 5 for examples of outlines.) The outline can add meaning and structure to material, and it simplifies and organizes complex information. The physical process of writing and organizing material creates a foundation for committing it to memory. Use section titles and paragraph headlines to provide a guide. Continue to write questions in the margin. (See **Worksheet 6.5** on page 208 for a blank format to use for a formal outline.)

5. **Identify key words and concepts.** Underline and highlight key words, definitions, facts, and important concepts. Write them in the margins and on note cards. Draw illustrations (or embellish those in the book) to help clarify the text. Use graphics and symbols to indicate difficult material, connections, and questions you need go over again. (Refer to Figure 5.5 on page 160 for common symbols used in note taking and reading.) A highlighter may be useful for calling out main points and marking sections that are important to review later. (See **Peak Progress 6.3** on using a highlighter.)

6. **Make connections.** Link new information with what you already know. Look for main ideas, supporting points, and answers to the questions you have developed. Integrate what you are reading into lecture notes and study group discussions. Asking yourself these questions may help you make associations and jog your memory:

   - What conclusions can I make as I read the material?
   - How can I apply this new material to other material, concepts, and examples?
   - What information does and does not match?
   - What do I know about the topic that may influence how I approach the reading?

7. **Talk with the author.** Pretend you are talking with the author and jot down points with which you agree or disagree. This exercises your critical thinking skills and helps you connect new information to what you already know. If there are points you disagree with, consider bringing them up in class (if it's appropriate) and see if other students feel the same.

8. **Compare notes.** Compare your textbook notes with your lecture notes. Compare your notes with those of your study team members. Ask your instructor to clarify confusing or difficult material and how much weight the textbook has on exams. Some instructors highlight important information in class and want students to read the text for a broad overview.

9. **Take frequent breaks.** Schedule short stretching breaks about every 40 minutes. A person's brain retains information best in short study segments.

To Highlight or Not to Highlight?

This is the age-old question. Fellow students may tell you not to highlight your text, as it's easier to sell back a "clean" text. Others recommend buying a used book that's already highlighted—the work is done for you.

However, these debates miss the point of highlighting. Whether you use a colored highlighter or underline words with a pen or pencil, highlighting is a very personal study strategy that can improve your ability to determine the important points within a reading. The simple act of highlighting makes you reread the information, helping you improve your comprehension, which benefits not just visual and tactile learners but also those with other learning styles as well. Highlighting helps you find key concepts more easily when reviewing and studying for exams. Research has also shown that students with learning disabilities or ADHD demonstrate a marked increase in their learning ability when they use a highlighter while reading.

Highlight?

Yes	No
• Your textbook. It's yours—use it!	• A library book; instead, make notes on stickies on the pages as well as record main points and page numbers in your notes
• Key points, names, important dates, new terms	
• Use different colors for main ideas vs. definitions vs. examples—but don't make the process too tedious or too confusing to follow	• Highlighting too fast before you truly know the main point(s)
• Use circles, arrows, and notes in the margins to make connections, add questions, etc.	• Entire sections or paragraphs
	• More than 10% of a page
• Read the chapter summary, which should point out the key points in case you missed them	• Relying on someone else's highlighting, especially in a used book

Don't struggle with unclear material now. You may need several readings to comprehend and interpret the material. Go back to the difficult areas later when you are refreshed and the creative process is not blocked.

10. **Integrate learning styles.** Read in alignment with your learning style, and integrate styles. For example, if you are a visual learner, take special note of pictures, charts, and diagrams. Develop mental pictures in your mind and actively use your imagination. Compare what you are reading with course lectures, overhead material, and notes on the board. If you are primarily an auditory learner, read out loud or into a digital recorder and then listen to it.

If you are a kinesthetic learner, read with a highlighter in hand to mark important passages and key words. Work out problems on paper and draw illustrations. Write your vocabulary, formulas, and key words on note cards. Read while standing up or recite out loud. The physical act of mouthing words and hearing your voice enhances learning. Integrate different learning styles by using all your senses. Visualize what something looks like, hear yourself repeating words, draw, and read out loud. Review your notes and summaries with your study team. This helps you integrate learning styles and increases your comprehension, critical thinking, and recall.

11. **Use the entire text.** As discussed in Chapter 4, a peak performer seeks out and uses available resources. Many textbooks include a number of resources that sometimes get overlooked, such as a glossary, chapter objectives, and study questions. Make sure you read (or at least initially scan) all the elements in your textbook, as they are included to help you preview, understand, review, and apply the material. (See **Peak Progress 6.4**.) After all, you've paid for the text, so use it! (Also see **Peak Progress 6.5** for tips on reading digital material.)

For practice on taking notes, take a look at **Figure 6.2** on page 188 and compare it with your notes for this page.

Reviewing Strategies

Reading isn't over with the turn of the last page. Take the time to review what you have read to make sure you understand and retain the information.

1. **Summarize in writing.** After you finish reading, close your book and write a summary in your own words. In just 4 or 5 minutes, write down everything you can recall about the chapter and the main topics. Writing is an active process that increases comprehension and recall. Write quickly and test yourself by asking questions such as these:

   - What is the major theme?
   - What are the main points?
   - What are the connections to other concepts?

2. **Summarize out loud.** Summarizing out loud can increase learning, especially if you are an auditory or a kinesthetic learner. Some students use an empty classroom and pretend they are lecturing. If need be, recite quietly to yourself, taking care not to disturb anyone, especially in the library or other populated areas. Review several times until you understand the material and can explain it to someone else. Review in your study teams and take turns listening to each other's summary. Remember that the best way to learn is to teach. As you recite and listen to each other, you can ask questions and clarify terms and concepts.

3. **Review and reflect.** You have previewed, developed questions, outlined main points, read actively, highlighted and underlined, written key words, and summarized in writing and aloud. Now it is important to review for understanding main ideas and to commit the information to long-term

Peak Progress

Using Your Textbook

Textbooks are developed with many features to help you preview, understand, review, and apply the material. As soon as you purchase your text, take a few minutes to flip through it to see how it is put together. Although textbooks vary, many include the following elements:

Preface. At the beginning of the text, you may find a preface, and some books include two prefaces: one for the instructor who is interested in using the text in the course and the other specifically for the student. Read through the student preface, as it will provide information to help you get off on the right foot. For example, at the beginning of this text, you will find a "Getting Started" section that explores many issues you may be facing the first few weeks of school (or even before the first day of school).

It's also a good idea to review the material designed for the instructor, which may give you insights into the overall approach of the text, as well as new developments or research in the field. It may also describe difficult concepts and challenges that your instructor faces when teaching the course, which can be helpful for you to know and prepare for.

Preview features. Many texts include features that let you know what you will learn in the chapter, such as learning outcomes, chapter outlines, and introductory statements or quotes. *What types of preview features can you find in this text?*

Applications. More effective texts not only provide the essential information but also give you opportunities to apply it. These applications can take the form of case studies, exercises, assessments, journal activities, websites, and critical thinking and discussion questions. *What are some features in this text that help you apply what you are learning?*

Review material. You may find features that reinforce and help you understand and review the material, such as section or chapter summaries; glossaries; important key points or words; bulleted lists of information; comprehensive tables; and review questions. *What features in this text are useful for reviewing the material?*

Resources beyond the text. Many texts have accompanying websites, workbooks, and DVDs that reinforce and apply what you are learning in the text and course. Often, connections to these resources appear in the text, reminding you to use the resource for specific information. *What resources are available with this text?*

Peak Progress

Digital Reading Material

As a student today, you have many digital options available that weren't offered even just a few years ago. Books, journals, newspapers, and textbooks are often delivered in a digital format. Communication media, such as Facebook, Twitter, and Wikipedia, have changed how we learn and interact.

Digital readers have become a popular alternative to print books. Amazon's Kindle, which sold out in 5½ hours upon its release in 2007, allows you to store and read digital media for use anywhere and features "electronic paper." Apple's iPad offers numerous applications, including the Internet, iTunes, and iBooks, in a portable format. Many textbooks are offered for use with these digital readers, as are subscriptions to newspapers and magazines.

As online reading becomes more popular, you may need to tweak your reading strategies. Following are a few things to consider:

- **Pace your reading.** Research indicates the average person reads from a computer screen about 10 percent slower than a printed text. If that's true for you, plan your reading schedule accordingly.
- **Adjust the page.** If you can, change the type size and font to one that is easier to read.
- **Use the built-in functions.** Learn how to use the highlighter and other note-taking features.
- **Print.** Make back-up copies of your digital notes and print key sections, in case you run into technical issues later. Annotate the hard copies to reinforce your understanding of the material.
- **Avoid ads.** Many articles are surrounded by advertisements and pop-up ads that can distract you. Turn on a pop-up blocker.
- **Protect against theft.** A tablet is a hot commodity and should be stored in a secure place.

Figure 6.2

Sample Notes

This illustration shows study notes you might take when reading page 186. Compare it with the notes you took on that page. *What are the similarities? What did you do differently? Do you have unique note-taking strategies that work for you?*

Integrate VAK

note cards. Read while standing up or recite out loud. The physical act of mouthing words and hearing your voice enhances learning. Integrate different learning styles by using all your senses. Visualize what something looks like, hear yourself repeating words, draw, and read out loud. Review your notes and summaries with your study team. This helps you integrate learning styles and increases your comprehension, critical thinking, and recall.

Use textbook features

What's in this book?

11. **Use the entire text.** As discussed in Chapter 4, a peak performer seeks out and uses available resources. Many textbooks include a number of resources that sometimes get overlooked, such as a glossary, chapter objectives, and study questions. Make sure you read (or at least initially scan) all the elements in your textbook, as they are included to help you preview, understand, review, and apply the material. (See **Peak Progress 6.4.**) After all, you've paid for the text, so use it! (Also see **Peak Progress 6.5** for tips on reading digital material.)

For practice on taking notes, take a look at **Figure 6.2** on page 188 and compare it with your notes for this page.

Reviewing Strategies

Reading isn't over with the turn of the last page. Take the time to review what you have read to make sure you understand and retain the information.

1. **Summarize in writing.** After you finish reading, close your book and write a summary in your own words. In just 4 or 5 minutes, write down everything you can recall about the chapter and the main topics. Writing is an active process that increases comprehension and recall. Write quickly and test yourself by asking questions such as these:

questions to ask
- What is the major theme?
- What are the main points?
- What are the connections to other concepts?

Good for AK

2. **Summarize out loud.** Summarizing out loud can increase learning, especially if you are an auditory or a kinesthetic learner. Some students use an empty classroom and pretend they are lecturing. If need be, recite quietly to yourself, taking care not to disturb anyone, especially in the library or other populated areas. Review several times until you understand the material and can explain it to someone else. Review in your study teams and take turns listening to each other's summary. Remember that the best way to learn is to teach. As you recite and listen to each other, you can ask questions and clarify terms and concepts.

3. **Review and reflect.** You have previewed, developed questions, outlined main points, read actively, highlighted and underlined, written key words, and summarized in writing and aloud. Now it is important to review for understanding main ideas and to commit the information to long-term

memory. You can increase your comprehension by reviewing the material within 24 hours of your first reading session. Reflect by bringing your own experience and knowledge to what you have learned with readings lectures, field trips, and work with your study team. You should review your outline, note cards, key words, and main points. Review headings, main topics, key ideas, first and last sentences in paragraphs, and summaries. Make sure you have answered the questions you created as you read the material. Carry your note cards with you and review them when you have a few minutes before class.

4. **Read and review often.** Reviewing often and in short sessions kicks the material into long-term memory. Review weekly and conduct a thorough review a week or so before a test. Keep a list of questions to ask your instructor and a list of possible test questions. The key is to stay on top of reading so it doesn't pile up, which should allow you enough time to review effectively.

Evan always waits until the last minute to tackle his reading assignments. At the eleventh hour—literally—he finally plops into an easy chair near midnight and begins to read. Not a morning person, Evan is sure he can focus and whip through it, until 30 minutes later, when his eyes are half closed and he realizes he doesn't remember a word.

- If Evan truly does his best work at night, what strategies should he use while reading to make sure he's alert, focused, learning, and retaining the material?
- Do you think Evan's last-minute strategy is an effective method of reading for class? What important steps from the Five-Part Reading System might he end up skipping for time's sake?
- Does Evan really understand the purpose of reading assignments? If not, can you explain it to him?

THINK *FAST*

Build Your Vocabulary

You will need a fundamental vocabulary to master any subject. To succeed in a career, you must know and understand the meaning of words you encounter in conversations, reports, meetings, and professional reading. People often judge the intelligence of another person by the ability to communicate through words, and an effective speaker who has a command of language can influence others. Try the following methods for building your vocabulary:

1. **Observe your words and habits.** You may be unaware that you fill your conversations with annoying words, such as *you know, OK, like,* and *yeah,* as well as inappropriate expletives.

2. **Be creative and articulate.** Use precise, interesting, and expressive words.

3. **Associate with articulate people.** Surround yourself with people who have effective and extensive vocabularies.

4. **Look up words you don't know.** Peak Progress 6.6 on page 190 shows you how to navigate around a dictionary.

5. **Write down new words.** Listen for new words and observe how they are used and how often you hear them and see them in print. Record them in your journal or on note cards.

6. **Practice mentally.** Say new words again and again in your mind as you read, and think of appropriate settings where you could use the words.

7. **Practice in conversation.** Use new words until you are comfortable using them.

> "If you wish to know the mind of a man, listen to his words."
> **CHINESE PROVERB**

> "I was reading the dictionary. I thought it was a poem about everything."
> **STEVEN WRIGHT**
> *Comedian*

Peak Progress

Look It Up! Using a Dictionary

Depending on the source you are using, many dictionary resources will provide at least some of the following:

Guide words: In a printed dictionary, boldface words at the top of the page indicate the first and last entries on the page. Online dictionaries will often provide the previous and subsequent words.

Pronunciation: This key shows how to pronounce the word. Online dictionaries will often provide an audio pronunciation.

Part of speech: If not spelled out, following are abbreviations for the parts of speech:

- **n.**—noun
- **adj.**—adjective
- **v.i.**—intransitive verb
- adv.—adverb
- conj.—conjunction
- prep.—preposition
- v.t.—transitive verb
- pron.—pronoun
- interj.—interjection

Etymology: This is the origin of the word, which is especially helpful if the word has a Latin or Greek root from which many other words are derived. Knowing the word's history can help you remember the word or look for similar words.

Syllabication: This shows how the word is divided into syllables.

Capital letters: This indicates if a word should be capitalized.

Definition: Definitions are listed chronologically (oldest meaning first).

Restrictive labels: Three types of labels are used most often in a dictionary. Subject labels tell you that a word has a special meaning when used in certain fields (mus. for music, med. for medicine, etc.). Usage labels indicate how a word is used (slang, dial. for dialect, etc.). Geographic labels tell you the region of the country where the word is used most often.

Homographs: A single spelling of a word has different meanings.

Variants: These are multiple correct spellings of a single word (example: *ax* or *axe*).

Illustrations: Drawings or pictures are used to help illustrate a word.

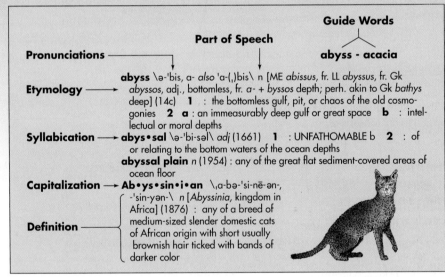

Source: By permission. From *Merriam-Webster's Collegiate® Dictionary*, 11th Edition © 2013 by Merriam-Webster, Inc. (www.Merriam-Webster.com).

8. **Look for contextual clues.** Try to figure out a word by the context in which it is used.

9. **Learn common word parts.** Knowing root words, prefixes, and suffixes makes it easier to understand the meaning of many new words. Also, in fields such as biology, knowing prefixes and suffixes helps you learn many new terms, such as *cardi* means "heart" (as in *cardiovascular*) and *calor* means "heat" (as in *calorie*, which is the energy content of food in the form of heat). Other examples follow:

Root	Meaning	Example
auto	self	autograph, autobiography
sub	under	submarine, submerge
circum	around	circumference, circumspect
manu	hand	manuscript, manual, manufacture

Also, learn to recognize syllables. Dividing words into syllables speeds up learning and improves pronunciation, spelling, and memory recall.

10. **Review great speeches.** Look at how Thomas Jefferson, Abraham Lincoln, John F. Kennedy, and Margaret Thatcher chose precise words. Read letters written during the Revolutionary and Civil wars. You may find that the common person at that time was more articulate and expressive than many people today.

11. **Invest in a vocabulary book.** Many are available, so you may want to ask your instructor for guidance. Also, if you have decided on your future career, see if any books are written for that field.

12. **Read.** The best way to improve your vocabulary is simply to read more.

Manage Language Courses

Building vocabulary is important if you are learning a new language. Following are a number of reading and study tips.

1. **Do practice exercises.** As with math and science, doing practice exercises is critical in learning any language.

2. **Keep up with your reading.** You must build on previous lessons and skills. Therefore, it is important to keep up with your reading; preview chapters, so that you have a basic understanding of any new words; then complete your practice sessions several times.

3. **Carry note cards with you.** Drill yourself on the parts of speech and verb conjugation through all the tenses, which is a significant part of learning a new language. Keep related terms grouped together on cards (such as "In the Kitchen" or "In the Home").

4. **Recite out loud.** This is especially important in a language course, as knowing a word's pronunciation is as important as understanding its meaning. Record yourself and play it back.

5. **Form study teams.** Meet with a study team and speak only the language you are studying. Recite out loud to each other, explain verb conjugation, and use words in various contexts.

6. **Listen to recordings.** Plug into CDs and downloads while commuting, exercising, and so on.

7. **Model and tutor.** Meet with a student whose primary language is the one you are studying. Speak only his or her native language. You can meet international students in classes for English as a second language, usually taught in local schools and communities.

8. **Have fun.** Do research on the country of the language you're studying. Invite your study group for an authentic meal, complete with music and costumes.

The same principles and strategies you use for reading English can be applied to reading and learning a different language. Your efforts will be worthwhile, especially when you are able to speak, read, and understand another language as you communicate in the real world. Remember, as you become a better reader, you will enjoy the new language more and more. (**Figure 6.3** offers additional tips for English speakers of other languages.)

Specialized Reading

Comprehending Technical Material

Some of your courses may include technical information. Science, math, computer science, accounting, and statistics courses tend to present their data in specialized formats. You may need to interpret graphs, charts, diagrams, tables, and spreadsheets. You may read technical material, such as the directions for a chemistry experiment, a flowchart in a computer program, the steps for administering medication, or the

Figure 6.3
Tips for ESL Students

Students whose first language is not English can try additional strategies for reading success. Also, there is a wealth of resources on the Internet for ESL readers. Search "ESL reading activities" or a similar phrase. *What challenges do you face if your home language is different from a community's prominent language?*

Get the "gist" of it: Don't worry about every word. Focus on main ideas, concepts, and key words.

Vary your reading materials: Language "styles" vary based on the purpose, such as a textbook vs. a magazine vs. a blog. The more variety you are exposed to, the more fluent you will become.

Discuss in your first language: Talk about the topic with family and friends, who will offer additional perspectives and questions to explore.

Make a list: Jot down unfamilliar words that seem important and look them up.

statistical analysis of a financial statement. Such material can be complicated. Many readers get discouraged and skip over it—which is a big mistake.

Instead, try these reading strategies when you encounter graphics in your studies or on the job:

1. Identify the type of graphic you are looking at. Is it a table, chart, graph, or other type of illustration? (See **Figure 6.4**.)

2. Read each element:
   • Graphic title
   • Accompanying captions
   • Column titles
   • Labels or symbols and their keys (usually provided at the bottom of the graph)
   • Data (percentages, totals, figures, etc.)

3. Identify the purpose of the graphic. Is it demonstrating similarities or differences, increases or decreases, comparisons or changes?

4. See a connection between the topic of the graphic and the chapter or section topic in which it appears.

5. Explain in your own words the information depicted on the graphic.

6. Share your interpretation of the graphic with your study group members. Do they feel your interpretation is clear and on target?

Reading Manuals

Technical writing professionals spend hundreds of hours writing instructions for everything from using your new toaster to troubleshooting why engine lights are

Figure 6.4
Illustration Examples

The table (left) and graph (right) include the same information but present it differently. *What key elements would you look for to understand the material? Which presentation is easier to understand—the table or the graph? Which one might be easier to remember? What conclusions might you draw from this information regarding future statistics?*

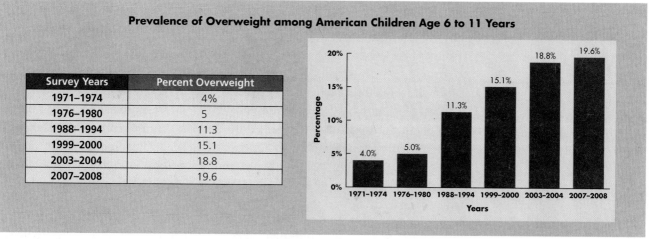

Survey Years	Percent Overweight
1971–1974	4%
1976–1980	5
1988–1994	11.3
1999–2000	15.1
2003–2004	18.8
2007–2008	19.6

Source: 2007–2008 National Health and Nutrition Examination Survey (NHANES).

coming on (i.e., your car's owner's manual). However, many people resist opening up the manual. For some, it's like stopping and asking for directions: "I can figure it out on my own!" For others, deciphering a manual is like reading a foreign language. They have no idea where to begin.

Although some manuals are better than others in providing thorough, step-by-step instructions, you should invest the time to at least scan through the manual as you get started. First review the table of contents to see how the instructions are set up (such as a description or an illustration of product components, assembling or starting the product, caution or warning signs, and maintenance issues). After that, follow these time-saving tips:

1. Compare the description with what you received and make sure all the pieces are there.

2. Follow step-by-step installation or assembly instructions. Often it is helpful to read the instructions aloud to yourself or someone else as you go along. Assembling a product incorrectly can cause it to fail, break, or become dangerous.

3. Go to the index and look up key words related to problems you encounter or specific tasks you want to do. For example, if you need to change the time on your car clock, the index will show the page where the manual explains the procedure.

4. If the manual that came with the product is too brief or doesn't address a problem you are having, look online by checking the company's website or searching the product's name. You may find more detailed instructions, as well as tips from other users.

5. The manual (or website) may include a frequently asked questions (FAQs) section, which includes issues you may encounter using the product. Read this even if the product appears to be working correctly, as it may warn you of potential problems or maintenance issues.

6. If the product came with access codes or other important information, record that in the manual and keep it in a place that you'll remember later.

The key to reading manuals is to be patient and not get frustrated. Approach the task as if you were solving a puzzle—eventually, you will put the pieces together.

Completing Forms

Whether you are entering school, applying for a job, filling out medical papers, or requesting a bank loan, you will probably have to complete some type of form. Although forms differ widely, many elements of information are requested on all of them. You may need to provide your name, address, Social Security number, proof of citizenship, phone numbers, e-mail address, and references. (Call ahead to find out what information and documents are needed.) Reading the form carefully and accurately can save time and prevent complications. For example, if the directions say to print your name in black or blue ink, do not use a pencil or write your name in cursive handwriting. And fill in all required boxes. Failure to "follow the rules" could result in you missing a deadline or losing out on a job offer or other opportunity.

AVOID CARELESSNESS

1 Scan the entire form before you begin to fill it out.

2 When filling out the form, read the small print directions carefully. Often, these directions appear in parentheses below a fill-in blank.

3 Fill in all the questions that pertain to you. Pay attention when you read the directions that tell you which sections of the form or application you should fill out and which sections are to be completed by someone else.

4 Write clearly—particularly numbers.

5 Reread your responses before submitting your form or application. If you are filling out a form online, check and recheck more than once before clicking "send" because you probably can't retrieve your form.

Overcome Obstacles

Reading Difficulties

Some students have specific reading challenges to overcome. Most reading difficulties are related to decoding, comprehension, and retention, with many experts believing the root of most reading problems is decoding. **Decoding** is the process of breaking words into individual sounds. Those with decoding problems may have trouble sounding out words and recognizing words out of context, can confuse letters and the sounds they represent, and ignore punctuation while reading. Dyslexics have difficulty decoding. Experts estimate dyslexia affects as many as 15 percent of all Americans, including celebrities Jay Leno, Tom Cruise, Patrick Dempsey, and Whoopi Goldberg. Albert Einstein, Thomas Edison, George Washington, Winston Churchill, and Sir Isaac Newton were also challenged with reading difficulties.

How do you know if your reading abilities need improvement? Although reading speeds vary, the average adult reads 250 to 300 words per minute. The key, however, is to balance your pace with comprehension. Flying through pages at lightning speed will do you no good if you can't articulate the main points of what you've just read. The following concerns also could signal reading difficulties:

- Making poor grades despite significant effort
- Needing constant, step-by-step guidance for tasks
- Having difficulty mastering tasks or transferring academic skills to other tasks

The good news is that you can improve your reading abilities. As discussed in Chapter 4, many resources are available, such as your school's learning center, if you are struggling with reading. Professionals there will help you understand your difficulty and provide specific tips to help you improve. Also, your instructor or physician (or even the local elementary school) can provide advice on additional resources in your community.

● **Finding Time to Read**
Investing time in reading pays off. Your reading skills improve when you read more. *How can you make time to read for pleasure?*

❝My alma mater was books, a good library . . . I could spend the rest of my life reading, just satisfying my curiosity.**❞**

MALCOLM X
Civil rights leader

Create a Positive Attitude

One of the greatest barriers to effective reading is attitude. Many people are not willing to invest the time it takes to become a better reader. If the material is difficult, seems boring, or requires concentration, they may not complete the reading assignment. So much instant entertainment is available that it is easy to watch a movie or television program or listen to the news instead of reading a newspaper or news magazine. Reading takes time, effort, concentration, and practice.

To create a positive attitude about reading, first pinpoint and dispel illogical thoughts, such as "I have way too much reading; I can never finish it all"; "I'm just not good at math"; or "I never will understand this material!" Many students have trouble reading certain subjects and may lack confidence. It takes time and patience to learn to ski, drive a car, become proficient with computers, or become a more effective reader. Use affirmations to develop confidence: "With patience and practice, I will understand this material." Use the ABC Method of Self-Management to dispel negative thinking and create a "can do" attitude.

Some students and career professionals say they have too much required reading and too little time for pleasure reading. Returning students have difficulty juggling reading, lectures, homework, job, and kids. They can't even imagine having time to read for pleasure. However, it is important to read for pleasure, even if you have only a few minutes a day. (See **Peak Progress 6.7** for ways to fit in reading with children around.) Carry a book with you or keep one in your car. Although you shouldn't study in bed, many people like to read for pleasure each night before turning in.

The more you read, the more your reading skills will improve. As you become a better reader, you will find you enjoy reading more and more. You will also find that, as your attitude improves, so does your ability to keep up on assignments, build your vocabulary, understand and retain what you have read, and learn more about areas that interest you.

Reading with Children Around

Concentrating on your reading can be challenging with children at your feet. However, it's essential to fit reading into your daily routine (as well as theirs). Try these ideas:

1. **Read in short segments.** Provide activities for your children and set a timer. Tell them that, when it goes off, you'll take a break from reading and do something enjoyable with them. Then set the timer again. In 10 or 15 minutes, you can preview a chapter, outline main ideas, recite out loud, or review. Don't fall into the trap of thinking you need 2 uninterrupted hours to tackle a chapter, or you may never get started.

2. **Read while they sleep.** Get up early and read, or try reading at night when your kids are sleeping. Even if you're tired, read actively or outline a chapter before you turn in. Resist doing the dishes or cleaning and save those activities for when reading and concentrating would be very difficult. Read a little each night and notice how it pays off.

3. **Take reading with you.** If your children are in after-school activities, such as sports or music, take your reading with you and make the most of your waiting time. This is also a nice time to visit with other parents, but you may need to devote that time to keeping up with your reading.

4. **Read to your children.** Get your kids hooked on reading by reading to them and having them watch you read out loud. Have family reading time, when everyone reads a book. After you read your children a story, ask them to read by themselves or to each other or look at pictures while you read your assignments. Remember to approach reading with a positive attitude, so that they will connect reading with pleasure.

TAKING CHARGE

Summary

In this chapter I learned to

- **Apply the Five-Part Reading System.** Like the Adult Learning Cycle, this system is useful for increasing my comprehension and recall. The steps are (1) prepare, (2) preview, (3) predict questions, (4) process information, and (5) paraphase and review. Scanning chapters gives me a quick overview of main concepts and ideas. I look for information I already know and link it to new information. I look for key words, main ideas, definitions, facts, and important concepts. I make questions out of chapter headings and definitions. I review the chapter to find answers and write them in the margin or on note cards and compare my answers with those of my study team.

- **Apply the SQ3R Reading System.** A five-step process, this method can improve my reading comprehension: S = Survey; Q = Question; R = Read; R = Recite; R = Review.

- **Be an active reader.** I clarify how I will use the information and set goals. I concentrate on main points and general understanding. I read difficult material out loud or standing up. I write in the margins, draw illustrations, underline, sketch, take notes, and dig out key points and key words. I pretend I'm talking with the author and jot down questions.

- **Outline main points and make connections.** Organizing information in an outline creates order, meaning, and understanding and helps me recall the material. It simplifies difficult information and makes connections clear. I link new information with what I already know and look for connections to what I don't know. I look for similarities and differences. I look for examples and read end-of-chapter summaries.

- **Summarize.** Summarizing in writing and out loud are powerful reading and memory strategies. I close the book at various times to write summaries and then check my brief summaries with the book. I summarize in writing after I finish a quick read of the chapter and then fill in with details.

- **Review.** I increase my comprehension by reviewing my outline, note cards, key words, main points, and summaries within 24 hours of reading and after lectures.

- **Build a strong vocabulary.** A good vocabulary is critical to success in school and my career. I can improve my vocabulary by learning and incorporating new words into my writing and conversations, using resources such as a dictionary or vocabulary book, and observing my speech habits.

- **Manage language courses.** Many of the same vocabulary-building strategies work for second-language courses. I can focus on key words, recite out loud, carry note cards, listen to recordings, keep up with the reading assignments, and use practice exercises.

- **Tackle specialized reading.** Thoroughness and precision are critical for reading technical information, graphs, manuals, and forms. Tips for technical information include identifying the purpose of the material, looking for connections, and explaining in my own words. Tips for manuals include reviewing the table of contents, looking up key words in the index, following step-by-step instructions, and reading aloud if necessary. Tips for forms include scanning before I begin, reading the small print, knowing what pertains to me, and asking questions when I'm unsure.

- **Address reading challenges.** I know to seek help with reading difficulties and create a positive attitude about improving my reading abilities, including reading for pleasure.

Performance Strategies

Following are the top 10 strategies for active reading:

- Find interest in the material.
- Outline the main points and identify key words.
- Gather information and predict questions.
- Take breaks and make reading physical.
- Reduce distractions and stay alert.
- Make connections and link information.
- Create a relationship with the author.
- Summarize in writing in your own words.
- Review consistently and as soon as possible.
- Teach by summarizing out loud and explaining the material to others.

Tech for Success

Take advantage of the text's website at **www.mhhe.com/ferrett9e** for additional study aids, useful forms, and convenient and applicable resources.

- **Books online.** Many of your textbooks can be purchased online and downloaded to your computer or electronic device. Most of these books are formatted to be read online, rather than printed. Do you prefer this format over reading from a printed text? List some of the advantages and disadvantages of both options.

- **All the news that's fit to click.** What's your source for the latest news? Most major newspapers are available online and archive previous articles. Take a poll of your classmates to see who still opts for newsprint, who prefers the local and cable networks, and who relies on the Web. Discuss the pros and cons. Do your classmates' preferences match their learning styles? Which sources do the more avid readers prefer?

Study Team Notes

Career *in* focus

Brian Singer
INFORMATION TECHNOLOGY SPECIALIST

Related Majors: Computer Science, Mathematics, Information Systems

Keeping Up-to-Date

Brian Singer is an information technology specialist, or computer programmer, for a major hospital group. His job is to write computer instructions that update financial records.

When writing a program, Brian must first break the task into various instructional steps that a computer can follow. Then he must code each step into a programming language. When finished, Brian tests the program to confirm it works accurately. Usually, he needs to make some adjustments, called debugging, before the program runs smoothly. The program must be maintained over time and updated as the need arises. Because critical problems can be intricate and time-consuming and must be fixed quickly, Brian usually works long hours, including evenings and weekends. Although his office surroundings are comfortable, Brian must be careful to avoid physical problems, such as eyestrain or back discomfort.

To stay current in his field, Brian reads about 300 pages of technical materials each week. Brian also took a class on reading technical information to improve his reading skills. Because he concentrates best when he is around people, Brian likes to read and study in a coffeehouse. When he has difficulty understanding what he reads, he gets on the Internet and asks for help from an online discussion group. To help him remember and better understand what he has read during the week, Brian tries to implement the new information in his work.

CRITICAL THINKING What strategies might help an information technology specialist when reading technical information?

Peak Performer PROFILE

Sonia Sotomayor

A culmination of a successful career in law and an early love of books led Sonia Sotomayor, born and raised in the Bronx by Puerto Rican parents, to a U.S. Supreme Court nomination in 2009. In this historic appointment, Sotomayor was the first Hispanic person and third woman to become a Justice on the Supreme Court. Sotomayor believes that the law and its inherent fairness enabled her to rise from the Bronx housing project where she grew up to become a member of the Supreme Court today. She is credited as being a "role model of aspiration, discipline, commitment, intellectual prowess, and integrity."

It was a love of books that initially led Sotomayor into pursuing law. She became an avid reader when, at the age of 9, she turned to books for solace after her father died. Nancy Drew mysteries especially captivated her and inspired her to want to become a detective. She soon discovered the *Perry Mason* television show. Because the lawyers were often involved in investigative work like Nancy Drew, she decided at the age of 10 that she would become a lawyer.

Sotomayor graduated valedictorian of her high school and attended Princeton University, where she felt like "a visitor landing in alien country," given the lack of female and Hispanic students at the time. With hard work and perseverance, Sotomayor excelled in her

classes and attended Yale Law School on a scholarship, where she graduated with a J.D. in 1979.

As an assistant district attorney in New York and later as the first Latina woman on the U.S. Court of Appeals of the Second Circuit, Sotomayor was known for her preparedness, fairness, and adherence to the law. In the courthouse, she works to empower young people with her Development School for Youth program, which sponsors workshops that teach inner-city students how to function successfully in a work setting. By following her own dreams from a very early age, Sotomayor hopes to encourage the next generation of lawyers, doctors, and, perhaps, detectives.

PERFORMANCE THINKING Books and other media not only offer opportunities for escape and personal reflection but also allow us to see a different view of a particular occupation we may not have seen before. When have you learned more about a career while reading a book or an article?

CHECK IT OUT Websites such as Flashlight Worthy Book Club Recommendations (**www.flashlightworthybooks.com/**), LitLovers Online Book Community (**www.litlovers.com**), and Book Movement Book Club Resources (**www.bookmovement .com/**) recommend books clubs and publish book reviews. Some connect members through forums, reading guides, or online courses. Find inspiration for what you'll read next. Through reading, you, too, may discover something new about yourself, as Sotomayor did with the Nancy Drew series.

Starting Today

At least one strategy I learned in this chapter that I plan to try right away is

_____

_____

_____

What changes must I make in order for this strategy to be most effective?

_____

_____

_____

Review Questions

Based on what you have learned in this chapter, write your answers to the following questions:

1. Name and describe each part of the Five-Part Reading System.

_____

_____

2. How does outlining the main points help you improve your reading?

_____

_____

3. Name three strategies for managing language courses.

_____

_____

4. Explain how building your vocabulary can be important to your career success.

_____

_____

5. What are important elements to look for when reading graphics?

_____

_____

To test your understanding of the chapter's concepts, complete the chapter quiz at **www.mhhe.com/ferrett9e.**

Effective Reading Habits

In the Classroom

Chris McDaniel struggles to keep up with her reading. She is overwhelmed by the amount of reading and the difficulty of her textbooks. She has never been much of a reader, spending most of her free time watching television. She sometimes reads in bed but often falls asleep. She realizes this is not the most productive way to study, but it has become a habit. Chris has noticed that, after reading for an hour or so, she can recall almost nothing. This has frustrated her, and she doubts her ability to succeed in college.

1. What habits should Chris change to improve her reading skills?

   _____

   _____

   _____

2. Suggest one or two specific strategies Chris could implement to become a better reader.

   _____

   _____

In the Workplace

Chris is now a stockbroker. She never thought she would work in this business, but a part-time summer job led her to a career in finance, and she really likes the challenge. She is surprised, however, at the vast amount of reading involved in her job: reports, magazines, and articles. She also reads several books and blogs on money management each month.

3. What strategies in this chapter would help Chris manage and organize her reading materials?

   _____

   _____

4. What are some specific reading strategies that apply to both school and work?

   _____

   _____

REVIEW AND APPLICATIONS | CHAPTER 6

Applying the ABC Method of Self-Management

In the Journal Entry on page 175, you were asked to describe a time when you enjoyed being read to. Why was the experience pleasurable? What types of books did you enjoy most? Did you have a favorite book or story?

_____

_____

_____

_____

Now think about your current experiences with reading. Do you enjoy reading? If so, what are the benefits to you? Visualize either a recent positive or a recent negative reading situation. Apply the ABC steps to visualize how the situation can enhance your reading skills.

A = Actual event:

_____

_____

B = Beliefs:

_____

_____

C = Challenge:

_____

_____

When you are in a positive state of mind, do you see yourself reading quickly and comprehending and recalling information effortlessly? Enjoy becoming an active reader.

PRACTICE SELF-MANAGEMENT

For more examples of learning how to manage difficult situations, see the "Self-Management Workbook" section of the Online Learning Center website at **www.mhhe.com/ferrett9e.**

CHAPTER 6

REVIEW AND APPLICATIONS

Attitudes and Reading

Read the following questions and write your answers on the lines provided.

1. What is your attitude toward reading?

   _____

   _____

2. What kind of books do you most like to read?

   _____

   _____

3. Do you read for pleasure?

   _____

   _____

4. Do you read the daily newspaper? (print or online)   Yes _____   No _____

   If yes, what section(s) do you read? _____

   _____

5. Do you read magazines?   Yes _____   No _____

   If yes, which magazines?

   _____

6. How would it benefit you to read faster?

   _____

   _____

7. What techniques can you learn to read faster and remember more?

   _____

   _____

   _____

Different Types of Reading

Find a sample of each of the following sources of reading material:

- Newspaper
- Chapter from a textbook
- Instructions such as for an appliance, an insurance policy, or a rental contract

Read each sample. Then answer the following questions.

1. How does the reading process differ for each type of reading?

_____

_____

_____

_____

_____

_____

_____

_____

_____

_____

_____

2. How does knowing your purpose for reading affect how you read? Why?

_____

_____

_____

_____

_____

_____

_____

_____

_____

_____

Summarize and Teach

1. Read the following paragraphs on Title IX. Underline, write in the margins, and write a brief summary of the paragraph. Compare your work with a study partner's work. There are many ways to highlight, so don't be concerned if yours is unique.

THE IMPACT OF TITLE IX

When Title IX of the Education Amendments was passed, gender was added to the list of categories protected by federal law. From then on, schools and colleges receiving any federal funds were prohibited from discriminating against either employees or students on the basis of their sex. Despite resistance in many forms, Title IX has slowly transformed education in the United States.

When people hear the words *Title IX,* they usually think of athletics and sports facilities. Indeed, in 1972, only about 294,000 American high school girls took part in interscholastic sports; today, about 3 million girls play sports. But Title IX is much more far-reaching than sports.

Prior to Title IX, girls who became pregnant were often forced to leave school or, at best, to attend segregated—and well-hidden—classes. Title IX prohibited that practice. Although schools can still offer voluntary classes for pregnant and parenting teens, no girl can be kept out of any program, class, or extracurricular activity because of bearing a child. These were no small victories in schools where girls who became pregnant were routinely expelled.

Source: James W. Fraser, *Teach: A Question of Teaching,* McGraw-Hill, 2011.

SUMMARY

_____

_____

_____

_____

_____

_____

_____

2. Work with a study partner in one of your classes. Read a chapter and write a summary. Compare your summary with your study partner's summary. Then summarize and teach the main concepts to your partner. Each of you can clarify and ask questions.

SUMMARY

_____

_____

_____

_____

_____

_____

_____

REVIEW AND APPLICATIONS | CHAPTER 6

Creating a Reading Outline

Outlining what you read can be a helpful study technique. Develop the habit of outlining. Use the following form as a guide. You may also develop your own form (see Chapter 5 for examples). Outline Chapter 6 on the following lines (or select another chapter in this or one of your other texts).

Course _____ Chapter _____ Date _____

I. _____

    A. _____

        1. _____

        2. _____

        3. _____

    B. _____

        1. _____

        2. _____

        3. _____

II. _____

    A. _____

        1. _____

        2. _____

        3. _____

    B. _____

        1. _____

        2. _____

        3. _____

III. _____

    A. _____

        1. _____

        2. _____

        3. _____

    B. _____

        1. _____

        2. _____

        3. _____

IV. _____

    A. _____

        1. _____

        2. _____

        3. _____

    B. _____

        1. _____

        2. _____

        3. _____

Analyzing Chapters

As you start to read the next chapter in this book, fill in this page to prepare for reading. You may need to add additional headings. List each heading and then phrase it as a question. Then summarize as you complete your reading. Use a separate sheet of paper if needed.

Course _____ Textbook _____

Chapter _____

Heading 1 _____

Question _____

Heading 2 _____

Question _____

Heading 3 _____

Question _____

Heading 4 _____

Question _____

SUMMARY OF SECTION

_____

_____

_____

_____

SUMMARY OF CHAPTER

_____

_____

_____

_____

Mind Map Your Text

Make a mind map of a section or chapter of one of your textbooks using the format provided here (and edit/change as necessary). Use **Figure 5.2** on page 155 as a guide.

For example, let's say you will map out a section from Chapter 3 of this text: "Manage Your Time." In the middle circle, you might put "Time-Management Strategies." In one of the surrounding circles, you might enter "Study everywhere and anywhere." In offshoot circles from that, you might put "Carry note cards," "Listen to recorded lectures," and "Avoid peak times in the library." Compare your mind maps with those drawn by other students in your class.

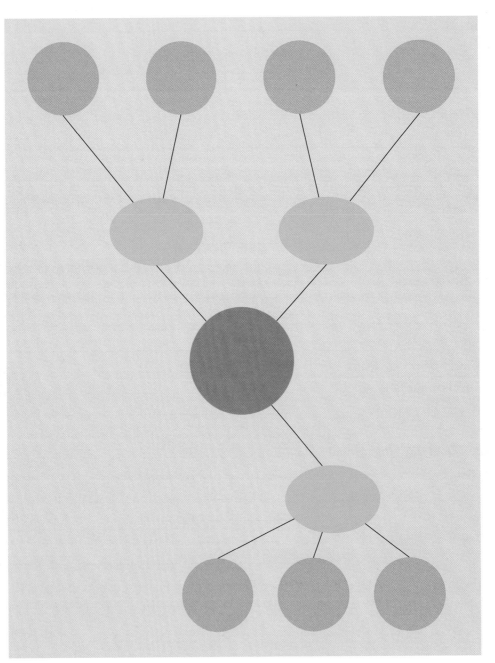

REVIEW AND APPLICATIONS | CHAPTER 6

Breaking Barriers to Reading

Following is a list of the common reasons that some students use for not reading effectively. Read this list; then add to it on the lines provided. Use creative problem solving to list strategies for overcoming these barriers.

Reasons for Not Reading	Strategies for Overcoming Reading Barriers
1. My textbooks are boring.	
2. I can't concentrate.	
3. I'm easily distracted.	
4. I fall asleep when I read.	
5. I never study the right material.	
6. There is too much information, and I don't know what is important.	
7. I read for hours, but I don't understand what I have read.	
8. I don't like to read.	

Demonstrating Competencies

Follow these steps and fill in the blanks to demonstrate your competencies. Then add this page to your Career Development Portfolio.

1. **Looking back:** Review your worksheets from other chapters to find activities from which you learned to read and concentrate.
2. **Taking stock:** Identify your strengths in reading and what you want to improve.
3. **Looking forward:** Indicate how you would demonstrate reading and comprehension skills to an employer.
4. **Documentation:** Include documentation of your reading skills.
5. **Inventory:** Make a list of the books you've read recently, including any classics. Use a separate sheet of paper.

Explain how you demonstrate these competencies:

Competencies	Your Demonstration
Active reading	_____
	_____
Critical reading	_____
	_____
Willingness to learn new words	_____
	_____
Improvement in technical vocabulary	_____
	_____
Articulation	_____
	_____
Expressiveness	_____
	_____
Ability to use a dictionary	_____
	_____
Positive attitude toward reading	_____
	_____
Technical reading	_____
	_____
Form reading	_____
	_____

Improve Your Memory Skills

LEARNING OUTCOMES

In this chapter, you will learn to:

7.1 Apply the five-step memory process

7.2 Describe memory strategies, including mnemonic devices

7.3 Summarize, review, and reflect for better retention and recall

SELF-MANAGEMENT

"I have been meeting so many new people. I wish I could remember their names, but I just don't have a good memory. How can I increase my memory skills and remember names, facts, and information more easily?"

Do you ever feel embarrassed because you cannot remember the names of new people you've met? Do you ever get frustrated because you don't remember material for a test? In this chapter, you will learn how to increase your memory skills.

JOURNAL ENTRY In **Worksheet 7.1** on page 236, describe a situation in which you needed to learn many new facts for a test. How did you fare? What factors helped you remember?

Technology has provided ample ways to store and retrieve information. No longer do we memorize and recite long stories in order to pass them down, as was done hundreds of years ago. In fact, many people don't even know their best friend's phone number, because it's programmed into their cell phone.

However, you can't whip out your phone when you take a test or run into a business acquaintance and can't remember his name ("Is it Bob or Bill? I know it starts with a *B*."). Although you may search the Internet to find information, you still determine what the information means, how it relates to other material, and how you will use it now and in the future. For this, your brain—not your computer, smartphone, or calculator—is the most essential "device."

Do you think some people are born with better memories than others? You will discover in this chapter that memory is a complex process that involves many factors you can control, such as your attitude, interest, intent, awareness, mental alertness, observation skills, senses, distractions, memory techniques, and willingness to practice. Most people with good memories say they mastered the skill by learning and continually practicing the strategies for storing and recalling information. This chapter will describe specific strategies that help you remember information.

WORDS TO SUCCEED

❝Memory . . . is the diary that we all carry about with us.❞

OSCAR WILDE
Dramatist

The Memory Process

The memory process involves five main steps:

1. Intention—you are interested and have a desire to learn and remember
2. Attention—you are attentive, observing information, and concentrating on details
3. Association—you organize and associate information to make sense of it
4. Retention—you practice until you know the information
5. Recall—you remember, teach, and share information with others

As you can see, this process is similar to the Adult Learning Cycle, which is explored throughout this text. (Read **Peak Progress 7.1** to see how you can use the Adult Learning Cycle to improve your memory skills.)

1. **Intention.** The first step in using memory effectively is to prepare mentally. As with learning any skill, your intention, attitude, and motivation are fundamental to success. Intention means being interested and willing to learn. You intend to remember by finding personal meaning and interest. Have you ever said, "I wish I could remember names," or "I can't remember formulas for math"? Instead, say, "I really want to remember JoAnne's last name."

   If you make excuses or program your mind with negative self-talk, your mind refuses to learn new information. If you think a subject is

Peak Progress

Applying the Adult Learning Cycle to Increasing Your Memory Skills

1. **RELATE. Why do I want to learn this?** I must become more proficient at remembering names, facts, and information. This is critical for success not only in school but also in work and social situations. What strategies do I already use to remember information?

2. **OBSERVE. How does this work?** Who is good at remembering names and information? What tips can I pick up from him or her? Who seems to struggle with remembering important information? I'll try using new strategies and observe how I'm improving.

3. **REFLECT. What does this mean?** What strategies seem to work best for me? What strategies are ineffective? Have I eliminated negative and defeating self-talk? I continue to look for connections and associations. I use humor, songs, rhymes, and other mnemonic techniques.

4. **DO. What can I do with this?** I will practice memory skills in many different situations and make a conscious commitment to improving my skills. I'll make games out of my practice and have fun. I'll find practical applications and use my new skills in everyday life. Each day, I'll work on one area. For example, I'll choose one class in which I'm having trouble recalling information and experiment with new strategies.

5. **TEACH. Whom can I share this with?** I'll talk with others and share my tips and experiences. I'll ask if they have any strategies they find useful that I might also try.

Congratulate yourself when you make improvements. The more you go through the cycle, the more interest and meaning recall will have for you, and the better your memory skills will become.

---

boring or unimportant, you will have difficulty remembering it. Make a conscious, active decision to remember, and state your intention with positive affirmations.

2. **Attention.** The second step in the memory process is to concentrate, observe, and be attentive to details. How often have you physically been in one place but mentally and emotionally were thousands of miles away? **Mindfulness** is the state in which you are totally in the moment and part of the process. Learning occurs when your mind is relaxed, focused, receptive, and alert. Focus your attention by concentrating briefly on one thing. Visualize details by drawing mental pictures. **Personal Evaluation Notebook 7.1** on page 216 helps you practice your observation skills.

3. **Association.** Nothing is harder to remember than unconnected facts, dates, or theories. Ask about how information is interconnected: How is this information similar to other information? How is it different?

   By associating and linking new material with old material, you make it meaningful. You cannot retain or recall information unless you understand it. Understanding means being able to see connections and relationships in information and to summarize and explain the material in your own words. Make associations by looking for similarities or differences. Create understanding by finding out why this information is important and how it relates to other information. Too often, students study just enough to get by on a quiz and then forget the information. It is much better to learn a subject, so that it becomes interesting and part of your long-term memory. (See **Peak Progress 7.2** on page 217 on short-term versus long-term memory.)

continued on page 218

> **"**An education isn't how much you have committed to memory, or even how much you know. It's being able to differentiate between what you know and what you don't.**"**
>
> ANATOLE FRANCE
> *Author*

WORDS TO SUCCEED

Personal Evaluation Notebook

Being Observant

Try the following experiments to determine if you are really observing the world around you.

EXPERIMENT 1

1. Look around the room.
2. Close your eyes.
3. Mentally picture what is in the room.
4. Open your eyes.
5. Did you remember everything? If not, what didn't you remember?

_____

_____

_____

EXPERIMENT 2

1. Look at a painting, photo, or poster for 1 minute.
2. Without looking back, write down the details you remember.
3. Compare your list of details with the painting, photo, or poster.
   a. What details did you remember? Colors? Faces? Clothing?

   _____

   _____

   b. What details didn't you remember?

   _____

   _____

   c. Did you remember the obvious things or did you remember subtle details?

   _____

   d. Why do you think those were the details you remembered?

   _____

   _____

Peak Progress

Short-Term and Long-Term Memory

People have two basic types of memory: short-term or active memory, and long-term or passive memory. Each type plays an important role in learning and the ability to respond effectively to life's challenges.

Before short-term memory can perform its wonders, information must flow into it. This can be new information entering through your natural senses, stored information you retrieve from long-term memory, or a combination of both. You might equate your natural senses with the zoom-in button on your camera, while you may think of long-term memory as your computer hard drive where you download and save your pictures. (See **Figure 7.1**.) Just as you make choices about which pictures to save on your computer, you determine which information becomes stored in your long-term memory. The information you choose to save in long-term memory has great value. It can be retrieved and used as it is, or it can be retrieved and combined with other information to create something entirely new.

When we consider the transfer of information back and forth in our memory system, think of the mind as a vast relational database. It is not enough merely to store information; for any database to be useful; the information stored in it must be organized and indexed for retrieval. This occurs naturally when we are predisposed to remember something, but what happens when we have to memorize information we just don't care about? Not only is that information more difficult to memorize but also it becomes nearly impossible to recall. The good news is that we can make such information more memorable by personally relating to it. For example, ask yourself, "How can I use this information in my life?" Answers to such questions can create meaning, which helps our mind to naturally organize information. When it comes time to use that information, such as during an examination, it will have been naturally indexed for easier recall.

Figure 7.1
Short-Term and Long-Term Memory

Think of your memory like taking pictures. First, you input information through your natural senses (such as pointing the camera and clicking). Your short-term memory is like the group of pictures in your camera, which can be deleted easily and gone forever. But, instead, you want to download your pictures onto your computer for long-term access, which can be organized, retrieved, printed, and viewed later (recall). *What material from this course may be in your short-term memory? In your long-term memory?*

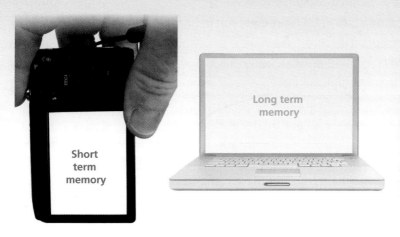

One way to organize material to look for connections is by outlining each chapter. As discussed in Chapter 5, use the Cornell System or a mind map (or whatever outline method works for you) to organize information. (See **Personal Evaluation Notebook 7.2** for a sample of a mind map.)

4. **Retention.** Repetition and practice help you retain information. Do it, and do it again. Repeat names or information aloud. Practice what you have learned, find new applications, and connect this information to other information you already know. Continue to ask questions and look for more examples.

5. **Recall. Memorization** is the transfer of information from short-term memory into long-term memory. Of course, the only reason to do this is so we can retrieve it in the future for use by our short-term memory. This transfer in the other direction is known as recall. To **recall** information means you not only have retained it but also can remember it when you need to.

Share information with others; introduce a person you have just met; practice giving summaries of chapters to your study team. Teach the information, write about it, talk about it, apply it to new situations, and demonstrate that you know it. This will make you more interested in the information, create more meaning for you, and build your confidence. Repeating this cycle will build your memory skills.

Memory Strategies

The following strategies will help you improve your memory skills.

1. **Write it down.** Writing is physical and enhances learning. When you write information, you are reinforcing learning by using your eyes, hand, fingers, and arm. Writing uses different parts of the brain than do speaking and listening.

   - Writing down a telephone number helps you remember it by providing a mental picture.
   - Planning your time in a day planner and creating a to-do list can trigger accomplishing tasks later in the day when you may have become overwhelmed with distractions.
   - Taking notes in class prompts you to be logical and concise and fills in memory gaps.
   - Underlining important information and then copying it onto note cards reinforces information.
   - Writing a summary in your own words after reading a chapter helps transfer information to long-term memory.

2. **Go from the general to the specific.** Many people learn and remember best by looking at the big picture and then learning the details. Try to outline from the general (main topic) to the specific (subtopics). Previewing a chapter gives you an overview and makes the topic more meaningful. Your brain is more receptive to details when it has a general idea of the main topic. Read, listen, and look for general understanding; then add details.

3. **Reduce information.** You don't have to memorize certain types of information, such as deadlines, telephone messages, and assignment due

Personal Evaluation Notebook

Using a Mind Map to Enhance Memory

Not only will a mind map help you organize information to be memorized, but also the physical act of writing will help you commit the material to memory. Use the map figure that follows as a guide, and in the space provided create a mind map of this chapter.

- Write the main topic in the middle and draw a circle or box around it.
- Surround the main topic with subtopics.
- Draw lines from the subtopics to the main topic.
- Under the subtopics, jot down supporting points, ideas, and examples.

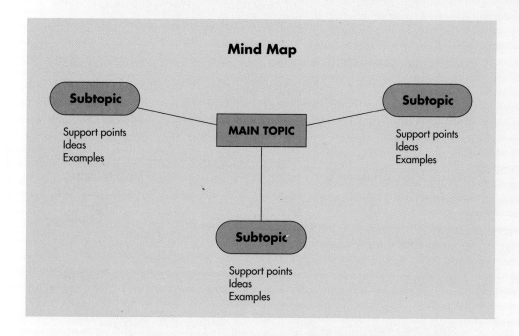

Create your own mind map.

Think of an essay question from an exam you have taken. How would using a mind map have helped you answer the question?

Take 3 minutes to organize your study area to prevent distractions:

- What assignments are completed and should be filed away?
- Which projects are due soon? Assemble all the necessary materials and put them in an accessible spot.
- Which readings must be completed this week? Pile those books together.

What else can you do in 3 minutes?

- Create file folders for all your courses.
- Scan today's lecture notes and read key points out loud.
- Empty all the trash and recycle old papers.

Take 3

dates. You just have to know where to find this information. Record deadlines and important information in your organizer, planner, or calendar, not on slips of paper, which can get lost. You can refer to any of this written information again if you need it.

4. **Eliminate distractions.** Distractions keep you from paying attention and remembering what you're trying to learn. One way to avoid distractions is to study in an uncluttered, quiet area, such as a library or designated study room. If it is noisy in class, ask the instructor to repeat information, or move closer to the front. The more effectively you focus your attention, the better you will create associations and recall information.

5. **Study in short sessions.** You will use the power of concentration more fully, and the brain retains information better, in short study sessions. After about 40 minutes, the brain needs a break to process information effectively. Break large goals into specific objectives and study in short sessions. For example, if you are taking a marketing course, preview a chapter in your textbook for 20 minutes and mind map the chapter for 20 minutes. Then take a 10-minute break. Stretch, drink a glass of water, or eat a small snack. Then return to complete your goal.

6. **Use all your senses.** Memory is sensory, so using all your senses (sight, hearing, touch, smell, and taste) will give your brain a better chance of retaining information.

   - *Visualize.* Because much of what you learn and remember reaches you through sight, it is important to visualize what you want to remember. The art of retention is the art of attention. Be a keen observer of details and notice differences and similarities. Suppose you are taking a medical terminology or vocabulary-building course. You may want to look at pictures and visualize images with the new terms or words. Look at illustrations, pictures, and information on the board.

   - *Listen.* You cannot remember a name or information in class if you are not attentive and listening. Actively listen in class, record lectures (ask for the instructor's permission), and play them back later. Recite definitions and information aloud.

   - *Move.* Whether you learn best by reading or listening, you will retain information better if you use all your senses and make learning physical. Read aloud; read while standing; jot down notes; lecture in front of the classroom to yourself or your study team; draw pictures, diagrams, and models; and join a study group. Practice reciting information while doing physical activity, such as showering or jogging. The more you use all your senses, the more information you will retain.

   Complete **Personal Evaluation Notebook 7.3** on page 222 to assess your memory and how your senses relate to your childhood memories. Complete

Personal Evaluation Notebook 7.4 on page 223 to determine how to use learning styles to improve recall.

7. **Use mnemonic devices. Mnemonic** (neh-mon-nik) devices are memory tricks that help you remember information. However, mnemonic devices have limits. Developing a memory trick takes time, and the trick will be hard to remember if it is too complicated. Because mnemonic devices don't help you understand the information or develop skills in critical thinking, they are best used for sheer rote memorization. Follow up by looking for associations, making connections, and writing summaries. Some mnemonic devices are

- *Rhymes and rhythms.* In elementary school, you might have learned the rhyme "In 1492 Columbus sailed the ocean blue" to remember the date of Columbus's voyage. Rhythms can also be helpful. Many people have learned to spell the word *Mississippi* by accenting all the *is* and making the word rhythmic. This is similar to the technique used in rap music and poetry, in which syllables are accentuated on an established beat.

- *Acronyms.* **Acronyms** are words formed from the first letters of a series of other words, such as HOMES for the Great Lakes (Huron, Ontario, Michigan, Erie, and Superior) and EPCOT (Experimental Prototype Community of Tomorrow).

- *Acrostics.* **Acrostics** are similar to acronyms, but they are made-up sentences in which the first letter stands for something, such as Every Good Boy Deserves Fun for remembering the sequence of musical notes: E, G, B, D, F. Another is My Very Easy Memory Jingle Seems Useful Now, which helps you remember the order of the planets from the sun (assuming you know that the first planet is Mercury and not Mars and that Pluto is no longer considered a planet. Can you name the rest with the help of the acrostic?) Acrostics are often used in poetry, where the first letter of every line combine to spell something, such as the poem's title. (See **Personal Evaluation Notebook 7.5** on page 224 to practice creating acronyms and acrostics.)

- *Association.* Suppose you are learning about explorer Christopher Columbus's three ships. Think of three friends whose names start with the same first letters as the ships' names: *Pinta, Santa Maria,* and *Nina* (e.g., Paul, Sandy, and Nancy). Vividly associate your friends' names with the three ships, and you should be able to recall the ships' names. Using associations can also be helpful in remembering numbers. For example, if your ATM identification number is 9072, you might remember it by creating associations with dates. Maybe 1990 is the year you graduated from high school and 1972 is the year you were born.

- *Chunking.* **Chunking,** or grouping, long lists of information or numbers can break up the memory task and make it easier for you. Most people can remember up to seven numbers in a row, which is why phone numbers are that long.

● Learning Memory
Focusing on your preferred learning style strengthens your memory skills. *How does your learning style affect the way in which you learn memory?*

❝No memory is ever alone; it's at the end of a trail of memories, a dozen trails that each have their own associations.❞

LOUIS L'AMOUR
Author

WORDS TO SUCCEED

Personal Evaluation Notebook

Memory Assessment

1. Sometimes your perceptions differ from reality, particularly when you are assessing your skills and personal qualities. Check Yes or No as it pertains to you.

   a. Do you remember names easily?   Yes _____ No _____
   b. Do you remember important information for tests?   Yes _____ No _____
   c. Do you often forget about due dates and appointments?   Yes _____ No _____
   d. Do you often "lose" things around the house?   Yes _____ No _____
   e. Did you use your senses more as a child?   Yes _____ No _____

2. Write a few lines about your earliest memory.

   _____

   _____

   _____

   _____

3. Does it help your memory to look at family photos or hear about your childhood? Why?

   _____

   _____

   _____

4. What sounds and smells do you remember most from home?

   _____

   _____

   _____

   _____

- *Stacking technique.* Visualize objects that represent points, and stack them on top of each other. For example, if you were giving a speech on time management, you would start with a clock with a big pencil on it to represent how much time is saved if you write information down. On top of the clock is a big calendar, which reminds you to make the point that you must set priorities in writing. On the calendar is a Time Log with the name Drucker on it. This will remind you to present a quote by Peter Drucker that you must know where your time goes if you are to be effective in managing your life. You stack an object to remind you of each of the key points in the speech.

Personal Evaluation Notebook

7.4

Learning Styles and Memory

Answer the following questions on the lines provided.

1. What is your preferred learning style? How can you use this information to enhance your memory?

   _____

   _____

   _____

   _____

   _____

2. How can you incorporate other learning styles to help you improve your recall?

   _____

   _____

   _____

   _____

   _____

- *Method-of-place technique.* As far back as 500 B.C.E. the Greeks were using a method of imagery called loci—the method-of-place technique. (*Loci* is Latin for "place.") This method, which is similar to the stacking technique, is still effective because it uses imagery and association to aid memory. Memorize a setting in detail and then place the item or information you want to remember at certain places on your memory map. Some people like to use a familiar street, their home, or workplace as a map on which to place their information. Memorize certain places on your map and the specific order or path in which you visit each place. Once you have memorized this map, you can position various items to remember at different points. **Personal Evaluation Notebook 7.6** on pages 225 and 226 gives you a chance to practice this technique.

8. **Recite.** Recite and repeat information, such as a name, poem, date, or formula. When you say information aloud, you use your throat, voice, and lips, and you hear yourself recite. This recitation technique may help when you are dealing with difficult reading material. Reading aloud and hearing the material will reinforce it and help move information from your short-term memory to your long-term memory. Use the new words in your own conversations. Write summaries in your own words and read to others. Study groups are

Personal Evaluation Notebook

Acronyms and Acrostics

An *acronym* is a word formed from the first letters of a series of other words. An *acrostic* is a made-up sentence, with the first letter of each word standing for something. Create one or more acronyms and acrostics based on information you are learning right now in your courses.

Acronym example: "NATO" stands for North Atlantic Treaty Organization.

Acronym _____

Stands for _____

Acrostic example: "Old People From Texas Eat Spiders" stands for the bones of the skull (occipital, parietal, frontal, temporal, ethmoid, sphenoid).

Acrostic _____

Stands for _____

✔ Use index cards for recording information you want to memorize. Write brief summaries and indicate the main points of each chapter on the backs of note cards.

✔ Carry the cards with you and review them during waiting time, before going to sleep at night, or any other time you have a few minutes to spare.

✔ Organize the cards according to category, color, size, order, weight, and other areas.

---

effective because you can hear each other, clarify questions, and increase understanding as you review information.

To remember names, when you meet someone, recite the person's name several times to yourself and out loud. **Peak Progress 7.3** on page 227 provides more tips for remembering names.

9. **Use note cards.** On note cards, the information is condensed and written, so the act of writing is kinesthetic and holding cards is tactile. Note cards are visual and, when the information is recited out loud or in a group, the auditory element enhances learning. Note cards are a great way to organize information and highlight key words.

10. **Practice, practice, practice!** You must practice information you want to remember. For example, when you first start driver training, you learn the various steps involved in driving. At first, they may seem overwhelming. You may have to stop and think through each step. After you have driven a car for awhile, however, you don't even think about all the steps required to start it and back out of the driveway. You check your mirror automatically before changing lanes, and driving safely has become a habit. Through repetition, you put information into your long-term memory. The more often you use the information, the easier it is to recall. You could not become a good musician without hours of practice. Playing sports, speaking in public, flying an airplane, and learning to drive all require

Personal Evaluation Notebook

A Walk Down Memory Lane

Creating a memory map is a visual way to enhance and practice your memory skills. The key to this method is to set the items clearly in your memory and visualize them. For example, a familiar memory map involves remembering the 13 original colonies. The memory map in this case is a garden with several distinct points. There is delicate chinaware sitting on the garden gate (Delaware); the birdbath contains a large fountain pen (Pennsylvania); in the gazebo is a new jersey calf (New Jersey); and sitting on the calf is King George (Georgia) with a cut on his finger (Connecticut). The flowerbed has a mass of flowers (Massachusetts); in the fountain, splashing, is Marilyn Monroe (Maryland); the garden sun dial is pointing south (South Carolina); a large ham is sitting on the garden bench (New Hampshire); and the gardener, named Virginia (Virginia), who is wearing an empire dress (New York), is watering the northern flowerbed (North Carolina). In the middle of the flowerbed is an island of rocks (Rhode Island). There you have the 13 original colonies in the order in which they joined the union.

YOUR MEMORY MAP

Create your own memory map using a familiar place, such as your neighborhood, the mall, or a store you often visit, such as a grocery store. Chances are, you navigate around these places the same way every time. You start out on the same path; you park near or enter the same door. You are very familiar with what you will see at each point. For example, you may enter the grocery store near the courtesy counter, grab a cart, and turn right towards the produce section. You can easily visualize where everything is located and what you will see along the "path." Draw a picture of your map in detail in the space provided.

(continued)

Personal Evaluation Notebook  7.6

A Walk Down Memory Lane *(concluded)*

Using your map, imagine you have a test coming up in your American government class and need to remember the first 4 (out of 10) amendments that make up the Bill of Rights:

1: Freedom of speech, press, religion, assembly, and petition

2: Right to keep and bear arms

3: Quartering of soldiers

4: Search and arrest

Now, follow these steps in the method-of-place technique:

1. Imagine your memory location, and think of each distinctive detail within the location.
2. Create a vivid image to help you remember each amendment. (If you are unfamiliar with the meaning of any of the amendments, do a quick search online or at the library.)
3. Associate each of the images representing the amendments with points in your map, and see the images at each location. Draw them in your map.
4. As you "stroll" through your map, create mental pictures of each of your items through association. Recite each one aloud as you visualize them.

To help you get started, you may think of a newspaper stand to remind you of freedom of speech or of the press, or protestors with signs to remember the right to assemble or petition. Place these images within your memory map, such as at the front door (so that you have to walk around the protestors to get in the door).

Be creative and make the images meaningful to you. If you really want to stretch your critical thinking skills, add images for Amendments 5 through 10:

5: Rights concerning prosecution in criminal cases

6: Right to a speedy and fair trial

7: Right to a trial by jury

8: Bail, fines, and punishment

9: Rights retained by the People

10: States' rights

skills that need to be repeated and practiced many times. Repetition puts information into long-term memory and allows for recall.

These strategies are very effective in strengthening your memory skills. Certain strategies might work better for you than others, depending on your personality and learning styles, personal strengths, and abilities. You can master the use of memory strategies with effort, patience, and practice. As you build your memory skills, you will also enhance your study habits and become more disciplined and aware of your surroundings.

Summarize, Review, and Reflect

Summarize a lecture or a section or chapter of a book in your own words as soon as possible after hearing or reading it. The sooner and more often you review information, the easier it is to recall. Ideally, your first review should be within the first hour after hearing a lecture or reading an assignment. Carry note cards with you and review them again during the first day. As discussed in Chapter 5, memory researchers suggest that, after only 48 hours, you may have forgotten 70 percent of what you have learned. However, if you review right after you hear it and again within 24 hours, your recall soars to 90 percent.

Go beyond studying for tests. Be able to connect and apply information to new situations. Uncover facts, interesting points, related materials, details, and fascinating aspects of the subject. Ask your instructor for related stories to enhance a point.

Definitely a "people person," Aleah just began her nursing program and can't wait to start working with real patients. She enjoys the hands-on lab section of her anatomy and physiology course but worries she'll never master all the basic terminology—the skeletal system, the muscle groups, the endocrine system, and on and on.

- Which mnemonic devices might be helpful in remembering human anatomy?
- How could Aleah use visualization techniques to help her recall information?
- What is Aleah's preferred learning style, and how can she use it to improve her recall? How can she use other styles to complement her learning?

Peak Progress

Remembering Names

Techniques that help you remember names can also be used to remember material in class, such as key people and events.

1. Imagine the name. Visualize the name clearly in your mind: Tom Plum. Clarify how the name is spelled: P-l-u-m.

2. Be observant and concentrate. Pay attention to the person's features and mannerisms.

3. Use exaggeration. Caricaturing the features is a fun and effective way to remember names. Single out and amplify one outstanding feature. For example, if Tom has red hair, exaggerate it to bright red and see the hair much fuller and longer than it is.

4. Visualize the red hair and the name Tom. See this vision clearly.

5. Repeat Tom's name to yourself several times as you are talking to him.

6. Recite Tom's name aloud during your conversation. Introduce Tom to others.

7. Use association. Associate the name with something you know ("Tom is the name of my cat") or make up a story using the person's name and add action and color. Tom is picking red plums that match his hair.

8. As soon as you can, jot down the name. Use a key word, or write or draw a description.

9. Use rhyming to help you recall: "Tom is not dumb; he's a plum."

10. Integrate learning styles. It may help if you see the name (visual), hear it pronounced (auditory), or practice saying it and writing it several times and connecting the name with something familiar (kinesthetic).

11. Ask people their names. If you forget, say your name first. "Hi, I'm Sam and I met you last week." If they don't offer their names, ask.

If you have time, read a novel on the subject or look in the library for another textbook that explains the subject from a different view. You will remember information more easily if you take time to understand and apply it.

Overcome Obstacles

A barrier to memory is disinterest. You have to want to remember. People often say, "If only I could remember names," or "I wish I had a better memory." Avoid using words such as *try, wish,* and *hope*. Overcome the barrier of disinterest by creating a positive, curious attitude; intending to remember; using all your senses; and using memory techniques. Related to disinterest is lack of attentiveness. You must be willing to concentrate by being an attentive listener and observe. Listen for overall understanding and for details. A short period of intense concentration will help you remember more than reading for hours.

Practice becoming more observant and aware. Suppose you want to learn the students' names in all your classes. Look at each student as the instructor takes roll, copy down each name, and say each name mentally as you look around the classroom. As you go about your day, practice becoming aware of your surroundings, people, and new information.

Finally, relax. Anxiety and stress can make you forget. For example, let's return to remembering names. Suppose you see Tom when you are with a good friend. You may be so anxious to make a good impression that Tom's name is lost for a moment. Relax by being totally in the moment instead of worrying about forgetting, how you

look, what others may think, or your nervousness. Take a deep breath. If you still can't remember, laugh and say, "Hi, my mind just went blank. I'm Jay; please refresh my memory."

Just as you need to exercise your physical body, keep your memory skills sharp by exercising your brain—stretch your imagination, flex your areas of interest, and jog your memory!

Can you answer yes?

✔ Do I want to remember?

✔ Do I have a positive attitude about the information?

✔ Have I eliminated distractions?

✔ Have I organized and grouped material?

✔ Have I reviewed the information often?

✔ Have I reviewed right after the lecture? Within 24 hours?

✔ Have I visualized what I want to remember?

✔ Have I used repetition?

✔ Have I summarized material in my own words?

✔ Have I used association and compared and contrasted new material with what I know?

✔ Have I used memory techniques to help me associate key words?

✔ Have I set up weekly reviews?

TAKING CHARGE

Summary

In this chapter, I learned to

- **Apply the five-step memory process.** Similar to the Adult Learning Cycle, the memory process consists of five steps: intention, attention, association, retention, and recall.

- **Intend to remember.** People who have better memories *want* to remember and make it a priority. It's important for me to increase my memory skills, and I take responsibility for my attitude and intention. I create personal interest and meaning in what I want to remember.

- **Be observant and alert.** I observe and am attentive to details. I am relaxed, focused, and receptive to new information. I reduce distractions, concentrate, and stay focused and mindful of the present. I look at the big picture, and then I look at details. Memory is increased when I pay attention.

- **Organize and associate information.** Organization makes sense out of information. I look for patterns and connections. I look for what I already know and jot down questions for areas that I don't know. I group similarities and look for what is different.

- **Retain information.** I write summaries in my own words and say them out loud. I jot down main points, key words, and important information on note cards. I study in short sessions and review often.

- **Recall.** I recall everything I know about the subject. I increase my recall by writing down information, reciting out loud, and teaching others. Practicing and reviewing information often are key to increasing recall. I reward myself for concentration, discipline, and effort.

- **Write it down.** The simple act of writing helps me create a mental picture.

- **Go from the general to the specific.** I first look at the big picture for gaining general, overall understanding and meaning. I then focus on the details and specific supporting information.

- **Reduce information and eliminate distractions.** Some information (such as e-mail addresses and phone numbers) does not have to be memorized; I just need to know where to find it easily. I also need to eliminate distractions that affect my ability to concentrate on what I'm trying to learn and remember.

- **Take frequent breaks.** I study in 40- to 60-minute sessions because I know that the brain retains information best in short study periods. I take breaks to keep up my motivation.

- **Use my senses and integrate learning styles.** I draw pictures and illustrations, use color, record lectures, play music, write out summaries, jot down questions, collect samples, give summaries to my study group, and recite out loud.

- **Try mnemonic devices.** I use various techniques, such as rhymes and rhythms, acronyms, acrostics, grouping, association, and the method-of-place technique to help me memorize and recall information.

- **Use note cards.** Using note cards is an easy and convenient way for me to review important facts, terms, and questions.

- **Find connections and recite.** I link new information with familiar material, and I summarize what I have learned, either out loud or in writing.

- **Practice!** If I want to understand and remember information, I must practice and review it again and again.

Performance Strategies

Following are the top 10 strategies for improving memory:

- Intend to remember and prepare yourself mentally.
- Be observant, be alert, and pay attention.
- Organize information to make it meaningful.
- Look for associations and connections.
- Write down information.
- Integrate learning styles.
- Study in short sessions.
- Use mnemonic devices.
- Summarize information in your own words.
- Practice, use repetition, and relax.

Tech for Success

Take advantage of the text's web site at **www.mhhe.com/ferrett9e** for additional study aids, useful forms, and convenient and applicable resources.

- **Acrostics online.** Many disciplines (especially in the sciences) have well-known acrostics that students and professionals use to remember key information (such as human anatomy). There are a number of online sites that have collected hundreds of useful acrostics.

- **Stored memory.** Your computer is one big memory tool, storing thousands of hours of your work and contact information. For example, if you use the "Favorites"

feature in your web browser to catalog web sites, consider how long it would take for you to reconstruct this information if it were suddenly wiped out. Do you have back-up plans in case your hard drive becomes inaccessible, or if you lose your cell phone containing countless stored numbers? Use these many tools and features to help you organize and save time, but don't forget to write down or keep hard copies of very important documents and contact information.

Study Team Notes

Diana Tanaka
JOURNALIST

Related Majors: Journalism, Communications, English, Social Studies

Integrating Learning Styles

As a journalist, Diana Tanaka's job is to find news-worthy local issues, collect accurate information from both sides of the story, and write an article that treats the subject fairly. As a general assignment reporter for an online news service, she covers stories on politics, crime, education, business, and consumer affairs.

Diana works closely with her editor when selecting a topic for an article. She often investigates leads for a story, only to realize later that she does not have enough information to make a strong story. She organizes the information she gathers, not knowing how or if it will fit into the article. Diana usually works on more than one story at a time, as some stories take weeks of research. Her hours are irregular. Diana might attend an early morning political breakfast and a school board meeting that evening.

Each week, Diana interviews a wide variety of people, including the mayor, the police chief, the school super-visor, and other community leaders. She always says hello to people, using their names. She prides herself on being able to remember names after only one meeting. When conducting an interview, the first thing Diana does is write down the name of the person, asking for the correct spelling. By doing this, she not only checks spelling but also sees the name in print. Because Diana is a visual learner, this helps her remember it. After an interview, Diana types her notes and memorizes pertinent information, such as the names of people, businesses, and locations and determines key follow-up questions. Diana knows that having good memory skills is essential for being a capable journalist.

CRITICAL THINKING Which learning styles help Diana remember pertinent information?

Peak Performer
PROFILE

David Diaz

In first grade, David Diaz knew he wanted to be a "drawer." However, he had no idea what that meant. He knew he liked to draw. It wasn't until high school that an instructor and a sculptor became instrumental in his selection of art as his career path. The art teacher encouraged him to enter art competitions; the sculptor, Duane Hanson, demonstrated by example the life of an artist.

Diaz attended the Fort Lauderdale Art Institute before moving across the country to California to start his prolific career in graphic design and illustration. For more than 25 years, he has been illustrating for national publications, book publishers, and corporations.

Success came early in his picture-book career when he was awarded the prestigious Caldecott Medal for illustrating Eve Bunting's *Smokey Nights,* a story about a boy's point of view of the Los Angeles riots in 1992. Critics and readers continue to appreciate the honest, vibrant, painterly quality of his work.

"I'm always thinking about how to make [the book] more of an experience, not just something you read," he said. His dynamic work comes through numerous revisions of looks and feels of the characters in the stories. He keeps working over an image to get it just right.

After all this time and success, Diaz still goes back to his roots: the foundations of drawing. "All the technique in the world can't save a bad drawing. As an artist, the challenge for me is to retain the spontaneity of an initial sketch or thumbnail drawing through the creation of the final image." Here is an artist, following his instinct, education, and passion through each phase of his career.

PERFORMANCE THINKING A career in the arts is often about paying careful attention to the world around you. Unique observations and an execution of talent are two keys to garnering attention for artistic merits. How might an artist find an activity like the Memory Map on page 219 helpful to his or her work? Why might memory be important to creating a piece of artwork?

CHECK IT OUT The largest library in the world, the Library of Congress, houses more than 130 million items and 530 miles of bookshelves. Visit the website **www.loc.gov** to search for various print, media, and online resources. Also available on the website is a section called "American Memory," which showcases historical information and resources on a number of topics, such as environment/conservation, immigration/American expansion, African American history, and women's history.

Starting Today

At least one strategy I learned in this chapter that I plan to try right away is

_____

_____

_____

What changes must I make in order for this strategy to be most effective?

_____

_____

_____

Review Questions

Based on what you have learned in this chapter, write your answers to the following questions:

1. What are the five main steps of the memory process?

_____

_____

2. Why is intending to remember so important to enhancing memory?

_____

_____

3. Why does writing down information help you remember it?

_____

_____

4. Name one mnemonic device and how it is used to help you remember. Give an example.

_____

_____

5. What is the purpose of reviewing information soon and often?

_____

_____

To test your understanding of the chapter's concepts, complete the chapter quiz at **www.mhhe.com/ferrett9e**.

Overcoming Memory Loss

In the Classroom

Erin McAdams is outgoing, bright, and popular, but she also has a reputation for being forgetful. She forgets appointments, projects, and due dates. She repeatedly loses her keys and important papers. She is often late and forgets meetings and even social events. She always tells herself, "I really am going to try harder to get more organized and remember my commitments." She blames her bad memory for doing poorly on tests and wishes that people would understand she's doing her best. She insists that she's tried but just can't change.

1. What would you suggest to help Erin improve her memory skills?

   _____

   _____

2. What strategies in this chapter would be most helpful?

   _____

   _____

   _____

In the Workplace

Erin is now in hotel management. She loves the excitement, the diversity of the people she meets, and the daily challenges. She has recently been assigned to plan and coordinate special events, which include parties, meetings, and social affairs. This new job requires remembering many names, dates, and endless details.

3. How can Erin learn to develop her memory skills?

   _____

   _____

4. Suggest a program for her that would increase her memory skills.

   _____

   _____

REVIEW AND APPLICATIONS | CHAPTER 7

Applying the ABC Method of Self-Management

In the Journal Entry on page 213, you were asked to describe a situation when you needed to learn many new facts for a test. How did you fare? What factors helped you remember?

_____

_____

_____

_____

Now describe a situation in which you forgot some important information or someone's name that you really wanted to remember. Work through the ABC Method and incorporate the new strategies you have learned in this chapter.

A = **Actual event:**

_____

_____

_____

B = **Beliefs:**

_____

_____

_____

C = **Challenge:**

_____

_____

_____

Relax, take a deep breath, and visualize yourself recalling facts, key words, dates, and information easily.

PRACTICE SELF-MANAGEMENT

For more examples of learning how to manage difficult situations, see the "Self-Management Workbook" section of the Online Learning Center web site at **www.mhhe.com/ferrett9e**.

REVIEW AND APPLICATIONS | CHAPTER 7

Memory

A. Quickly read these lists once. Read one word at a time and in order.

1	2
the	Disney World
work	light
of	time
and	and
to	of
the	house
and	the
of	packages
light	good
of	praise
care	and
the	coffee
chair	the
and	of

B. Now cover the lists and write as many words as you can remember on the lines that follow. Then check your list against the lists in Part A.

_____   _____

_____   _____

_____   _____

_____   _____

_____   _____

_____   _____

_____   _____

_____   _____

_____   _____

(continued)

1. How many words did you remember from the beginning of each list? List them.

_____

_____

2. How many words did you remember from the middle of each list? List them.

_____

_____

3. How many words did you remember from the end of each list? List them.

_____

_____

4. Did you remember the term *Disney World?*   Yes _____   No _____

Most people who complete this exercise remember the first few words, the last few words, the unusual term *Disney World,* and the words that were listed more than once (*of, the,* and *and*). Did you find this to be true about yourself?   Yes _____   No _____

C. Remembering names

1. Do you have problems remembering names?   Yes _____   No _____

2. What are the benefits of remembering names now and in a career?

_____

_____

_____

D. Which memory techniques work best for you and why?

_____

_____

_____

_____

_____

_____

_____

_____

Mental Pictures

Use various techniques to recall the following information:

In World War II, the major Axis powers were Germany, Italy, and Japan. The Allied powers were led by Great Britain, the Union of Soviet Socialist Republics (USSR), and the United States of America.

1. Think of mental images that would help you remember each of the following during an exam:

Axis Powers   **Allied Powers**

Germany _____   Great Britain _____

_____   _____

Italy _____   USSR _____

_____   _____

Japan _____   USA _____

_____   _____

2. Create a memory map using the method-of-place technique. Either place these mental images in the map or create new images that may work better using this technique.

3. Now create an acrostic or acronym to remember each grouping (all three Axis powers and all three Allied powers). Refer to pages 221 to 223 to refresh your memory on these mnemonic devices.
   - Axis powers: _____
   - Allied powers: _____

Applying Memory Skills

Assess your memory skills by answering the following questions. Add this page to your Career Development Portfolio.

1. **Looking back:** Review an autobiography you may have written for this or another course. Indicate the ways you applied your memory skills.

   _____

   _____

2. **Taking stock:** What are your memory strengths and what do you want to improve?

   _____

   _____

3. **Looking forward:** How would you demonstrate memory skills for employers?

   _____

   _____

4. **Documentation:** Include examples, such as poems you have memorized, literary quotes, and techniques for remembering names.

   _____

   _____

5. **Assessment and demonstration:** Critical thinking skills for memory include the following. When have you demonstrated these?

   - Preparing yourself mentally and physically
   - Creating a willingness to remember
   - Determining what information is important and organizing it
   - Linking new material with known information (creating associations)
   - Integrating various learning styles
   - Asking questions
   - Reviewing and practicing

   _____

   _____

   _____

   _____

   _____

Excel at Taking Tests

LEARNING OUTCOMES

In this chapter, you will learn to

8.1 Prepare for tests

8.2 Describe strategies for taking tests

8.3 Use test results

8.4 Take different types of tests

8.5 Use special tips for math and science tests

8.6 Overcome test anxiety

SELF-MANAGEMENT

"I studied very hard for my last test, but my mind went blank when I tried to answer the questions. How can I reduce my anxiety and be more confident about taking tests?"

Have you ever felt anxious and worried when taking tests? Do you suffer physical symptoms, such as sweaty palms, an upset stomach, headaches, or an inability to sleep or concentrate? Everyone experiences some anxiety when faced with a situation involving performance or evaluation. Peak performers know that the best strategy for alleviating feelings of panic is to be prepared. In this chapter, you will learn ways to decrease your anxiety and test-taking strategies that will help you before, during, and after tests.

JOURNAL ENTRY In **Worksheet 8.1** on page 266, describe a time when you did well in a performance, sporting event, or test. What factors helped you be calm, feel confident, and remember information?

Successful athletes and performers know how important it is to monitor their techniques and vary their training programs to improve results. Taking tests is part of school; performance reviews are part of a job; and tryouts and performing are part of being an athlete, a dancer, or an actor. In fact, just about any job involves some assessment of skills, attitudes, and behavior. Many fields also require you to pass rigorous exams before you complete your education (such as the LSAT for law) and certification exams (as in athletic training). In this chapter, we explore specific test-taking strategies that will help you both in school and your career.

Test-Taking Strategies

Before the Test

Test taking starts long before sitting down with pencil in hand (or in front of a computer) to tackle an exam. The following tips will help you prepare for taking a test.

4 **Start on day one.** The best way to do well on tests is to begin preparing on the first day of class. Set up a review schedule on the first day and attend all classes, arrive on time, stay until the end of class, and create a positive frame of mind about succeeding.

Test-Taking Skills

1 Prepare yourself both mentally and physically

2 Determine what information is important

3 Process information

4 Link new material with known information

5 Create associations

6 Create a willingness to remember

7 Stay focused

8 Reason logically

9 Overcome fear

10 Evaluate test results

Personal Evaluation Notebook

Test Taking

Your instructor will often give clues in class as to what will be covered on tests. Watch for

- Information that is repeated or emphasized
- Illustrations on the board, PowerPoint presentations, or handouts
- Intensified voice or hand gestures and eye contact
- Examples and pauses for students to take notes
- Points covered while introducing or summarizing a topic

1. With classmates or study team members, use the list of clues as a guide to create a list of topics you think might be covered on the next exam.

   _____

   _____

   _____

2. As a team, approach your instructor to see if your list is on target. Ask your instructor what kinds of questions to expect on the test. Write that information on the following lines. (See pages 249–253 for types of test questions.)

   _____

   _____

   _____

2. **Know expectations.** On the first day of class, most instructors outline the course and clarify the syllabus and expectations concerning grading, test dates, and types of tests. During class or office hours, ask your instructors about test formats, sample questions, a study guide, or additional material that may be helpful. Also ask how much weight the textbook has on tests. Some instructors cover key material in class and assign reading for a broad overview. Observe your instructors to see what they consider important and what points and key words they stress. As you listen to lectures or read your textbook, ask yourself what questions might be on the examination. A large part of fear and anxiety comes from the unknown, so, the more you know about what is expected, the more at ease you will be. **Personal Evaluation Notebook 8.1** gives you a guide for approaching your instructors about upcoming tests. (**Worksheet 8.3** on pages 268 and 269 also provides a detailed guide for tracking test information.)

3. **Ask questions in class.** If you are unclear about a point, raise your hand and ask for clarification. Or ask your instructor or another student at the end of class. Don't assume all of the lecture will be covered in the textbook.

4. **Keep up.** Manage your time and keep up with daily reading and assignments. (Use your time-management strategies from Chapter 3.) Don't wait until the night before to prepare for an exam. (**Worksheet 8.2** on page 267 is a handy form for keeping track of your exams.)

5. **Review immediately.** Start the review process by quickly previewing chapters before classes and taking a few minutes to review your notes right after class. When information is fresh, you can fill in missing pieces, make connections, and raise questions to ask later. Refer to your review schedule and make sure you have time to review notes from all your classes each day. Review time can be short; 5 or 10 minutes for every class is often enough. When reviewing each day, scan reading notes and items that need memorization. This kind of review should continue until the final exam.

6. **Review weekly.** Spend about an hour per subject to investigate and review not only the week's assignments but also what has been included thus far in the course. These review sessions can include class notes, reading notes, chapter questions, note cards, mind maps, flash cards, a checklist of items to study, and summaries written in your own words. To test your understanding, close your book after reading and write a summary; then go back and fill in missing material.

7. **Do a final review.** A week or so before a test, commit to a major review. (Some instructors recommend allocating at least 2 hours per day for 3 days before the exam.) This review should include class and book notes, note cards, and summaries. You can practice test questions, compare concepts, integrate major points, and review and recite with your study team. Long-term memory depends on organizing the information. Fragmented information is hard to remember or recall. When you understand the main ideas and connect and relate information, you transfer the material into long-term memory.

8. **Use memory techniques.** Determine which memory techniques will help you recall information, especially if you need to remember key dates, names, or lists. (Refer to Chapter 7 for descriptions of effective memory techniques.)

9. **Create sample tests.** Pretest yourself by predicting questions and creating and taking sample tests. Chapter objectives, key concepts, summaries, and end-of-chapter questions and exercises provide examples of possible test questions. Also, many textbooks have accompanying DVDs or websites that include sample test questions (as you will find at **www.mhhe.com/ferrett9e**). Review and rehearse until you have learned the material and feel confident. Save all quizzes, course materials, exercise sheets, and lab work. Ask if old tests or sample tests are available at the library.

10. **Summarize.** Pretend the instructor allows you to take one note card to the test. Choose the most important concepts, formulas, key words, and points, and condense them onto one note card. Chances are, you will do better on the test even if you cannot use the note card during the test. If you go beyond memorizing facts to summarize in your own words, you will understand the material.

11. **Use your study team.** You may be tempted to skip studying one night, but you can avoid temptation if you know other people are depending on your contribution. Have each member of the study team provide 5 to 10 potential test questions. Share these questions and discuss possible answers. Word the questions in different formats—multiple-choice, true/false, matching, and essay. Then simulate the test-taking experience by taking, giving, and correcting each other's timed sample tests.

12. **Use all available resources.** If your instructor offers a review before the exam, attend it, take good notes, and ask clarifying questions. Consider getting a tutor; check with

the learning center, academic departments, or student services. A tutor will expect you to attend all classes, keep up with reading and homework assignments, and be motivated to learn. Your tutor will not do your work for you but will review assignment expectations, explain concepts, help you summarize and understand terms and definitions, and help you study for tests.

13. **Assemble what you will need.** Pack sharpened pencils, pens, paper clips, and any other items you may need, such as a watch, calculator, or dictionary. Get a good night's sleep, eat a light breakfast, and make sure you set an alarm. You don't want to be frantic and late for a test. Arrive a few minutes early.

Take 3 minutes to create sample test questions for one of your courses:
- Which events, people, or ideas did the instructor stress?
- Was some material covered in the text but not in lectures (or vice versa)?
- What main points could be addressed in essay questions?

What else can you do in 3 minutes?
- Summarize the course thus far onto one note card.
- Ask your instructor what types of questions to expect on the next exam.
- Find out where the learning center is and what kinds of resources it offers.

Take 3

During the Test

The following strategies will help you take a test. See **Peak Progress 8.1** for specific tips on taking online exams.

1. **Read and listen to all instructions.** Many mistakes result from a failure to follow directions correctly. For example, your instructor may require that you use a pen and write on only one side of the paper. Make sure you understand what is expected in each section of the test. If you are unsure, ask your instructor immediately. (See **Figure 8.1** on page 246 on how to take a Scantron test.)

Peak Progress   8.1

Taking Online Exams

Although the preparation may be similar, taking an online exam may involve more coordination than a traditional pencil-and-paper exam.

- Double-check your computer's settings before you start the test, so that you avoid problems.
- Unless the test must be taken at a certain time or specific date, do not wait until the last day to take it. If you have technical difficulties or lose your connection, you may not have time to solve the problem.
- Shut down all other programs not needed during the exam, including e-mail.
- If your test is timed, make sure you can easily see the timer or the computer's clock.
- If allowed, have your text and any other materials nearby and easily accessible. Put key information, dates, or formulas on sticky notes next to the screen.

- Wait until the test is fully loaded before answering questions.
- Set the window size before you start. Resizing later may refresh your screen and cause the test to reload and start over.
- To avoid being accidentally kicked out of the exam, do not click outside the test area or click the back arrow. Only use functions within the testing program to return to previous questions.
- If there is a save option, save often throughout the exam.
- If more than one question is on a page, click "Submit" or the arrow button only after all questions on that page have been answered.
- Click "Submit" only once at the end of the test, and confirm that the test was received.

Figure 8.1
Fill in the Bubbles

You have probably taken a number of Scantron tests (named after the company that distributes them), or "bubble" tests. Using a #2 pencil, you must completely fill in the circles. Fill in only one bubble per line, and completely erase any changes. Be careful not to skip a line, or all the rest of your answers may be wrong. *Would all of the answers in this figure be acceptable?*

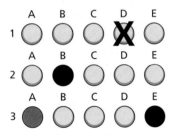

2. **Write down key information.** As soon as you get the test, write your name on it and jot down key words, facts, formulas, dates, ideas, concepts, statistics, and other memory cues in pencil on the back of your paper or in the margins. If you wait until you are reading each question, you may forget important material while under pressure.

3. **Scan the entire test.** Before you start answering questions, you need to
   - Look at the point value for each question and determine the importance of each section. For example, you will want to spend more time on an essay worth 25 points than on a multiple-choice section worth 5.
   - See which questions are easiest and can be answered quickly.
   - Underline or put a star by key names and themes that pop out. These may stimulate your memory for another question.
   - Set a plan and pace yourself based on the amount of time allowed.

4. **Answer objective questions.** Sometimes objective questions contain details you can use for answering essay questions. Don't panic if you don't know an answer right away. Answer the easiest questions, and mark questions you want go back to later.

5. **Answer essay questions.** Answer the easiest subjective or essay questions first, and spend more time on the questions with the highest value. Underline or circle key words or points in the question. If you have time, do a quick outline in pencil, so that your answer is organized. Look for defining words, and make sure you understand what the question is asking. For example, are you being asked to justify, illustrate, compare and contrast, or explain? Write down main ideas and then fill in details, facts, and examples. Be complete, but avoid filler sentences that add nothing.

6. **Answer all remaining questions.** Unless there is a penalty for guessing, answer all questions. Rephrase questions you find difficult. It may help if you change the wording of a sentence. Draw a picture or a diagram, use a different equation, or make a mind map and write the topic and subtopics. Use association to remember items that are related.

7. **Review.** Once you have finished, reread the test carefully and check for mistakes or spelling errors. Stay the entire time, answer extra-credit and bonus questions, fill in details, and make any necessary changes. (See **Peak Progress 8.2** to learn specific strategies for math and science tests.)

After the Test

The test isn't over when you hand it in. Successful test taking includes how you use the results.

1. **Analyze and assess.** When you receive the graded test, analyze the grade and your performance for many things, such as the following:
   - *Confirm your grade.* Confirm that your score was calculated or graded correctly. If you believe there is a mistake in your grade, see your instructor immediately and ask to review it.
   - *Determine common types of mistakes.* Were your mistakes due to carelessness in reading the instructions or lack of preparedness on certain

Special Strategies for Math and Science Tests

1. **Use note cards.** Write formulas, definitions, rules, and theories on note cards and review them often. Write out examples for each theorem.

2. **Write key information.** As soon as you are given the test, jot down theorems and formulas in the margins.

3. **Write the problem in longhand.** Translate into understandable words—for example, for $A = 1/2bh$, "For a triangle, the area is one-half the base times the height."

4. **Make an estimate.** A calculated guess will give you an approximate answer. This helps you when you double-check the answer.

5. **Illustrate the problem.** Draw a picture, diagram, or chart that will help you understand the problem—for example, "The length of a field is 6 feet more than twice its width. If the perimeter of the field is 228 feet, find the dimensions of the field."

   Let l = the length of the field

   Let w = the width of the field

   Then $l = 2w + 6$

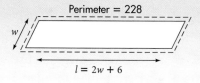

$$w + 2w + 6 + w + 2w + 6 = 228$$

So $6w + 12 = 228$

$(w + 2w + 6 + w + 2w + 6)$

$6w + 12 = 228$

$6w = 216$

$w = 36$

So $l = 2w + 6 = 2(36) + 6 = 78$

Translating: The width of the field is 36 ft. and its length is 78 ft.

Checking: The perimeter is $2w + 2l = 2(36) + 2(78) = 72 + 156 = 228$

6. **Ask yourself questions.** Ask, "What is being asked? What do I already know? What are the givens? What do I need to find out? How does this relate to other concepts? What is the point of the question?"

7. **Show your work.** If allowed, write down the method you used to get to the answer, which will help you retrace your steps if you get stuck. Your instructor may give you partial credit, even if the answer is incorrect. In some cases, you are expected to show your work (and will lose points for not showing complete or accurate work). Make sure you know what your instructor requires.

8. **Do a similar problem.** If you get stuck, try something similar. Which formula worked? How does this formula relate to others?

9. **State answers in the simplest terms.** For example, 4/6 instead should be answered as 2/3.

10. **Pay attention to the sign.** Note if a number is actually a negative number.

11. **Check your work.** Does your answer make sense? Is your work correct and systematic?

12. **Review.** Review your test as soon as you get it back. Where did you make mistakes? Did you read the problems correctly? Did you use the correct formulas? What will you do differently next time?

topics? **Figure 8.2** on page 248 identifies common reasons for incorrect answers on tests. Are there patterns in your mistakes? If so, determine how to correct those patterns.

- *Learn what to do differently next time.* Your test will provide valuable feedback, and you can learn from the experience. Be a detached, curious, receptive observer and view the results as feedback that is essential for improvement. (See **Peak Progress 8.3** on page 248 for a checklist on how to assess your testing performance in order to improve your skills.)

> **"** 'Obvious' is the most dangerous word in mathematics. **"**
>
> ERIC TEMPLE BELL
> *Mathematician, author*

WORDS TO SUCCEED

Figure 8.2

Reasons for Incorrect Test Answers

As you review your test results, check if any of these problems affected your performance. *How can you use this list to prepare for future exams?*

Common errors

- ✓ I did not read and/or follow the directions.
- ✓ I misread or misunderstood the question.
- ✓ I did not demonstrate reasoning ability.
- ✓ I did not demonstrate factual accuracy.
- ✓ I did not demonstrate good organization.
- ✓ My answer was incomplete.
- ✓ My answer lacked clarity.
- ✓ My handwriting was hard to read.
- ✓ I used time ineffectively.
- ✓ I did not prepare enough.
- ✓ I studied the wrong information.
- ✓ I knew the information but couldn't apply it to the questions.
- ✓ I confused facts or concepts.
- ✓ The information was not in my lecture notes.
- ✓ The information was not in the textbook.

66 We learn more by looking for the answer to a question and not finding it than we do from learning the answer itself. 99

LLOYD ALEXANDER
Author

2. **Review with your instructor.** If you honestly don't know why you received the grade you did, ask your instructor to review your answers with you. Approach the meeting with a positive attitude, not a defensive one. Ask for clarification and explain your rationale for answers. Ask for advice on preparing for the next test.

3. **Review the test with your study team.** This will help you see common errors and how others approached answering the questions, which will give you insights into how to study more effectively and answer questions better on the next test.

Remember, a test is feedback on how you are doing, not an evaluation of you as a person. You cannot change unless you understand your mistakes. Assess what you did wrong and what you will do right the next time.

Peak Progress

8.3

Using Test Results

Determine if your study strategy is working and what to do differently next time. Ask yourself the following questions:

1. Did I read the test before I started?
2. What were my strengths? What did I do right?
3. What questions did I miss?
4. Did I miss clues in the test? Did I ask the instructor for clarification?
5. How well did I know the content on which I was being tested?
6. What should I have studied more?
7. Did I anticipate the style and format of the questions?
8. What didn't I expect?
9. Did I have trouble with certain types of questions?
10. Did I test myself with the right questions?
11. Did I handle test anxiety well?
12. Would it have helped if I had studied with others?
13. What changes will I make in studying for the next test?

Taking Different Types of Tests

Objective Tests

TRUE/FALSE TESTS

1. **Read the entire question carefully before answering.** For the question to be true, the entire question must be true. If any part of the statement is false, the entire statement is false.

2. **Pay attention to details.** Read dates, names, and places carefully. Sometimes the numbers in the dates are changed around (1494 instead of 1449) or the wording is changed slightly. Any such changes can change the meaning.

3. **Watch for qualifiers.** Watch for such words as *always, all, never,* and *every.* If you can think of just one exception, then the statement is false. Does the statement over- or understate what you know is true?

4. **Watch for faulty cause and effect.** Two true statements may be connected by a word that implies cause and effect, and this word may make the statement false—for example, "Temperature is measured on the centigrade scale *because* water freezes at zero degrees centigrade."

5. **Always answer every question.** Unless there is a penalty for wrong answers, answer every question. You have a 50 percent chance of being right.

6. **Trust your instincts.** Often, your first impression is correct. Don't change an answer unless you are certain it is wrong. Don't spend time pondering until you have finished the entire test and have time to spare.

MULTIPLE-CHOICE TESTS

1. **Read the question carefully.** Are you being asked for the correct answer or the best choice? Is there more than one answer? Preview the test to see if an answer is included in a later statement or question.

2. **Rephrase the question.** Sometimes it helps to rephrase the question in your own words, which may trigger reading or hearing the initial discussion.

3. **Cover the potential answers.** Cover the answers (called "distractors") as you read the question and see what answer first comes to you. Then look at the answers to see if your answer is one of the choices.

4. **Eliminate choices.** Narrow your choices by reading all of them and eliminating those you know are incorrect, so that you can concentrate on real choices.

5. **Go from easy to difficult.** Go through the test and complete the questions for which you know the answers. Don't spend all your time on a few questions. With a pencil, mark the questions that you are unsure of, but make certain you mark your final answer clearly.

6. **Watch for combinations.** Read the question carefully; don't just choose what appears to be the one correct answer. Some questions offer a combination of choices, such as "all of the above" or "none of the above."

7. **Look at sentence structure.** The grammatical structure of the question should match that of your choice.

Sample Matching Question

Match the following mnemonic devices with their definition:

A. Acronym
B. Acrostic
C. Rap
D. Chunking
E. Method-of-Place
1. grouping information
2. uses rhythm
3. words formed from first letters of other words
4. sentences in which the first letter of each word stands for something
5. memory map

Which are the easiest answers to match up first?

Sample Fill-in-the-Blank Question

The term that describes when it is legal and ethical to use a direct quote from the Internet or another source is _____ _____.

What clues help you determine the answer?

MATCHING TESTS

1. **Read carefully.** Read the question carefully before matching items, and make sure you understand what you are being asked to match.
2. **Eliminate.** Go through and match all the items you are absolutely sure of first. Cross out items as you match them unless the directions mention that an item can be used more than once.
3. **Look for clues.** Should the pair include a person's name, a date, or an event? Is chronological order important? Look for commonalities in sentence structure. Does it make sense?

FILL-IN-THE-BLANK TESTS

1. **Watch for grammatical clues.** If the word before the blank is *an,* the word in the blank generally begins with a vowel. If the word before the blank is *a,* it probably begins with a consonant.
2. **Count the number of blanks.** The number of blanks often indicates the number of words in an answer. Think of key words that were stressed in class.
3. **Watch for the length of the blank.** A longer blank may indicate a longer answer.

OPEN-BOOK TESTS

Students often think open-book tests will be easy, so they don't study or prepare their book. Generally, these tests go beyond basic recall and require critical thinking and analysis. Put markers in your book to indicate important areas. Write formulas, definitions, key words, sample questions, and main points on note cards. Bring along your detailed study sheet. You will need to find information quickly. However, use your own words to summarize—don't copy from your textbook.

Essay Tests

Being prepared is essential when taking an essay test. Make certain you understand concepts and relationships, not just specific facts. (See **Figure 8.3** for a sample essay test.) In addition, use the following strategies to help you take an essay test.

1. **Budget your writing time.** Look over the whole test, noticing which questions are easiest. Allot a certain amount of time for each essay question, and include time for review when you're finished.
2. **Read the question carefully.** Be sure you understand what the question is asking. Respond to key words, such as *explain, classify, define,* and *compare.* Rephrase the question into a main thesis. Always answer what is being asked directly—don't skirt around an issue. If you are asked to compare and contrast, do not describe, or your answer will be incorrect. **Peak Progress 8.4** on page 252 lists key words used in many essay questions.
3. **Create an outline.** Organize your main points in an outline, so that you won't leave out important information. An outline will provide a framework to help

Figure 8.3
Sample Essay Test

When answering an essay question, a detailed outline may also be required, as in this example. *In what situations would a mind map work better to develop your thoughts rather than a formal outline?*

Intro to Economics Quiz   March 16, 2014

Steve Hackett

ESSAY QUESTION: Describe the general circumstances under which economists argue that government intervention in a market economy enhances efficiency.

THESIS STATEMENT: Well-functioning competitive markets are efficient resource allocators, but they can fail in certain circumstances. Government intervention can generate its own inefficiencies, so economists promote the forms of government intervention that enhance efficiency under conditions of market failure.

OUTLINE:

I. Well-functioning competitive markets are efficient.

    A. Firms have an incentive to minimize costs and waste.

    B. Price approximates costs of production.

    C. Effort, quality, and successful innovation are rewarded.

    D. Shortages and surpluses are eliminated by price adjustment.

II. Markets fail to allocate scarce resources efficiently under some circumstances.

    A. Externalities affect other people.

        1. Negative externalities, such as pollution

        2. Positive externalities and collectively consumed goods

    B. Lack of adequate information causes failure.

    C. Firms with market power subvert the competition.

III. Government intervention can create its own inefficiencies.

    A. Rigid, bureaucratic rules can stifle innovative solutions and dilute incentives.

    B. Politically powerful groups can subvert the process.

IV. Efficient intervention policy balances market and government inefficiencies.

ESSAY RESPONSE:

Well-functioning competitive markets allocate resources efficiently in the context of scarcity. They do so in several ways. First, in market systems, firms are profit maximizers and thus have an incentive to minimize their private costs of production. In contrast, those who manage government agencies lack the profit motive and thus the financial incentive to minimize costs. Second, under competitive market conditions, the market price is bid down by rival firms to reflect their unit production costs. Thus, for the last unit sold, the value (price) to the consumer is equal to the cost to produce that unit, meaning that neither too much nor too little is produced. Third, firms and individuals have an incentive to work hard to produce new products and services preferred by consumers because, if successful, these innovators will gain an advantage over their rivals in the market-place. Fourth, competitive markets react to surpluses with lower prices and to shortages with higher prices, which work to resolve these imbalances.

Markets can fail to allocate scarce resources efficiently in several situations. First, profit-maximizing firms have an incentive to emit negative externalities (uncompensated harms generated by market activity that fall on others), such as pollution, when doing so lowers their production costs and is not prevented by law. Individual firms also have an incentive not to provide positive externalities (unpaid-for benefits) that benefit the group, such as police patrol, fire protection, public parks, and roads. A second source of market failure is incomplete information regarding product safety, quality, and workplace safety. A third type of market failure occurs when competition is subverted by a small number of firms that can manipulate prices, such as monopolies and cartels. Government intervention can take various forms, including regulatory constraints, information provision, and direct government provision of goods and services.

Government intervention may also be subject to inefficiencies. Examples include rigid regulations that stifle the incentive for innovation, onerous compliance costs imposed on firms, political subversion of the regulatory process by powerful interest groups, and lack of cost-minimizing incentives on the part of government agencies. Thus, efficient government intervention can be said to occur when markets fail in a substantial way and when the particular intervention policy generates inefficiencies that do not exceed those associated with the market failure.

Peak Progress

Important Words in Essay Questions

Analyze	Explain the key points, parts, or process and examine each part.	**Enumerate**	Present the items in a numbered list or an outline.
Apply	Show the concept or function in a specific context.	**Evaluate**	Carefully appraise the problem, citing authorities.
Compare	Show similarities between concepts, objects, or events.	**Explain**	Make an idea or a concept clear, or give a reason for an event.
Contrast	Show differences between concepts, objects, or events.	**Identify**	Label or explain.
Critique	Present your view or evaluation and give supporting evidence.	**Illustrate**	Clarify by presenting examples.
		Interpret	Explain the meaning of a concept or problem.
Define	Give concise, clear meanings and definitions.	**Justify**	Give reasons for conclusions or argue in support of a position.
Demonstrate	Show function (how something works); show understanding physically or through words.	**List**	Enumerate or write a list of points, one by one.
Describe	Present major characteristics or a detailed account.	**Outline**	Organize main points and supporting points logically.
Differentiate	Distinguish between two or more concepts or characteristics.	**Prove**	Give factual evidence and logical reasons for why something is true.
Discuss	Give a general presentation of the issue with examples or details to support main points.	**Summarize**	Present core ideas in a brief review that includes conclusions.

you remember dates, concepts, names, places, and supporting material. Use **Personal Evaluation Notebook 8.2** to practice outlining key words and topics.

4. **Focus on main points.** Your opening sentence should state your thesis, followed by supporting information.

5. **Write concisely and correctly.** Get directly to the point, and use short, clear sentences. Remember that your instructor (or even teaching assistants) may be grading a pile of tests, so get to the point and avoid filler sentences.

6. **Use key terms and phrases.** Your instructor may be looking for very specific information in your answer, including terms, phrases, events, or people. Make sure you include that information—don't just assume the instructor knows to whom or what you are referring.

7. **Answer completely.** Reread the question and be sure you answered it fully, including supporting documentation. Did you cover the main points thoroughly and logically?

8. **Count your words.** Double check that your response meets any required length criteria. Note if the essay must meet a minimum or maximum word count, number of paragraphs, or pages.

9. **Write neatly.** Appearance and legibility matter. Use an erasable pen. Use wide margins and don't crowd your words. Write on one side of the paper only. Leave space between answers, so that you can add to an answer if time permits.

Personal Evaluation Notebook

Essay Test Preparation

Pretend you are taking an essay test on a personal topic—your life history. Your instructor has written the following essay question on the board:

Write a brief essay on your progress through life so far, covering the highs and lows, major triumphs, and challenges.

1. Before you begin writing, remind yourself of the topics you want to cover in this essay. List key words, phrases, events, and dates you would jot in the margin of your paper on the lines provided.

   _____

   _____

   _____

   _____

   _____

2. In the following space, create a mind map or an outline of the events or topics you would cover in your essay.

10. **Use all the available time.** Don't hurry. Pace yourself and use all the available time for review, revisions, reflection, additions, and corrections. Proofread carefully. Answer all questions unless otherwise directed.

Last-Minute Study Tips

Cramming is not effective if you haven't studied or attended classes. But the following activities will help you make the most of the last hours and minutes before a test.

Ashish failed his midterm. He thought he had studied enough before the test, but he quickly realized he should have paid more attention to the online readings. His mind went blank when he tried to formulate an answer to the essay question that was worth 50 percent of the total exam.

- What questions could he have asked his instructor before the test to clarify expectations?
- What could Ashish have done as he started the essay section to help him formulate his thoughts?
- How can he use the test results to improve for the final exam?

1. **Focus on a few points.** Instead of trying to cram everything into a short study session, decide what are the most important points or formulas, key words, definitions, and dates. Preview each chapter quickly; read the chapter objectives or key concepts and the end-of-chapter summary.

2. **Intend to be positive.** Don't panic or waste precious time being negative. State your intention of being receptive and open, gaining an overview of the material, and learning a few supporting points.

3. **Review your note cards.** The physical (and visual) act of reading and flipping note cards will help you review key information.

4. **Review your notes.** Look for words or topics you have highlighted or written on the side. Reread any summaries or mind maps you created after class.

5. **Affirm your memory.** The mind is capable of learning and memorizing material in a short time if you focus and apply it. Look for opportunities to connect information.

6. **Do *not* pop pills.** Adderall is a drug often prescribed to people with ADHD who have trouble focusing. Too many students are illegally taking this highly addictive drug, oftentimes before tests, believing it will help them remember information. There are too many health risks, including serious side effects, for this to even be considered a "smart drug" as it is often called. Rely on your own motivation, strength of character, and test preparation—not a bottle—to excel.

Overcome Obstacles

Some students see tests and performance assessments as huge mountains—one slip, and they tumble down the slope. Even capable students find that certain tests undermine their confidence. Just the thought of taking a math or science test causes anxiety in some people and sends others into a state of panic. A peak performer learns to manage anxiety and knows that being prepared is the road to test-taking success.

Test Anxiety

Test anxiety is a learned response to stress. The symptoms include nervousness, upset stomach, sweaty palms, and forgetfulness. Being prepared is the best way to reduce anxiety. As we discussed earlier in this chapter, you will be prepared if you have attended every class; previewed chapters; reviewed your notes; and written, summarized, and studied the material each day. Studying with others is a great way to rehearse test questions and learn through group interaction.

The attitude you bring to a test affects your performance. Approach tests with a positive attitude. Tests let you practice facing fear and transforming it into positive energy. Tests are chances to show what you have mastered. Following are more suggestions that might help:

1. **Dispute negative thoughts and conversations.** Some people have negative or faulty assumptions about their abilities, especially in courses such as math and science, and may think, "I just don't have a logical mind." Replace negative

self-talk with affirmations, such as "I am well prepared and will do well on this test" or "I can excel in this subject." Talk to yourself in encouraging ways. Practice being your own best friend! Also, avoid negative conversations that make you feel anxious—for example, if someone mentions how long he or she studied.

2. **Rehearse.** Athletes, actors, musicians, and dancers practice for hours. When they perform, their anxiety is channeled into focused energy. If you practice taking sample tests with your study team, you should be more confident during the actual test.

3. **Get regular exercise.** Aerobic exercise and yoga reduce stress and tension and promote deeper, more restful sleep. Build regular exercise into your life, and work out the day before a test, if possible.

4. **Eat breakfast.** Eat a light, balanced breakfast that includes protein, such as cheese or yogurt. Keep a piece of fruit or nuts and bottled water in your backpack for energy. Limit your caffeine intake; too much can make you more nervous or agitated.

5. **Visualize success.** See yourself taking the test and doing well. Imagine being calm and focused. Before getting out of bed, relax, breathe deeply, and visualize your day unfolding in a positive way.

6. **Stay calm.** Make your test day peaceful by assembling your books, supplies, pens, and keys the night before. Review your note cards just before you go to sleep, repeat a few affirmations, and get a good night's rest. Set an alarm, so that you'll be awake in plenty of time. Last-minute, frantic cramming creates a hectic climate and increases anxiety. To alleviate stress, practice relaxation techniques (see Chapter 11).

7. **Get to class early.** Get to class early enough that you are not rushed and can use the time before the test to take a few deep breaths and review your note cards. While waiting for the start of class, the instructor will sometimes answer questions or explain material to students who arrived early.

8. **Focus.** When your attention wanders, bring it gently back. Stay in the present moment by focusing on the task at hand. Concentrate on answering the questions, and you won't have room in your mind for worry.

9. **Keep a sense of perspective.** Don't exaggerate the importance of tests. Tests do not measure self-esteem, personal qualities, character, or ability to contribute to society. Even if the worst happens and you do poorly on one test, it is not the end of your college career. You can meet with the instructor to discuss options and possibly do extra work, retake the test, or retake the class, if necessary.

10. **Get help.** If you are experiencing severe anxiety that prevents you from taking tests or performing well, seek professional help from the learning center or see a counselor at your school. Services often include support groups, relaxation training, and other techniques for reducing anxiety. Taking tests and being evaluated are essential parts of school and work, so it's important to get your fears under control. (See **Peak Progress 8.5** on preparing for a performance appraisal.)

● **Keeping Calm**
Test anxiety can cause some people to feel overwhelmed and even panicked. *How can you reduce the feeling of anxiety before you take a test?*

Peak Progress

Preparing for a Performance Appraisal

If you are employed, at some time you will probably receive a performance appraisal. This can be a valuable tool for informing you about how your employer perceives the quality of your work, your work ethic, and your future opportunities. It also allows you to ask similar questions of your manager or reviewer. Often, employees are asked to evaluate their own performance, which is similar to answering an essay question. You want to address the question fully and provide supporting, factual evidence (and often suggest outcomes, such as new goals and challenges).

The following questions will help you focus on getting the most out of your performance appraisal.

- Review your job description, including the duties you perform. What is expected of you? What additional duties do you perform that are not listed?
- How do you view your job and the working climate?
- List your goals and objectives and the results achieved.
- What documentation demonstrates your results and achievements?
- What areas do you see as opportunities for improvement?

- What are your strengths, and how can you maximize them?
- What are your advancement possibilities?
- What additional training would be helpful for you?
- What new skills could assist in your advancement?
- How can you increase your problem-solving skills?
- How can you make more creative and sound decisions?
- What can you do to prepare yourself for stressful projects and deadlines?
- How have you specifically contributed to the company's profits?
- What relationships could you develop to help you achieve results?
- Do you work well with other people?
- What project would be rewarding and challenging this year?
- What resources do you need to complete this project?
- Do you have open and effective communication with your supervisor and co-workers?
- How does your assessment of your work compare with your supervisor's assessment?

Reflect and use critical thinking to describe your test anxiety experiences in **Personal Evaluation Notebook 8.3**. **Peak Progress 8.6** on page 259 explores how you can apply the Adult Learning Cycle to improve your test-taking skills and reduce anxiety.

Cheating

A central theme of this book is that character matters. Honesty during test taking demonstrates to your instructor, your classmates, and, most important, yourself that you are trustworthy—a person of integrity. Cheating includes

- Looking at someone's paper during a test
- Passing or texting answers back and forth
- Getting notes from someone who has just taken the same test
- Stealing tests from an office
- Using electronic devices (such as a calculator) when not allowed
- Taking or receiving pictures of test questions via cell phone
- Having someone else complete online work for you

Personal Evaluation Notebook

Test Anxiety

Read through each statement and reflect on past testing experiences. You may wish to consider all testing experiences or focus on particular subjects (history, math, science, etc.) one at a time. Indicate how often each statement describes you by choosing a number from 1 to 5.

Never	Rarely	Sometimes	Often	Always
1	2	3	4	5

_____ I have visible signs of nervousness, such as sweaty palms and shaky hands, right before a test.

_____ I have butterflies in my stomach before a test.

_____ I feel nauseated before a test.

_____ I read through the test and feel that I do not know any of the answers.

_____ I panic before and during a test.

_____ My mind goes blank during a test.

_____ After I leave a testing situation, I remember the information that escaped my mind during the test.

_____ I have trouble sleeping the night before a test.

_____ I make mistakes on easy questions or put answers in the wrong places.

_____ I have trouble choosing answers.

Add together your scores for each statement to find your total score. Totals will range from 10 to 50.

- **10–19 points:** You do not suffer from test anxiety. If your score was extremely low (close to 10), a little more anxiety may be healthy to keep you focused and get your blood flowing during exams.

- **20–35 points:** Although you exhibit some of the characteristics of test anxiety, the level of stress and tension you're experiencing is probably healthy.

- **Over 35 points:** You are experiencing an unhealthy level of test anxiety. Evaluate the reason(s) for the distress and determine strategies to help you handle the anxiety.

Source: From NIST. *Developing Textbook Thinking*, 5E. © 2002 Wadsworth, a part of Cengage Learning, Inc. Reproduced by permission. www.cengage.com/permissions

1. In what classes do you experience the most anxiety? Why?

   _____

   _____

2. What physical symptoms do you most often experience? (Examples include headaches, nausea, extreme body temperature changes, excessive sweating, shortness of breath, light-headedness or fainting, rapid heartbeat, and dry mouth.)

   _____

   _____

(continued)

Test Anxiety *(concluded)*

3. Which emotional symptoms do you most often experience? (Examples include excessive feelings of fear, disappointment, anger, depression, helplessness, or uncontrollable crying or laughing.)

_____

_____

4. Do you have different feelings about nonacademic tests, such as a driving test or a medical test, than academic tests, such as quizzes and exams? If so, why?

_____

_____

Even if you haven't fully prepared for an exam, there is no excuse for cheating. Cheating only hurts you because it

● **Cheating Only Hurts You**

There is never an excuse to cheat. *If this student is caught cheating, what are some of the repercussions he could face?*

- **Violates your integrity.** You begin to see yourself as a person without integrity; if you compromise your integrity once, you're more likely to do it again.
- **Erodes confidence.** Cheating weighs on your conscience and sends you the message that you don't have what it takes to succeed. Your confidence and self-esteem suffer.
- **Creates academic problems.** Advanced courses depend on knowledge from earlier courses, so cheating only creates future academic problems. You are paying a lot of money not to learn essential information.
- **Increases stress.** You have enough stress in your life without adding the intense pressure of worrying about being caught.
- **Brings high risks.** Possible consequences of cheating and plagiarism include failing the class, being suspended for the semester, and even being expelled from school permanently. Cheating can mess up your life. It is humiliating, stressful, and completely avoidable.

There is never a legitimate reason to cheat. Instead, be prepared, use the resources available to help you succeed, and practice the strategies offered in this book to become a peak performer.

Peak Progress

Applying the Adult Learning Cycle to Improving Your Test-Taking Skills and Reducing Test Anxiety

1. **RELATE. Why do I want to learn this?** I need to reduce my test anxiety and want to do better on tests. Knowing how to control anxiety will help me when taking tests and in other performance situations. Do I already apply specific test-taking strategies? What are some of my bad habits, such as last-minute cramming, which I should change?

2. **OBSERVE. How does this work?** Who does well on tests, and does that person seem confident when taking tests? What strategies can I learn from that person? Who does poorly on tests or seems full of anxiety? Can I determine what that person is doing wrong? I can learn from those mistakes. I'll try new strategies for test taking and observe how I'm improving.

3. **REFLECT. What does this mean?** What strategies are working for me? Have I broken any bad habits, and am I more confident going into tests? Has my performance improved?

4. **DO. What can I do with this?** I will map out a plan before each major test, determining what I need to accomplish in order to be prepared and confident. I won't wait until the last minute to prepare. Each day, I can practice reducing my anxiety in many stressful situations.

5. **TEACH. Whom can I share this with?** I'll talk with others and share what's working for me. Talking through my effective strategies reinforces their purpose.

Now return to Stage 1 and think about how it feels to learn this valuable new skill. Remember to congratulate and reward yourself when you achieve positive results.

TAKING CHARGE

Summary

In this chapter, I learned to

- **Prepare for test taking.** The time before a test is critical. I must prepare early, starting on the first day of class. I keep up with the daily reading and ask questions in class and while I read. I review early and often, previewing the chapter before class and reviewing the materials after class. I save and review all tests, exercises, and notes and review them weekly. I rehearse by taking a pretest, and I predict questions by reviewing the text's chapter objectives and summaries. I summarize the chapter in my own words (in writing or out loud), double-checking that I've covered key points. I recite my summary to my study team and listen to theirs. We compare notes and test each other.

- **Take a test effectively.** Arriving early helps me be calm and focused on doing well. I get organized by reviewing key concepts and facts. I write neatly and get to the point with short, clear responses. I read all the instructions, scanning the entire test briefly and writing formulas and notes in the margins. I pace myself by answering the easiest questions first, and I rephrase difficult questions and look for associations to remember items. At the end, I review to make certain I've answered what was asked and check for mistakes or spelling errors. I stay the entire time that is available.

- **Follow up a test.** I will analyze and assess how I did on the test. Did I prepare enough? Did I anticipate questions? What can I do differently for the next test? I'll use creative problem solving to explore ways to do better on future tests.

- **Be successful on different kinds of tests.** Objective tests include true/false, multiple-choice, matching, fill-in-the-blank, and open-book. I must read the question carefully, watch for clues, and look at sentence structure. Essay tests focus on my understanding of concepts and relationships. I outline my response, organize and focus on the main points, and take my time to deliver a thorough, neat, well-thought-out answer.

- **Use last-minute study tips.** I know it's not smart to wait until the last minute, but a few important things I can do include focusing on a few key points and key words, reviewing note cards, looking for connections to memorize, and not wasting time by panicking.

- **Overcome test anxiety.** A positive attitude alleviates anxiety before and during a test. I should prepare as much as possible, avoid last-minute cramming, practice taking a sample test, get to class early, stay calm, listen carefully to instructions, preview the whole test, and jot down notes.

- **Practice honesty and integrity when taking tests.** I know that cheating on exams hurts me by lowering my self-esteem and others' opinions of me. Cheating also has long-term repercussions, including possible expulsion from school. There is never an excuse for cheating.

Performance Strategies

Following are the top 10 strategies for successful test taking:

- Prepare early.
- Clarify expectations.
- Observe and question.
- Review.
- Apply memory techniques.
- Create sample tests.
- Use your study team.
- Answer easier questions first.
- Spend more time on questions worth the most points.
- Analyze your test results to learn how to improve.

Tech for Success

Take advantage of the text's website at **www.mhhe.com/ferrett9e** for additional study aids, useful forms, and convenient and applicable resources.

- **Online tutors.** Various organizations provide online tutors and live tutorial services. Your school or public library may also offer access to this kind of service. Often, these are paid services and may be worth the fee. However, you may be able to get limited assistance for free through a professional organization or related site.

Ask your librarian for advice and explain how much help you think you need and in what content areas.

- **Textbook accompaniments.** Many of your textbooks have accompanying websites that provide study materials, such as online study guides, animated flash cards, and possible essay questions. Often, this material is free when you purchase a new text. Take advantage of these resources to test your understanding of the information prior to taking the real test.

Study Team Notes

Answers to Questions on Pages 249 and 250
True/false: False
Multiple-choice: C
Matching: A/3; B/4; C/2; D/1; E/5
Fill-in-the-Blank: fair use

Career *in* focus

Tests in the Workplace

Carlos Fuentes is a physical therapist. A physical therapist works closely with physicians to help patients restore function and improve mobility after an injury or illness. Their work often relieves pain and prevents or limits physical disabilities.

When working with new patients, Carlos first asks questions and examines the patients' medical records, then performs tests to measure such items as strength, range of motion, balance and coordination, muscle performance, and motor function. After assessing a patient's abilities and needs, Carlos implements a treatment plan, which may include exercise, traction, massage, electrical stimulation, and hot packs or cold compresses. As treatment continues, Carlos documents the patient's progress and modifies the treatment plan.

Carlos is self-motivated and works independently. He has a strong interest in physiology and sports, and he enjoys working with people. He likes a job that keeps him active and on his feet. Carlos spends much of his day helping patients become mobile. He often demonstrates an exercise while teaching how to do it correctly. His job sometimes requires him to move heavy equipment or lift patients. Because Carlos is pursuing a master's degree in physical therapy, he works only 3 days a week.

Although his job does not require him to take tests, Carlos does undergo an annual performance appraisal with his supervisor. After 8 years of service, Carlos is familiar with the types of questions his supervisor might ask and keeps those in mind as he does his job throughout the year.

Carlos Fuentes
PHYSICAL THERAPIST

Related Majors: Physical Therapy, Athletic Training, Biology

CRITICAL THINKING How might understanding test-taking skills help Carlos work more effectively with his patients? How would test-taking skills help him prepare more effectively for performance appraisals?

Peak Performer

PROFILE

Ellen Ochoa

When astronaut Ellen Ochoa was growing up in La Mesa, California, in the 1960s and early 1970s, it was an era of space exploration firsts: the first walk in space, the first man on the moon, the first space station. Even so, it would have been difficult for her to imagine that one day she would be the first Hispanic woman in space, because women were excluded from becoming astronauts.

By the time Ochoa entered graduate school in the 1980s, however, the sky was the limit. Having studied physics at San Diego State University, she attended Stanford and earned a master's of science degree and a doctorate in electrical engineering. In 1985, she and 2,000 other potential astronauts applied for admission to the National Aeronautics and Space Administration (NASA) space program. Five years later, Ochoa, 18 men, and 5 other women made the cut. The training program at the Johnson Space Center in Houston, Texas, is a rigorous mix of brain and brawn. Ochoa tackled subjects such as geology, oceanography, meteorology, astronomy, aerodynamics, and medicine. In 1991, Ochoa officially became an astronaut and was designated a mission specialist. On her first mission in 1993, Ochoa carried a pin that read "Science Is Women's Work."

From 1993 to 2002, Ochoa logged in four space shuttle missions. Her first and second missions focused on studying the sun and its impact on the earth's atmosphere. Her third mission involved the first docking of the shuttle *Discovery* on the International Space Station. Her latest flight experience was the first time crewmembers used the robotic arm to move during spacewalks.

Ochoa enjoys talking to young people about her experiences. Aware of her influence as a woman and a Hispanic, her message is that "education is what allows you to stand out"—and become a peak performer.

PERFORMANCE THINKING Ochoa had to excel in many difficult academic courses in order to realize her dream of becoming an astronaut. What are some important personal characteristics that helped her reach the top? What are some specific testing strategies she may have used to get through her coursework, as well as to prove she had the "right stuff"?

CHECK IT OUT Ochoa is among a number of space pioneers profiled by NASA at **www.nasa.gov**. This site includes a wealth of media downloads, news articles, and activities for young and old space adventurers. Also visit the "Careers@NASA" section, which describes the types of internships, cooperative programs, and positions available. According to the first female astronaut in space, Sally Ride, the "most important steps" she followed to becoming an astronaut started with studying math and science in school.

Starting Today

At least one strategy I learned in this chapter that I plan to try right away is

_____

_____

_____

What changes must I make in order for this strategy to be most effective?

_____

_____

_____

Review Questions

Based on what you have learned in this chapter, write your answers to the following questions:

1. Describe five strategies for preparing for a test.

_____

_____

_____

2. Why is it important to pace yourself while taking a test?

_____

_____

3. What should you do after taking a test?

_____

_____

4. Describe three strategies for taking math and science tests.

_____

_____

5. Describe three ways in which cheating hurts you.

_____

_____

To test your understanding of the chapter's concepts, complete the chapter quiz at **www.mhhe.com/ferrett9e.**

Coping with Anxiety

In the Classroom

Sharon Martin is a bright, hardworking student. She studies long hours, attends all her classes, and participates in class discussions. Sharon is very creative and especially enjoys her typography course. When taking tests, however, she panics. She stays up late, cramming; tells herself she might fail; and gets headaches and stomach pains. Her mind goes blank when she takes the test, and she has trouble organizing her thoughts. Sharon could get much better grades and enjoy school more if she reduced her stress and applied some test-taking strategies.

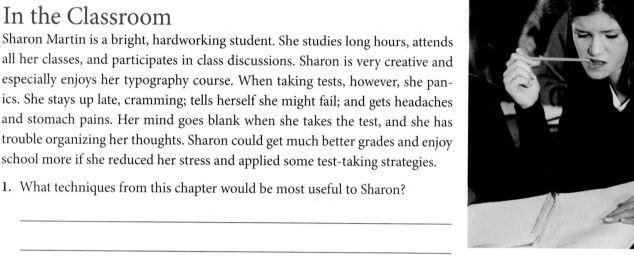

1. What techniques from this chapter would be most useful to Sharon?

   _____

   _____

   _____

2. What one habit could she adopt that would empower her to be more successful?

   _____

   _____

   _____

In the Workplace

Sharon now works as a graphic designer for a large company. She likes having control over her work and is an excellent employee. She is dedicated, competent, and willing to learn new skills. Her job involves great pressure to meet deadlines, learn new techniques, and compete with other firms. She handles these responsibilities well unless she is being evaluated. Despite her proficiency, Sharon panics before performance appraisals. She feels pressure to perform perfectly and has trouble accepting criticism or even advice.

3. What strategies in this chapter would be most helpful to Sharon?

   _____

   _____

   _____

4. What would you suggest she do to control her performance anxiety?

   _____

   _____

   _____

Applying the ABC Method of Self-Management

In the Journal Entry on page 241, you were asked to describe a time when you did well in a performance, sporting event, or test. Write about that, and indicate the factors that helped you be calm, confident, and focused.

_____

_____

_____

_____

Now consider a situation in which your mind went blank or you suffered anxiety. Apply the ABC Method to visualize a result in which you are again calm, confident, and focused.

A = Actual event:

_____

_____

_____

B = Beliefs:

_____

_____

_____

C = Challenge:

_____

_____

_____

Practice deep breathing with your eyes closed for just 1 minute. See yourself calm, centered, and relaxed as you take a test or give a performance. See yourself recalling information easily. You feel confident because you have learned to control your anxiety. You are well prepared and know how to take tests.

PRACTICE SELF-MANAGEMENT

For more examples of learning how to manage difficult situations, see the "Self-Management Workbook" section of the Online Learning Center website at **www.mhhe.com/ferrett9e.**

Exam Schedule

Fill in the following chart to remind you of your exams as they occur throughout the semester or term.

Course	Date	Time	Room	Type of Exam
Student Success 101	November 7	2:15 p.m.	1012A	Essay

REVIEW AND APPLICATIONS | CHAPTER 8

Preparing for Tests and Exams

Before you take a quiz, a test, or an exam, fill in this form to help you plan your study strategy. Certain items will be more applicable, depending on the type of test.

Course _____

Date of test _____ Test number (if any) _____

- Pretest(s)   Date given _____   Results _____

                 Date given _____   Results _____

                 Date given _____   Results _____

- Present grade in course_____
- Met with instructor   Yes _____   No _____   Date(s) of meeting(s) _____
- Study team members   Date(s) of meeting(s) _____

   Name _____   Phone /e-mail _____

   Name _____   Phone /e-mail _____

   Name _____   Phone /e-mail _____

   Name _____   Phone /e-mail _____

- Expected test format (circle; there can be more than one test format)

   Essay   True/false   Multiple-choice   Fill-in-the-blank

   Other _____

- Importance (circle one)

   Quiz   Midterm   Final exam   Other

- Chapters covered in the test _____

   Date for chapter review _____

- Chapter notes (use additional paper)

   _____

   _____

   _____

- Date for review of chapter notes _____
- Note cards   Yes _____   No _____   Date note cards reviewed _____
- List of key words

Word _____ Meaning _____

Word _____ Meaning _____

Word _____ Meaning _____

Word _____ Meaning _____

(continued)

- Possible essay questions

1. Question _____

   Thesis statement _____

   Outline _____

      I. _____

        A. _____

        B. _____

        C. _____

        D. _____

      II. _____

        A. _____

        B. _____

        C. _____

        D. _____

   - Main points

     _____

     _____

   - Examples

     _____

     _____

2. Question _____

   Thesis statement _____

   Outline _____

      I. _____

        A. _____

        B. _____

        C. _____

        D. _____

      II. _____

        A. _____

        B. _____

        C. _____

        D. _____

   - Main points

     _____

     _____

   - Examples

     _____

     _____

REVIEW AND APPLICATIONS | CHAPTER 8

Assessing Your Skills and Competencies

The following are typical qualities and competencies that are included in many performance appraisals.

- Communication skills (writing, speaking, reading)
- Integrity
- Willingness to learn
- Decision-making skills

- Delegation
- Planning
- Organizational skills
- Positive attitude
- Ability to accept change

- Working with others
- Quality of work
- Quantity of work
- Personal growth and development
- Use of technology

On the following lines, describe how you currently demonstrate each of the listed skills and competencies to an employer. Consider how you can improve. Add this page to your Career Development Portfolio.

1. How do you demonstrate the listed skills?

_____

_____

_____

_____

_____

_____

_____

_____

_____

2. How can you improve?

_____

_____

_____

_____

_____

_____

_____

_____

_____

_____

REVIEW AND APPLICATIONS | CHAPTER 8

Express Yourself in Writing and Speech

LEARNING OUTCOMES

In this chapter, you will learn to

9.1 Explain the five-step writing process for developing effective papers and speeches

9.2 Research information through the library and online

9.3 Use strategies for giving effective presentations

9.4 Overcome speech anxiety

SELF-MANAGEMENT

"I put off taking the required public speaking class because I hate getting up in front of people. My mind goes blank, I get butterflies, and my palms sweat. How can I decrease stage fright and be more confident about speaking in public?"

Have you ever had a similar experience? Do you feel anxious and worried when you have to make a presentation or give a speech? Do you suffer physical symptoms, such as sweaty palms, upset stomach, headaches, or an inability to sleep or concentrate, even days before the event? In this chapter, you will learn how to communicate effectively and develop public speaking skills.

JOURNAL ENTRY In **Worksheet 9.1** on page 298, describe a time when you did well on a speaking assignment or leading a discussion. What factors helped you remain calm and confident?

Famed sportswriter Red Smith once commented, "Writing is very easy. All you do is sit in front of a typewriter keyboard until little drops of blood appear on your forehead." For some people, few things in life cause as much anxiety as writing research papers and public speaking. Just the thought of speaking in front of a group can produce feelings of sheer terror. In fact, research indicates that public speaking is the greatest fear for most people, outranking even fear of death. For many students, writing not only produces feelings of doubt but also demands their focused attention, intense thinking, and detailed research. You can't avoid writing or speaking in school or at work, but you can learn strategies that will make them easier and more effective.

The Importance of Writing and Speaking

The ability to communicate clearly, both orally and in writing, is the most important skill you will ever acquire. Peter Drucker, noted management expert and author, remarked, "Colleges teach the one thing that is perhaps most valuable for the future employee to know. But very few students bother to learn it. This one basic skill is the ability to organize and express ideas in writing and speaking."

You may be asked to do research on new ideas, products, procedures, and programs and compile the results in a report. You will most likely write business correspondence. You may give formal speeches before a large group, preside at meetings, or present ideas to a project team. You will be expected to present written and spoken ideas in a clear, concise, and organized manner. Writing papers and preparing speeches in school give you a chance to show initiative, use judgment, apply and interpret information, research resources, organize ideas, and polish your style. Public speaking skills also help you inform and persuade others. Good writers and speakers are not born, and there is no secret to their success. Like other skills, speaking and writing can be learned with practice and effort.

The Writing Process

This chapter will give you strategies for handling every step of the paper-writing and speech-giving process, from choosing a topic to turning in the paper or delivering the speech. Keep these five basic steps in mind as you develop your paper or speech: (1) prepare; (2) organize; (3) write; (4) edit; (5) review.

Prepare

Whether you are writing a paper or a speech, preparation includes several tasks:

1. **Set a schedule.** Estimate how long each step will take, and leave plenty of time for proofing. You may think that the bulk of your time will be spent writing your first draft (step 3). However, you should allot about half your time to Steps 1, 2 and 3 and the other half to Steps 4 and 5. To develop a schedule,

❝ The pages are still blank, but there is a miraculous feeling of the words being there, written in invisible ink and clamoring to become visible. **❞**

VLADIMIR NABOKOV
Author

Term Paper for Criminal Justice 101, Due April 3	
Final Check. Print.	April 2
Edit, revise, and polish.	March 29 (Put away for one or two days)
Complete bibliography.	March 28
Revise.	March 26
Edit, review, revise.	March 24 (Confer with instructor)
Final draft completed.	March 22 (Proof and review)
Complete second draft.	March 20
Add, delete, and rearrange information.	March 17
First draft completed.	March 15 (Share with writing group)
Write conclusion.	March 12
Continue research and flesh out main ideas.	February 16
Write introduction.	February 10
Organize and outline.	February 3
Gather information and compile bibliography and notes.	January 29
Narrow topic and write thesis statement.	January 23
Do preliminary reading.	January 20
Choose a topic.	January 16
Brainstorm ideas.	January 15
Clarify expectations and determine purpose.	January 14

Figure 9.1
Sample Schedule

This schedule for preparing a term paper starts where the paper is finished. *Why does this schedule begin at the due date of the term paper?*

consider working backward from the due date, allowing yourself ample time for each step. See **Figure 9.1** for an example.

2. **Choose a general topic.** Choose a topic that meets your instructor's requirements, interests you, and is narrow enough to handle in the time available. Talk with your instructor about any questions you have concerning expectations for the topic, length, format and style, purpose, and method of citation. Use the tips in **Peak Progress 9.1** on page 274 to help you come up with a topic.

3. **Determine your purpose.** Do you want your reader or listener to think, feel, or act differently or be called to action? Is your purpose to entertain, inform, explain, persuade, gain or maintain goodwill, gain respect and trust, or gather information?

4. **Do preliminary reading and research.** Gather general information by reviewing reference materials, such as articles or an encyclopedia. Check the list of related references at the end of reference books and articles. Your

Peak Progress

How to Generate Topic Ideas

- *Brainstorm.* Brainstorming is generating as many ideas as possible without evaluating their merit. You can brainstorm ideas alone, but the process works well in small groups. Your goal is to list as many creative ideas as you can in the allotted time without defending or judging ideas. Because ideas build on each other, the more ideas the better. Within 10 minutes, you can often generate a sizable list of potential topics.

- *Go to the library.* Look in the *Readers' Guide to Periodical Literature* for possible ideas. Look through newspapers, magazines, and new books.

- *Search online.* Do a number of key word searches to see what topics pop up.

- *Keep a file.* Collect articles, quotes, and a list of topics you find interesting. Listen to good speeches and collect stories or ideas from current newspapers that you could research and write about from a different perspective. Think of possible topics as you read, watch television and movies, and talk with friends. What topics are in the news? What are people talking about?

- *Complete a sentence.* Brainstorm endings to open-ended sentences such as these:

  The world would be better if _____
  Too many people _____
  In the future _____
  A major problem today is _____
  The best thing about _____
  What I enjoy most is _____
  I learned that _____
  It always makes me laugh when _____
  If I had unlimited funds, I would buy _____
  I get through a tough day by _____

- *Free write.* For one or more potential topics, start jotting down as many related items as you can as fast as you can. Include examples, descriptions, and key events. Sometimes the original topic leads to a better topic.

- *Mind map.* For a potential topic, sketch a mind map (described in Chapters 5 and 6). Include supporting points and examples.

---

initial research is intended to give you an overview of the subject and key issues. Later, you will want to look at specific facts and data. Develop a list of questions that can lead to new directions and additional research:

- What do I already know about the topic? What do I want to know?
- What questions do I want to explore? What interests me most?
- What is the point I want to research?

5. **Narrow your topic.** After you have finished your preliminary reading, you can focus on a specific topic. For example, instead of "health problems in America," narrow the subject to "cigarette smoking among teenage girls" or "should cigarette advertising be banned?"

6. **Write a thesis statement.** The thesis is the main point, or central idea, of a paper. In one sentence, your thesis should describe your topic and what you want to convey about it. A good thesis statement is unified and clear—for example, "Smoking among teenage girls is rising due to influences by peers and advertising that glamorizes smoking." Remember, you can always revise your thesis statement as you do more research.

7. **Take notes.** Determine the most convenient way to record support, such as quotations, ideas, reports, and statistics that clarify your research topic. An "old school" way is to use 3 × 5 notecards, writing the topic at the top and one

idea per card so that you can organize your ideas easily. (This method may be effective for kinesthetic learners or if you are unsure of your overall outline or where your research may lead you.) You can also keep your research documented in a notebook or on computer or tablet. (Having a digital file is probably best to avoid misplacing your work.) No matter which method of organization works best, you will need exact information for your final bibliography or footnotes (discussed in more detail later); thus, the more complete you can be in your initial research, the less backtracking you will need to do to plug in holes. Record the following information in your research notes (examples are provided here):

- **Topic:** Indicate what this source supports, which can be general at this point.
  Example: Food addictions: Caffeinated drinks

- **Author's full name:** Include all authors and the order they are listed. If it is an image, include the photographer or right's owner.
  Example: Mayo Clinic Staff (no individuals listed)

- **Title of article, book, or report:** Include any subtitles as well.
  Example: Caffeine content for coffee, tea, soda and more

- **Publisher:** Include the main source for the material, such as the publishing company, journal, news service, or website. Copy the direct link to the article if it's from an online source and the date you accessed it. Also include any original research sources cited in the article.
  Example: Mayo Clinic website (Nutrition and Healthy Eating section) www.mayoclinic.com/health/caffeine/AN01211; retrieved on June 19, 2013. Original sources: Adapted from Journal of Food Science, 2010; American Academy of Pediatrics, 2011; USDA National Nutrient Database for Standard Reference, Release 23, 2010; Consumer Reports, 2011; Mayo Clinic Proceedings, 2010.

- **Summary:** In your own words, summarize the point of the source.
  Example: The amount of caffeine in everyday drinks varies widely. One popular energy drink has about 10 times the caffeine content as other energy drinks—more than 200 milligrams per 2 ounce serving. In comparison, a 12-ounce cola has 35 milligrams. High amounts of caffeine can cause headaches and anxiety. Experts recommend no more than 500 milligrams for adults and 100 milligrams for adolescents per day.

- **Relevance:** Include why you think this makes sense to include.
  Example: Article provides compiled data on caffeine content, which most likely is much higher than the average consumer realizes. Specific energy drinks and espresso have extremely high amounts of caffeine, which have become popular drinks for teens as well as adults.

- **Quotations:** If you are quoting, record the author of the quote or comment, use quotation marks, and write the words exactly as they appear in the source, including the page number or date if applicable. If there is an error in the text (such as the speaker used a word incorrectly or there was a grammatical mistake in the text), in brackets write the term *sic*, which means "thus in the original." If you omit words, indicate missing words with ellipsis points (three periods).
  Example: November 1, 2013: Personal interview with Ava Simpson, age 19, who has drunk energy drinks since high school: "At first, I drank them for

the novelty—the buzz you would feel. Now, I can barely make it through the day without a couple cans. Sometimes I'm so wired at night, I can't sleep. I feel like a yo-yo, bouncing around all day. I hate it."

Along with your notes, print or make a copy of the original article or book section. This isn't usually required, but is tremendously helpful if the online source moves or is taken down or if the book you used is checked out and you need to read the material again. (Conducting your research is discussed in further detail later in this chapter.)

8. **Don't just cut and paste.** As we'll discuss further in this chapter in regard to plagiarism, be careful about simply cutting and pasting material, especially from online sources. Either reword the material as you write it or make note that you will need to rework the material later when you write your paper.

9. **Prepare a bibliography.** A bibliography is a list of books, articles, Internet sources, interviews, and other resources about a subject or by a particular author that you plan to use as support for information in your paper. A bibliography page or section appears at the end of a research paper or book. Most instructors expect you to include a complete list of your sources, so record them accurately and thoroughly as you do your research.

Organize

Now that you have done the preliminary legwork, you'll want to create a writing plan.

1. **Develop an outline.** Organize your notes into a logical order using either a traditional or mind map outline. This outline should contain main points and subtopics and serve as a road map that illustrates your entire project and keeps you focused. (See the sample outline in the margin.) Use **Personal Evaluation Notebook 9.1** to help you organize your paper.

2. **Do in-depth research.** Look for specific information and data that support your main points and thesis. Research further the books and articles you recorded in your initial research. (We will discuss research skills in more detail later in the chapter.)

3. **Revise your outline as needed.** You may also refine your writing strategy by considering how best to accomplish your purpose. What is your major topic? What subtopics do you want to include? What examples, definitions, quotations, statistics, stories, or personal comments would be most interesting and supportive? Keep looking for specific information to support your thesis.

Write

Now is the time to organize all your notes according to sections and headings and write your first draft in your own words according to your revised outline. Write freely and don't worry about spelling, grammar, or format. The key is to begin writing and keep the momentum going. Both papers and speeches should have three sections: an introduction, a main body, and a conclusion.

1. **Introduction.** The introduction should be a strong opening that clearly states your purpose, captures the audience's attention, defines terms, and sets the stage for the main points. Use an active, not a passive, voice. For example, "More than 450,000 people will die this year from the effects of cigarette smoking" is a stronger introduction than "This paper will present the dangers of smoking."

Sample Outline

Thesis statement: Smoking among teenage girls is rising due to influences by peers and advertising that glamorizes smoking.

I. Smoking among teenage girls is increasing.
   A. Smoking has increased by 24 percent.
      1. Supporting information
      2. Supporting information
   B. Girls are smoking at younger ages.
      1. Supporting information
      2. Supporting information

II. Advertising targets young girls directly.
   A. Examples of advertising
      1. Supporting information
      2. Supporting information
   B. Effects of advertising
      1. Supporting information
      2. Supporting information

Personal Evaluation Notebook

9.1

Preparing Research Papers

Use this form to prepare and organize your upcoming paper. Jot down preliminary notes to get started.

Topic _____   Due Date _____

Main Point (Thesis) _____

_____

_____

How do the topic and thesis fulfill the assignment? _____

_____

_____

Review your outline and notes for these elements and provide examples or descriptions of how they will be addressed in the paper:

Main Body

- Background of topic _____
- Main points and arguments _____
- Supporting points _____
- Terminology, facts, data _____
- Key words _____

Conclusion

- Restate thesis. _____
- Summarize key points. _____
- Present a clear and strong conclusion. _____

2. **Main body.** The main body is the heart of your paper or speech. Each main point should be presented logically and stand out as a unit (see **Figure 9.2** on page 278). Explain main points in your own words and use direct quotes when you want to state the original source. Your research notes will help you find support elements. If you find gaps, do more research.

3. **Conclusion.** Your final paragraph should tie together important points. The reader or listener should now have an understanding of the topic and believe that you have achieved your purpose. You might use a story, quotation, or call to action. You may want to refer again to the introduction, reemphasize main points, or rephrase an important position. Keep your conclusion brief, interesting, and powerful. (**Figure 9.3** provides hints on overcoming writer's block.)

Figure 9.2
Writing Pyramid

Start at the top of the pyramid with your major topic, and move down to each subtopic and its main points. Provide support for your main points, including examples and statistics. End with a powerful conclusion that summarizes the paper or speech. *Why are "support" elements so important?*

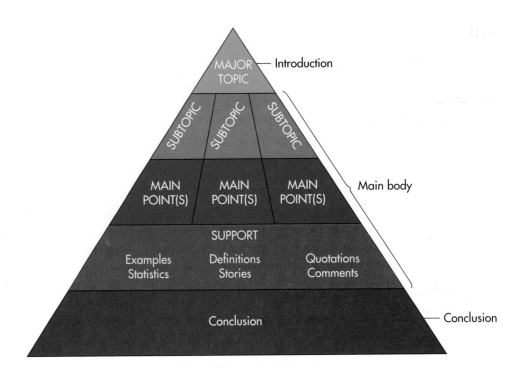

Figure 9.3
Overcoming Writer's Block

There are a number of ways to jump start your writing. *Which tips have worked best for you?*

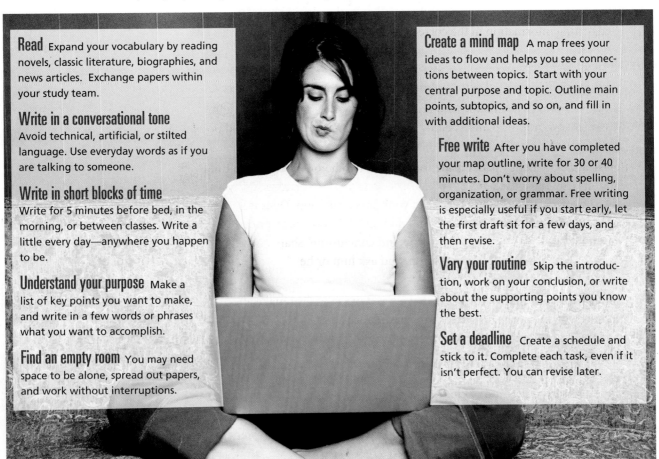

Read Expand your vocabulary by reading novels, classic literature, biographies, and news articles. Exchange papers within your study team.

Write in a conversational tone Avoid technical, artificial, or stilted language. Use everyday words as if you are talking to someone.

Write in short blocks of time Write for 5 minutes before bed, in the morning, or between classes. Write a little every day—anywhere you happen to be.

Understand your purpose Make a list of key points you want to make, and write in a few words or phrases what you want to accomplish.

Find an empty room You may need space to be alone, spread out papers, and work without interruptions.

Create a mind map A map frees your ideas to flow and helps you see connections between topics. Start with your central purpose and topic. Outline main points, subtopics, and so on, and fill in with additional ideas.

Free write After you have completed your map outline, write for 30 or 40 minutes. Don't worry about spelling, organization, or grammar. Free writing is especially useful if you start early, let the first draft sit for a few days, and then revise.

Vary your routine Skip the introduction, work on your conclusion, or write about the supporting points you know the best.

Set a deadline Create a schedule and stick to it. Complete each task, even if it isn't perfect. You can revise later.

Edit

A thorough edit can turn good papers into excellent papers.

1. **Revise.**

   - Do a word count. Most papers have a minimum or maximum word count objective or may require a specific number of paragraphs or pages, either single or double-spaced. Check to make sure you are within these parameters. Keep this objective in mind throughout all stages of revision. Not meeting length criteria set by your instructor may result in lost points.

   - Read your paper out loud to get an overall sense of meaning and the flow of words. Vary sentence lengths and arrangements to add interest and variety. For example, don't start each sentence with the subject or overuse the same words or phrases.

   - Rework paragraphs for clarity and appropriate transitions. Does each paragraph contain one idea in a topic sentence? Is the idea well supported? Transitions should be smooth and unobtrusive. In a speech, they should be defined clearly, so that listeners stay focused. Take out unnecessary words. Ask yourself if a phrase or sentence contributes to your purpose.

   - Recheck your outline. Have you followed your outline logically and included supporting information in the correct places? Break up the narrative with lists if you are presenting series of data. As you revise, stay focused on your purpose, not on the ideas that support your conclusion. Be sure your points are clearly and concisely presented with supporting stories, quotes, and explanations.

   - Review sentence structure, punctuation, grammar, and unity of thought. Correct typographical and spelling errors, grammatical mistakes, and poor transitions. As you work, remember to save your work frequently.

2. **Revise again.** Set your paper aside for a day or two before you give it a final revision with a fresh view. Go through your entire paper or speech. Is your central theme clear and concise? Read your paper out loud. Does it flow? Could it use more stories or quotes to add flair? Is it too wordy or confusing? Does it have an interesting introduction and conclusion? Share your paper with a friend or member of your study team, and ask him or her to proofread your work. Others provide a fresh viewpoint and can sometimes see errors you miss.

3. **Confer with your instructor.** If you have not done so earlier, make an appointment with your instructor to review your paper. Some students make an appointment after completing their outline or first draft, while others like to wait until they have proofed their second draft. Most instructors will review your paper with you and make suggestions. Discuss what to add, what to revise, and the preferred method of citation. Also, many colleges have a writing center staffed with English majors who will read your rough drafts and help you revise.

4. **Prepare your final draft.** Following your instructor's guidelines, prepare your final draft. Leave a margin of 1 inch on all sides, except for the first page,

---

Take 3 minutes to express your thoughts in a daily journal:

- What good things happened to you today?
- What "lessons" did you learn? Describe any negative experiences, and use the ABC Method to find positive outcomes and relieve lingering stress.
- Free write about any interesting ideas you have, and stretch your vocabulary with unusual words and phrases.

What else can you do in 3 minutes?

- Brainstorm ideas for your next writing assignment.
- Spellcheck your class paper.
- Create a writing schedule for an upcoming project.

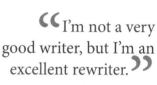

Take 3

> **"** I'm not a very good writer, but I'm an excellent rewriter. **"**
>
> JAMES MICHENER
> *Author*

Peak Progress

Writing Do's: The Seven *C*'s of Effective Writing

Be concise. Eliminate unnecessary words. Write in plain language and avoid wordiness. Cut any phrases that do not support your purpose.

Be concrete. Use vivid action words rather than vague, general terms. The sentence "Jill wrote the paper" is in the active voice and is easy to understand; "The paper was written by Jill" is in the passive voice and sounds weak. Avoid vague adjectives and adverbs, such as *nice, good, greatly,* and *badly.*

Be clear. Never assume that the audience has prior information. Avoid technical terms, clichés, slang, and jargon. If you must be technical, include simple definitions for your audience.

Be correct. Choose precise words and grammatically correct sentences. Verify that supporting details are factual and correctly interpreted. Make certain you cite another's work. Check spelling and punctuation carefully.

Be coherent. Your message should flow smoothly. Transitions between topics should be clear, logical, and varied in word choice. Also vary the length of sentences for interest and a sense of rhythm. Include stories, examples, and interesting facts.

Be complete. Include all necessary information. Will your listeners or readers understand your message? Reread your speech or paper from their point of view. What questions might the audience have? Answer any unanswered questions.

Be considerate. Respect your reader by presenting a professional paper. Neatness counts, and papers should always be typed. Use a respectful tone; don't talk down to your audience or use pompous or prejudiced language. Write with courtesy and consideration, and avoid using words that are biased in terms of sex, disabilities, or ethnic groups.

Instead Of	You Can Substitute
mankind	humanity, people, humankind
manmade	manufactured, handcrafted
policeman	police officer
fireman	firefighter
housewife	homemaker
crippled, disabled	physically challenged
Indian (American)	Native American
Oriental	Asian
Chicano	Latino

which should have a 3-inch margin at the top of the paper. Double-space your entire paper, except for the footnotes and bibliography, which are often single-spaced. Make corrections, revise, run a spell-check, and print out a clean, corrected copy on good-quality paper (if submitting a hard copy versus online). Also proofread this hard copy, as it's easy to miss errors on a computer screen. See **Peak Progress 9.2** for writing tips. (Also see **Peak Progress 9.3** if you are writing online.)

5. **Cite your sources.** Always cite your sources when you quote or use another person's words or ideas. **Plagiarism** is using someone else's words or ideas

Peak Progress

Online Writing

The Internet opened the floodgates of communication opportunities, as **blogging** (writing personal thoughts online, usually about a specific topic, for others to view and often comment on) and chatting on social networking sites have become popular writing activities. Many courses require students to manage their own blogs (for example, to report on service learning experiences) or to communicate with other class members via discussion boards.

When posting material online, the purpose is usually the same as for writing a class paper—to succinctly communicate your main message—and the techniques are very similar, including providing supporting material and examples. Following are some specific tips to help focus your online writing:

1. The point of your writing (especially with a blog) is to express your own opinion, so do it respectfully (without slander or profanity) and as briefly as possible.

2. Write a creative headline that conveys your main message.

3. Limit your words to no more than 250.

4. If your message is longer than three paragraphs, break it up with subheads, so that the post is easy to scan.

5. Use bullets for examples or to stress information, which catches the reader's attention.

6. If your goal is to attract readers to your posting, include many key terms that would pop up during word searches.

7. Link to supporting, credible websites.

8. Copyedit before you post. Nothing hurts your credibility more than typos and grammatical mistakes.

9. Now that you've started the line of communication, be prepared to follow up on feedback, if necessary.

---

and trying to pass them off as your own. It can have serious consequences, such as a failing grade or expulsion from school. You can put the person's exact words in quotation marks, or you can **paraphrase** by using your own words to restate the author's ideas. You can give credit in the text of the paper or in a note, either at the bottom of the page as a footnote or at the end of the paper as an endnote. (See **Peak Progress 9.4** on pages 282 and 283 for a discussion of citation styles.)

For example, you may choose to use the following source when writing a paper on the history of the funeral industry. This is the exact quote from the text along with one method of citation:

"Simplicity to the point of starkness, the plain pine box, the laying out of the dead by friends and family who also bore the coffin to the grave—these were the hallmarks of the traditional funeral until the end of the nineteenth century."[1]

[1]Mitford, Jessica. *The American Way of Death.* New York: Simon & Schuster, 1963.

Instead, you may choose to paraphrase the information from the book:

In her book *The American Way of Death*, Jessica Mitford says one myth that is sold by the funeral industry is that today's elaborate and expensive funeral practices are part of the American tradition. In truth, prior to the end of the nineteenth century, the average American funeral was inexpensive and often consisted of a pine box and a simple ceremony.

You do not need to credit general ideas that are considered to be part of common knowledge, such as the suggestion that people who exercise reduce their stress levels. However, when in doubt, it's best to cite your source. Read **Personal Evaluation Notebook 9.2** on page 284 to get a better understanding of plagiarism and how to avoid it.

6. **Add a title page and page numbers.** If required, create a title page by centering the title one-third of the page from the top. Two-thirds from the top, center your name, the instructor's name, the course title, and the date. Do not

Writing Citations

There are many ways to write citations. Ask your instructor which documentation style is preferred. Each academic discipline has its preferred format. The Modern Language Association (MLA) of America format is often preferred for the humanities (philosophy, languages, arts, and so on). The American Psychological Association (APA) format is commonly used for the social sciences, psychology, and education. The style of the Council of Biology Editors (CBE) is primarily used for the natural and physical sciences. Computer programs are available to help you format citations according to some styles.

Reference notes can be placed at the bottom of a page as footnotes or listed together at the end of the paper as endnotes. A bibliography, which lists all the sources (such as books, articles, websites, and personal communication) referenced in a paper, may include works for background and further reading. A reference list, on the other hand, cites works that specifically support an article. Bibliographies and reference lists are found at the end of a paper after endnotes, if there are any. In the MLA format, the bibliography appears under the heading "Works Cited." For more information on MLA format, visit the MLA website at **www.mla.org/style_faq.**

The various citation formats are similar. The MLA style uses the simplest punctuation and is acceptable in many situations. The elements of an MLA citation are author, book title, place of publication, publisher, year of publication, and page number.

The APA style generally uses a combination of in-text citations and a reference list. Text citations use an author-date system (such as Nelson, 2004). Items in the reference list usually contain the following elements: author, year of publication, title of the work, place of publication, and publisher. For more information about APA style, visit the APA website at **www.apastyle.org/faqs.html.**

Several excellent websites can guide you through a generally acceptable way to cite sources. Your local or school library may also post citation information on its website. Following is a guide for most types of sources you will cite:

For Footnotes

MLA   1. Lee, Ann. <u>Office Reference Manual</u>. New York: Irwin, 1993.

APA   (Lee, 1993)
Note: In the APA's author-date system, the last name(s) of the author(s) and the year of publication are inserted in the text at the appropriate point.

For Reference List or Works Cited

Book: One Author

MLA   Henley, Patricia. <u>Hummingbird House</u>. Denver: MacMurray, 1999.

APA   Henley, P. (1999). *Hummingbird house.* Denver: MacMurray.

Book: Two or More Authors

MLA   Gillespie, Paula, and Neal Lerber. <u>The Allyn and Bacon Guide to Peer Tutoring</u>. Boston: Allyn, 2000.

APA   Gillespie, P., & Lerber, N. (2000). *The Allyn and Bacon guide to peer tutoring.* Boston: Allyn.

Government Publication

MLA   United States Department of Health and Human Services. <u>Pressure Ulcers in Adults: Prediction and Prevention</u>. Rockville, MD: Publisher, 1992, 28.

APA   U.S. Department of Health and Human Services. (1992). *Pressure ulcers in adults: Prediction and prevention* (AHCPR Publication No, 92-0047). Rockville, MD: Author.

Journal

MLA   Klimoski, Richard I., and Susan Palmer. "The ADA and the Hiring Process in Organization." <u>Consulting Psychology Journal: Practice and Research</u>, 45.2 (1993) 10–36.

APA   Klimoski, R. I., & Palmer, S. (1993). The ADA and the hiring process in organization. *Consulting Psychology Journal: Practice and Research, 45*(2), 10–36.

Nonprint Source (website)

MLA   Stolley, Karl. "MLA Formatting and Style Guide." The OWL at Purdue. 10 May 2006. Purdue University Writing Lab. 12 May 2006 <http://owl.english.purdue.edu/owl/resource/557/01/>.

APA   Stolley, K. (2006). MLA formatting and style guide. Retrieved May 12, 2006, from Purdue University Writing Lab website: http://owl.english.purdue.edu/owl/resource/557/01/

(continued)

Writing Citations *(continued)*

Nonprint Source (Online Journal)

MLA Wheelis, Mark. "Investigating Disease Outbreaks under a Protocol to the Biological and Toxin Weapons Convention." <u>Emerging Infectious Diseases</u> 6.6 (2000): 33 pars. 8 May 2006 <www.cdc.gov/ncidod/eid/vol6no6/wheelis.htm>.

APA Wheelis, M. (2000). Investigating disease outbreaks under a protocol to the biological and toxin weapons convention. *Emerging Infectious Diseases*, 6. Retrieved May 8, 2006, from **www.cdc.gov/ncidod/eid/vol6no6/vvwheelis.htm**

Nonprint Source (DVD)

MLA Reaven, Gerald, and Meenakshi Aggarwal. <u>Heart Disease and South Asians: A Population at Risk.</u> DVD. CustomFlix, 2006.

APA Reaven, G., & Aggarwal, M. (2006). *Heart Disease and South Asians: A Population at Risk.* [DVD]. CustomFlix.

Nonprint Source (App)

MLA Prentice, William E., Amanda Andrews Benson, and Linda Stark Bobo. <u>Athletic Trainer</u> <u>Plus.</u> Van Brien & Associates. 2013. Electronic application. June 19, 2013.

APA Van Brien & Associates. (2013). *Athletic Trainer Plus.* [Mobile application software]. Retrieved from http://itunes.apple.com

Letter to the Editor

MLA Berkowitz, A. D. Letter. "How to Tackle the Problem of Student Drinking." <u>The Chronicle of Higher Education</u>. 24 Nov 2000: B20.

APA Berkowitz, A. D. (2000, November 24). How to tackle the problem of student drinking [Letter to the editor]. *The Chronicle of Higher Education*, p. B20.

Encyclopedia or Other Reference Work

MLA Bergmann, Peter G. "Relativity." <u>The New Encyclopaedia Britannica</u>. 15th ed. 1993.

APA Bergmann, P. G. (1993). Relativity. In *The new encyclopaedia britannica* (Vol. 26, pp. 501–508). Chicago: Encyclopedia Britannica.

Note: In MLA style, titles of whole works may be underlined or italicized.

---

number this page. Number all remaining pages in the upper right-hand corner 1/2 inch from the top of the page. Number your endnotes and bibliography as part of the text. (Refer to any guidelines your instructor may have given you regarding formatting preferences.)

Review

Proofread by carefully reading through your work one more time. Peak Progress 9.5 on page 285 provides a handy checklist to use as you finalize. Be prepared to submit your paper or give your speech by the due date. Delaying just adds to the anxiety and may result in a lower grade. Keep back-up copies (a hard copy and a digital file) of your final paper or speech, in case your instructor loses the original.

Review your graded paper or speech when it is returned to you, and make sure you understand what you could have done differently to have received a better grade. If you are unsure, ask your instructor for tips on improving your work. Keep copies of your major research papers in your Career Development Portfolio to show documentation of your writing, speaking, and research skills.

> **"** Proofread carefully to see if you any words out. **"**
>
> AUTHOR UNKNOWN

WORDS TO SUCCEED

Conducting Research

Conducting research requires the same skills you've been learning throughout this book: observing, recording, reviewing, and using critical thinking to assess and evaluate. The purpose of research is to find information and ideas about a topic beyond what

Personal Evaluation Notebook

That's Not Fair (Use)

One survey reported that 36 percent of teens admitted they had used the Internet to plagiarize an assignment. However, it's likely that even more are committing plagiarism without realizing it because of the confusion over what constitutes plagiarism versus "fair use."

Fair use is the legal and ethical use of a direct quote from the Internet or another source, including a book, in something you claim as your own work. According to the U.S. Copyright Office, fair use is limited to the "quotation of excerpts in a review or criticism for purposes of illustration or comment; quotation of short passages in a scholarly or technical work, for illustration or clarification of the author's observations; use in a parody of some of the content of the work parodied; summary of an address or article, with brief quotations," and similar use. Even when the quotation is within the fair use guidelines, it is essential to give a reference through a footnote or other indication that these words were written by someone other than you. Because of the prevalence of plagiarism, many instructors use online services to check for it, including having students deliver their papers via an online site, such as turnitin.

To test your understanding, consider the following scenarios*:

1. This morning, you read an editorial in the local newspaper and totally agreed with the author's 10-step approach to improving high school graduation rates. You include all 10 suggestions in your presentation to your Introduction to Education class but reword each one slightly and don't cite the author. Is this plagiarism?

   yes _____   no_____

2. You cut and paste a lengthy article from a reputable online news service into your paper and add a new introduction and a brief summary. You include a complete citation in your source information. Is this plagiarism?

   yes _____   no_____

3. Last semester, you wrote a stellar paper for your English composition class, in which you compared and contrasted a number of local businesses. You decide to hand in the same paper this week for an Economics 101 assignment. Is this plagiarism?

   yes_____   no_____

Sources: Josephson Institute Center for Youth Ethics, "The Ethics of American Youth—2008 summary," http//charactercounts.org/programs/reportcard/, accessed August 14, 2009.

U.S. Copyright Office—Fair Use, www.copyright.gov/fls/fl102.html, revised May 2009.

*Answers are on page 293.

you already know. Research helps you support opinions and information with facts and data. Your initial research will give you an overview of the subject and help you define your thesis statement. Additional research will uncover specific facts about your subject.

Using the Library for Research

As discussed in Chapter 4, the library contains a wealth of information. Reference librarians are trained to find information about every subject. They can often order materials

Peak Progress

Checklists for Writing Papers and Giving Speeches

Papers and Speeches

_____ Appropriate and focused topic

_____ Attention-getting introduction

_____ Clear thesis statement

_____ Appropriate word choice

_____ Plenty of factual support

_____ Good examples

_____ Good visuals

_____ Sources credited

_____ Smooth transitions

_____ Effective summary/ conclusions

Papers

_____ Spelling and grammar checked

_____ Proofread at least twice

_____ Pages numbered

_____ Neat appearance/ format

_____ Deadline met

Speeches

_____ Eye contact

_____ Appropriate voice level and tone

_____ No slang or distracting words

_____ Relaxed body language

_____ Appropriate attire

_____ Access to watch or clock

---

from other libraries or direct you to other sources. Asking for their guidance at the beginning of your search can save you hours of time and frustration. When planning your research strategy, remember the basic types of sources found in most libraries:

- **Books.** Books make up a large part of every library. They treat a subject in depth and offer a broad scope. In your research project, use books for historical context, detailed discussions of a subject, or varied perspectives on a topic.

- **Periodicals.** A periodical is a regularly issued publication, such as newspapers, news magazines, professional and scholarly journals, and trade and industry magazines. For your research, use periodicals when you need recent data.

- **Reference materials.** Reference materials may be in print or digital. Examples include encyclopedias, dictionaries, chronologies, abstracts, indexes, and compilations of statistics. In your research strategy, use reference materials when you want to obtain or verify specific facts.

The _Readers' Guide to Periodical Literature_ is a helpful source for locating articles. Other standard reference materials that may give you a general understanding of specific topics and help you develop questions include the _Encyclopaedia Britannica,_ and the indexes of _The New York Times_ and _Wall Street Journal._

Check these sources for historical speeches:

- _Speech Index_
- _Index to American Women Speakers, 1828–1978_
- Representative _American Speeches_
- _Facts on File_
- _Vital Speeches of the Day_
- _Public Papers of the Presidents of the United States_

Search by author or subject through the library's online catalog. Often, the electronic source will include only a summary, so you may need to go to the library stacks or periodicals to read the book or article.

A Good Source
Libraries provide the most research options, with books, periodicals, reference materials, online access, and trained librarians. _What's the best source for recent data?_

Taking Your Search Online

Before you start a search online, think about a precise question you want to answer, such as "How does education affect smoking by college students?" Identify the key words and ideas in this question—for example, *smoking, education,* and *addiction.* Directories such as Yahoo.com (**www.yahoo.com**) are often helpful when starting your research because they are organized by subject. Other sites, such as google.com (**www.google.com**), combine directories with search engines. Type your key words into the search box, select from the options that pop up, or hit the return key and wait for a list of web pages to appear. If they don't answer your question, rephrase your question and search again using other key words. Each search site offers links that will explain how to do advanced searches. Bookmark websites that you use often.

Although searching for information on the Internet by using key words or key phrases may seem relatively easy and efficient, you must verify that what you choose to use comes from a reliable source. See **Peak Progress 9.6** for tips on evaluating

Peak Progress   9.6

Evaluating Online Information

With millions of web pages to choose from, how do you know which sites are reliable? Use the following checklist when evaluating online information for research and personal use.

Is It Credible?

- Is the page's author clearly identified? Does he or she have the credentials for writing about this topic?
- Is the author affiliated with an organization? If so, what is the organization's nature or purpose?
- Is there a link to the organization's home page or some other way to contact the organization and verify its credibility (a physical address, phone number, or e-mail address)?
- Is the page geared for a particular audience or level of expertise?
- Is the primary purpose to provide information, sell a product, make a political point, or have fun?
- Is the page part of an edited or peer-reviewed publication?
- Does the domain name provide clues about the source of the page?
- Does the site provide details that support the data?
- Is there a bibliography or other documentation to corroborate the information? When facts or statistics are quoted, look to see whether their source is revealed.

Is It Accurate?

- Are there obvious typographical or spelling errors?
- Based on what you already know or have just learned about this subject, does the information seem credible?
- Can factual information be verified?
- Is it comprehensive, or does it focus on a narrow range of information?
- Is it clear about its focus?
- Has the site been evaluated?

Is It Timely?

- Can you tell when the information was published? Is it current?
- When was the page last updated?
- If there are links to other web pages, are they current?

Is It Objective?

- Is the source of factual information consistent and stated clearly?
- Does the page display a particular bias? Is it clear and forthcoming about its view of a particular subject?
- If the page contains advertisements, are they clearly distinguishable from the content of the information?

Source: Used by permission of the University of Texas System Digital Library, The University of Texas at Austin.

online material. As with other sources, you must also cite material you find on the Internet.

Public Speaking Strategies

Public speaking is an essential school and job skill. In school, you will ask and answer questions in class, lead discussions, summarize topics, introduce other students, present your academic plan or thesis, and interview for internships or jobs. On the job, you may introduce a guest, present the results of a group project, make a sales pitch, demonstrate a new product, present goals and objectives, entertain clients, talk with upper management, or accept an award.

Many of the strategies for choosing a topic and organizing and writing a speech are like those for writing papers. Following are additional strategies specifically for public speaking:

1. **Understand the occasion.** Why are you speaking? Is the occasion formal or informal? How much time do you have? What is your purpose? Do you want to inform, entertain, inspire, or persuade?

2. **Think about your topic.** If a topic hasn't been assigned, what are you interested in talking about? Prepare a thesis statement, such as "My purpose is to inform the Forestry Club on the benefits of our organization."

3. **Know your audience.** You don't need to know them personally, but you should have a sense of their backgrounds and why they are in the room. For example, if you are giving a speech on cutting-edge technology and the majority of your audience barely knows how to turn on a computer, chances are you are going to lose them quickly unless you present the topic at a level they can relate to, with benefits they can appreciate.

4. **Get the audience's attention.** Write an introduction that gets attention, introduces the topic, states the main purpose, and briefly identifies the main points.

5. **Get the audience involved.** Consider asking a question, which may help personalize the topic, encourage participation, or keep the audience interested.

6. **Look at the audience.** Establish eye contact and speak to the audience members. Smile, develop rapport, and notice when your audience agrees with you or looks puzzled or confused.

7. **Outline your speech.** Organize the body of your speech to include supporting points and interesting examples.

8. **Write a good conclusion.** The audience should have a clear picture of what your main point is, why it's important, and what they

Izzy's blog has become an instant hit with fans of local cuisine. Majoring in food science, Izzy loves to give (and ask for) opinions on hot spots, new chefs, menu makeovers, and dining experiences—the good and the bad. However, as much as Izzy enjoys voicing her thoughts online in elaborate detail, writing a term paper is as appealing to her as a trip to the dentist.

- How do Izzy's personality and learning styles influence her online writing success?
- If Izzy enjoys writing her blog, why does she view other writing opportunities differently? How are they different? How are they similar?
- What tips would you give Izzy to help her tackle her more structured writing projects?

THINK FAST

● **Eye Contact**

When you look at the audience as you speak, you create a rapport that makes everyone more comfortable. *What other strategies can help you become a good speaker?*

should do about it. You may want to end with a story, strong statement, or question.

9. **Develop visuals.** When appropriate, use overheads, a PowerPoint presentation, handouts, and demonstrations to focus attention and reinforce your speech. Make sure the projection equipment works, and you have practiced working with the visual aids. See **Figure 9.4** for tips on creating effective PowerPoint presentations.

10. **Prepare your prompters.** Don't memorize the speech, but be well acquainted with your topic, so that you are comfortable talking about it. Prepare simple notes to prompt yourself. Write key phrases, stories, and quotes in large letters on note cards.

11. **Practice.** Rehearsal is everything! Practice the speech aloud several times in front of a mirror, an empty classroom, or friends. Practice speaking slowly, calmly, and louder than usual. Vary the pitch and speed for emphasis. Practice will also help you overcome stage fright. (See the next section on speech anxiety.)

12. **Relax.** Take a deep breath as you walk to the front of the room. During the speech, speak loudly and clearly, don't rush, and gesture when appropriate to help you communicate.

13. **Watch your time.** If you have a time limit, make sure there is a clock you can glance at during your presentation. Pace yourself, so that you finish on time.

14. **Be in the present.** Look at your audience and smile. Keep your purpose in mind, and stay focused on the message and the audience. Pause at important points for emphasis and to connect with your audience.

15. **Avoid unnecessary words.** Use clear, concise wording. Don't use pauses as fillers, irritating nonwords, or overused slang, such as *uh, ur, you know, stuff like that, sort of,* and *like.*

16. **Review your performance.** Ask your instructor and fellow students for feedback. Use the sample speech evaluation form shown in **Figure 9.5** to help you improve your performance or as you are listening to others.

See **Peak Progress 9.7** on page 290 to explore how you can apply the Adult Learning Cycle to becoming more proficient at public speaking.

Overcoming Speech Anxiety

Most beginning public speakers feel nervous about speaking in front of others. This kind of nervousness is called speech anxiety, stage fright, or communication apprehension—and it is normal. A little apprehension is good for public speaking. It adds energy and can sharpen your awareness and focus. Too much anxiety, however, can be harmful. Speech anxiety has both mental and physical components. Mentally, you might think of all the ways you will fail. As you worry about the speech, your negative thoughts can work you into a state of real anxiety. Physical symptoms include butterflies-in-the-stomach, irregular breathing, sweaty palms, dry mouth, nausea, mental blocks, flushed skin, tense muscles, and shaky hands. Some people have even fainted. Extreme anxiety can prevent you from doing your best.

PowerPoint Tips

WORDS:
1. Title each screen with a 35-45-point font
2. Select sans-serif fonts, 24-point or larger
3. Use linear (outline) or topical organization
4. No more than 6-8 words per line
5. Bullet points:
   - 1 thought per line
   - 6 words per line maximum
   - 6 lines per slide maximum
6. Use colors, sizes, and styles (**bold**, <u>underline</u>) for impact

PowerPoint Tips

VISUALS:
1. Keep a consistent background
2. Use dark text on light background or light text on dark background
3. Use quality graphics sparingly
4. Avoid flashy graphics, transitions, and noisy animations
5. Limit the number of colors on a single screen

Figure 9.4
PowerPoint Presentations

When developing a PowerPoint presentation, include only essential words and images. The text has to be big enough to be read from the back of the room. Do not read from your presentation, but use it as a guide to follow as you speak. *Do you feel more comfortable giving a presentation with or without an accompanying PowerPoint?*

You can become more confident and overcome speech anxiety with these tips:

1. **Practice.** The more prepared you are, the less nervous you're likely to be. Practice out loud, in front of a mirror, with a friend and in the room where you'll be speaking, if possible.

2. **Use visuals.** Visual aids can prompt you during the presentation and direct the spotlight away from you.

3. **Dispute irrational thoughts.** You might think, "People will laugh at me" or "My mind will go blank." In reality, others are also apprehensive (and more concerned about their own performance) and want you to do your best. Counter your "catastrophic" thinking by considering, "What's the worst thing that can happen?" and follow with affirmations. "I am well prepared. I am relaxed. I am comfortable talking with others. The audience is on my side."

Name _____ **Topic** _____

Introduction
— Gained attention and interest
— Introduced topic
— Topic related to audience
— Established credibility
— Previewed body of speech

Body
— Main points clear
— Organizational pattern evident
— Established need
— Presented clear plan
— Demonstrated practicality
— Language clear
— Gave evidence to support main points
— Sources and citations clear
— Reasoning sound
— Used emotional appeals
— Connectives effective

Delivery
— Spoke at an appropriate rate
— Maintained eye contact
— Maintained volume and projection
— Avoided distracting mannerisms
— Used gestures effectively
— Articulated clearly
— Used vocal variety and dynamics
— Presented visual aids effectively
— Departed appropriately
— Other:

Conclusion
— Prepared audience for ending
— Reinforced central idea
— Called audience to agreement/action
— Used a vivid ending

Suggestions
_____
_____
_____
_____
_____
_____
_____
_____

General Notes
_____
_____
_____
_____
_____
_____
_____

Key: Superior (1), Effective (2), Average (3), Weak (4)

Figure 9.5
Speech Evaluation Form

Feedback on your speaking skills can help you improve. *How would you assess your last speech in a class?*

Peak Progress

Applying the Adult Learning Cycle to Improving Your Public Speaking

Increasing your public speaking skills takes time, effort, and practice.

1. **RELATE. Why do I want to learn this?** I admire people who are confident speaking in front of others, and I want to feel as confident, poised, and in control. Becoming an effective public speaker will be a valuable skill for both school and career. What areas do I need to work on? What are my physical symptoms of anxiety?

2. **OBSERVE. How does this work?** I can learn by observing people who confidently give effective speeches. What makes them successful? Do I understand the message? I'll also analyze ineffective speeches. Did stage fright play a role? Did the speaker seem nervous? I'll try using new techniques and strategies for dealing with stage fright and observe how I'm improving.

3. **REFLECT. What does this mean?** What strategies are working for me? Am I more confident and relaxed? Am I reducing anxiety and negative self-talk?

4. **DO. What can I do with this?** I will practice my public speaking skills whenever possible. I'll find practical applications for my new skills. Each day, I'll work on one area. For example, I'll choose less stressful situations, such as my study group or a club meeting, and offer to give a presentation on an interesting topic. I will ask for feedback.

5. **TEACH. Whom can I share this with?** I'll talk with others and share my tips and experiences and listen to theirs in return. I'll volunteer to help other students in my study group.

Now, return to Stage 1 and think about how it feels to learn this valuable new skill. Remember, the more you practice speaking in front of others, the more relaxed and confident you will become.

---

4. **Use stress-reduction techniques.** Relax your muscles by tensing and then quickly releasing them. Do head rolls. Put your shoulders way up and then drop them. Take deep breaths, and concentrate on expanding your stomach with each breath and exhaling fully. Don't rush right into your speech. Take several slow, deep breaths before going up to speak. Relax and smile.

If your anxiety is severe and prevents you from succeeding, see the learning center or counseling center for individualized tips. Complete **Personal Evaluation Notebook 9.3** to determine how you handle stage fright and writer's block.

Personal Evaluation Notebook  9.3

Controlling Stage Fright and Writer's Block

A. Use your critical thinking skills to answer the following questions. Be prepared to discuss your answers in your study team.

1. Describe your typical physical reaction to giving a speech.

   _____

   _____

2. What has helped you control stage fright?

   _____

   _____

3. Describe the processes of writing that are easiest for you and those that are hardest.

   _____

   _____

B. Read the following common reasons and excuses that some students give for not writing effective speeches. Use creative problem solving to list strategies for overcoming these barriers.

REASONS/EXCUSES

1. I have panic attacks before I write or give speeches.
   Strategy _____

   _____

2. I can't decide on a topic.
   Strategy _____

   _____

3. I don't know how to research.
   Strategy: _____

   _____

4. I procrastinate until the last minute.
   Strategy: _____

   _____

5. I don't know what my instructor wants.
   Strategy: _____

   _____

6. My mind goes blank when I start to write or give a speech.
   Strategy: _____

   _____

TAKING CHARGE

Summary

In this chapter, I learned to

- **Become a more effective writer and speaker.** Being a good communicator is the most important skill I will ever acquire. Although public speaking can be stressful, I can learn to reduce my anxiety and become more successful if I prepare, organize, write, edit, and review my presentation carefully.

- **Prepare effectively.** When writing a paper or presentation, I first set a schedule. I carefully and thoughtfully choose my topic and do the preliminary reading and information gathering. I can then narrow my topic and write a thesis statement that clarifies what I plan to cover. I prepare a bibliography of references and original sources, and take notes that support my topic.

- **Organize my writing plan.** I must organize my thoughts and research into a coherent outline. I continue to look for specific data that support my main points. I revise my outline as necessary as I consider the subtopics that support my main theme. I include interesting and supportive examples, definitions, quotations, and statistics.

- **Write a draft of my paper or presentation.** After finishing the preliminary research and outline, I prepare a draft, writing freely and with momentum. My draft includes an introduction, the main body, and a conclusion. The introduction clearly states the purpose or theme, captures attention, and defines terms. The main body includes the subtopics that support the main theme, as well as visual aids. The conclusion ties the important points together and supports the overall theme of the presentation.

- **Revise and edit my paper or presentation.** Now that I have prepared a draft, I must revise it often. I make sure the overall theme and supporting points are clear and revise my outline when necessary. I correct spelling and grammatical mistakes and review transitions and sentence structure. I read it out loud to make sure the writing is varied and interesting. I verify that I have accurately prepared the bibliography, and I ask my instructor to review my paper. I then finalize my paper, number the pages, and add a title page if required.

- **Review and assess my paper or presentation.** After a final check of my paper, I make a copy for my Career Development Portfolio. I submit it on time, go over my graded results, and ask my instructor for tips for improvement.

- **Use the library and Internet for research.** The library provides a wealth of resources, and reference librarians can assist in my search. The Internet is the world's largest information network, providing access to a myriad of resources, including databases.

- **Incorporate new strategies for effective public speaking.** When I speak in public, it's important for me to be prepared, establish eye contact with my audience, develop visual aids, and prepare simple notes or cues to prompt myself. I avoid unnecessary words and fillers, and I connect with my audience. Rehearsing is key to a successful presentation, and I review my performance by asking others for feedback.

Performance Strategies

Following are the top 10 strategies for writing papers and giving speeches:

- Determine your purpose and set a schedule.
- Choose and narrow your topic.
- Read and research. Prepare a bibliography.
- Organize information into an outline.
- Write a draft.
- Refine your purpose and rewrite the draft.
- Edit and proof.
- Use your study team to practice and review.
- Revise and polish.
- Practice. Practice. Practice.

Tech for Success

Take advantage of the text's website at **www.mhhe.com/ferrett9e** for additional study aids, useful forms, and convenient and applicable resources.

- **Visual aids.** As many of your instructors do, you will want to enhance your presentations with visual aids, such as handouts and PowerPoint presentations. Many employers do not provide training for presentation software but knowing how to incorporate them into business meetings and presentations is often expected. Thus, learning at least the basics of PowerPoint or a similar program will be a valuable skill you can use both in school and on the job.

- **Spell-check, spell-check, spell-check.** As e-mail has replaced the traditional memo, it's much easier to send out correspondence quickly to a group of people. However, it's not uncommon to receive important e-mails that are riddled with typos, grammatical mistakes, and texting jargon. Get in the habit of using the spell-check function before you send e-mails or any documents. The few seconds it takes to check your outgoing correspondence can save you from unnecessary embarrassment.

Study Team Notes

Answers to Personal Evaluation Notebook 9.2 on page 284:

1. Yes. Using someone else's ideas and presenting them as your own—whether from a written or a verbal source—is considered plagiarism unless credit is given to the original source.
2. Yes. Even though the source is cited, a significant amount of material has been used and is being presented as original work. The ideas can still be included in your work (as long as the source is cited), but the material should be revised in your own words.
3. Yes. This is considered "self-plagiarism," and multiple submission of material is often considered unethical in an academic situation.

Lori Benson
HUMAN RESOURCES DIRECTOR

Related Majors: Human Resources, Personnel
Administration, Labor Relations

Communication Skills

Lori Benson is the human resources director for a small advertising firm. Lori is her company's only human resources employee. Besides recruiting and interviewing potential employees, Lori also develops personnel programs and policies. She serves as her company's employee benefits manager by handling health insurance and pension plans. Lori also provides training in orientation sessions for new employees and instructs classes that help supervisors improve their interpersonal skills.

Possessing excellent communication skills is essential for Lori's job. To recruit potential employees, Lori contacts local colleges to attract recent graduates and places ads on online job search sites. In addition, Lori often sends e-mails to the employees at her company to notify them about new policies and benefits. This kind of writing must be clear, accurate, and brief. She usually asks the CEO to review the ads and press releases sent to the media.

Lori does research to find out what programs and policies other companies are offering. She uses public speaking strategies when preparing for training and other classes. First she makes notes and then writes prompts to help her remember what she wants to say. Lori practices her presentation several times and reviews her notes before each class. She keeps her notes on file for the next time she gives a class on the same subject.

CRITICAL THINKING How does Lori incorporate the communication skills she learned in college into the workplace?

Peak Performer PROFILE

Toni Morrison

Her books have been described as having "the luster of poetry" illuminating American reality. However, one reader once commented to acclaimed novelist Toni Morrison that her books were difficult to read. Morrison responded, "They're difficult to write." The process, Morrison sums up, "is not [always] a question of inspiration. It's a question of very hard, very sustained work."

An ethnically rich background helped provide Morrison's inspiration. The second of four children, she was born Chloe Anthony Wofford in a small Ohio steel town in 1931 during the Great Depression. The family's financial struggle was offset by a home strengthened by multiple generations and traditional ties. Storytelling was an important part of the family scene and black tradition.

In the late 1940s, Morrison headed to the East Coast. After earning a bachelor's degree in English from Howard University and a master's degree from Cornell University, she was still years away from literary recognition. While working as an editor at Random House in New York City, she began her writing career in earnest, and in 1970 her first novel, *The Bluest Eye,* was published.

Since then, Morrison has produced a body of work described as standing "among the 20th century's richest depictions of Black life and the legacy of slavery." In 1987, she won the Pulitzer Prize for her fifth novel, *Beloved.* Based on a true incident that took place in 1851, this novel has been read by millions. Then, in 1993, Morrison was awarded the Nobel Prize in Literature. She is the first black woman and only the eighth woman to receive this supreme honor.

Through Morrison's writing skills and self-expression, she has provided insight into American cultural heritage and the human condition.

PERFORMANCE THINKING The novel *Beloved* is dedicated to "Sixty Million and more." What is Morrison trying to express?

CHECK IT OUT "Toni Morrison's novels invite the reader to partake at many levels, and at varying degrees of complexity. Still, the most enduring impression they leave is of empathy, compassion with one's fellow human beings," said Professor Sture Allén as he presented Toni Morrison with the Nobel Prize for Literature for 1993. At **www.nobelprize.org**, select "Nobel Prizes" and then choose the Literature section to read about the many laureates who have received this highest honor. You can also listen to acceptance speeches and Nobel lectures, including Morrison's eloquent prose, "We die. That may be the meaning of life. But we do language. That may be the measure of our lives."

Starting Today

At least one strategy I learned in this chapter that I plan to try right away is

_____

_____

_____

What changes must I make in order for this strategy to be most effective?

_____

_____

_____

Review Questions

Based on what you have learned in this chapter, write your answers to the following questions:

1. What is the one basic skill taught in college that Peter Drucker feels is the most valuable for a future employee to know?

   _____

   _____

2. How should you establish a schedule to research and write a paper?

   _____

   _____

3. What are three questions to ask when evaluating information on the Internet?

   _____

   _____

4. Describe four strategies you can use to overcome writer's block.

   _____

   _____

5. What are five public speaking strategies?

   _____

   _____

To test your understanding of the chapter's concepts, complete the chapter quiz at **www.mhhe.com/ferrett9e**.

Learning Communication Skills

In the Classroom

Josh Miller is a finance student at a business college. He likes numbers and feels comfortable with order, structure, and right-or-wrong answers. As part of the graduation require-ments, all students must take classes in speech and writ-ing. Josh becomes nervous about writing reports or giving speeches and doesn't see the connection between the required class and his finance studies. One of Josh's biggest stumbling blocks is thinking of topics. He experiences writer's block and generally delays any project until the last possible minute.

1. What strategies in this chapter would help Josh think of topics and meet his deadlines?

_____

_____

2. What would you suggest to help him see the value of speaking and writing well?

_____

_____

In the Workplace

Josh has recently been promoted to regional manager for an investment firm. He feels very secure with the finance part of his job but pressured by new promotion requirements. He will need to present bimonthly speeches to top management, run daily meetings, and write dozens of reports. He must also give motivational seminars at least twice a year to his department heads. Josh wants to improve his writing skills and make his presentations clear, concise, and motivational.

3. What suggestions would you give Josh to help make his presentations more professional and interesting?

_____

_____

4. What strategies could he use to improve his writing?

_____

_____

REVIEW AND APPLICATIONS　|　CHAPTER 9

Applying the ABC Method of Self-Management

In the Journal Entry box on page 271, you were asked to describe a time when you did well in a speaking assignment or leading a discussion. What factors helped you be calm and confident?

_____

_____

_____

Now describe a situation in which your mind went blank or you suffered stage fright. How would increasing your presentation or public speaking skills have helped you? Apply the ABC Method to visualize a result in which you are again calm, confident, and focused.

A = **Actual event:**

_____

_____

_____

_____

B = **Beliefs:**

_____

_____

_____

C = **Challenge:**

_____

_____

_____

Practice deep breathing with your eyes closed for 1 minute. See yourself calm, centered, and relaxed as you give a performance or make a speech. See yourself presenting your ideas clearly, concisely, and confidently. You feel confident because you have learned to control stage fright, are well prepared, and know how to give speeches.

PRACTICE SELF-MANAGEMENT

For more examples of learning how to manage difficult situations, see the "Self-Management Workbook" section of the Outline Learning Center website at **www.mhhe.com/ferrett9e.**

Practice Paraphrasing

Because it's so easy to cut and paste material from the Internet, it's also too easy to pick up someone else's work and use it as your own. It's essential to paraphrase (and cite) material originally developed by others.

Read the following excerpt and then attempt to rewrite in your own words what the author has said:

Are you among the millions of Americans who take vitamin supplements? If your answer is "yes," why do you use them? Many people take multiple vitamin/mineral supplements as an "insurance policy" in case their diets are not nutritionally adequate. Other people use specific vitamin supplements because they think this practice will result in optimal health. Vitamin supplements are effective for treating people with specific vitamin deficiency diseases, metabolic defects that increase vitamin requirements, and a few other medical conditions. However, scientific evidence generally does not support claims that megadoses of vitamins can prevent or treat everything from gray hair to lung cancer.

(Source: Wendy J. Schiff: *Nutrition for Healthy Living*, 2009, McGraw-Hill.)

Now, write the essence of what the author has said:

_____

_____

_____

_____

_____

_____

_____

_____

_____

_____

_____

_____

_____

_____

_____

_____

_____

_____

_____

REVIEW AND APPLICATIONS | CHAPTER 9

Your Writing and Speaking Skills

Looking Back

1. Recall any activities and events through which you learned to write and speak. Jot down examples of classes, presentations, essays, journals, and papers.

   _____

   _____

2. What are your strengths in writing and speaking?

   _____

   _____

3. What would you like to improve?

   _____

   _____

4. What are your feelings about writing and speaking?

   _____

   _____

Looking Forward

5. How can you demonstrate to employers that you have effective writing and speaking skills?

   _____

   _____

6. Include in your portfolio samples of speeches you have given. List the titles on the following lines.

   _____

   _____

7. Include in your portfolio samples of your writing. List the titles.

   _____

   _____

8. Include in your portfolio samples of your research. List the titles.

   _____

   _____

Add this page to your Career Development Portfolio.

Become a Critical Thinker and Creative Problem Solver

LEARNING OUTCOMES

In this chapter, you will learn to

10.1 Define Bloom's Taxonomy

10.2 Explain the problem-solving process

10.3 Practice critical thinking and problem-solving strategies

10.4 Describe common fallacies and errors in judgment

10.5 Explain the importance of creativity in problem solving

10.6 Use problem-solving strategies for mathematics and science

10.7 Overcome math and science anxiety

SELF-MANAGEMENT

"I dropped a class, thinking I could take it next semester, but it's offered just once a year, so I won't graduate when I had planned to. I didn't realize one decision could have such an impact."

Have you ever made a decision without thinking through all the consequences? How does your attitude affect your thinking and creativity? In this chapter, you will learn to use your critical thinking and creative problem-solving skills and learn strategies for making sound decisions in all areas of life.

JOURNAL ENTRY In **Worksheet 10.1** on page 328, think of a decision you made that has cost you a lot of time, money, or stress. How would critical thinking and creative problem solving have helped you make better decisions?

"A problem is a picture with a piece missing; the answer is the missing piece."

JOHN HOLT
Educator, author

Problem solving—coming up with possible solutions—and **decision making**—deciding on the best solution—go hand-in-hand. You have to make decisions to solve a problem; conversely, some problems occur because of a decision you made. For example, you may decide to smoke cigarettes; later, you face the problem of nicotine addiction, health problems, and a lot of your budget spent on cigarettes. In school, a decision not to study mathematics and science because they seem too difficult will close off the chance to choose certain majors and careers. Many events in life do not just happen; they are the result of our choices and decisions. We make decisions every day; even not deciding is making a decision. For example, if you avoid going to class, that shows you have decided the class is unimportant or not worth the time. You may have not formally dropped the class or not thought through the consequences, but the result of deciding not to go to class is an *F* grade.

In this chapter, you will learn to use critical thinking and creativity to help you solve problems and make effective and sound decisions. Mathematics and science will be discussed, as these are key areas which rely on your critical thinking and problem-solving skills. You will also learn to overcome math anxiety and develop a positive attitude toward problem solving.

Essential Critical Thinking Skills

As discussed in Chapter 1, critical thinking is a logical, rational, systematic thought process necessary for understanding, analyzing, and evaluating information in order to solve a problem. In the 1956 text *Taxonomy of Educational Objectives,* Benjamin Bloom and his colleagues outlined a hierarchy of six critical thinking skills that college requires (from lowest- to highest-order): knowledge, comprehension, application, analysis, synthesis, and evaluation. (See **Figure 10.1.**)

"The value of a problem is not so much coming up with the answer as in the ideas and attempted ideas it forces on the would-be solver."

I. N. HERSTEIN
Mathematician

1. **Knowledge.** In most college courses, you have to memorize lists, identify facts, complete objective tests, and recognize and recall terms and information.
2. **Comprehension.** You also need to demonstrate that you understand the material. You may be asked to state ideas in your own words, outline key ideas, and translate an author's meaning.
3. **Application.** You will be asked to apply what you've learned to a new situation. You may explore case studies, solve problems, and provide examples to support your ideas. You can learn application by applying ideas to your own life. For example, how can you apply political science concepts to issues in your state?
4. **Analysis.** You will be asked to break apart ideas and relate them to other concepts, answer essay questions, identify assumptions, and analyze values. You will compare and contrast ideas or subjects, such as economic theories or two works of art.

Evaluation ↑	Make judgments about the information
Synthesis ↑	Combine selected parts to create new information
Analysis ↑	Separate understood information into parts
Application ↑	Make practical use of the understood information
Comprehension ↑	Understand the significance of the information
Knowledge	Recall information

CRITICAL THINKING SKILLS

Figure 10.1
Bloom's Taxonomy

Actively participating in college will require you to use six core critical thinking skills. *Which skills are you using as you complete current projects or assignments?*

5. **Synthesis.** You will be asked to integrate ideas, build on other skills, look for interconnections, create and defend a position, improve on an existing idea or design, and develop creative ideas and new perspectives. You might compose a song or research ways that a community project affects other areas of the community.

6. **Evaluation.** You will be asked to criticize a position, form conclusions and judgments, list advantages and disadvantages of a project or an idea, and develop and use criteria for evaluating a decision. You can develop evaluation skills by using standards for evaluating speeches in class, evaluating group projects, and being open to suggestions from your study group and instructors.

To excel in school and make sound decisions in life, you must move beyond simple knowledge and comprehension and be able to apply, analyze, synthesize, and evaluate questions and problems you are faced with. See **Peak Progress 10.1** on page 304 for an example of moving from knowledge to evaluation.

Problem-Solving Steps

You must exercise and apply your critical thinking skills when solving problems and making decisions. The problem-solving process can be broken down into four major steps: (1) Define the problem, (2) gather and interpret information, (3) develop and implement a plan of action, and (4) evaluate the plan.

1. **Define the problem.** Do you understand and can you clearly state the problem? What are you trying to find out? What is known and unknown? What is the situation, or context? What decision are you asked to make? Can you separate the problem into various parts? Organize the problem, or restate the decision or problem in your own words—for example, "Should I go on a study abroad exchange or do an internship?"

Peak Progress

From Knowledge to Evaluation

If you can recall the number 8675309, but you attach no significance to the number, you have mere *knowledge*. Not tremendously useful, is it?

However, if you are familiar with a particular song performed by Tommy Tutone, you may recognize this number as the telephone number of a girl named Jenny, which the songwriter had found penned on a wall. Now you have *comprehension*. Still, you wonder, "So what?"

Maybe you are intrigued enough to actually call the number to see whether Jenny answers. This is *application*. Unfortunately, unless you happen to be in an area code where this telephone number exists, you will probably get a telephone company recording.

Next you break down the number into its component parts. You see that it has a 3-digit prefix and a 4-digit suffix. The prefix is 867. You have just performed a simple *analysis*.

In order to track Jenny down, you will need to combine other bodies of information with what you already know. You know Jenny's phone number, but there could be many identical phone numbers throughout the country. What you need to find is a list of area codes that includes this number. You have then performed *synthesis*.

Before you go any further, ask yourself how important it is to find Jenny. How many matching telephone numbers did you turn up in the previous step? Are you going to dial each of them? How much is it going to cost you in long-distance charges? How much of your time will it take? Is it worth it? You have just made an *evaluation*.

Courtesy T. C. Stuwe, Salt Lake Community College, © 2002.

---

2. **Gather and interpret information.** What are all the possibilities? Be sure you have all the information you need to solve the problem and make a decision. Try to see the problem from different angles. "I have visited the career center and the study abroad office. I have listed pros and cons for each choice. I have included cost and expenses." Are there other options, such as a paid internship or student teaching abroad? When choosing a plan of action, consider all options and then narrow the list.

3. **Develop and implement a plan of action.** How would this plan work? Eventually, you need to act on your decision and choose an appropriate strategy. Ask yourself what information would be helpful. "I have gathered information and talked to people in my chosen field. Most career professionals have suggested that I go on an exchange as a way to broaden my worldview. I found out I can apply for an internship for the following term. Because I can learn a second language and take valuable classes, I am going on the study abroad exchange and will do everything possible to make this experience valuable." Your intention to make this decision succeed is key.

4. **Evaluate your plan.** Why is this plan better for you than other options? Is there one right answer? What consequences are likely if you choose this approach? "I made valuable contacts and am learning so much from this experience. I'll do an internship when I return. This was the best choice for me at this time." Observe the consequences of this decision over time, and reflect on what other options may have worked better. See **Personal Evaluation Notebook 10.1** to explore the consequences of everyday decisions.

Problem-Solving Steps

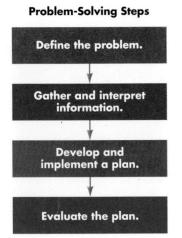

Define the problem.

Gather and interpret information.

Develop and implement a plan.

Evaluate the plan.

Personal Evaluation Notebook

Think It Through

Often we make decisions without considering the consequences. It may be because we're only thinking about the immediate result or benefit. Or maybe the decision seems so minor that the consequences are insignificant. However, a series of poor "small" decisions can lead to big problems later.

Exercise your decision-making and problem-solving skills by teaming up with classmates to consider decisions you make every day. For example, let's say you've missed a couple of classes lately. One person should state the problem or issue. Then go through the problem-solving steps, ask questions, explore possibilities, and use critical thinking to make a sound decision:

1. **Define the problem.**
   - I've missed three classes in the past 2 weeks.

2. **Gather and interpret the information.**
   - The reasons are [such as my babysitter canceled, car broke down, alarm didn't go off, or I hate 8:00 a.m. classes].
   - The consequences for missing this class are
   - If I drop the class, what could happen?
   - If I keep missing the class, what could happen?

3. **Develop and implement a plan of action.**
   - What are some creative possibilities to help me get to class?
   - What is the best plan of action?

4. **Evaluate the plan.**
   - What decision is best for my goals and priorities?
   - How will I ensure that this decision succeeds?

Come up with other situations you may encounter daily, such as relationship issues and spending decisions, and work through them using the problem-solving steps.

Critical Thinking and Problem-Solving Strategies

Critical thinking and problem solving will help you make day-to-day decisions about relationships, courses to take, jobs to apply for, places to live, ideas for speeches and papers, and resolutions to conflicts. You can apply the following strategies to ensure you are fully using your critical thinking and problem-solving capabilities:

1. **Have a positive attitude.** Critical thinking requires a willingness and passion to explore, probe, question, and search for answers and solutions. (See **Figure 10.2**.) Your attitude influences how you solve a problem or make a decision. Think of problems as puzzles to solve, rather than difficulties to avoid. Instead of delaying, making a knee-jerk decision, or looking for the one "right answer," focus on

Figure 10.2
Critical Thinking Qualities

Thinking critically is important for understanding and solving problems. *Do you apply any of the attributes of a critical thinker when you need to solve a problem?*

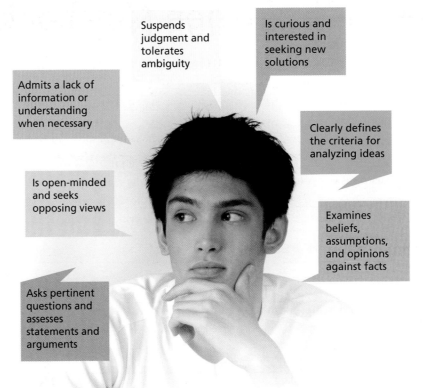

A Critical Thinker . . .

Suspends judgment and tolerates ambiguity

Is curious and interested in seeking new solutions

Admits a lack of information or understanding when necessary

Clearly defines the criteria for analyzing ideas

Is open-minded and seeks opposing views

Examines beliefs, assumptions, and opinions against facts

Asks pertinent questions and assesses statements and arguments

problem-solving strategies. For example, you may have a negative attitude toward math or science, considering it irrelevant or too difficult. Choose to see a problem or situation in the best possible light. Complete **Personal Evaluation Notebook 10.2** to practice turning negatives into positives.

2. **Ask questions.** It's difficult to solve a problem without knowing all the facts and opinions—or at least as many as you can find out. **Peak Progress 10.2** on page 308 offers tips for formulating effective questions.

3. **Persistence pays off.** You won't solve every problem with your first effort. Sometimes you'll need a second or third try. Analytical thinking requires time, persistence, and patience. Sometimes it pays to sleep on an important decision instead of bowing to pressure. Effective problem solvers are not beaten by frustration but look for new ways to solve problems.

4. **Use creativity.** As we will explore later in this chapter, you should learn to think in new and fresh ways, look for interconnections, and brainstorm many solutions. Good problem solvers explore many alternatives and evaluate their strengths and weaknesses.

5. **Pay attention to details.** Effective problem solvers show concern for accuracy. They think about what could go wrong, recheck calculations, and look for errors. They gather all relevant information and proofread or ask questions. They are willing to listen to arguments, create and defend positions, and can distinguish among various points of view.

6. **See all sides of the issue.** Think critically about what you read, hear, and see in newspapers and on the Internet. As you read, question sources and viewpoints. For example, when you read an article about Social Security or tax cuts, ask yourself what biases politicians or special interest groups might have regarding

Personal Evaluation Notebook

10.2

Using Critical Thinking to Solve Problems

Stating a problem clearly, exploring alternatives, reasoning logically, choosing the best alternative, creating an action plan, and evaluating your plan are all involved in making decisions and solving problems.

Look at the common reasons or excuses given by some students for not solving problems creatively or making sound decisions. Create strategies for overcoming these barriers.

1. I'm not a creative person.

   Strategy: _____

   _____

2. Facts can be misleading; I like to follow my gut instinct.

   Strategy: _____

   _____

3. I avoid conflict.

   Strategy: _____

   _____

4. I postpone making decisions.

   Strategy: _____

   _____

5. I worry that I'll make the wrong decision.

   Strategy: _____

   _____

these issues. Does the argument appeal to emotion rather than to logic? Talk to people who have different opinions or belong to a different political party. Really listen to their views, and ask them to explain their opinions and why they support certain issues.

7. **Use reasoning.** We are constantly trying to make sense of our world, so we make inferences to explain and interpret events. Effective problem solvers check their inferences to see if they are sound, not based on assumptions, which often reflect their own experiences and biases. Ask yourself, "What makes me think this is true? Could I be wrong? Are there other possibilities?" Effective problem solvers do not jump to conclusions.

   Inductive reasoning is generalizing from specific concepts to broad principles. For example, you might have had a bad experience with a math class in high school and, based on that experience, might reason inductively that all math classes are hard and boring. When you get into your college math class, you may discover that your conclusion was incorrect and that you actually like mathematics. In contrast, **deductive reasoning** is drawing conclusions based on going from the general to the specific—for example, "Because all mathematics classes at this college must be taken for credit and this class is a math class, I

Asking Questions

"Why is the sky blue?" "Where do babies come from?" When we were children, our days were filled with endless questions, reflecting curiosity about the world around us. As adults, some of us have become reluctant and sometimes even nervous to ask for help or insightful answers. It's not that there are no questions left to ask—just the contrary. Attending college opens up the floodgates of new information to comprehend, process, apply, and question.

This reluctance can stem from possible embarrassment, as the information may have already been covered (and you were daydreaming, didn't read the assignment, didn't see the connections, etc.) and others will think you're behind for one reason or another. Or, when simply talking with friends, you may think asking questions will seem like you are prying or are "nosey," or behind on the latest trends.

Whatever your reasons, you must overcome your reluctance and learn how to formulate questions. Most careers require asking questions and persistence in finding answers. A sales representative asks customers what their needs are and tries to fulfill those needs with his or her product. A physician asks patients questions about their medical history, symptoms, and reactions to medications.

WHO CAN BEST ANSWER YOUR QUESTION?

Before asking a question, determine whom or what you should be consulting. Could the information be found more easily or quickly by looking it up online, in the library, or in another source? Is it a question more appropriate for your instructor, advisor, or financial aid officer? Is there a local "expert" in this area?

WHAT TYPE OF QUESTION SHOULD YOU ASK?

State your question quickly and succinctly, and provide background information only if your question isn't clear. Based on the type of response you are looking for, there are several ways to formulate your question:

- **Closed question.** Use this type of question when you want either a yes/no answer or specific details—for example, "Which planet is closer to the sun—Earth or Mars?"
- **Fact-finding question.** This is aimed at getting information on a particular subject, usually when your core materials (such as the textbook or lecture) haven't provided the information—for example, "Which battle had the most casualties, and was that considered the turning point in the war?"
- **Follow-up question.** This question clarifies a point, gathers more information, or elicits an opinion—for example, "So, what side effects might I experience from this medication?"
- **Open-ended question.** Use this to invite discussion and various viewpoints or interpretations of an issue—for example, "What do you think about the ordinance to ban smoking in local restaurants?"
- **Feedback question.** Use this when you want someone to provide you with constructive criticism—for example, "What sections of my paper supported my main points effectively, and what sections needed more back-up?"

WHEN SHOULD YOU ASK THE QUESTION?

Ask your question as soon as possible after the speaker has completed his or her point. Most likely, your instructor has guidelines for class (such as saving questions for the last 10 minutes). If so, jot down your questions during the lecture, so that you can return to them or to add answers if the content is covered in the meantime. Open-ended and feedback questions may be more appropriate outside a typical class discussion but can often provide the most thoughtful answers.

---

must take it for credit." However, don't assume that the main premise is always true. In this example, there may be math labs, workshops, or special classes offered for no credit. Practice inductive versus deductive reasoning in **Personal Evaluation Notebook 10.3** on page 310.

Common Errors in Judgment

Some thoughts and beliefs are clearly irrational, with no evidence to support them. For example, if you believe people cannot change, you could get stuck in unhealthy situations and accept that there is no solution for your problems. Solving problems requires critical thinking and frequent self-assessment of your thoughts and beliefs. Ask questions to help clarify your thinking and apply the ABC Method of Self-Management to dispel myths and irrational thoughts.

Here are some common errors in judgment or faulty thinking that interfere with effective critical thinking:

Brandon has really enjoyed his first semesters of college and has gotten good grades in the wide variety of classes he has taken. Now at the end of his sophomore year, the pressure is on for him to choose a major.
- Which school resources should he contact to find out more about selecting a major?
- What questions should he ask his advisor?
- Help Brandon walk through the problem-solving process to figure out which major best suits him.

THINK FAST

- *Stereotypes* are judgments held by a person or group about the members of another group—for example, "All instructors are absentminded intellectuals." Learn to see individual differences between people.

- *All-or-nothing thinking* means seeing events or people in black or white, such as turning a single negative event into a pattern of defeat: "If I don't get an *A* in this class, I'm a total failure." Be careful about using the terms *always* and *never*.

- *Snap judgments* are decisions made before gathering all the necessary information or facts. An example is concluding that someone doesn't like you because of one comment or because of a comment made by someone else. Instead, find out the reason for the comment. Perhaps you misinterpreted the meaning.

- *Unwarranted assumptions* are beliefs and ideas you assume are true in different situations. For example, your business instructor allows papers to be turned in late, so you assume that your biology instructor will allow the same.

- *Projection* is the tendency to attribute to others some of your own traits in an attempt to justify your own faulty judgments or actions—for example, "It's OK if I cheat, because everyone else is cheating."

- *Sweeping generalizations* apply one experience to a whole group or issue. For example, if research has been conducted using college students as subjects, you cannot generalize the results to the overall work population.

- The *halo effect* is the tendency to label a person good at many things based on one or two qualities or actions. For example, Serena sits in the front row, attends every class, and gets good grades on papers. Based on this observation, you decide she is smart, organized, and a great student in all her classes. First impressions are important in the halo effect and are difficult to change. You can make this work for you. Suppose you start out the semester by giving it your all; you go to every class, establish a relationship with the instructor, participate in class, and work hard. Later in the semester, you may need to miss a class or ask to take an exam early. Your instructor has already formed an opinion of you as a good student and may be more sympathetic, because you have created a positive impression.

- *Negative labeling* is focusing on and identifying with shortcomings, either yours or others. Instead of saying, "I made a mistake when I quit going to my math study group," you tell yourself, "I'm a loser." You may also pick a single negative trait or detail and focus on it exclusively. You discount positive qualities or accomplishments: "I've lost my keys again. I am so disorganized. Yes, I did organize a successful club fundraiser, but that doesn't count."

Personal Evaluation Notebook

Inductive versus Deductive Reasoning

Practice creating inductive and deductive statements.

INDUCTIVE EXAMPLES

- No one should consider buying a car with a sunroof. Mine leaked every time it rained.
- Nadia ended up in the hospital with food poisoning the day after the party. I'm sure that's why Cara and Brendan said they were sick the next day, too.

_____

_____

_____

_____

DEDUCTIVE EXAMPLES

- Everyone who attended the review session for the first test received an *A*. If I attend the next session, I'm bound to get an *A*.
- All the men in our family are over 6 feet tall. I'm sure my baby son will be as tall when he's an adult.

_____

_____

_____

_____

Creative Problem Solving

Creativity is thinking of something differently and using new approaches to solve problems. Many inventions have involved a break from traditional thinking and resulted in an "aha!" experience. For example, Albert Einstein used many unusual approaches and "riddles" that revolutionized scientific thought. (Several websites include "Einstein's Riddle." Locate one and test yourself to see if you can answer "who owns the fish?")

Use creativity to explore alternatives, look for relationships among different items, and develop imaginative ideas and solutions. Try the following strategies to unlock your mind's natural creativity:

1. **Expect to be creative.** Use affirmations that reinforce your innate creativity:
   - I am a creative and resourceful person.
   - I have many imaginative and unusual ideas.

Copyright © 2015 The McGraw-Hill Companies

- Creative ideas flow to me many times a day.
- I act on many of these ideas.
- I act responsibly, use critical thinking, check details carefully, and take calculated risks.

2. **Challenge the rules.** Habit often restricts you from trying new approaches to problem solving. Often, there is more than one solution. List many alternatives, and imagine the likely consequences of each. Empty your mind of the "right" way of looking at problems, and strive to see situations in a fresh way. How often have you told yourself you must follow certain rules and perform tasks a certain way? If you want to be creative, try new approaches, look at things in a new order, break the pattern, and challenge the rules. Practice a different approach by completing the Nine-Dot Exercise in **Personal Evaluation Notebook 10.4** on page 312.

3. **Use games, puzzles, and humor.** Rethinking an assignment as a puzzle, challenge, or game instead of a difficult problem opens your mind and encourages your creative side. Creative people often get fresh ideas while having fun engaging in an unrelated activity. When your defenses are down, your brain is relaxed and your subconscious is alive; creative thoughts can flow.

4. **Brainstorm.** Brainstorming is a common strategy for freeing the imagination. You can brainstorm alone, but a group may be more effective for generating as many ideas as possible. Brainstorming encourages the mind to explore without judging the merit of new ideas. In fact, even silly and irrelevant ideas can lead to truly inventive ideas. While brainstorming ideas for a speech, one study group started joking about the topic, and new ideas came from all directions.

5. **Change mindsets.** It is difficult to see another frame of reference once your mind is set. The exercise in **Personal Evaluation Notebook 10.5** on page 313 is an "aha" exercise. It is exciting to watch people see the other picture. Perceptual exercises of this kind demonstrate that you see what you focus on and when you reframe. You are conditioned to see certain things, depending on your beliefs and attitudes. Rather than seeing facts, you may see your interpretation of reality. Perceptual distortion can influence how you solve problems and make decisions. For example, John was told that his Spanish instructor was aloof, not student-oriented, and boring. John went to his first class with that mindset, sat in the back of class, and did not ask questions or get involved. He later found out that his friend had been referring to another instructor. John realized that his mindset was influencing how he viewed his instructor.

Copyright © 2015 The McGraw-Hill Companies

Personal Evaluation Notebook

10.4

Nine-Dot Exercise

Connect the following nine dots by drawing only four (or fewer) straight lines without lifting the pencil from the paper. Do not retrace any lines. The solution is on page 322.

He reframed his impression and developed a positive relationship with the instructor.

6. **Change your routine.** Try a different route to work or school. Read different kinds of books. Spend time with people who are different from you. Occasionally break away from your daily routine, and take time every day to relax, daydream, and renew your energy. Look at unexpected events as a chance to retreat from constant activity and hurried thoughts. Perhaps this is a good time to brainstorm ideas for a speech assignment or outline an assigned paper.

7. **Use both sides of the brain.** You use the logical, analytical side of your brain for certain activities and your imaginative and multidimensional side for others. When you develop and integrate both sides of your brain, you become more imaginative, creative, and productive.

8. **Acknowledge your style.** Your personality type or learning style may coincide with the way you approach problem solving. Recall Figure 1.3 on page 21, which lists the characteristics of personality types. If you tend to be a *judger*, for example, your thinking style may be to tackle problems quickly, looking for objective facts and precedents to support your decision. In contrast to a *perceiver*, you may not consider the "human toll" or circumstances that could take the decision in another direction. As in the case of learning, which you can enhance by recognizing your preferred style and mixing it up by incorporating other styles, you can enhance problem solving by adding styles to the one you prefer. To think out of the box, recognize how you normally think and respond to problems, assess if your style clouds or limits your thinking, and determine how to expand your abilities. Based on your earlier assessment of your personality type and learning style (which you may have modified since then), how would you characterize your "thinking style"?

9. **Keep a journal.** Keep a daily journal of creative ideas, dreams, and thoughts. Collect stories of creative people and what they do that is unique. Write in your journal about risks you take and what you have learned from the experience.

handshakes by solving it for 2 people instead of 5. When each person initiates a handshake, 2 people shake hands a total of 2 times. Using the formula determined in number 4, you see that the equation is $2 \times 1 = 2$. Fill in the rest of the table on the previous page.

Along the same lines, when working on homework, studying in your group, or taking a test, always do the easiest problems first. Confident that you can solve one kind of problem, you gain enthusiasm to tackle more difficult questions or problems. Also, an easier problem may be similar to a harder problem.

6. **Translate words into equations.** Highlight visual and verbal learning by showing connections between words and numbers. Write an equation that models that problem. For example, Sarah has a total of $82.00, consisting of an equal number of pennies, nickels, dimes, and quarters. How many coins does she have in all? You know how much all of Sarah's coins are worth and you know how much each coin is worth. (In the following equation, p = pennies, n = nickels, d = dimes, and q = quarters.)

$$p + 5n + 10d + 25q = 8,200$$

We know that she has an equal number of each coin; thus, $p = n = d = q$. Therefore, we can substitute p for all the other variables:

$$1p + 5p + 10p + 25p = 41p = 8,200, \text{ so } p = 200$$

Sarah has 200 pennies, 200 nickels, 200 dimes, and 200 quarters. Therefore, she has 800 coins.

7. **Estimate, make a reasonable guess, check the guess, and revise.** Using the example in number 6, if you were told that Sarah had a large number of coins that added up to $82.00, you could at least say that the total was no more than 8,200 (the number of coins if they were all pennies) and no less than 328 (the number of coins if they were all quarters).

8. **Work backwards and eliminate.** For example, what is the largest 2-digit number that is divisible by 3 whose digits differ by 2? First, working backwards from 99, list numbers that are divisible by 3:

99, 96, 93, 90, 87, 84, 81, 78, 75, 72, 69, 66, 63, 60, . . .

Now cross out all numbers whose digits do not differ by 2. The largest number remaining is 75.

9. **Summarize in a group.** Working in a group is the best way to integrate all learning styles, keep motivation and interest active, and generate lots of ideas and support. Explain the problem to your group and why you arrived at the answer. Talking out loud, summarizing chapters, and listening to others clarifies thinking and helps you learn.

10. **Take a quiet break.** If your group can't find a solution to the problem, take a break. Sometimes it helps to find a quiet spot and reflect. Working on another problem or relaxing for a few minutes while listening to music helps you return to the problem refreshed.

Overcome Math and Science Anxiety

Many people suffer from some math and science anxiety—having a preconceived notion that the material is difficult to learn, over their heads, or too precise (only

● **Anxiety about Math and Science**
Some students are nervous about taking courses in math and science, even though the basic principles have many everyday applications. *What are some tasks you do daily that involve knowledge of basic math and science?*

one correct answer). As with the fear many experience with public speaking, the first step in learning any subject is to use critical thinking and creative problem solving to manage and overcome these anxieties.

Anxiety is a learned emotional response—you were not born with it. Because it is learned, it can be unlearned. In Chapter 9, we explored strategies for overcoming speech anxiety, and many apply to math and science as well. Here are some additional strategies:

1. **Do your prep work.** Don't take a math or science class if you haven't taken the proper prerequisites. It is better to spend the summer or an additional semester gaining the necessary skills, so that you don't feel overwhelmed and discouraged.

2. **Keep up and review often.** If you prepare early and often, you will be less anxious. Use the night before a test for reviewing, not learning new material.

3. **Discipline yourself.** Focus your attention away from your fears, and concentrate on the task at hand. Jot down ideas and formulas, draw pictures, and write out the problem. Reduce interruptions and concentrate fully for short periods. Time yourself on problems to increase speed and make the most of short study sessions.

4. **Study in groups.** Learning does not take place in isolation but, rather, in a supportive environment where anxiety is reduced and each person feels safe to use trial-and-error methods. Group study encourages creativity, interaction, and multiple solutions. You will build confidence as you learn to think out loud, brainstorm creative solutions, and solve problems. See **Peak Progress 10.4** for a comprehensive checklist of questions to use as you solve problems.

5. **Have a positive attitude.** As mentioned earlier, a positive attitude is key to learning any subject. Do you get sidetracked by negative self-talk about your abilities or the reason for learning math skills? Choose to focus on the positive feelings you have when you are confident and in control. Replace negative and defeating self-talk with positive "I can" affirmations. Math anxiety, like stage fright and other fears, is compounded by negative self-talk. Approach math and science with a positive "can do," inquisitive attitude.

6. **Dispute the myths.** Many times, fears are caused by myths, such as "Men do better than women in math and science" or "Creative people are not good at math and science." There is no basis for the belief that gender determines math ability, nor is skill in math and science unfeminine. Success in math and science requires creative thinking. As mathematician Augustus De Morgan said, "The moving power of mathematics is not reasoning, but imagination."

7. **Ask for help.** Don't wait until you are in trouble or frustrated. Talk with the instructor, visit the learning center, get a tutor, and join a study group. If you continue to feel anxious or lost, visit the counseling center. Try taking a summer refresher course. You'll be prepared and confident when you take the required course later.

See **Peak Progress 10.5** to apply the Adult Learning Cycle to overcoming anxiety.

Peak Progress

Problem-Solving Checklist

When you enroll in any course, including math or science, consider these questions:

- Have you approached the class with a positive attitude?
- What do you want to know, and what are you being asked to find out?
- Have you separated essential information from the unessential?
- Have you separated the known from the unknown?
- Have you asked a series of questions: How? When? Where? What? If?
- Have you devised a plan for solving the problem?
- Have you gone from the general to the specific?
- Have you made an estimate?
- Have you illustrated or organized the problem?
- Have you made a table or a diagram, drawn a picture, or summarized data?
- Have you written out the problem?

- Have you discovered a pattern to the problem?
- Have you alternated intense concentration with frequent breaks?
- Have you tried working backwards, completing similar problems, and solving small parts?
- Have you determined if you made careless errors or do not understand the concepts?
- Have you asked for help early?
- Have you been willing to put in the time required to solve problems?
- Have you analyzed the problem? Was your guess close? Did your plan work? How else can you approach the problem?
- Have you brainstormed ideas on your own? In a group setting?
- Have you rewarded yourself for facing your fears, overcoming anxiety, and learning valuable skills that will increase your success in school, in your job, and in life?

Peak Progress

Applying the Adult Learning Cycle to Overcoming Math and Science Anxiety

1. **RELATE. Why do I want to learn this?** I want to be confident in math and science. Avoiding math and science closes doors and limits opportunities. More than 75 percent of careers use math and science, and these are often higher-status, better-paying jobs. This is essential knowledge I'll use in all facets of life.

2. **OBSERVE. How does this work?** I can learn a lot about applying critical thinking and creative problem solving to mathematics and science by watching, listening, and trying new things. I'll observe people who are good at math and science. What do they do? I'll also observe and learn from the mistakes of people who experience anxiety and don't do well. I'll try new critical thinking techniques for dealing with fear and observe how I'm improving.

3. **REFLECT. What does this mean?** I'll apply critical thinking to mathematics and science. What works and doesn't work? I'll think about and test new

ways of reducing anxiety and break old patterns and negative self-talk. I'll look for connections and associations with other types of anxiety and apply what I learn.

4. **DO. What can I do with this?** I will practice reducing my anxiety. I'll find practical applications for connecting critical thinking and creative problem solving to math and science. Each day I'll work on one area. For example, I'll maintain a positive attitude as I approach math and science classes.

5. **TEACH. Whom can I share this with?** I'll form a study group and share my tips and experiences. I'll demonstrate and teach others the methods I've learned. I'll reward myself when I do well.

Remember, attitude is everything. If you keep an open mind, apply strategies you have learned in this chapter, and practice your critical thinking skills, you will become more confident in your problem-solving abilities.

TAKING CHARGE

Summary

In this chapter, I learned to

- **Appreciate the importance of critical thinking.** Critical thinking is fundamental to understanding and solving problems in coursework, my job, and the rest of my life. I have learned to examine beliefs, assumptions, and opinions against facts, ask pertinent questions, and analyze data.

- **Apply essential critical thinking skills.** Bloom's Taxonomy outlines the six critical thinking skills that college requires (from lowest- to highest-order): knowledge, comprehension, application, analysis, synthesis, and evaluation.

- **Use the problem-solving process.** When I problem solve, I will (1) define the problem; (2) gather and interpret information; (3) develop and implement a plan of action; and (4) evaluate the plan or solution.

- **Incorporate problem-solving strategies.** My attitude affects how I approach problem solving. I have developed a positive, inquisitive attitude and a willingness to explore, probe, question, and search for answers and solutions. I will replace negative self-talk with affirmations. I will use my critical thinking skills and be persistent in solving problems. I will participate in a supportive group environment, such as a study group.

- **Avoid errors in judgment.** I will avoid using stereotypes, all-or-nothing thinking, snap judgments, unwarranted assumptions, projection, sweeping generalizations, the halo effect, and negative labeling. I will not project my habits onto others to justify my behavior or decisions.

- **Use creative problem solving.** I will use creative problem solving to approach problems from a different direction and explore new options. What problems are similar? Is there a pattern to the problem? I will brainstorm various strategies. I will act out the problem, move it around, picture it, take it apart, translate it, and summarize it in my own words. I will solve easier problems before tackling harder problems.

- **Apply strategies to math and science courses.** What model, formula, drawing, sketch, equation, chart, table, calculation, or particular strategy will help? I choose the most appropriate strategy and outline a step-by-step plan. I show all my work, so that I can review.

- **Overcome anxiety for math and science.** If I am anxious about taking math and science courses, I will try to maintain a positive attitude, use available resources, take control, and focus on the task at hand.

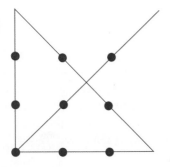

Solution to the Nine-Dot Exercise on Page 312

Most people try to solve this problem by remaining within the boundaries of the dots. However, when you move outside the confines of the dots and the boundaries are reset, you can easily solve the puzzle. This exercise helps illustrate that some problems cannot be solved with traditional thinking.

Performance Strategies

Following are the top 10 strategies for critical thinking and creative problem solving:

- Define the problem.
- Gather and interpret information.
- Develop and implement a plan of action.
- Evaluate your decisions.

- Ask questions.
- Brainstorm creative options.
- Pay attention to details.
- Consider all sides of an issue.
- Use reasoning and avoid errors in judgment.
- Have a positive attitude.

Tech for Success

Take advantage of the text's website at **www.mhhe.com/ferrett9e** for additional study aids, useful forms, and convenient and applicable resources.

- **Work on weak areas.** Various online programs can help you determine the mathematical areas where you need the most work. ALEKS (**www.aleks.com/highered**) is a tutorial program that identifies your less proficient areas and then focuses on improvement through practice and targeted problems.

- **Math at your fingertips.** In your studies, you will come across many standard calculations and formulas, most of which can be found online and downloaded. Although this should not replace working through the formulas yourself to make sure you understand their applications, it does make incorporating math into your everyday life much easier.

Study Team Notes

Marina and Josef Koshetz
RESTAURANT OWNERS

Related Majors: Restaurant and Food Service Management, Business

Creativity at Work

Marina Koshetz and her husband, Josef, have recently opened a small restaurant that serves foods from their homeland of Russia. Starting their restaurant was a great deal of work. They had to get the correct permits, remodel an existing building, purchase equipment, and plan the menu. The couple works long hours, 6 days a week. Before opening the restaurant at 11 a.m., Marina makes bread while Josef mixes together the traditional dishes they will serve. Then Marina remains in the kitchen to cook and prepare dishes while Josef waits tables and runs the cash register. At the end of the day, the couple washes the dishes and cleans the restaurant together. Although the restaurant is closed on Mondays, Marina and Josef use that day to plan the next week's specials and purchase food and other supplies.

Despite their hard work, the couple has made only enough money to cover costs. On a recent Monday afternoon, the two restaurateurs brainstormed ways to attract more customers. The restaurant is located in a quiet neighborhood on the edge of a district where many Russian immigrants live. So far, almost all of their customers have been Russian. Josef and Marina realized they needed to do more to attract other residents to their restaurant. They decided to host an open house and invite everyone living within a mile radius of the restaurant. Then they decided to add a couple of popular American dishes and offered a discount on Groupon. Soon their restaurant was attracting more customers, and the business began to show a profit.

CRITICAL THINKING How did Josef and Marina use creativity and critical thinking to improve their business?

Peak Performer

PROFILE

Scott Adams

He's been described as a techie with the "social skills of a mousepad." He's not the sort of fellow you'd expect to attract media attention. However, pick up a newspaper, turn to the comics, and you'll find him. He's Dilbert. Cartoonist Scott Adams created this comic-strip character who daily lampoons corporate America and provides a humorous outlet for employees everywhere.

Though Adams was creative at a young age, his artistic endeavors were discouraged early on. The Famous Artists School rejected him at age 11. Years later, he received the lowest grade in a college drawing class. Practicality replaced creativity. In 1979, Adams earned a B.A. in economics from Hartwick College in Oneonta, New York, and, in 1986, an MBA from the University of California at Berkeley. For the next 15 years, Adams settled uncomfortably into a series of jobs that "defied description." Ironically, the frustrations of the workplace—power-driven co-workers, inept bosses, and cell-like cubicles—fueled his imagination. Adams began doodling, and Dilbert was born.

Encouraged by others, Adams submitted his work to United Media, a major cartoon syndicate. He was offered a contract in 1989, and "Dilbert" debuted in 50 national newspapers. Today, "Dilbert" appears in 2,000

newspapers in 70 countries and was the first syndicated cartoon to have its own website.

With such mass exposure, coming up with new ideas for cartoons could be a challenge. However, Adams found the perfect source: He gets hundreds of messages a day from workers at home and abroad. His hope is that, through his creative invention, solutions will develop for the problems he satirizes.

PERFORMANCE THINKING Of the creative problem-solving strategies on pages 310–316, which one do you think has been most helpful for Scott Adams and why?

CHECK IT OUT According to Scott Adams, "Creativity is allowing yourself to make mistakes. Art is knowing which ones to keep." Adams is no stranger to taking chances and voicing his views on management—both in the workforce and in the government. At **www.dilbert.com,** you can read (and respond to, if you like) Adams' blog and "mash up" one of his comics by creatively inserting your own words into the frames.

Starting Today

At least one strategy I learned in this chapter that I plan to try right away is

_____

_____

_____

What changes must I make in order for this strategy to be most effective?

_____

_____

_____

Review Questions

Based on what you have learned in this chapter, write your answers to the following questions:

1. Name six critical thinking skills necessary for success in college.

_____

_____

2. What are the attributes of a critical thinker?

_____

_____

3. What are the four steps of problem solving?

_____

_____

4. Name five strategies for becoming more creative.

_____

_____

5. Name five strategies for problem solving in math and science.

_____

_____

To test your understanding of the chapter's concepts, complete the chapter quiz at **www.mhhe.com/ferrett9e.**

Conquering Fear of Failure

In the Classroom

Gloria Ramone is a single mom who works part-time and lives and attends school in the inner city. She is eager to complete her education, begin her career, and earn a higher salary. She is a medical records student who wants her classes to be practical and relevant. Her school requires a class in critical thinking, but she is resisting it because she sees no practical application to her job. Her attitude is affecting her attendance and participation.

1. Offer ideas to help Gloria see the importance of critical thinking in decision making.

_____

_____

2. Help her connect decisions in school with job decisions.

_____

_____

In the Workplace

Gloria is now an office assistant for a team of doctors. She is also taking evening classes, working toward a health care administration degree. She has received praise for her work but wants to eventually move up to office manager or work for a health care company. Gloria is very interested in the insurance industry and loves to solve problems. New issues arise every day, and she has decisions to make. She has lots of practice predicting results and using critical thinking to solve problems. Gloria enjoys most of her courses but dreads the classes in finance and statistics, because she has math anxiety.

3. What strategies in this chapter could help Gloria overcome math anxiety?

_____

_____

4. What are some affirmations Gloria could use to help her develop a positive attitude about math?

_____

_____

_____

Applying the ABC Method of Self-Management

In the Journal Entry on page 301, you were asked to describe a decision you made that cost you a lot of time, money, or stress. How would critical thinking and creative problem solving have helped you make better decisions?

_____

_____

_____

    Now that you know more strategies for critical thinking and creative problem solving, apply the ABC Method to a difficult situation you have encountered, such as a financial dilemma, rigorous course, or personal crisis. Use your critical thinking skills to work through the situation and arrive at a positive result.

A = Actual event:

_____

_____

_____

B = Beliefs:

_____

_____

_____

C = Challenge:

_____

_____

_____

Use positive visualization and practice deep breathing with your eyes closed for just 1 minute. See yourself calm, centered, and relaxed, learning formulas, practicing problem solving, and using critical thinking to work through problems. You feel confident because you have learned to control your anxiety and maintain a positive attitude.

PRACTICE SELF-MANAGEMENT

For more examples of learning how to manage difficult situations, see the "Self-Management Workbook" section of the Online Learning Center website at **www.mhhe.com/ferrett9e.**

Apply Bloom's Taxonomy

Different situations call for different levels of thinking. Although many, if not all, of these skills are required in every course you take, jot down classes or situations where you might rely more on a particular thinking skill. For example, in a speech class, you may be asked to evaluate others' speeches.

Critical Thinking Skill	Task	Class or Situation
Knowledge	Recite; recall; recognize	
Comprehension	Restate; explain; state; discuss; summarize	
Application	Apply; prepare; solve a problem; explore a case study	
Analysis	Break ideas apart and relate to other ideas; complete an essay	
Synthesis	Integrate ideas; create new ideas; improve on design	
Evaluate	Critique; evaluate; cite advantages and disadvantages	

REVIEW AND APPLICATIONS | CHAPTER 10

Preparing for Critical Thinking

Brainstorm alternative approaches and solutions to the problems that arise in your day-to-day activities at school, on the job, or at home. Consider things such as the potential consequences of certain decisions, timing, and related costs.

ISSUE/PROBLEM

_____

_____

_____

_____

_____

SOLUTION 1: _____

Pros	Cons

SOLUTION 2: _____

Pros	Cons

SOLUTION 3: _____

Pros	Cons

BEST SOLUTION AND WHY:

_____

_____

_____

You Can Solve the Problem: Sue's Decision

Every day, life brings problems and choices. The kinds of choices you make can make your life easier or harder. Often, you do not know which direction to take. Use these six steps to work through the following case study:

Step 1   Know what the problem really is. Is it a daily problem? Is it a once-in-a-lifetime problem?
Step 2   List what you know about the problem. List what you don't know. Ask questions. Get help and advice.
Step 3   Explore alternate choices.
Step 4   Think about the pros and cons for the other choices. Arrange them from best to worst choice.
Step 5   Pick the choice you feel good about.
Step 6   Study what happens after you have made your choice. Are you happy about the choice? Would you make it again?

Case Study: Sue

Sue has been diagnosed with cancer. Her doctor has told her that it is in only one place in her body. The doctor wants to operate. He thinks he will be able to remove all of it, but he wants Sue to undergo 4 months of chemotherapy, which will make her feel very sick. It will make her tired, but it may also help keep the cancer from coming back and spreading.

Sue is not sure what to do. She has two small children who are not in school. Sue's husband works days and cannot help care for the children during the day. The rest of Sue's family lives far away, and she cannot afford day care. She wonders, "How will I be able to care for my children if I'm sick?"

The doctor has told Sue that she must make her own choice. Will she undergo the chemotherapy? She will talk with her husband, and they will make a choice together.

What is Sue's problem? What are her choices? What would you decide? Apply the six steps to help Sue make a good decision by writing responses to the following questions and statements.

Step 1   The problem is

_____

_____

_____

_____

(continued)

Step 2

a. You know these things about the problem:

_____

_____

_____

_____

b. You don't know these things about the problem:

_____

_____

_____

_____

Step 3   The other choices are

_____

_____

_____

_____

Step 4   Rank the choices, best to worst.

_____

_____

_____

_____

Step 5   Pick a choice the family might feel good about and explain why.

_____

_____

_____

_____

Step 6   What might happen to Sue and her family?

_____

_____

_____

_____

Assessing and Demonstrating Your Critical Thinking Skills

1. **Looking back:** Review your worksheets to find activities that helped you learn to make decisions and solve problems creatively. Jot down examples. Also, look for examples of how you learned to apply critical thinking skills to math and science.

   _____

   _____

   _____

   _____

   _____

2. **Taking stock:** What are your strengths in decision making and critical thinking? Are you creative? What areas would you like to improve?

   _____

   _____

   _____

   _____

   _____

3. **Looking forward:** How would you demonstrate critical thinking and creative problem-solving skills to an employer?

   _____

   _____

   _____

   _____

   _____

4. **Documentation:** Document your critical thinking and creative problem-solving skills. Which instructor or employer would write a letter of recommendation? Indicate here which person you'll contact. Add this letter to your portfolio.

   _____

   _____

   _____

   _____

Add this page to your Career Development Portfolio.

Create a Healthy Mind, Body, and Spirit

LEARNING OUTCOMES

In this chapter, you will learn to

11.1 Explain the connection among the mind, body, and spirit

11.2 Make healthy choices in your diet

11.3 Incorporate regular physical activity

11.4 Manage stress and reduce anxiety

11.5 Make sound decisions about alcohol and other drugs

11.6 Recognize depression and suicidal tendencies

11.7 Protect yourself from disease, unplanned pregnancy, and acquaintance rape

SELF-MANAGEMENT

"I'm stressed out with doing so much homework and trying to juggle everything. I haven't been getting enough sleep, and I'm gaining weight from eating too much fast food and not exercising. What can I do to manage my stress and be healthier?"

Do you feel overwhelmed and stressed by too many demands? Do you lack energy from too little sleep or exercise or from excess calories? In this chapter, you will learn how to manage stress and create healthy habits to last a lifetime. You will see yourself healthy and in charge of your mental, physical, and spiritual life.

JOURNAL ENTRY In **Worksheet 11.1** on page 366, describe a time when you had lots of energy, felt healthy and rested, and were in control of your weight. What factors helped you be calm, confident, and healthy? How did your attitude help you be in control?

> " He who has health has hope; and he who has hope has everything. "
>
> ARABIC PROVERB

reating balance, managing stress, increasing energy, and providing time for renewal are essential to becoming a peak performer. In this world of multitasking, we need to slow down, become mindful of our purpose, and focus on important priorities. In this chapter, we will present principles and guidelines to help you develop the most effective methods of maintaining your health while learning how to cope with daily demands.

Redefining Health: Connecting the Mind, Body, and Spirit

Many people think of health as the absence of disease. However, optimal health—or **wellness**—means living life fully with purpose, meaning, and vitality. Your overall wellness is largely determined by your decisions about how you live your life and the measures you take to avoid illness. Although genetics, age, and accidents also influence your health and are beyond your control, you can optimize your health by understanding the connection among your mind, body, and spirit. The habits you develop now will affect not only how long you live but also the quality of life you enjoy.

The Mind

Peak emotional and intellectual wellness requires that you develop the mind's thinking and feeling aspects. It is important to develop critical thinking and creative problem-solving skills, good judgment, common sense, and self-control. It's also important to develop and manage your emotional qualities, such as a positive attitude, optimism, confidence, coping skills, and rapport building. You need to understand and be able to express emotions, have empathy for others, manage yourself, and develop healthy relationships.

The Body

Peak physical wellness requires eating healthy foods, exercising, getting plenty of sleep, recognizing the symptoms of disease, making responsible decisions about sex, avoiding harmful habits, improving your immune system, and taking steps to prevent illness and physical harm. None of this information is new; however, many people have difficulty putting these good habits into practice.

The Spirit

Peak spiritual wellness requires thinking about and clarifying your values and questioning the purpose, beliefs, and principles that give your life meaning. Spirituality may include your religious beliefs or a belief in a higher power, but also it encompasses your willingness to serve others; your sense of ethics and honesty;

your relationship to people, nature, and animals; your definition of the purpose of life; the legacy you want to leave; and how you fit into this universe. In Chapter 2, we discussed Maslow's hierarchy of needs. At the highest level, self-actualized people achieve fulfillment, creativity, and greater spiritual growth. Some physicians believe spirituality is the essence of wellness and wholeness. The body, mind, and spirit are interconnected. For example, if you are optimistic and live with love, honesty, and forgiveness, you are more likely to be physically well.

Understanding the connection among the mind, body, and spirit will help you develop skills for coping with the demands of school and work. Reports, deadlines, tests, performance reviews, conflicts, committees, commuting, family responsibilities, and presentations are all part of life. These and other demands create a great deal of stress. Stress is not an external event but part of a larger system, and it affects all aspects of your mind, body, and spirit.

Awareness and Prevention

The first step in managing your health is awareness. You may not even realize you eat every time you watch television, drink several cans of diet cola while you study, or nibble while you fix dinner. You may be drinking alcohol or smoking when you're under stress instead of learning healthy coping skills. Improving your health begins with observing your daily habits and replacing unproductive ones with beneficial choices.

CANCER

It's important to observe how your body feels, the thoughts going through your mind, and your stress level. Have you recently experienced discomfort or a change in your body? If you can identify symptoms and early-warning signs of an illness, you can take action to protect yourself from diseases, such as cancer. One in three people will develop cancer in his or her lifetime. At **www.cancer.org**, the American Cancer Society provides guidelines for the early detection of specific cancers, such as skin cancer, which is diagnosed more than 1 million times each year. Signs and symptoms such as unexplained weight loss of 10 pounds or more, persistent fever, fatigue, pain, and skin changes can be caused by a range of conditions, including cancer, and should be taken seriously. **Figure 11.1** on page 338 includes more specific signs and symptoms of cancer. While these are the most common, there are many other signs. If you notice any major changes in the way your body functions or looks or the way you feel, especially if it persists or gets worse, tell someone, including your doctor.

DIABETES

Although more than 11 million people are living with cancer in the United States, an estimated 23.6 million people (almost 8 percent of the population) have diabetes, making it one of the fastest-growing health issues. Several factors are involved (including genetics), but the rise in rates of obesity (more than 33 percent of U.S. adults over age 20 are considered obese) probably contributes to the increase in cases of diabetes. Obesity is a risk factor for many illnesses (including heart disease and cancer) and costs almost $150 billion in medical expenses each year.

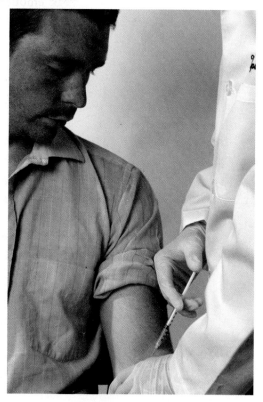

● **Fighting the Flu**
Each year, 36,000 people in the United States die from seasonal flu-related causes, making it important to understand how to protect yourself from contracting the flu. *Do you know what to do to decrease your risk of getting the flu?*

Figure 11.1
Cancer Caution Signs

Although these are the most common specific signs of cancer, they could be symptoms of other health issues. *Do you routinely discuss any concerns with your physician?*

See your doctor if you experience any of the following:

- Change in bowel habits or bladder function
- Sores that do not heal
- Unusual bleeding or discharge
- Thickening or lump in breast or other parts of the body
- Indigestion or trouble swallowing
- Recent change in a wart or mole
- Nagging cough or hoarseness

Source: American Cancer Society.

Strategies for Good Health Management

1. **Eat healthy foods.** Eat a nutritious diet daily to control your weight and blood pressure and to reduce depression, anxiety, headaches, fatigue, and insomnia. The *Dietary Guidelines for Americans,* published jointly every 5 years by the Department of Health and Human Services and the U.S. Department of Agriculture, provides authoritative advice about how good dietary habits can promote health and reduce risk for major chronic diseases. The latest edition can be found at **www.health.gov/dietaryguidelines**. Additionally, the following general guidelines will help you make healthy choices in your diet:

   - *Eat a variety of foods.* Include whole grains, lots of fruits and vegetables, milk, meats, poultry, fish, and breads and cereals in your diet. **See Peak Progress 11.1** for suggested descriptions of various balanced diets.

   - *Increase your fiber.* Having a healthy digestive system helps reduce your risk of constipation, diverticulosis, hemorrhoids, high cholesterol, obesity, colon cancer, diabetes, and heart disease. Many grains, beans, fruits, and vegetables are good sources of fiber.

   - *Reduce the amount of animal fat in your diet.* Too much animal fat can increase the level of cholesterol in your blood, which can affect your cardiovascular system, causing your body to get less oxygen.

   - *Broil or bake rather than frying.* If you do fry, use olive oil or another monounsaturated fat instead of butter.

   - *Cut down on salt.* Salt is an ingredient in many prepared foods. You may be surprised that white bread is the leading source of sodium in the average diet. Be aware of how much salt you consume.

   - *Cut down on sugar and refined carbohydrates.* Eating refined sugar creates a sudden drop in blood sugar, shakiness, and a need for more glucose. This can lead to type 2 diabetes, obesity, and other health problems. Substitute whole grains and fresh fruit and vegetables for white bread and sweets.

Eating for Health and Energy

MEDITERRANEAN DIET

Researchers have studied the effects of diet for years and have tried to agree on the best diet for most people. In 1993, scientists and nutritionists from the United States and Europe met to look at the traditional Mediterranean diet, which may have prolonged life and prevented disease for centuries in Mediterranean countries. The experts released a model similar to that of the U.S. Department of Agriculture's (USDA's) original food guide pyramid. (See pyramid illustrations below.) The Mediterranean model suggests eating more beans and legumes than animal-based proteins and advocates using olive oil daily.

MYPLATE

The food guide pyramid developed by the USDA has continued to change over the years, and in 2011 it was replaced with a plate, helping consumers understand how their meals should be divided among the various food groups. Each "color" on the plate is tied to a specific food group (orange = grains, green = vegetables, etc.). To determine your needs and create a good eating plan, go to **www.choosemyplate.gov** and look for the SuperTracker application, which can help you plan, analyze, and track your diet and physical activity. You can also use Worksheet 11.3 on page 369 to get a snapshot of your eating habits.

DASH

Dietary Approaches to Stop Hypertension (DASH) is designed to combat high blood pressure and is widely recommended by physicians, the *Dietary Guidelines for Americans*, and the American Heart Association. The goal is to eventually eliminate the need for medications by eating a diet high in potassium, magnesium, calcium, and fiber, and that is moderately high in protein and low in saturated fat and total fat. Although these can be found in fruits, vegetables, grains, and low-fat dairy, many consumers need help initially determining the best food sources and serving sizes. Go to **www.dashdiet.org** for more information.

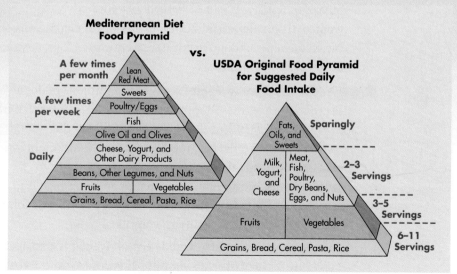

Source: U.S. Department of Agriculture, U.S. Department of Health and Human Services.

- *Restrict the "diet" foods.* Research indicates that diet soft drinks may actually hamper your efforts to control calories, confusing your body as to how many calories it has consumed. And 100-calorie serving sizes may help you control how much you eat—as long as you stop after one package. Oftentimes, we trick ourselves into thinking that we've done such a good job cutting calories that a little more won't hurt.

- *Cut down on caffeine.* A small amount of caffeine can enhance alertness and effectiveness for some people. However, many people don't stop with just one or two cups. More than 20 percent of Americans consume heavy amounts of caffeine (600 milligrams, or approximately four or more servings per day), especially with the popularity of "energy" drinks and supersized servings. Too much caffeine can make you nervous, jittery, irritable, and prone to insomnia. It may deplete your body of the B vitamins, minerals, and other nutrients it needs to cope with stress. Caffeine can also be addictive: The more you consume, the more it takes to produce the desired burst of energy. If you experience caffeine-induced symptoms, reduce your intake, but do so gradually. Headaches can result from rapid caffeine withdrawal. Try substituting decaffeinated coffee and tea (green tea is especially high in antioxidants) or plain water. Check labels to confirm that your substitutions are caffeine-free.

- *Take a multivitamin supplement.* Many experts advise taking vitamin and mineral supplements for optimal health. Some recommend extra C, E, B-complex, and A vitamins if you are under stress.

- *Use alcohol in moderation.* If you drink alcoholic beverages, do it in moderation: one or two drinks no more than three times a week. Too much alcohol increases the risk for certain cancers, cirrhosis of the liver, damage to the heart and brain, and strokes. Never drink and drive.

- *Drink water.* It's important to keep yourself hydrated, as about 60 percent of your body is made up of water. Fluid needs differ based on overall health, exercise levels, and so on, but a good rule of thumb is to drink as many ounces of water as about 30 percent of your body weight. For a 150-pound woman, that means drinking about 45 ounces per day. Choose water as your mealtime beverage, and drink a glass between meals. Also hydrate before, during, and after exercise.

2. **Maintain your ideal weight.** People spend millions of dollars every year on diet programs, exercise equipment, and promises of a quick fix. If you need to lose weight, don't try to do it too quickly with fad diets or fasting. Consult a physician to discuss the best method for you. Slow weight loss is more effective and helps you keep the weight off longer. Support groups for weight control can also be very helpful. Building energy by nourishing and caring for the body takes a long-term commitment to good habits. The following general guidelines will help you maintain your ideal weight:

   - *Exercise.* If you want to lose and keep off weight and increase your energy, build physical activity into your life. If you have time and are in a safe area, park your car a little farther out in the parking lot and walk a few extra steps. Sign up for an exercise class, or jog on a track. Find out what fitness resources are offered free by your school or community.

"More die in the United States of too much food than of too little."

JOHN KENNETH GALBRAITH
Economist

● **Coffeehouse Blues**
The caffeine in coffee can be pleasurable in moderate amounts, but, because it is addictive, there's a downside to drinking too much. *What are some other ways to increase your energy besides consuming caffeine?*

- *Eat only when you're hungry.* Eat to sustain your body, not because you are depressed, lonely, bored, or worried.

- *Don't fast.* When a person fasts, the body's metabolic rate decreases, so the body burns calories more slowly. At a certain point, the body has an urge to binge, which is nature's way of trying to survive famine.

- *Eat regularly.* Establish a pattern of three meals a day or five small meals. Don't skip meals, especially breakfast. You must eat regularly to stoke your metabolism, lose weight, and keep it off. If you are really rushed, carry fruit, raw vegetables, or nuts with you.

- *Create healthy patterns.* Eat slowly and enjoy your food. Eat in one or two locations, such as the dining room or at the kitchen table. Resist the urge to eat on the run, sample food while you are cooking, munch in bed, or snack throughout the day. Use critical thinking as you explore your eating patterns in **Personal Evaluation Notebook 11.1** on page 342.

- *Get help.* Do you have a problem with weight control, or are you overly concerned with being thin? Do you have a problem with eating too little or with fasting (such as anorexia nervosa)? Do you eat and then vomit as a way to control your weight (as with bulimia nervosa)? Anorexia and bulimia are serious illnesses that require medical treatment. You might feel isolated and powerless, but many resources offer help. Confide in a friend or family member. Go to the counseling or health center and discuss your problem with a medical professional. (See **Peak Progress 11.2** on page 343.)

3. **Renew energy through rest.** Most people need between 6 and 9 hours of sound sleep each night. The key is not to focus on the number of hours but, rather, whether you feel rested, alert, and energized. Some people wake up rested after 5 hours of sleep; others need at least 9 hours to feel refreshed. If you wake up tired, try going to bed earlier for a night or two, and then establish a consistent bedtime. Notice if you are using sleep to escape conflict, depression, or boredom. Also find time to relax each day. Use critical thinking in **Personal Evaluation Notebook 11.2** on page 343 to assess your commitment to getting rest.

Personal Evaluation Notebook

Reviewing Your Health

Read the following and write your comments on the lines provided.

1. Do you maintain your ideal weight? If not, how can you achieve your ideal weight?

   _____

   _____

   _____

2. Describe a few of your healthy eating habits.

   _____

   _____

   _____

3. Describe a few of your unhealthy eating habits.

   _____

   _____

   _____

4. Do you feel you have control over your eating? Explain.

   _____

   _____

   _____

5. What can you do to make positive and lasting changes in your eating habits?

   _____

   _____

   _____

4. **Increase physical activity.** Regular exercise reduces stress and strengthens every organ in the body. It reduces heart disease risk, strengthens the immune system, stimulates the lymphatic system, and increases functional capacity. Exercise burns calories and stimulates the brain to release endorphins, natural chemicals that increase feelings of well-being. National physical activity guidelines recommend at least 150 minutes of moderate intensity (30 minutes, 5 days) or 75 minutes of vigorous aerobic exercise (25 minutes, 3 days) per week. These two types of aerobic exercise can be combined to meet national goals. Exercise to build strength, muscular endurance, and flexibility is recommended 2 to 3 days per week for building healthy bones and further enhancing health benefits. The key is to accumulate the recommended

Personal Evaluation Notebook

11.2

Getting Proper Rest

Read the following and write your comments on the lines provided.

1. Do you generally wake up in the morning feeling rested and eager to start the day or tired with little energy? _____

2. How many times do you hit the snooze button before getting out of bed? _____

3. What prevents you from getting enough rest?

   _____

   _____

4. Besides sleep, what activities can renew your body and spirit?

   _____

   _____

Peak Progress

11.2

Eating Disorders

Known as a perfectionist, 20-year-old Jill was a bright, social college sophomore who seemed to have it all together, coping with the stress of college and part-time work. In just a few months, however, she broke up with her boyfriend, her sister married and moved away, and she felt pressured to choose a college major before the semester ended. In addition, she lost control of her car on an icy road and her car was totaled, although she wasn't seriously hurt. She began to feel depressed and out of control. She loved to exercise, so she started running twice as much as usual. She withdrew from family and friends and didn't feel like eating, so she gradually eliminated most foods from her diet, except fruits, yogurt, and salads. She continued to lose weight until her family insisted she get counseling and weigh in at the health center every day. Jill didn't think she had an eating disorder because she wasn't obsessed with being thin, but she was diagnosed as suffering from anorexia nervosa.

Most *anorexics* are white, young, middle-class women who have a distorted body image and want to be thin. Some anorexics are perfectionists, grew up in families with high expectations, and feel overwhelmed that they cannot meet these expectations, so they turn to something they can control—their weight.

Bulimia nervosa is another eating disorder; it involves binge eating and purging through forced vomiting or the use of laxatives. It can cause long-term dental damage and chemical imbalances, both of which can lead to organ damage and failure, bone loss, and even death. Many people with eating disorders also suffer from depression, anxiety, or substance abuse.

The National Association of Anorexia Nervosa and Associated Disorders estimates that approximately 8 million people in the United States have anorexia nervosa, bulimia nervosa, and related eating disorders. Essentially, about 3 of every 100 people in this country eat in a way disordered enough to warrant treatment. Ninety percent of those dealing with eating disorders are women. Research suggests that about 4 of every 100 college-age women have bulimia nervosa.

If you are dealing with an eating disorder, or suspect a friend or a family member is struggling with a disorder, seek help immediately. To learn more, visit the National Eating Disorders Association website at **www.nationaleatingdisorders.org** or call (800) 931-2237.

Melissa is determined not to succumb to the "freshman 10" and gain weight at school. In fact, she does the opposite and eats little all day before going out at night with her friends. She believes she looks good and doesn't have to worry about the extra calories she eats (and drinks) late at night because she's hardly eaten during the day.

- What negative psychological and physical patterns regarding food is Melissa displaying?
- How might her diet affect her success in school?
- What should Melissa do differently to meet her goal of a healthy weight?

THINK FAST

● **Increasing Energy**
Whether your physical activity routine includes power walking around your neighborhood or daily CrossFit workouts, establish a consistent pattern of exercise. *How can you fit in 150 minutes of moderate or 75 minutes of vigorous exercise per week?*

minutes. Consider moderate activities (such as brisk walking), vigorous aerobic activities (swimming, dancing, jogging), vigorous sports and recreation (tennis, hiking), muscle fitness (resistance training) and flexibility exercises (yoga, stretching). Start slowly, build gradually, commit to smart personal goals, and be consistent. If you experience pain beyond normal soreness while exercising, stop and consult your physician. Assess your commitment to exercise in **Personal Evaluation Notebook 11.3.**

5. **Establish healthy relationships.** Sharing a good talk or wonderful evening with a friend is deeply satisfying. So is the sense of accomplishment after completing a team project. Indeed, other people can help us think through problems, develop self-confidence, conquer fears, develop courage, brainstorm ideas, overcome boredom and fatigue, and increase our joy and laughter. But sometimes we:

- Get so busy at school and work that we ignore friends and family
- Are shy and find it difficult to build friendships
- Approach friendship as a competitive sport

It takes sensitivity and awareness to value others' needs. It also takes courage to overcome shyness. The key is to see the enormous value of friendships. Friends bring great joy and fellowship to life. Life's sorrows and setbacks are lessened when you have friends to support you through difficult times. (We'll further discuss building healthy relationships in Chapter 12.)

Manage Stress

College students face many demands: papers, tests, deadlines, studying, finances, relationships, and conflicts. Coping with stress means being able to manage difficult circumstances, solve problems, resolve conflicts, and juggle the daily demands of school, work, and home. Stress is the body's natural reaction to external events (e.g., taking an exam or giving a speech) and internal events (e.g., fear, worry, or unresolved anger). Everything you experience stimulates your body to react. Stress is normal and, in fact, necessary for a vital life. With too little positive stress, many people are bored and unproductive. The key is knowing how to cope with demands, avoid burnout, and channel stress instead of dealing with it in unproductive ways, such as:

- Denying, ignoring, or repressing feelings or problems, so that you don't have to face them
- Lashing out at other people
- Using alcohol, tobacco, or other drugs to reduce tension
- Eating too much or too little
- Thinking you can handle your problems without help

Life is a series of changes, and they require adaptive responses. The death of a close family member or friend, a serious illness or accident, exams, divorce, relationship changes, financial problems, and loss of a job all require adjustment and cause stress. It is important to realize, however, that your perception of and reaction to

Personal Evaluation Notebook

Committing to Exercise

Read the following and write your comments on the lines provided.

1. Describe your current commitment to physical activity.

   _____

   _____

   _____

2. What are your excuses for not exercising? What can you do to overcome these barriers?

   _____

   _____

   _____

3. Set your exercise goal.

   _____

   _____

   _____

these life events determine how they affect you. Even positive events can be stressful. Marriage, a promotion, the birth of a baby, a new romantic relationship, and even vacations may be demanding for some people and therefore stressful. Public speaking may be exciting and fun for one person but causes anxiety in another.

> **❝**Man should not try to avoid stress any more than he would shun food, love, or exercise.**❞**
>
> **HANS SELYE**
> *Endocrinologist*

WORDS TO SUCCEED

Symptoms of Burnout

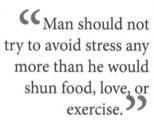

- Frequent headaches, back and neck pain, stomachaches, or tense muscles
- Insomnia or disturbed sleep patterns
- No sense of humor; nothing seems fun
- Fatigue, listlessness, or hopelessness
- Increase in drug or alcohol use or smoking
- Depression or moodiness
- Racing heart
- Appetite changes (eating too much or too little)
- Frequent colds, flu, or other illnesses
- Anxiousness, nervousness, difficulty concentrating
- Irritability, losing your temper, and overreacting
- Lack of motivation, energy, or zest for living
- A feeling that you have too much responsibility
- Lack of interest in relationships

You can choose to see stress as a challenge or something to avoid. You can adopt a positive, optimistic outlook; use resources; and rechannel energy in productive ways. You can learn to manage stress with coping strategies:

1. **Become attuned to your body and emotions.** The transition to college forces you to become more self-sufficient, which can cause stress. Recognize if you are having physical symptoms of stress, such as frequent headaches, difficulty relaxing, or a depressed or irritable mood. Give yourself permission to feel several different emotions, but also learn strategies to pull yourself out of a slump. You might set a time limit: "I accept that I'm feeling overwhelmed or down today. I will allow a few hours to feel these emotions; then I will do what I know makes me feel better."

2. **Exercise regularly.** Exercise is one of the best ways to reduce stress, relax muscles, and promote a sense of well-being. Most people have more energy when they exercise regularly.

3. **Dispute negative thoughts.** We've discussed the importance of self-management and monitoring your self-talk. Using the ABC Method of Self-Management helps you challenge self-defeating thoughts and replace them with positive, realistic, hopeful thoughts. Pessimists tend to describe their stressful situations with such words as *always* and *never*, and they imagine the worst possible outcomes. Negative thinking can lead to a self-fulfilling prophecy; if you say you're going to fail, you probably will. Change these negative thoughts to confident, positive thoughts and actions.

4. **Rest and renew your mind, body, and spirit.** Everyone needs to rest, not only through sleep but also through deep relaxation. Too little of either causes irritability, depression, inability to concentrate, and memory loss. Yoga and pilates are great ways to unwind, stretch and tone the muscles, and focus energy. Many people find that meditation promotes relaxation and renewal. You don't have to practice a certain type of meditation; just create a time for yourself when your mind is free to rest and quiet itself. Go for a walk, listen to music, create art, dance, sing, or get a massage. Visualization is another powerful technique for relaxing your body and reducing anxiety.

5. **Use breathing methods.** Deep breathing reduces stress and energizes the body. Many people breathe in short, shallow breaths, especially when under stress. Begin by sitting or standing up straight; breathe through your nose, fill your lungs completely, push out your abdomen, and exhale slowly and fully. Focus on a word, a sound, or your breathing, and give it your full attention. You can

DEEP RELAXATION

Sit in a quiet place and breathe deeply, fill your lungs, and exhale completely. Tense and relax your body by clenching one fist and then relaxing it; now the other fist. Then shrug your shoulders, wrinkle your forehead, squint your eyes, clench your jaw, and tighten your thighs and toes, followed by relaxing each muscle.

do a variation of this anytime during the day, even if you can't escape to a quiet spot.

6. **Develop hobbies and interests.** Sports, crafts, reading, and collecting can add fun and meaning to your life. Many get satisfaction from developing an interest in a cause or need, such as the environment, the elderly, politics, animals, or the homeless. Investigate volunteering opportunities in your area.

7. **Create a support system.** The support and comfort of family and friends can help you clear your mind and make better decisions. Express your feelings, fears, and problems to people you trust. A support group of people with similar experiences and goals can give you a sense of security, personal fulfillment, and motivation.

8. **Take mini-vacations.** When you are waiting on hold or in line, pull out a novel and enjoy a few moments of reading. Practice deep breathing or head rolls, or visualize the tension flowing out of your body. Get up and stretch periodically while you're studying. These mini-vacations can keep you relaxed, expand your creativity, and make you grateful for being alive.

9. **Rehearse a feared event.** When you mentally rehearse a stressful event beforehand, your fears become known and manageable.

10. **Exercise and stretch the mind.** Mental exercise is important—read, complete crossword puzzles, and play challenging board games. Attend lectures, take workshops and seminars, and brainstorm creative ideas or current subjects with well-read friends. Make friends with creative people who inspire you and renew your perspective.

11. **Create balance in your life.** Peak performers recognize the importance of balance between work and play. Assess whether your activities are distractions or opportunities. Say no to requests that do not enrich your life or the lives of others. (recall Peak Progress 3.3 on page 94). Set time limits on work, demands from others, and study; reward yourself for finishing tasks.

12. **Develop a sense of humor.** Nothing reduces stress like a hearty laugh or spontaneous fun. Laughing produces endorphins, natural chemicals that strengthen the immune system and produce a sense of well-being. Laughter also increases oxygen flow to the brain and causes other positive physiological changes.

13. **Plan; don't worry.** A disorganized life is stressful. Write down what has to be done each day; don't rely on your memory. Take a few minutes the night before to pack your lunch and list the next day's priorities. Get up 20 minutes early, so that you don't have to rush. Set aside time each day to plan, solve problems, and explore solutions. When your time is up, leave the problems until your next scheduled session.

14. **Be assertive.** Stand up for your rights, express your preferences, and acknowledge your feelings. Assertive communication helps you solve problems, rather than build resentment and anger, and increases your confidence and control over your life.

Take 3 minutes for a stress break:
- Turn off the lights (if you can) and any other distractions. Sit in a comfortable place and close your eyes.
- Where do you feel tense? Relax your muscles and drop your shoulders.
- Concentrate on your breathing, following it from deep in your stomach all the way out your nose or mouth. (If a meditating stress break doesn't work for you, put on some music and dance around the room and sing—find what makes you peaceful and happy.)

What else can you do in 3 minutes?
- Do stomach crunches or knee-bends, or use hand weights or water bottles to do arm curls.
- Make a grocery list of healthy foods to pick up at the store.
- Boost your energy by snacking on a handful of walnuts or almonds.

15. **Keep a journal.** A journal can give you insight into what types of situations you find stressful and how you respond to them. Be honest with yourself, and record daily events and your reactions.

16. **Get professional help.** Grief after a loss or major transition is normal. Allow yourself time to grieve in order to experience and release your emotional pain. However, if your sadness, depression, or anger continues despite your best efforts, or if you are suicidal, get professional help. With a counselor's guidance, you can gain insight into your pattern of reacting to stress and modify your perception and behavior. (See **Peak Progress 11.3** on using the Adult Learning Cycle to create a more healthy balance.)

Unhealthy Addictions

Unfortunately, many college students turn to alcohol, other drugs, or cigarettes to relieve stress. One of the biggest concerns health professionals have about students smoking or drinking every day is that it delays developing coping skills, resulting in serious problems. Rather than looking for quick fixes, practice coping strategies, such as facing your problems head on, resolving conflicts through communication, and finding creative solutions. Unhealthy behaviors will only escalate your problems.

Alcohol Abuse

Because it is a drug, alcohol can alter moods, become habit-forming, and cause changes in the body. It depresses the central nervous system, delaying reaction times and clouding personal judgment. Just one night of heavy drinking can impair your ability to think abstractly for up to 30 days.

There are more than 25 million alcoholics in the United States and most began drinking in high school and college. Although one in five college students report that they don't drink at all, the Core Institute, an organization that surveys college drinking practices, reports that almost one-third of college students admit to having missed at least one class because of alcohol use. Nearly 160,000 students will drop out of school due to alcohol- or other drug-related reasons, and 300,000 of today's college students will eventually die of alcohol-related causes, such as drunk driving accidents, cirrhosis of the liver, various cancers, and heart disease.

THE COSTS OF ALCOHOL

- In 2010, 10,228 fatalities were caused by alcohol-related crashes—almost 31 percent of all fatal crashes.
- Three out of 10 Americans may be involved in an alcohol-related crash.
- In 2010, 1.4 million people were arrested in the United States for driving under the influence of alcohol or narcotics (1 out of every 139 licensed drivers).
- According to the Department of Justice, each year 37 percent of rapes and sexual assaults involve alcohol use by the offender, as do 15 percent of all robberies, 27 percent of all aggravated assaults, and 25 percent of all simple assaults.

Sources: National Highway Traffic Safety Association; National Center for Statistics and Analysis; www.factsontap.org/collexp/stats.htm; U.S. Department of Justice, *Alcohol and Crime: An Analysis of National Data on the Prevalence of Alcohol Involvement in Crime.*

Applying the Adult Learning Cycle to Creating a Healthier Lifestyle

1. **RELATE. Why do I want to learn this?** I know I must reduce my stress, control my eating habits, exercise, and maintain my ideal weight. What areas do I struggle with, and what would I like to improve? Strong physical energy will boost my mental energy.

2. **OBSERVE. How does this work?** Who do I know with a healthy lifestyle? What behaviors do I want to emulate? What benefits will motivate me to improve my health behaviors? I'll try developing new habits and using new techniques and strategies, and I'll observe how I'm improving.

3. **REFLECT. What does this mean?** What strategies are working, and where do I continue to struggle? What tools or information would keep me motivated?

4. **DO. What can I do with this?** I will make a commitment to improve my health by eating right and exercising. Each day, I'll work on one area. For example, I'll use time-management skills and find ways to build exercise into my day. I'll practice reducing my stress in different situations. I'll use my new skills in everyday life.

5. **TEACH. Whom can I share this with?** I'll look for a partner with similar interests, and we'll keep each other motivated. I'll share my tips and experiences.

Living a healthy lifestyle is a life-long commitment. You will repeat the cycle many times to stay focused and successful.

For most adults, a glass of wine or a beer at dinner is not a problem, but even a small amount of alcohol can cause slowed reactions and poor judgment. See **Figure 11.2** on how to "party with a plan."

Students often believe there's no problem if they drink just beer, but a six-pack of beer contains the same amount of alcohol as six drinks of hard liquor—or one beer is equivalent to one shot of hard liquor. **Binge drinking** means consuming five or more drinks in a row for men, or four or more drinks in a row for women, at least once in the previous 2 weeks. Binge drinking can lead to serious problems, including fights, injuries, academic problems, suspension, sexual assault, DUIs, blackouts, and even death.

Alcoholism is a chronic disease that can be progressive and even fatal. It can begin as early as childhood and is often influenced by peer pressure. A major life lesson is to think for yourself and be responsible for your choices and behavior.

Party with a Plan

0 = No drinking if you are pregnant, driving, underage, or taking medications

1 = No more than one drink per hour (12 oz. beer; 4 oz. wine; 1 oz. shot)

2 = No more than two times per week

3 = No more than three drinks in one day

Used by permission from Randy Speaks, Inc. copyright 2006.

Figure 11.2
Party with a Plan

Motivational speaker Randy Haveson has created Party with a Plan®—a quick guide for drinking alcohol sensibly. See **www.partywithaplan.org** for a complete description.

Cigarette Smoking

It is hard to believe that anyone would smoke after seeing the public awareness campaigns that present the risks of cigarette smoking, yet 46 million adults in the United States smoke. Perhaps the billions of dollars spent to promote cigarettes each year convince them that smoking makes them sexier, cooler, and calmer. Such claims are in stark contrast to the actual facts about smoking.

THE COSTS OF SMOKING

- Cigarette smoking-related diseases cause about 443,600 deaths each year in the United States, killing more Americans than alcohol, car accidents, suicide, AIDS, homicide, and illegal drugs combined.
- Cigarette smoking is directly responsible for 87 percent of all lung cancer cases.
- The Environmental Protection Agency estimates that secondhand smoke causes about 3,400 lung cancer deaths and 46,000 heart disease deaths in nonsmokers each year.
- Nonsmokers married to smokers have a 30 percent greater risk for lung cancer than those married to nonsmokers.
- Secondhand smoke contains more than 4,000 chemicals: 200 are poisons and 63 cause cancer.
- Smoking costs the United States more than $190 billion each year in health care costs and lost productivity.
- On average, adults who smoke cigarettes die 14 years earlier than nonsmokers.

Illegal Drug Use

The cost of drug abuse to American society is approximately $50 billion a year. Almost 80 percent of people in their mid-twenties have tried illegal drugs.

Marijuana is the most commonly used illegal drug. Although some people think they are smoking a harmless "weed," marijuana use has many negative effects, including loss of coordination and memory and increases in heart rate and blood pressure. Besides experiencing the respiratory problems that cigarette smokers also develop, habitual marijuana users tend to inhale deeper and hold the smoke in their lungs longer, releasing five times more carbon dioxide and three times more tar into their lungs than tobacco does.

K2 (also known as "spice" or synthetic marijuana) is a newer drug that is also dangerous, even though it is legal in many places and sold as incense or potpourri. Symptoms of its use mimic marijuana use, such as a rapid heartbeat, dangerously elevated blood pressure, pale skin, and vomiting. It also is believed to affect the central nervous system, causing severe, potentially life-threatening hallucinations and seizures.

Prescription and Over-the-Counter Medication Abuse

When used as directed, medications can be beneficial. However, roughly one in five people in the United States have used prescription drugs for nonmedical reasons.

Likewise, over-the-counter (OTC) drugs are abused for the high or other effects they produce—but often with serious consequences, especially when taken in large doses or combined with other drugs. Medicines containing dextromethorphan (DXM), such as cold medications, are the most abused OTC drugs. Excessive doses can lead to hallucinations, seizures, brain damage, and death. As mentioned in Chapter 8, Adderall is often abused by students who think it gives them an edge while studying, helping them to focus. However, the potential side effects far outweigh any benefits.

Overcoming Addictions

Addictive behavior comes in many forms, not just substance abuse. Just as an alcoholic feels happy when drinking, a food addict feels comforted when eating, a sex addict gets a rush from new partners, a shoplifter feels a thrill with getting away with stealing, an addictive shopper feels excited during a shopping spree, a gambler feels in control when winning, and a workaholic feels a sense of importance while working late at night or on weekends. Addiction is an abnormal relationship with an object or event and involves repeatedly using a substance or performing a behavior. Beginning as a pleasurable act or a means of escape, it progresses until it becomes a compulsive behavior that causes significant problems. Do you have a pattern of addiction? If you don't get this under control now, it will only get worse.

A person trying to overcome an addiction may experience anxiety, irritability, or moodiness. Some people switch addictions as a way to cope and give them the illusion that they have solved the problem. For example, many former alcoholics become chain smokers. Some people take up gambling as a way to have fun and get a rush, but then it becomes a problem. Compulsive gambling can leave people deeply in debt and devastate families and careers. Warning signs include secrecy; a change in discipline, mood, or work habits; a loss of interest in hobbies or school; and altered eating and sleeping habits. You may become withdrawn, depressed, or aggressive. You must take the initiative to get help. Ask your school counselor or go to the health center.

Here are some additional steps to take to deal with an addiction:

- *Admit there is a problem.* The first step in solving a problem is to face it. Many people with addictions react to problems with denial. They may do well in school or hold down a job and, therefore, don't see a problem. If you think you have lost control or are involved with someone who has, admit it and take charge of your life. Look at how you handle stress and conflict. Do you solve problems, deny them, or look for an escape?

- *Take responsibility for addiction and recovery.* You are responsible for and can control your life. Several support groups and treatment programs are available for various addictions. Search the Internet for resources in your area, or contact the following:

  Alcoholism: Alcoholics Anonymous: **www.aa.org**

  Distracted driving: U.S. Department of Transportation website for Distracted Driving: **www.distraction.gov**

  Drug abuse: National Institute on Drug Abuse: **www.drugabuse.gov**

  Gambling: National Council on Problem Gambling: **www.ncpgambling.org**

● **The Last Text**
Many people find it hard to put down their phone, even when driving. However, 3,331 people were killed and almost 390,000 injured in 2011 due to distracted driving. Drivers who use handheld devices are four times more likely to get into crashes serious enough to injure themselves. This is the last text University of Northern Colorado student Alexander Heit was typing before he lost control of his car and fatally crashed. *Do you text and drive? Do you agree with laws that prohibit use of digital devices while driving?*

"One trait of addictive families is that we never recognize our own addictions."

LORNA LUFT
Entertainer

Sexual behavior: The Society for the Advancement of Sexual Health: **www.sash.net**

Smoking: Centers for Disease Control and Prevention, Smoking and Tobacco Use: **www.cdc.gov/tobacco**

Codependency

Even if you do not abuse alcohol or other drugs, your life may be affected by someone who does. A common term used to describe nonaddicted people whose lives are affected by an addict is **codependency.** Codependent people exhibit numerous self-defeating behaviors, such as low self-esteem; lack of strong, emotionally fulfilling relationships; lack of self-control; and overcontrolling behavior. A codependent person may

- *Avoid facing the problem of addiction.* Denying, making excuses, justifying, rationalizing, blaming, controlling, and covering up are all games that a codependent person plays in an effort to cope with living with an addict.
- *Take responsibility for the addict's life.* This may include lying; taking over a job, an assignment, or a deadline; or somehow rescuing the addict.
- *Be obsessed with controlling the addict's behavior.* A codependent person may hide bottles; put on a happy face; hide feelings of anger; confuse love and pity; and feel that, if only he or she could help more, the addict would quit.

If you feel you have problems in your life as a result of growing up in an alcoholic family or may be codependent, get help. Organizations such as Adult Children of Alcoholics (ACA) address the issues of people who grew up in alcoholic homes. There are many agencies and groups that can make a difference.

Emotional Health

Everyone has the blues occasionally. However, sometimes stress and emotional problems interfere with your goals or ability to cope. Approximately 40 million U.S. adults are affected by anxiety disorders, and there has been a 264 percent rise in mental health drug use among women ages 20 to 44 during the past 10 years. A variety of emotional problems affect college students and professionals in all walks of life.

Depression

Depression is an emotional state of sadness ranging from mild discouragement to utter hopelessness. Each year, more than 60 million people suffer from mild depression, which is relatively short-term. Severe depression is deeper and may last months or years. More than 6 million Americans suffer serious depression that impairs their abilities, accounting for 75 percent of psychiatric hospitalizations. Fifty percent of college students report they have felt so depressed they found it difficult to function during the last school year; yet 80 percent who need mental health services won't seek them. Depression can occur as a response to the following situations:

- *Loss.* The death of a loved one, divorce, the breakup of a relationship, the loss of a job, involvement in a robbery or an assault, or any other major change, loss, disappointment, or violation can trigger depression.

- *Health changes.* Physical changes, such as a serious illness, an injury, childbirth, or menopause, can produce chemical changes that can cause depression.

- *An accident.* A car accident can be very traumatic, leading to feelings of being out of control and depression. Even if you were not seriously injured, feelings of hopelessness or guilt can result from an accident.

- *Conflicts in relationships.* Unresolved conflicts in relationships can cause depression.

- *Loneliness.* Loneliness can seem like a physical illness—painful or as dark as if someone has thrown a heavy blanket over your life. It is often felt by freshmen who have left home and haven't yet rebuilt a social network. (We'll discuss loneliness in more detail in Chapter 12.) Get involved in school activities and in the community, get a part-time job, practice listening, and try to develop new relationships.

- *Peer pressure.* You may feel pressured to get involved in alcohol, other drugs, smoking, or sex. When you have doubts, stop and think about the consequences. Ask why you are allowing others to define your values and boundaries. When you do something you are uncomfortable with, you may experience depression or sadness as if you have lost a sense of who you really are.

- *Daily demands.* You may feel overwhelmed by too many demands, such as deadlines or the pressure to choose a major. Nontraditional, or re-entry, students often must juggle school, work, family, and care of their home. Set priorities, ask for help, and try to eliminate or reduce unimportant or routine tasks. Delegate whenever possible.

Depression can be triggered by many events. Some of these relate to certain stages in life. For example, adolescents are just beginning to realize who they are and are trying to cope with the responsibilities of freedom and adulthood. Someone facing middle age may regret the loss of youth or unrealized career goals or may miss children who are leaving home. For an elderly person, the loss of physical strength, illness, the death of friends, and growing dependency may prompt depression. When depression causes persistent sadness and continues beyond a month, severe depression may be present.

WARNING SIGNS OF DEPRESSION

- Sleep disturbance (sleeping too much or too little, constantly waking up)
- Increase in or loss of appetite
- Overuse of alcohol or prescription and/or nonprescription drugs
- Withdrawal from family and friends, leading to feelings of isolation
- Avoidance of teachers, classmates, and co-workers and lack of attendance
- Recurring feelings of anxiety
- Anger and irritability for no apparent reason
- Loss of interest in formerly pleasurable activities
- A feeling that simple activities are too much trouble
- A feeling that other people have much more than you have

WARNING SIGNS OF SUICIDE

- Excessive alcohol or other drug use
- Significant changes in emotions (hyperactivity, withdrawal, mood swings)
- Significant changes in weight or in sleeping, eating, or studying patterns
- Feelings of hopelessness or helplessness
- Little time spent with or a lack of close, supportive friends
- Nonsupportive family ties
- Rare participation in group activities
- Recent loss or traumatic or stressful events
- Suicidal statements
- A close friend or family member who committed suicide
- Attempted suicide in the past
- Participation in dangerous activities
- A plan for committing suicide or for giving away possessions

Suicide

More than 4,000 people in the United States between ages 16 and 25 die from suicide each year, making it the third leading cause of death for young people. Suicidal thoughts occur when a feeling of hopelessness sets in and problems seem unbearable. Suicidal people think the pain will never end, but they usually respond to help. You should be concerned if you know someone who exhibits several warning signs. If you do know someone who is suffering from depression and seems suicidal, take the following steps:

1. Remain calm.
2. Take the person seriously; don't ignore the situation.
3. Encourage the person to talk.
4. Listen without moralizing or judging. Acknowledge the person's feelings.
5. Remind the person that counseling can help and is confidential.
6. Remind the person that reaching out for help shows strength, not weakness.
7. Call a crisis hot line, health center, school or community counseling center, or mental health department for a list of agencies that can help. Get the name of a counselor for the person to call, or make the call with him or her.
8. Stay with the person to provide support when he or she makes the contact. If possible, walk or drive the person to the counselor.
9. Seek support yourself. Helping someone who is suicidal is stressful.

Protecting Your Body

Reliable information about sex can help you handle the many physical and emotional changes you will experience in life. Although sex is a basic human drive and

natural part of life, there are dangers, including sexually transmitted infections, unplanned pregnancies, and rape. Your level of sexual activity is a personal choice and can change with knowledge, understanding, and awareness. Having been sexually active at one time does not rule out a choice to be celibate now. No one should pressure you into sexual intercourse. If you decide to be sexually active, you need to make responsible decisions and be aware of the risks.

Sexually Transmitted Infections (STIs)

Sexually transmitted infections, or STIs, are spread through sexual contact (including genital, vaginal, anal, and oral contact) with an infected partner. An infected person may appear healthy and symptom-free. See **Figure 11.3** on page 356 for a list of STIs and their symptoms, treatments, and risks. Despite public health efforts and classes in health and sexuality, STIs infect significant numbers of young adults. Even if treated early, STIs are a major health risk and can have devastating effects, such as damage to the reproductive organs, infertility, or cancer.

Human papillomavirus (HPV) is the most common STI. Approximately 79 million Americans are currently infected with HPV, and 14 million people become newly infected each year. Anyone participating in vaginal, anal, or oral sex can contract HPV. HPV is so common that nearly all sexually active men and women get it at some point in their lives, with 90 percent of infections clearing up on their own. There are more than 40 types of HPV that can infect both men and women, leading to genital warts and cancer of the cervix, genitals, and throat. The vaccine Gardasil is offered to males and females ages 11 to 26 to prevent HPV prior to becoming sexually active. Cervarix is another vaccine for young females to protect against the types of HPV that cause most cervical cancers.

Acquired immune deficiency syndrome (AIDS) is a fatal STI. It weakens the immune system and leads to an inability to fight infection. AIDS is transmitted through sexual or other contact with the semen, blood, or vaginal secretions of someone with human immunodeficiency virus (HIV) or by sharing nonsterile intravenous needles with someone who is HIV-positive (24 percent of U.S. cases are caused this way). Occasionally, it is contracted through a blood transfusion. About 1.3 million people are living with HIV in the United States, with around 50,000 new infections each year. Half of new infections in the United States occur in people age 25 or younger.

AIDS is most commonly spread by heterosexual intercourse. AIDS cannot be transmitted by saliva or casual contact, such as sharing utensils or shaking hands. Therapies using a combination of drugs have succeeded in controlling the progression of the disease. Although there is currently no cure for AIDS, there is help. Go to the student health center or local health department for testing. The Public Health Service has a toll-free AIDS hot line (800-342-AIDS), and local and state hot lines are available.

To avoid contracting any STI, follow these guidelines:

- Know your partner. It takes time and awareness to develop a healthy relationship.

- Ask a prospective partner about his or her health. Don't assume anything based on looks, class, or behavior.

Figure 11.3
STIs: Symptoms, Treatments, and Risks

Because STIs are a serious health risk, it is important to separate fact from myth when considering your options for protection. *In what ways can knowing the facts about STIs protect you?*

Sexually Transmitted Infections	What Are the Common Symptoms?	What Is the Treatment?	What Are the Risks?
AIDS/HIV	No symptoms for years; some carriers can be HIV+	No known cure; medical treatments can slow the disease	Weakening of the immune system; life-threatening infections
Chlamydia	Known as the "silent" disease because most infected people have no symptoms; others may experience discharge from genitals or a burning sensation when urinating	Antibiotics	More susceptible to developing pelvic inflammatory disease and infertility, and to having premature babies; can infect baby's eyes and respiratory tract during delivery
Genital herpes	Ulcers (sores) or blisters around the genitals	No cure; antiviral medications can shorten and prevent outbreaks	Highly contagious; become more susceptible to HIV infection; can also be spread via oral sex
Genital warts	The virus (human papillomavirus, or HPV) lives in the skin or mucous membranes and usually causes no symptoms; some will get visible genital warts	No cure, although the infection usually goes away on its own; cancer-related types of HPV are more likely to persist	Higher risk of cervical cancer
Gonorrhea	Symptoms include a painful or burning sensation when urinating; men may have a white, yellow, or green discharge from the penis or painful or swollen testicles; women may have an increased vaginal discharge or vaginal bleeding between periods; however, most women have no symptoms	Antibiotics	More susceptible to pelvic inflammatory disease, infertility, and HIV
Syphilis	Early symptoms include one or multiple sores; later symptoms vary from a rash to fever, hair loss, sore throat, and fatigue	Antibiotics	Untreated, can lead to damage of internal organs, paralysis, blindness, and death
Trichomoniasis	Men may experience temporary irritation inside the penis, mild discharge, or slight burning after urination or ejaculation; women may have a yellow-green vaginal discharge with a strong odor	Prescription drugs	More susceptible to contracting HIV; giving birth to premature or underweight babies

Source: Centers for Disease Control and Prevention, Division of Sexually Transmitted Diseases, www.cdc.gov/std.

- No matter what the other person's health status is, explain that you always use safety precautions. (Keep in mind that, if you are having unprotected sex, you are essentially being exposed to everyone your partner has had sex with in the past.)
- Latex condoms and dental dams can help protect against most sexually transmitted diseases. However, abstinence is the only totally effective method of preventing the spread of STIs, as well as pregnancy.

Birth Control

If your relationship is intimate enough for sex, it should be open enough to discuss birth control and pregnancy if birth control fails. Both men and women need to stop and ask, "How would an unwanted pregnancy change my life?"

Many contraceptives are available, but only abstinence is 100 percent foolproof. Current contraceptives include birth control pills, condoms, diaphragms, sponges, spermicidal foams, cervical caps, intrauterine devices (IUDs), and long-term implants. Douching and withdrawal do not prevent pregnancy and should not be used for birth control. Discuss birth control methods with your partner and with a qualified health professional. Make an informed decision about what is best for you.

Understanding and Preventing Acquaintance Rape

Katie, a sophomore living off campus, is on her third date with Jeff, who is in her English class. They have been having a great time together, and Jeff is attentive and loving. In fact, Katie has told friends that he puts her on a pedestal. After a movie, they are sitting on her living room couch, drinking wine, talking, and sharing hugs and kisses. Jeff's kissing becomes more aggressive, and Katie pushes his hands away several times. Finally, she tells him she feels uncomfortable, wants to take the relationship slowly, and asks him to leave. Jeff blows up, accuses her of being a tease and leading him on, holds her down, and rapes her.

A typical image about rape involves a stranger lurking around a dark corner or deserted street. Although this does occur and requires safety precautions, most sexual assaults are committed by assailants known by the victim, and many occur in the victim's home. On college campuses, 84 percent of rape is acquaintance rape; 57 percent happens on dates (i.e., date rape). According to the FBI, up to 90 percent of rapes are not reported because the victim fears retaliation and social ostracism, fears not being believed, and, like Katie, blames herself because she had too much to drink or wonders if she said or did something to give the attacker the wrong idea. Make no mistake about it—date rape is rape.

One in three women in the United States will be a victim of sexual assault in her lifetime. All women are vulnerable to rape, no matter their age, race, class, or physical appearance. Rape is an act of aggression. A rapist seeks a person he can dominate and control. Check with the counseling center, health center, or local police for ways to protect yourself from date rape. Here are a few preventive measures:

1. **Make your expectations clear.** Send clear messages and make certain that your body language, tone of voice, and word choices match your feelings. In a direct, forceful, serious tone, let others know when their advances are not welcome. If you don't want to get physically intimate, don't allow anyone to talk you into

it. Be aware of your limits and feelings, and communicate them assertively. Say, "No," loudly and clearly. Scream for help if you need it.

2. **Meet in public places.** Until you know someone well, arrange to meet where others will be around. Double date whenever possible or go out with a group of friends. Have an agreement with friends that you will not leave a party alone or with someone you do not know well.

3. **Trust your intuition.** Be aware of your surroundings, and trust your instincts. If the situation doesn't feel right, leave and get help as soon as you can. If you feel ill, get help immediately. If you plan to go to a movie, to a party, or for a walk, ask a friend to go with you. If you're on a date, tell others when you expect to be back, take your cell phone, and leave your date's name. If something doesn't feel right, contact your roommate or a friend.

4. **Take your time.** It is impossible to spot a rapist by appearance, race, occupation, or relationship to you. The attacker might be your date, your lab partner, an instructor, a friend of a friend, or a neighbor down the hall. Take time to know a person before you spend time alone with him or her. Don't take chances because someone looks nice or knows someone you know. Don't invite anyone to your home unless you know this person well. Otherwise, make certain a roommate or friends are around. Relationships that start slowly are built on friendship and are healthier and safer.

5. **Recognize that alcohol and other drugs can be dangerous.** They can inhibit resistance, increase aggression, and impair decision-making skills. If you are intoxicated, you may not be able to protect yourself or notice the signals that should warn you of danger. In some cases, date rapists have added so-called date rape drugs, such as Rohypnol (also called Roofies), GHB, Ecstasy, or Ketamine, to the victim's drink, causing the victim to become confused, drowsy, and dizzy; to have impaired judgment; or to experience temporary amnesia. It can cause loss of consciousness and even a coma or death. Never leave your drink unattended, and do not accept drinks from a common container.

6. **Learn to read the danger signals of an unhealthy relationship.** Be concerned if you are dating someone who
   - Pressures you sexually
   - Refers to people as sex objects
   - Drinks heavily or uses drugs and pressures you to drink or take drugs
   - Doesn't respect your wants, needs, or opinions
   - Is possessive or jealous
   - Wants to make decisions for you—tells you whom you may be friends with or what clothes to wear
   - Has a temper and acts rashly
   - Is physically abusive
   - Is verbally and emotionally abusive through insults, belittling comments, or "sulking" behavior
   - Becomes angry when you say, "No"

7. **Be safe and vigilant.** Make wise choices, use common sense, and do everything possible to protect yourself. Don't go jogging alone or in isolated areas, lock your doors and windows, and don't pick up hitchhikers. Know your campus and community well, and stay out of dark, secluded areas. If you are taking a night class, find the safest place to park your car. Use a campus escort, or arrange to walk to your car with a friend or group from your class. Contact the local recreation center or police to learn if a self-defense course is available.

8. **Get professional help.** Unfortunately, even the most diligent and safety-minded people can be raped. Report a rape immediately by calling 911, a rape crisis center, or the police. Preserve evidence by not bathing or changing clothes. Make certain you get counseling to deal with the trauma. Remember, it is not your fault!

Rape is not just a woman's problem. Men as well as women can become victims of physical, sexual, and mental abuse. Understand how your own attitudes and actions perpetuate sexism and violence, and work to change them. Speak up against stereotypical attitudes that rape victims asked for it and that women are sex objects. You can challenge demeaning and cruel jokes and attitudes by taking a mature, caring stand against violence.

TAKING CHARGE

Summary

In this chapter, I learned to

- **Connect my mind, body, and spirit.** I envision my mind, body, and spirit as a whole system and realize that everything is connected. I observe my thoughts, how my body feels, my level of stress, my negative habits, what I eat and drink, and changes or discomfort in my body.

- **Eat a variety of healthy foods in moderation.** I increase my consumption of fresh fruits and vegetables, include good fiber sources, limit animal fat, avoid fried foods, cut down on salt, sugar, "diet" foods, and caffeine, and take a multivitamin supplement every day. This helps me maintain my ideal weight, increases my self-esteem, and gives me energy.

- **Exercise regularly.** I combine moderate and vigorous intensity aerobic exercise each week. I also choose activities 2 to 3 days per week that build strength, muscular endurance, and flexibility. I balance rest and relaxation with active sports, such as bicycling, dancing, or swimming. Being active helps me maintain my ideal weight, gives me energy, and increases my sense of well-being.

- **Develop healthy relationships.** Spending time with friends who are supportive and share my interests is a great source of satisfaction, and it adds to my energy and enjoyment of life. Friendships bring great joy and fellowship.

- **Reduce stress.** I have developed strategies for reducing stress, including exercising, doing deep breathing, disputing negative thoughts and beliefs, developing a sense of humor, rehearsing feared events, and creating balance in my life.

- **Use critical thinking to avoid drugs.** Alcohol is a toxin. Heavy drinking can damage the brain, increase the risk of heart disease, depress the immune system, and cause liver failure. Alcohol and other drugs can cause memory loss and impair reasoning.

- **Get help for addictions.** I recognize the signs of addiction to food, gambling, and alcohol and other drugs and when to seek help. I know that campus and community resources can help me or someone I know who has a drinking or other drug problem.

- **Observe my emotional health.** Although I know life has its ups and downs, I am aware of times when I don't bounce back after a disappointment or loss. Some warning signs of depression are changes in sleep patterns and appetite, drug use, and feelings of anxiety, anger, isolation, and disinterest. Severe depression and suicidal tendencies occur when feelings are extreme.

- **Protect my body.** I protect myself from illness, sexually transmitted infections, unwanted pregnancies, and rape. I am knowledgeable, aware, and proactive. I visit the health center, use safety precautions, and learn self-defense techniques.

Performance Strategies

Following are the top 10 tips for achieving a healthy lifestyle:

- Be aware of your body, your emotions, your unhealthy habits, and unexpected changes.
- Focus on healthy eating and a balanced diet.
- Maintain your ideal weight.
- Get enough rest and renewal time.
- Increase physical activity.

- Develop supportive and healthy relationships.
- Develop coping strategies for managing stress.
- Avoid addictive substances, such as cigarettes, alcohol, and other drugs.
- Get help immediately for depression and mental distress.
- Protect yourself from sexually transmitted infections and unwanted pregnancy.

Tech for Success

Take advantage of the text's website at **www.mhhe.com/ferrett9e** for additional study aids, useful forms, and convenient and applicable resources.

- **Health on the Web.** More sites on the Internet are devoted to health than any other topic. However, how do you know which sites provide accurate information? Start with government, professional organization, and nonprofit sites. Many of these offer questions to ask or red flags to look for when consulting with physicians or purchasing products on the Internet.

- **Assess yourself.** You will find a vast array of free personal assessment tools on the Internet. You can explore everything from ideal body weight to your risk of developing a certain cancer. Use assessments to help you

identify patterns and behaviors you want to change. As with all information on the Internet, check the source or research behind the assessment tool.

- **Just what is in that burger?** The website of almost every fast-food chain provides the caloric breakdown of its most popular items. Before your next trip to your favorite restaurant, look up the calories and fat content of your usual order. Is it what you expected, or even higher? Does this information affect your selections?

- **Music to my ears.** You may enjoy listening through headphones or earbuds, but follow the 60/60 rule to preserve your hearing: no more than 60 percent volume for no more than 60 minutes at a stretch.

Study Team Notes

Career *in* focus

Preventing Stress and Fatigue at Work

Tony Ferraro has been a member of his city's fire department for 25 years. Three years ago, he was promoted to captain. He and the other firefighters at his station respond to fire alarms using various techniques to put out fires. They also respond to medical emergencies by providing emergency medical assistance until an ambulance arrives. When not out on calls, Tony and his crew maintain their equipment, participate in drills and advanced fire fighting classes, and keep physically fit.

Tony works two or three 24-hour shifts a week, during which time he lives and eats at the fire station. Because fire fighting involves considerable risks for injury or even death, the job is stressful and demanding. Being alert, physically fit, calm, and clear-headed is critical for making sound decisions. To stay healthy mentally and physically, Tony studies a form of karate that helps him not only stay in shape but also remain calm and focused. In addition, he drinks no more than one to two cups of coffee a day and has given up smoking.

As captain of his fire station, Tony has initiated better eating habits in the kitchen by posting a food guide and talking to the other firefighters about reducing fat and salt in their diet. In addition, he observes the firefighters for signs of stress and makes suggestions when needed, such as taking time off or getting more rest. The company's health insurance policy includes coverage for counseling. Once after a particularly stressful period, Tony invited a stress counselor to speak and offer services at the station.

Tony Ferraro
FIREFIGHTER

Related Majors: Fire Science, Public Administration

CRITICAL THINKING Why do firefighters need to work toward goals for physical, emotional, and mental health?

Peak Performer

PROFILE

Mark Herzlich Jr.

When Sandon Mark Herzlich Jr. found out he had Ewing's Sarcoma, a rare form of cancer, he went home and sulked for 2 hours. After those 2 hours were over, Herzlich realized "This [cancer] has got to be something I overcome. Once I made that decision, I was ready."

Herzlich, a linebacker with the Boston College Eagles football team, had already beaten the odds in his sports career. As a college freshman, he received Freshman All-American team honorable mention from the *College Football News*. In his junior season, Herzlich was named a First-team All-American, the ACC Defensive Player of the Year, and a finalist for the Lott Trophy. He was ranked as the 45th best prospect for the 2009 NFL Draft before announcing his decision to return to Boston College the following season to finish his degree.

After his diagnosis in May 2008, Herzlich returned to school, and to the field, to provide others help during his illness. He ran with the team at the beginning of games, and served as a right-hand man for the team coach. His behind-the-scenes work was even more valuable. He spent his time providing orientation to incoming freshmen, counseling kids with cancer, and raising about $200,000 through "Uplifting Athletes," an agency which raises awareness of rare diseases.

Herzlich has said of his volunteer activities, "I like this being part of me. It's something that's exciting, in that I get to be able to help other people." He was, however, also excited for his return as a player for the Boston College Eagles, after his cancer-free diagnosis in October of 2009. Now a professional football player, he takes care of himself by not taking any risks that could hurt his recovering body, and routinely checks for any lingering effects of the cancer and its treatment. In all areas, Herzlich defines a peak performer: in mind, body, and spirit.

PERFORMANCE THINKING How did Herzlich's refusal to "sulk" put him onto a path towards self-determination and success over cancer? How do his actions personify those characteristics of a peak performer? If you have anything troubling you in your life, how can you use Herzlich's example to help better your own situation?

CHECK IT OUT At www.mademan.com/mm/10-famous-athletes-disabilities.html, you can read about the 10 most famous athletes with disabilities. Do you recognize any of the names? What else might these athletes have overcome? Think not only of bodily limitations but the limitations of other people's perceptions, attitudes, and other regulating guidelines.

Starting Today

At least one strategy I learned in this chapter that I plan to try right away is

_____

_____

_____

What changes must I make in order for this strategy to be most effective?

_____

_____

_____

Review Questions

Based on what you have learned in this chapter, write your answers to the following questions:

1. What are five strategies for good health management?

_____

_____

2. What are some of the benefits of aerobic exercise?

_____

_____

3. Why is it important to manage your stress?

_____

_____

4. Cite two statistics or facts about alcohol.

_____

_____

5. List four symptoms of depression.

_____

_____

To test your understanding of the chapter's concepts, complete the chapter quiz at **www.mhhe.com/ferrett9e.**

Increasing Your Energy Level

In the Classroom

Danny Mendez, a business major in marketing, works part-time at a sporting goods store, is president of his fraternity, and is on the soccer team. This demanding schedule is manageable because Danny's energy is high. However, around midterm he feels overwhelmed with stress. He needs to find ways to increase his energy, maintain his good health, and manage his stress.

1. What strategies would you suggest to help Danny reduce his stress?

_____

_____

2. What could you suggest to Danny to increase his energy level?

_____

_____

In the Workplace

Danny is now a marketing manager for a large advertising agency. He often travels to meet with current and prospective clients. When Danny returns, he finds work piled on his desk—advertising campaign issues, personnel problems, and production delays. Danny's energy has always been high, but lately he eats too much fast food, has started smoking again, and rarely exercises anymore. He keeps saying he'll get back on track when he has time.

3. What habits should Danny adopt to reduce his stress and fatigue?

_____

_____

4. What strategies in this chapter can help him increase his energy?

_____

_____

Applying the ABC Method of Self-Management

In the Journal Entry on page 335, you were asked to describe a time when you had lots of energy, felt healthy and rested, and were in control of your weight. What factors helped you be calm, confident, and healthy?

_____

_____

_____

Describe a situation in which you suffered from lack of sleep, were not eating healthy, or were stressed out. Apply the ABC Method to work through the scenario and achieve a positive outcome.

A = Actual event:

_____

_____

_____

B = Beliefs:

_____

_____

_____

C = Challenge:

_____

_____

_____

Use visualization to see yourself healthy and in charge of your physical, mental, and emotional life. You feel confident because you have learned to invest time in exercising, eating well, and being rested.

PRACTICE SELF-MANAGEMENT

For more examples of learning how to manage difficult situations, see the "Self-Management Workbook" section of the Online Learning Center website at **www.mhhe.com/ferrett9e**.

Stress Performance Test

Read the following list of situations. Then think back over the last few months. Have you experienced these situations? If so, put a check mark in the column that best indicates how you coped with the experience.

	Overwhelmed (3)	Moderately Stressed (2)	Handled Effectively (1)	Did Not Experience/ Not Applicable (0)
1. No time for goals	_____	_____	_____	_____
2. Lack of money	_____	_____	_____	_____
3. Uncomfortable living and study areas	_____	_____	_____	_____
4. Long working hours	_____	_____	_____	_____
5. Boring, uninteresting job	_____	_____	_____	_____
6. Conflict with roommate, family, etc.	_____	_____	_____	_____
7. Conflict with instructors	_____	_____	_____	_____
8. Too many responsibilities	_____	_____	_____	_____
9. Deadline pressures	_____	_____	_____	_____
10. Boring classes	_____	_____	_____	_____
11. Too many changes in life	_____	_____	_____	_____
12. Lack of motivation	_____	_____	_____	_____
13. Difficulty finding housing	_____	_____	_____	_____
14. Little emotional support from family	_____	_____	_____	_____

(continued)

REVIEW AND APPLICATIONS | CHAPTER 11

	Overwhelmed (3)	Moderately Stressed (2)	Handled Effectively (1)	Did Not Experience/ Not Applicable (0)
15. Poor grades	_____	_____	_____	_____
16. Parents/partners have set standards and expectations that are too high	_____	_____	_____	_____
17. Unclear on goals	_____	_____	_____	_____
18. Too many interruptions	_____	_____	_____	_____
19. Health problems	_____	_____	_____	_____
20. Dependency on alcohol, other drugs	_____	_____	_____	_____
21. Too much socializing	_____	_____	_____	_____
22. Lack of career/life goals	_____	_____	_____	_____
23. Speaking/test-taking anxiety	_____	_____	_____	_____
24. Lack of relationships, friends	_____	_____	_____	_____
25. Lack of self-esteem	_____	_____	_____	_____
Subtotals	_____	_____	_____	_____

Add your 1s, 2s, and 3s to give yourself a total score:

Totals   _____ + _____ + _____ = _____

Total score

SCORES

25–36   Peak performer (you have learned how to function effectively under stress)

37–48   Persistent coper (you handle stress in most situations but have some difficulty coping and feel overwhelmed sometimes)

49–60   Stress walker (you often feel overwhelmed and exhausted, which affects your performance)

60+   Burnout disaster (you need help coping; stress is taking a toll on your health and emotions, and you risk burning out)

I Am What I Eat

This exercise aims to make you aware of your food choices. Starting on Monday, record *everything* you consume for one week, including water. Exact measurements aren't necessary. "Other" includes additional snacks, a water break, etc. (For a complete diet analysis, create a profile at **www.choosemyplate.gov** or another online program designed to track and analyze your food intake and physical activity.)

Meal	Monday	Tuesday	Wednesday	Thursday	Friday	Saturday	Sunday
Breakfast							
Snack							
Lunch							
Snack							
Dinner							
Other							

1. Which type of liquid did you drink most often (water, coffee, milk, juice, etc.)? _____

2. How many soft drinks did you consume each day? (Use 12 ounces—the size of a soft drink can—as one drink, and divide by the number of days to get an average.) Are they usually diet or nondiet drinks? _____

3. How many drinks were caffeinated? _____

4. About how many times per day (or week) do you consume the following?
   - whole grains _____
   - green, leafy vegetables _____
   - fried foods _____
   - red meat _____
   - foods high in sugar _____
   - alcohol _____

5. Do you tend to eat fewer but bigger meals each day or many smaller meals? Or another pattern? _____

6. How many meals were bought at a restaurant, including via a drive thru or convenience store? _____

7. Of those meals, how many would you consider healthy choices? Did you consciously make a healthier selection versus something else you would have normally ordered? _____

8. Compare your eating and drinking habits on the weekend with the rest of the week. Are there obvious differences? If yes, explain. _____

9. Based on your food choices this week, what changes should you make to improve your diet? How easy or difficult will it be to make healthier choices? _____

REVIEW AND APPLICATIONS | CHAPTER 11

Inventory of Interests

Developing outside interests can help reduce stress in your life. Interests are activities that you enjoy and pique your curiosity. Besides reducing stress, they may help you determine your life's work and career path. For example, an interest in the outdoors may lead to a major in natural resources, then to a career as a park ranger. A passion for working with cars may lead to a certificate in auto mechanics and thus to your own auto repair shop.

Fill in the following inventory to help you determine a career that coincides with activities you enjoy. Review this later to see if your interests change.

1. My interests are

_____

_____

_____

_____

2. Answer the following questions:

a. What websites, blogs, and news sources do I like to visit and read?

_____

_____

_____

_____

b. What kinds of books and magazines do I like to read?

_____

_____

_____

_____

c. When I have free time, what do I like to do? (Check the areas that interest you.)

Reading	_____	Working with people	_____
Writing	_____	Working with computers	_____
Sports	_____	Building or remodeling	_____
Outdoor activities	_____	Creating artwork	_____
Traveling	_____	Public speaking	_____

Other Activities

_____

_____

_____

REVIEW AND APPLICATIONS | CHAPTER 11

Build Supportive and Diverse Relationships

SELF-MANAGEMENT

"I never realized I would interact with so many new people at college. It's exciting but frightening. I've been so focused on planning my coursework that I'm not prepared to think beyond my own little world."

College offers many new experiences and exposes you to a wide variety of people with different backgrounds, opinions, and interests. It also gives you an opportunity to become a better communicator and an effective participant in social and group settings. In this chapter, you will learn how to create healthy relationships, solve conflicts, work effectively in a team, become more assertive, and handle criticism. You will see yourself communicating clearly, concisely, and confidently.

JOURNAL ENTRY In **Worksheet 12.1** on page 402, describe a difficult or confrontational situation in which you felt comfortable communicating your needs and ideas in an assertive, direct, and calm manner. What factors helped you be confident and respectful?

N o one exists in a vacuum. You can learn to read efficiently, write fluid prose, score high on tests, or memorize anything you want, but success will elude you if you cannot communicate and build rapport with different people. People spend nearly 70 percent of their waking hours communicating and interacting with others. SCANS lists interpersonal relationships, communication, an understanding of diversity, and team skills as essential for job success. In this chapter, we will discuss ways to get better at understanding and relating to people, solving conflicts, and being an effective team member.

The Importance of Effective Communication and Rapport

Communication is the giving and receiving of ideas, feelings, and information. Note the word *receiving*. Some people are good at speaking but are not effective listeners. Poor listening is one of the biggest barriers to effective communication. Miscommunication wastes billions of dollars in business and damages relationships.

What do you really want when you communicate with someone else? Do you want people to listen to you, understand your feelings, and relate to your message? Building **rapport** is more than just giving and receiving information. It is finding common ground with another person based on respect, empathy, and trust. Finding **common ground** means having an intent to focus on similarities in interests and objectives and appreciate diverse core values, seeing other viewpoints, and building bridges to understanding.

Some people have a knack for building rapport and making others feel comfortable and accepted. They are sensitive to nonverbal cues and the responses they elicit from other people. They have developed empathy and make people feel valued. They are comfortable with themselves and with people from different cultures and backgrounds. They can put their egos aside and focus on the other person with genuine interest and appreciation. You can learn this skill, too. People will want to be near you because you make them feel good about themselves, treat them as important, and create a comfortable climate. People who build rapport not only look for similarities in others but also appreciate and celebrate differences.

Strategies for Building Communication and Rapport

1. **Be willing to find common ground.** The first step in building rapport is to assess your intention to find common ground. If your goal is to build understanding and acceptance, it will usually be reflected in your tone, body language, and style. If you are judgmental, however, this message will come through, regardless of your words. Even if you insist you want to find common ground, others will sense your intention to prove yourself right, scold, judge, instruct, embarrass, or put down.

2. **Be an attentive listener.** In Chapter 5, we explored how to be an effective listener by using strategies such as the following:

- *Listen; don't talk.* Don't change the subject unless the speaker is finished. Be patient and don't interrupt. Listen for feelings, undertones, and meanings in what people are saying. Observe nonverbal cues: posture, tone of voice, eye contact, body movements, and facial expressions.

- *Put the speaker at ease.* Create a supportive, open climate by being warm and friendly, showing interest, and smiling.

- *Withhold criticism.* Criticizing puts people on the defensive and blocks communication. Arguing almost never changes someone's mind, and it may widen the communication gap.

- *Paraphrase.* Restating in your own words what the speaker has said shows you are interested in the other person's point. Then ask for feedback: "Did I understand you correctly?"

- *Know when you cannot listen.* If you know you do not have time to pay close attention to the speaker, say so. For example, if you have a lot of studying to do and your roommate wants to talk about a date, you may want to say respectfully, "I'd like to know more about your date, but I have to read this chapter. Can we talk about it when I'm done"? You also may want to delay discussions when you are angry, tired, or stressed. Just make sure to respond in a respectful tone of voice.

● **Your Body Is Talking**
What message is this student sending to his instructor?

3. **Pay attention to body language.** Look at the speaker and appear attentive, interested, and alert. In contrast, crossing your arms, frowning, leaning back in your chair, avoiding eye contact, sighing, and shaking your head say, "I don't like you and I don't want to listen." When your eyes wander, you appear uninterested or bored. Instead, create an attentive, supportive climate: Look at the other person, relax and uncross your arms, and lean slightly toward the person. Some experts say that 70 percent of what is communicated is done through nonverbal communication, or body language. If you intend to build rapport, your words must match your body language.

4. **Be respectful.** Many organizations are training employees in the importance of business etiquette—respect for and consideration of the feelings and needs of others. Good manners and respect are the basis of all healthy relationships. People need to feel they are getting the consideration and appreciation they deserve, whether in the classroom, on the job, or at home. See **Peak Progress 12.1** on page 374 on applying these principles to communicating online.

5. **Use warmth and humor.** Avoid sarcasm and jokes at the expense of another person's feelings, but don't take yourself too seriously. Humor puts people at ease and can dissipate tension. Wit and a sincere smile create warmth and understanding and can open the door to further effective communication.

6. **Relate to a person's personality style.** As mentioned in Chapter 1, people learn, think, and relate differently. Knowing this can help you interact and work more

Peak Progress

Socially Acceptable Technology

The use of technology has replaced face-to-face communication for many people. Not only has a short e-mail or text become more convenient than a phone call or a stroll down the hallway, but many social networking services, such as Facebook and Twitter, provide the tremendous opportunity to communicate instantly with designated groups of people.

As popular and convenient as these communication sites have become, they also have their pitfalls. Because you are looking at a screen, it's easy to forget you are interacting with human beings. Misunderstandings can occur, because there are no nonverbal cues and voice inflections. More serious ramifications can happen if you don't follow some important guidelines:

- *Be respectful to others.* This may seem obvious, but many have used technology as a means to belittle, threaten, and harass others, which is considered **cyberbullying** or **cyberstalking**. The Internet should not be considered a convenient place to vent your frustrations and anger or to torment others. If you

find yourself a victim of cyber attacks, tell someone, including the site owner.

- *Do not provide personal information.* Not only could your identity be compromised financially but it also could be used by a predator to rob or physically harm you. If you are selling products on sites such as eBay or craigslist, never meet the buyer or seller alone.

- *Do not send inappropriate material.* Although **sexting** (exchanging sexually explicit material, often via cell phone) seems harmless to some, it can be considered pornography and lead to criminal prosecution, especially if a participant is a minor. Some statistics suggest that one-third of young adults have been sexted at least once, often with the embarrassing pictures forwarded to others.

- *If you think you shouldn't send it, don't.* Remember that virtual material can be available forever. If you think someone could take an e-mail or a posting the wrong way, it's better to take the time to reword it or not send it at all.

---

effectively with diverse groups of people. For example, if your boss has the personality of an analyzer or a thinker, you will want to base your reports on facts and deliver clear, concise, and correct presentations.

7. **Relate to a person's learning or teaching style.** For example, perhaps your instructor prefers the visual mode. She writes on the board, shows videos and PowerPoint presentations, and uses phrases such as "Do you see what I'm saying?" For an instructor who prefers a visual mode, enhance your visual presentation. Turn in an especially attractive paper by being extra careful about neatness and spelling and using illustrations whenever appropriate. Try to maintain eye contact while this instructor is lecturing, and return visual clues, such as nods, smiles, and other reassurances.

8. **Be a team player.** You must pull your weight on a team, whether at school or at work. You build team rapport not by being fun, charming, and a good conversationalist but by being clear on expectations, deadlines, commitment, and follow-through. Excuses do not build rapport, and no one likes a slacker. Check in often with your team and know when you will meet again, what work should be accomplished by individual team members, and what resources each person needs in order to produce results. The foundation of teamwork is effective communication and responsibility.

Assertive Communication

Assertive communication is expressing yourself in a direct, above-board, and civil manner. You may not always feel you have the right to speak up for what you need, particularly in new situations where you see yourself as powerless and dependent. However, only you can take responsibility for clarifying your expectations, expressing your needs, and making your own decisions. You might tend to act passively in some situations, aggressively in others, and assertively in still others. In most situations, however, strive to communicate in an assertive and respectful manner.

- *Passive* people rarely express feelings, opinions, and desires. They have little self-confidence and low self-esteem, have difficulty accepting compliments, and often compare themselves unfavorably with others. Sometimes they feel that others take advantage of them, which creates resentment.

- *Aggressive* people are often sarcastic, critical, and controlling. They want to win at any cost and sometimes blame others for making them angry. They may resort to insults and criticisms, which breaks down communication and harms relationships.

- *Passive-aggressive* people appear passive but act aggressively. For example, a passive-aggressive student will not respond in class when asked if there are any questions but will then go to the dean to complain that instructions aren't clear. A passive-aggressive roommate will leave nasty notes or complain to others rather than confront you directly.

- *Assertive* people state their views and needs directly; use confident body language; speak in a clear, strong voice; and take responsibility for their actions. Assertive people respect themselves and others.

Practice developing assertive responses in **Personal Evaluation Notebook 12.1** on page 376.

ASSERTIVENESS TIPS:

1 **State the problem in clear terms.**
Be clear on your position and what you want " I cannot study with the music so loud."

2 **Express your feelings.**
Use "I" messages instead of "You" messages: "I feel frustrated when the music is too loud, because I have to study for a test tommorrow."

3 **Make your request.**
"Please turn the music down . I especially need it quiet after ten o'clock."

4 **Use assertive body language.**
Stay calm, use direct eye contact, square your shoulders, and speak in a clear, low tone.

5 **State the consequences.**
Always start with the positive: "If you will turn down the volume on your music, I can study better and our relationship will be more positive." If you don't get the results you want, try saying, "I'm going to have to go to our landlord to discuss this problem."

Personal Evaluation Notebook

Assertive Communication Role-Playing

Read the following situations. Then develop an assertive response for each one.

1. **Situation:** You receive a *B* on your test, and you think you deserve an *A*. What would you say to your instructor?

   Assertive response: _____

2. **Situation:** A friend asks you to read her term paper. She tells you it is the best paper she has ever written. However, you find several glaring errors.

   Assertive response: _____

3. **Situation:** Your roommate asks to borrow your new car. You don't want to lend it.

   Assertive response: _____

4. **Situation:** An acquaintance makes sexual advances. You are not interested.

   Assertive response: _____

5. **Situation:** You go to a party and your date pressures you to drink.

   Assertive response: _____

6. **Situation:** Your roommate's friend has moved in and doesn't pay rent.

   Assertive response: _____

7. **Situation:** Your sister borrowed your favorite sweater and stained it.

   Assertive response: _____

8. **Situation:** A friend lights up a cigarette, and you are allergic to smoke.

   Assertive response: _____

9. **Situation:** You want your roommate or spouse to help you keep the apartment clean.

   Assertive response: _____

10. **Situation:** Your mother wants you to go home for the weekend, but you have to study for a major test.

    Assertive response: _____

Communicating with Instructors and Advisors

Develop professional relationships with your instructors and advisors, just as you would with your supervisor at work. Try a few of these tips to increase rapport:

1. **Clarify expectations.** Make certain you understand the objectives and expectations of your instructors and advisors. Most instructors will give you extra help and feedback if you take the initiative. For instance, before a paper is due, hand in a draft and say, "I want to make sure I'm covering the important points in this paper. Am I on the right track? What reference sources would you like me to use? What can I add to make this an *A* paper?"

2. **Clarify concerns.** If you don't understand or you disagree with a grade on a test or paper, ask for an appointment with the instructor. Approach the situation with a supportive attitude: "I like this course and want to do well in it. I don't

know why I got a *C* on this paper, because I thought I had met the objectives. Could you show me what points you think should be changed? Could I make these corrections for a higher grade?" Show respect and appreciation for your instructor's time and help, as your instructor may be teaching many courses with many students. Follow basic rules of etiquette when communicating with your instructor by e-mail. (See **Peak Progress 12.2** on page 378.)

3. **Adapt to your instructor's teaching style.** Approach each class with a positive attitude, and don't expect that all instructors will teach according to your learning style. (See Chapter 1, page 29, for specific tips.)

4. **Be open to learning.** Attend every class with an inquisitive, open mind. Some instructors may be less interesting, but be as supportive of the instructor as possible. If you are a returning student, you may find that the instructor is younger than you are and may lack life experiences. Be open to learning and valuing the training, education, and knowledge the instructor brings to class. The same rule applies to the workplace.

5. **Take responsibility for your own learning.** Don't expect your instructor to feed you information. You are ultimately responsible for your own learning and career. You may be tempted to cut classes, but you will miss valuable class discussions, question-and-answer sessions, explanations, reviews of concepts, expectations about tests, contact with students, and structure to help you stay focused.

6. **Take an interest in your instructors.** Visit them during office hours to discuss your work, goals, grades, and future coursework. When appropriate, ask about your instructors' academic backgrounds as a guide for yours. Ask about degrees, colleges attended, work experience, and what projects they are working on for professional growth. A large part of building rapport is showing genuine interest, appreciation, and respect.

7. **Network.** Building your professional network begins in college. Form professional relationships with other students, your advisor, a few key instructors, club advisors, administrators, and so on. Exchange e-mails and ask people on campus (who know you well) if you may use them as a reference or if they would be willing to write a letter of recommendation for graduate school, an internship, or your first job.

● **Connecting with Your Instructor**

Develop a rapport with your instructor by taking the initiative to ask for feedback and help when you need it and in plenty of time to put the advice into action. *Are you working on assignments or papers right now that you should be consulting with your instructor about?*

Conflict

Conflicts can occur between family members, co-workers, neighbors, roommates, friends, teammates, and instructors and students. Some common causes are strong emotions, unsatisfied needs, misperceptions and stereotypes, miscommunication, repetitive negative behavior, and differing expectations, opinions, beliefs, and values. Although conflict can impede communication and damage relationships, it can also bring problems to the surface and lead to creative solutions when the conflict is understood and coped with appropriately. Use your observation and critical

Peak Progress

E-mail Etiquette with Instructors

Although you may have established a friendly, personable relationship with your instructor or advisor, you should always treat him or her with the respect due to any employer or evaluator of your performance or behavior. Because technology has allowed us to communicate more quickly, we often forget to practice the basic rules of communication etiquette. When e-mailing your instructor for help, clarification, or advice, keep in mind the following:

1. **Use proper spelling, grammar, and punctuation.** Although you may be used to text messaging in lowercase letters, proper e-mail etiquette calls for writing the e-mail just as you would a letter or paper. Start each sentence with a capital letter, and end each sentence with punctuation (period, question mark, etc.). It's also common e-mail knowledge that you should not write in all capital letters, which designates "shouting" or intense urgency. Always use the spell-check before sending, and read it through at least once more.

2. **Avoid using slang, abbreviations, or "smileys."** You wouldn't say "ADN" (for "any day now") in a letter to a potential employer or include little smiley faces (emoticons). Those are fine in messages to friends, but not to instructors or employers. Also, your instructor may lose your meaning because he or she doesn't know what "BTW" ("by the way") stands for.

3. **Use proper greetings.** You wouldn't start a letter to your instructor with "Hey, Dr. Smith." "Dear Dr. Smith" is appropriate; "Hello, Dr. Smith" is also acceptable in most cases.

4. **Make it clear who you are.** Because instructors interact with many people daily, they can't decipher who you are by your e-mail account (bhappy16@aol.com). Quickly make it clear who you are ("I'm Beatrice Jones in your English 305 course"). Put your full name (and phone number, if necessary) at the end of your e-mail.

5. **Be smart about your e-mail address.** Although you may think hot2trot@aol.com gets attention, it won't garner much respect (and possibly even response) from an instructor or a future employer. Plus, with the myriad of spam messages and computer viruses, your instructor may even be hesitant to open your e-mail.

6. **Be concise and to the point.** Remember that your instructor has many people to respond to during the day: students, other faculty members, and administrators (not to mention people involved in their research work, professional memberships, and consulting obligations). In your message subject line, clearly state the overall point: "Question about today's discussion on learning styles." In one or two paragraphs, briefly ask your question or make your point. Include just the essential details. If you feel your point may be lost, either put your question at the very beginning or highlight it in bold or another color.

7. **Respectfully include a "due date," if necessary.** Never say to an instructor, "I must hear from you by . . ." However, your issue may be time-sensitive for a reason, such as a registration deadline. If you need a response by a certain time, indicate that politely: "It would be great to have your response by this Friday, as I have to turn in my forms by that afternoon." If you haven't received a response, send a follow-up: "Just checking to make sure you received my e-mail." When something is urgent, e-mail may not be the appropriate mode of communication. Call the instructor, drop by his or her office, catch him or her in class, or schedule an appointment. Do not let e-mail be an excuse for not getting an important answer.

8. **Leave in the message thread.** If there has been a string of e-mails to this point, it's always better to leave them in if you can, in case the recipient needs to refresh his or her memory about the issue.

9. **Do not use graphics.** Unless necessary, do not be creative with the typeface, graphics, or backgrounds in your e-mails. They only make the e-mail harder to read and increase the file size.

10. **Always say, "Thank you."** Get in the habit of ending e-mails with a *thank you, thanks,* or *I appreciate your help.* People will respond to you faster and more often if their efforts are acknowledged and appreciated.

thinking skills to complete **Personal Evaluation Notebooks 12.2** and **12.3** on pages 380 and 381 about conflict resolution.

The common responses to conflict are to avoid it, compromise, accommodate others, or cooperate with others. Following are a few suggestions that focus on cooperation as a means of resolving conflict.

1. **Define the conflict as a concrete problem to be solved.** Focus on the problem, not the other person: "The conflict is that Joe is doing most of the talking in my study group and I want to move on and solve the problem, so that the group can be more productive."

2. **Convert "You" statements into "I" statements.** Making "I" statements instead of "You" statements effectively communicates information without pointing the finger at the other person and putting him or her on the defensive. Instead of saying, "You talk too much," say, "I feel angry when one person does all the talking, because we need to hear the opinions of other people before we can make an informed decision." Use a three-part formula: "I FEEL (emotions) _____WHEN (behavior) _____ BECAUSE (reason) _____."

3. **Attentively listen to the other person's concerns and criticism.** Don't interrupt or start your defense. Really concentrate on the other person's perceptions, feelings, and expectations. Give physical cues that you are listening. Listen to what is said, how it is said, and when it is said. Listen also for what is not being said. Ask for clarification, avoid jumping to assumptions, and don't hurry the speaker.

4. **Develop empathy.** Empathy is the ability to share another's emotions, thoughts, or feelings in order to understand the person better. By taking the role of the other, you can develop the ability to see and feel the situation through his or her eyes. Sympathy is feeling compassion for a person, which can border on pity or condescension. An empathetic attitude says, "I am here with you." Empathy allows for the distance needed to maintain objectivity, so that the problem can be solved.

5. **Stay calm.** Control your emotions and don't lose your temper. Ask the other person to calm down: "I see you are upset, and I really want to know what your concerns are. Please talk more slowly." Listen to the message without overreacting or becoming defensive.

6. **Focus on the problem.** Don't use detours and attack the person—for example, "You think I'm messy. Look at your room. You're a real pig." Instead, focus on the problem: "If I do the dishes the same evening I cook, will you feel more comfortable?" Trust that you can both speak your minds calmly and nondefensively without damaging your relationship.

7. **Ask for specific details and clarification.** The key is to understand the issue at hand: "Can you describe a specific incident when you think I was rude?"

Take 3 minutes to thank someone for making a difference:

- Pick someone, such as a coach, teacher, boss, friend, relative, or group leader, with whom you've interacted.
- How has this person helped you or others? Has this person sacrificed personal time to fulfill the commitment?
- Write a note or an e-mail to the person, thanking him or her for the contribution, mentioning how you have been affected.

What else can you do in 3 minutes?

- Check the school's website or search online for information about your major instructors. See what types of research they are involved in.
- Send a "thinking of you" e-mail to a friend you haven't corresponded with lately.
- Say "hi" to everyone you pass on the way into class.

Personal Evaluation Notebook

12.2

Observing Conflict

Read the following questions and write your answers on the lines provided.

1. Observe how others handle conflict, compliments, and criticism. What ineffective behaviors do you notice?

   _____

   _____

2. What behaviors do you use under stress that you would like to change?

   _____

   _____

3. What do you intend to do the next time you are in a conflict with someone?

   _____

   _____

8. **Create solutions.** You might say, "I can see that this is a problem. What can I do to solve it? What procedures or options can we explore?"

9. **Apologize.** If you think the situation warrants it, apologize: "I'm sorry. I was wrong." It defuses anger and builds trust and respect.

10. **Forgive.** There are times when a conflict just can't be resolved, even though you have been hurt by the words or actions of someone else. Rather than holding onto that anger and resentment, you may need to let go of those feelings and forgive the other person and simply move on. **Forgiveness** does not mean you discount the situation or absolve the other person from responsibility, but you accept that the circumstances cannot be changed and decide to focus on the positive aspects in your life.

Constructive Criticism

Part of effective communication is being open to feedback and criticism. Start with the attitude that the critic has good intentions and is offering constructive criticism—criticism meant to be supportive and useful for improvement. Unconstructive criticism is negative and harsh; it doesn't offer options and can create defensiveness and tension.

GIVING CONSTRUCTIVE CRITICISM

Your feedback will be asked for more often if you give it in a nurturing way.

1. **Establish a supportive climate.** People need to feel safe when receiving feedback or criticism. Choose a convenient time and a private place to talk. If possible, sit next to the person instead of behind a barrier, such as a desk.

Personal Evaluation Notebook

Conflict Resolution

Describe a conflict you have not yet resolved. Think of resolution techniques that would be helpful. Respond to the following statements.

1. Describe the problem.

   _____

   _____

2. Express your feelings.

   _____

   _____

3. State what you want.

   _____

   _____

4. Predict the consequences.

   _____

   _____

2. **Ask permission to offer criticism.** Don't blindside someone with your feedback. First ask if he or she would like to hear your impressions and suggestions for improvement.

3. **Focus on the behavior, not the person.** Define the specific behavior you want to change. Don't hit the person with several issues at once.

4. **Stay calm.** Look at the person, keep your voice low and calm, use positive words, and avoid threats. Be brief and to the point.

5. **Be balanced.** Let the other person know you like him or her and appreciate the person's good qualities or behaviors. Avoid words such as *always* and *never*.

6. **Explain.** Explain why the behavior warrants criticism and why a change is in order. Talk about options and offer to help.

RECEIVING CRITICISM

Learning to accept and grow from constructive criticism is important for school and job success. Here are some tips:

1. **Listen with an open mind.** Reminders that you aren't perfect are never pleasant. However, try to listen with an open mind when your instructor, boss, co-worker, roommate, spouse, or classmate points out mistakes, mentions concerns, or makes suggestions. Don't talk until you have heard all the details.

> **"Minds are like parachutes. They only function when they are open."**
>
> SIR JAMES DEWAR
> *Chemist and physicist*

WORDS TO SUCCEED

Think about what is being said and whether the criticism is constructive. You may want to ask for time to think it through. Do others feel the same way? Have you heard similar criticism before? If so, it may be valid.

2. **Pay attention to nonverbal cues.** Sometimes people have difficulty expressing criticism, so they express it nonverbally. If the person is aloof, angry, or sad, you might ask if you did something to offend the person. If he or she is sarcastic, perhaps there is underlying hostility. If appropriate, you can say, "You've been very quiet today. Did I do something to offend you?"

3. **Ask for clarification.** Be sure you understand the criticism—for example, "Professor Walker, you gave me a *C* on this paper. Could you explain what points you consider to be inadequate?"

4. **Ask for suggestions.** If the criticism is constructive, ask for suggestions—for example, "How can I improve this paper?" Summarize the discussion and clarify the next steps. Know what you need to do to correct the situation. Don't make excuses for your behavior. If the criticism is true, change your behavior.

5. **Explain your viewpoint.** If the criticism feels unfair, discuss it openly. Don't let resentments smolder and build. Practice saying, "Thank you for your viewpoint and your courage in telling me what is bothering you. However, I don't think the criticism is fair." Criticism reflects how another person views your behavior at a certain time. It is not necessarily reality but an interpretation. Relax and put it in perspective.

Dealing with Shyness

Shyness is common, especially on college campuses, where people are adjusting to new situations and meeting new people. Shyness is not a problem unless it interferes with your life. It is perfectly acceptable to enjoy your privacy, prefer a few close friends to many, and even embarrass easily. However, if shyness keeps you from speaking up in class, getting to know your instructors and other students, giving presentations, or making new friends, it is interfering with your success. In school and in the workplace, it is important to speak up and ask questions, clarify assignments, and ask for help. You can overcome shyness, build rapport, and be an effective conversationalist by following these strategies:

1. **Use positive self-talk.** Instead of saying, "I can't change," tell yourself, "I'm confident, people like me, and I like people. I enjoy getting to know people. I am accepted, appreciated, and admired."

2. **Use direct eye contact.** Many shy people look down or avoid eye contact. Direct eye contact reinforces your confidence and shows interest in and empathy with others. Look at your instructors and show interest in what they are presenting.

3. **Ask questions and show genuine interest.** You don't have to talk a lot to be an effective conversationalist. In fact, you don't want to deliver monologues. Ask open-ended questions, show genuine interest, and give others a chance to talk. For example, instead of asking Jennifer if she is finished with an assigned term paper (yes/no), ask her how she is progressing with the paper (open-ended

question). See **Peak Progress 12.3** for tips on making small talk and initiating conversations.

4. **Listen to other points of view.** Even if you don't agree with other people's points of view, listen and respond tactfully and thoughtfully. You have something to contribute, and exchanging different views is a great way to learn and grow. Ask others how they developed their point of view.

5. **Use humor.** Most people like to laugh. Poking good-natured fun at yourself lightens the conversation, as does a funny joke or story. Just make certain to be sensitive; don't tell off-color or racial jokes or stories.

6. **Focus on the benefits.** Making friends helps you develop your sense of community and belonging. It can ease the loneliness many students feel.

Peak Progress

12.3

Making Small Talk

Whether you are meeting students in class, a business client, a first date, or the patient next to you in the doctor's office, the art of small talk can help you get to know people better and overcome awkward situations.

- *Ask questions to get the conversation rolling.* Most people love to talk about themselves, and you can learn a lot about someone. Follow up on phrases. If someone answers, "How are you?" with "Excellent," respond with "It sounds like you're having a great day! May I ask why?" If the person's mood isn't positive, though, be careful about asking too much, or you will seem to be prying.

- *Mention current events.* Bring up recent happenings in the news, sports, your community, or politics. However, avoid getting into a heated debate (especially a political one).

- *Comment on a piece of clothing or an accessory you like.* Ask where it came from or the significance. Everyone appreciates honest flattery.

- *Talk about television shows, movies, books, or other pop culture.* Share your interests to see what you might have in common or can learn from each other.

- *Mention places in the community.* Ask if the person has had a chance to see the new stadium or a jazz club that just opened. What restaurant would the person recommend to someone visiting from out of town?

- *Listen and pay attention.* Not paying attention during casual conversation makes a bad impression.

The other person will think you aren't interested and are just killing time.

- *Use your body language.* Keep your arms uncrossed and relaxed. Make direct eye contact and smile.

- *Be positive and friendly.* No one likes to be around people who are negative or rude. Use appropriate humor, not sarcasm, humor that belittles others, or offensive language.

- *Use the person's name.* If this isn't your first meeting, using the person's name makes him or her feel more important. Follow up on your last conversation: "How did your son's team do in that soccer tournament?" or "Were you happy with your grade on the economics paper?" People are impressed when you remember something about them.

- *Stay on common ground.* If you are stuck trying to come up with something to say, talk about whatever you know you have in common, such as a class.

- *If all else fails, use the weather.* It may be a cliché, but initiate a conversation by talking about the surroundings or situation: "Can you believe this hot spell we're having?" Segue into related topics: "I'm sure the baseball team is feeling the heat. Do you ever go to their games?" or "I've had to use the inside track for walking lately. Do you use the rec center, too?" The weather may help you find some common interests.

7. **Take action.** Join clubs and activities. Volunteer in an organization that sponsors service learning. Join study groups or ask one of your classmates to study with you. Get a part-time job or get involved in community organizations. Try out for a play or choir—really stretch yourself. Reach out to others and make friends with a broad range of people.

Overcome Obstacles to Effective Communication

The greatest barrier to effective communication is the assumption that the other person knows what you mean. It is easy to think that what you say is what your listener hears, but communication is a complex system, with so many barriers to overcome that it is a wonder anyone ever really communicates. Other barriers include poor listening skills, the need to be right all the time, and cultural, religious, social, and gender differences.

However, communication is the lifeblood of personal relationships and the foundation of effective teams and work groups. Learning to work effectively with your study team, advisors, instructors, roommates, co-workers, and supervisors is essential for success at school, at work, and in personal relationships. Look for patterns that seem to occur in your relationships as you complete **Personal Evaluation Notebook 12.4.**

Build Healthy Relationships

Problems in relationships can consume time and energy, and they may affect your self-esteem. Because feeling good about yourself is one key to all-around success, it is important to assess how you handle relationships with partners, friends, and family.

Romantic Relationships

Success in life can be even more meaningful when you are part of a loving, supportive relationship. However, too often we define ourselves by success in romantic endeavors rather than understanding what we gain emotionally by a rewarding relationship. Following are tips for building healthy relationships.

1. **Progress slowly.** Take time to get to know the other person and how he or she feels and reacts to situations. Relationships that move too fast or are based on intense and instant sexuality often end quickly. Some people go from casual to intimate in one date. Solid relationships need time to develop through the stages of companionship and friendship.

2. **Have realistic expectations.** Some people think a good romantic relationship will magically improve their lives, even if they make no effort to change their thinking or behavior. If you are a poor student, are unmotivated, are depressed, or lack confidence, you will still have these problems even if you have a great relationship. A relationship can't solve life's problems; only you

" Lots of people want to ride with you in the limo, but what you want is someone who will take the bus with you when the limo breaks down. **"**

OPRAH WINFREY
Talk show host, actor, publisher

Personal Evaluation Notebook

Patterns in Relationships

Look for patterns in your relationships. Recall situations that occur again and again. For example, you may have the same problem communicating with instructors or advisors. You may have had conflicts with several roommates, co-workers, or supervisors. Once you see the patterns and consequences of your interactions, you can begin to think and act differently. When you take responsibility for changing your inner world of beliefs and thoughts, your outer world will also change. Write about what seems to be a recurring theme or pattern in your relationships.

_____

_____

_____

_____

_____

_____

_____

_____

_____

can solve your problems. Put more energy into improving your life than into looking for someone else to do it.

3. **Be honest.** You certainly don't want to reveal your entire past to a casual acquaintance or first date. At the appropriate time, however, you need to be honest about your feelings, basic values, and major life experiences. For example, if you are an alcoholic or have been married before, the other person should know that as your relationship progresses.

4. **Be supportive and respectful.** A healthy relationship is mutually supportive of the growth and well-being of each partner and is based on respect for the other person's feelings and rights. An unhealthy relationship is not. No one owns another person, nor does anyone have a right to harm another physically or emotionally. An unhealthy relationship is possessive, controlling, and lacks trust.

● **Equal Parts**
A healthy relationship is based on honesty, trust, and mutual support. *Why do some partners have a difficult time ending an unhealthy relationship?*

5. **Know that change can occur.** Emotionally healthy people know that not all relationships will develop into romantic and intimate commitments. Knowing how to end or let go of a relationship is as important as knowing how to form healthy relationships. It is acceptable and normal to say no to an acquaintance who asks you out or to decide you don't want a romantic relationship or friendship to continue after a few dates. No one should date, have sex, or stay in a relationship out of guilt, fear, or obligation. It is harder to terminate a relationship if it progressed too fast or if the expectations for the relationship differ. Talk about your expectations, and realize that your worth does not depend on someone's wanting or not wanting to date you.

6. **Keep the lines of communication open.** Trouble occurs in relationships when you think you know how the other person feels or would react to a situation. For example, you may assume that a relationship is intimate, but the other person may regard it as casual. Make your expectations clear.

Communication in a healthy relationship is open enough to discuss even sensitive topics, such as birth control, sexually transmitted diseases, and unplanned pregnancy. Take a moment to reflect on your relationships in **Personal Evaluation Notebook 12.5.**

Relationships with the People You Live With

If you share your living space with a roommate, partner, or family member, it's important to create an open environment for communicating needs, problems, and solutions. The following suggestions will help you create rapport and improve communication with your roommates and family members.

1. **Clarify expectations of a roommate.** List the factors you feel are important for a roommate on your housing application or in an ad. If you don't want a smoker or pets, say so. Sometimes it is best not to live with a good friend—rooming together has ruined more than one friendship. Plus, getting to know new people with different backgrounds and experiences is a great opportunity.

2. **Discuss expectations when first meeting your roommate.** Define what neatness means to you. Discuss how both of you feel about overnight guests, drinking, drugs, choice and volume of music, housework, food sharing, quiet times, and so on. Consider developing a "roommate contract," which specifies certain expectations and responsibilities (including financial ones, if need be).

3. **Clarify concerns and agree to communicate with each other.** Don't mope or whine about a grievance or leave nasty notes. Communicate honestly and kindly. It's important to understand each other's views and expectations and try to work out conflicts. If your roommate likes to have the dishes done after each meal, try to comply rather than prove that he or she is a neat freak. If you like to have friends over but your roommate goes to bed early or is studying, entertain in the early evenings, be quiet, or go out in the late evenings.

4. **Treat your roommate and family members with respect and civility.** Don't give orders or make demands. Calmly listen to each other's needs.

Personal Evaluation Notebook

12.5

Healthy Relationships

Read the following statements and questions, and respond to them on the lines provided.

1. List the factors you believe are essential for a healthy relationship.

   _____

   _____

2. What do you believe contributes to unhealthy relationships?

   _____

   _____

3. Who are your friends?

   _____

   _____

4. Describe some of your other relationships, such as in study teams and with instructors.

   _____

   _____

5. List the ways that your relationships support you and your goals.

   _____

   _____

6. List the ways that unhealthy relationships may undermine you and your goals.

   _____

   _____

Think about your tone of voice, body language, and choice of words. Sometimes we treat family, friends, and roommates with less respect than strangers.

5. **Don't borrow unless necessary.** A lot of problems result over borrowing money, clothes, jewelry, cars, and so on. The best advice is not to borrow. However, if you must borrow, ask permission first and return the item in good shape or replace it if you lose or damage it. Fill the tank of a borrowed car with gas, for instance. Immediately pay back all money you borrow.

6. **Keep your agreements.** Make a list of chores, agree on tasks, and do your share. When you say you will do something, do it. When you agree on a time, be punctual. Try to be flexible, however, so that annoyances don't build.

Max is at the breaking point. He has walked into the kitchen to make breakfast, only to find that his roommate, Jimmy, must have had the late-night munchies again, as evidenced by the dirty pans on the stove, grated cheese on the floor, and a half-eaten taco abandoned on the coffee table beside Jimmy, who is passed out on the couch.

- If you were Max, would you wake up Jimmy and discuss the situation now?
- Develop some "I" statements that Max can use to discuss the situation with his roommate.
- If Jimmy's behavior doesn't change, what should Max do?

THINK FAST

7. **Accept others' beliefs.** Don't try to change anyone's beliefs. Listen openly and, when necessary, agree that your viewpoints are different.

8. **Respect others' privacy.** Don't enter each other's bedroom or private space without asking. Don't pry, read personal mail, or eavesdrop on conversations. Be cautious about posting photos of your roommate on social media sites. Ask permission first or be certain your roommate approves of the photo.

9. **Get to know each other.** Set aside time for occasional shared activities. Cook a meal, take a walk, or go to a movie. You don't need to be your roommate's best friend, but you should feel comfortable sharing a room or an apartment. Appreciate your roommate and/or family members, and try not to focus on little faults or inconveniences.

Appreciate Diversity

Colleges and workplaces reflect the changing **diversity** in our society—in gender, race, age, ethnicity, sexual orientation, physical ability, learning styles and abilities, social and economic background, and religion. We tend to surround ourselves with people who are similar to us and to see the world in a certain way. However, college is an excellent place to fully appreciate diversity by getting to know, understand, and value other cultures and people with different life experiences, talents, and political and social views. Expand your horizons and cultivate a wide variety of friends and acquaintances who see the world differently. Communication breaks down walls, corrects false beliefs, and enriches your life.

As a contributing member of society and the workforce, it is essential that you use critical thinking to assess your assumptions, judgments, and views about people who are different from you. Cultural sensitivity is the foundation for building common ground with diverse groups. (See **Figure 12.1**.)

● **Working Together**
The composition of the workforce will continue to change and diversify. To be effective and get along with co-workers, people need to deal with any prejudices they've learned. *What can companies do to help employees understand and appreciate diversity?*

Communication Strategies for Celebrating Diversity

Here are some strategies you can use for developing effective communication with diverse groups of people. (See **Peak Progress 12.4** on how to apply the Adult Learning Cycle to making the best use of your strategies.)

1. **Be aware of your feelings and beliefs.** If you have a negative attitude or reaction to a group or person, examine it and see where it is

Culturally Biased	Culturally in Denial	Culturally Aware	Culturally Sensitive and Respectful	Culturally Responsible and Active
Believes different groups have positive and negative characteristics as a whole	Believes there is no problem; everyone should be the same	Tries to understand and increase awareness; is aware that experiences differ for people based on their culture	Respects people from diverse cultural and social backgrounds; seeks out contact with people from diverse backgrounds; encourages people to value and respect their cultural identity	Acts on commitment to eliminate oppression; seeks to include full participation of diverse cultural groups in decision making

Figure 12.1
Cultural Understanding

Different categories of cultural understanding are seen in our society. *In what column do you believe you fit and why?*

coming from. (See **Figure 12.2** on page 390.) Unfortunately, **discrimination**—treating someone differently based on a characteristic—still occurs and varies by society. **Sexism** (a belief or an attitude that one sex is inferior or less valuable), **homophobia** (an irrational fear of gays and lesbians), and **racial profiling** (using racial or ethnic characteristics in determining whether a person is considered likely to commit a particular type of crime or an illegal act) are just a few examples of what we personally experience and impose on others daily. Be aware of how you talk to yourself about other people, and be willing to admit your own prejudices. This is the first step toward change and a willingness to build rapport.

2. **See the value in diversity.** We are a rich nation because of different races, cultures, backgrounds, and viewpoints. Having knowledge and understanding

Peak Progress   12.4

Applying the Adult Learning Cycle to Becoming a Better Communicator

1. **RELATE. Why do I want to learn this?** Effective communication is the most important skill I can acquire, practice, and perfect. By being more assertive, I avoid resentment and thoughts that I'm being taken advantage of. I can succinctly express my views, wants, and impressions, as well as my innovative ideas and decisions.

2. **OBSERVE. How does this work?** I admire people who are assertive and confident when expressing themselves and their views. What techniques or mannerisms do they use when communicating? I'll also observe people who are passive or aggressive and learn from their mistakes. How do others respond? I'll try using new strategies for dealing with fear, resentment, and anger.

3. **REFLECT. What does this mean?** What seems to work for me? Do I feel more confident and

comfortable interacting with others? Do I believe I'm presenting my ideas so that others understand my point of view? Am I more respectful of others' opinions and feelings? I'll continue to avoid negative self-talk and focus on a positive attitude and outlook.

4. **DO. What can I do with this?** I will practice being more assertive. I will make a commitment to be direct, kind, and respectful. Each day, I'll work on one area. For example, when my roommate plays music too loudly, I'll express my needs assertively and respectfully.

5. **TEACH. Whom can I share this with?** I'll ask others if they have ever felt misunderstood and what they changed to express themselves better. I'll share my experiences and the strategies that have worked for me. I'll volunteer to help others in my study group.

Now return to Stage 1 and continue to monitor your progress and think of new ways to enhance your communication skills.

Figure 12.2
Understanding the Meaning

Attitudes are thoughts and feelings. *Behaviors* are what we do—how we act out our thoughts and feelings. If we work on eliminating stereotypes and prejudices, we can affect the outcome: discrimination. *Have you ever felt prejudice? How have you dealt with that feeling?*

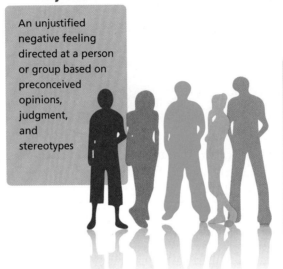

Stereotype

A mental or emotional picture held in common by members of a group that represents an oversimplified belief, opinion, or judgment about members of another group

Prejuduce

An unjustified negative feeling directed at a person or group based on preconceived opinions, judgment, and stereotypes

Discrimination

An unjustified negative behavior toward a person or group based on preconceived opinions, judgment, and stereotypes

of others helps to break through barriers, allowing us to appreciate different views and develop tolerance. Sharing different viewpoints teaches you new and interesting ways of seeing situations and approaching problems. Do you accept others and appreciate our diversity? Complete **Personal Evaluation Notebook 12.6** to determine your attitudes.

If the world were a village of 100 people . . .

61 villagers would be Asian (including **20** who would be Chinese and **17** who would be Indian), **14** would be African, **11** would be European, **9** would be Latin or South American, and **5** would be North American.

At least **18** villagers would be unable to read or write, but **33** would have cell phones and **16** would use the Internet.

There would be **18** cars in the village.

There would be an equal number of males and females.

33 villagers would be Christians, **20** would be Muslims, **13** would be Hindus, **6** would be Buddhists, **2** would be atheists, **12** would be nonreligious, and the remaining **14** would be members of other religions.

1 villager would have AIDS, **26** villagers would smoke, and **14** villagers would be obese.

63 villagers would have inadequate sanitation.

53 villagers would live on less than two U.S. dollars a day.

By the end of a year, one villager would die and two new villagers would be born, increasing the population to **101.**

Source: Adapted from Matt Rosenberg, "If the World Were a Village . . ." About. com , August 5, 2007; retrieved May 24, 2010 from http://geography.about. com/od/obtainpopulationdata/a/worldvillage.htm .

Personal Evaluation Notebook

12.6

Appreciating Diversity

A. Read the following, and write your comments on the lines provided.

1. What is your attitude toward people who differ from you in gender, race, sexual orientation, or culture? Is your attitude one of acceptance or exclusion?

   _____

2. Have you ever attended a political event for a party other than the one you support? If so, what are some of your viewpoints that differed from those of the other party?

   _____

3. Would you speak up if someone's gender, cultural, racial, sexual, or ethnic background were discussed in a stereotypical manner? How?

   _____

4. Do you consider yourself to be sensitive and respectful? Why or why not?

   _____

5. How do you show a sensitive, respectful attitude even when someone sees the world differently? For example, how can you discuss abortion or gay marriage with someone who has an opposite view and find common ground?

   _____

B. Look at the excuses some students use for not meeting different people. Write strategies for overcoming these excuses.

1. **Excuse:** I'm afraid of rejection or of getting into an argument.

   Strategy:_____

2. **Excuse:** People who are different want to stick with their own kind.

   Strategy:_____

3. **Excuse:** You can't change people's minds or beliefs, so what is the point?

   Strategy:_____

4. **Excuse:** I might say something embarrassing. I feel uncomfortable around people who are different from me.

   Strategy:_____

5. **Excuse:** People who are different from me wouldn't want me in their group.

   Strategy:_____

3. **See and treat people as individuals.** Each one of us is unique. Look beyond preconceived notions and see people as individuals, not members of a particular group. See **Personal Evaluation Notebook 12.7** on page 392 to determine your uniqueness.

4. **Treat people with respect and consideration.** You can be respectful even if someone's behavior is unacceptable or you don't agree with him or her.

5. **Focus on similarities.** As humans, we all experience similar emotions, fears, and needs for appreciation and respect. Don't let differences dominate your

What Do You Want to Be Called?

White, Black, Hispanic, Asian, Native American, Pacific Islander. At some point in your life, you've probably had to check off your race or ethnicity on a form. But what if none of those categories truly reflects your personal identity or accommodates those of us (the majority) who have come from multiple backgrounds? Some people of Central and South American origin prefer to be called Hispanic; others prefer Latino. Many prefer to use their specific place of origin—Guatemalan, Mexican, Puerto Rican, Cuban, and so on. In the same way, some descendents of the first residents of the United States prefer American Indian, others prefer First Peoples, and others prefer Native American. Many prefer specific tribal names, such as Sioux, Navajo, Apache, or Wampanoag. Today, many people are from families of mixed racial/ethnic origins and do not want to be called by the name of any one group. "Blasian" is used by many of Black and Asian descent.

In general, most people agree that all people have a right to be called what they want to be called and not have a group name imposed on them by someone else. How would you "label" yourself in one (or many) words?

_____

_____

Source: James W. Fraser, *Teach: A Question of Teaching* (McGraw-Hill, 2011).

> **"** People are pretty much alike. It's only that our differences are more susceptible to definition than our similarities. **"**

LINDA ELLERBEE
Journalist

interactions. However, don't act as if people were all alike and share the same experiences. Values and experiences differ based on a person's culture, religion, background, and experiences.

6. **Get involved.** Take a cultural diversity course or workshop at college or in the community. Visit with people from other religions. Go to lectures, read, and look for opportunities to become acquainted with other cultures.

7. **Take risks.** Don't avoid contact with other cultures because you fear making a mistake, saying the wrong thing, or inadvertently offending someone. Cultivate friendships with people of different cultures, races, and viewpoints. Share your own culture's foods and customs with others. Knowledge of other cultures can help you appreciate your own roots.

8. **Apologize when you make a mistake.** Mistakes happen, even with the best intentions. Occasionally, strong feelings or misunderstandings result from past experiences with racism or sexism. Thus, don't take it personally if someone does not respond as positively as you had hoped. Sometimes bridging the gap requires extra effort. Apologize, seek to understand, and move on.

9. **Speak out.** It is not enough to be aware that values and experiences differ from culture to culture; you must act on this knowledge. Speak out whenever you hear or see discrimination in school or at work.

10. **Encourage representation.** Encourage active participation by members of diverse cultural and social groups in clubs, student and local government, college meetings, community groups, and decision-making teams. Don't hold a self-righteous attitude that says, "I belong to the right political party, religion, or social cause." Open your mind and explore different views with a sincere willingness to learn.

11. **Study abroad.** Look into a national or an international exchange program. A semester abroad is a tremendous learning experience. You can also get to know students on your campus from other countries or states. Attend events sponsored by the exchange programs. Check out internships in different locations.

Diversity in the Workplace

As the workplace has become more diverse, it has become a more inclusive environment. **Inclusion** is a sense of belonging—feeling respected and valued for who you are. You feel you have support and commitment from others, so that you can do your best work. Attitudes and behavior from top management can set this tone for the whole company. Many top managers approach this by asking themselves, "How can I instruct others to tolerate differences in race, gender, religion, and sexual orientation?" Perhaps a better question would be "How can I set an example, create a climate of respect, and encourage people to value differences?"

As a result of our cultural explosion, many organizations offer diversity awareness training to help employees relate comfortably to each other and appreciate diversity. These programs give employees a chance to develop and strengthen critical thinking skills and reduce stereotypical thinking and prejudice. Firm guidelines clearly communicate the consequences for discrimination, which is illegal and can be grounds for court action.

Organizations are obligated to ensure that all employees know what behaviors are illegal and inappropriate, as well as the consequences for such behavior. Top managers are responsible for establishing procedures and need to offer a safe atmosphere for complaints. In short, companies must provide education, create guidelines and procedures, and set a tone of serious concern and respect for differences in the workplace. Think about what you learned about personality and team styles in Chapter 1. Diversity can have many positive effects on team effectiveness. Consider your study or work teams as you complete **Peak Progress 12.5** on page 394.

Sexual Harassment at School and Work

Sexual harassment is behavior that is unwelcome, unwanted, and degrading. It can be destructive to the school and work climate. It is also costly. Employee turnover, loss of productivity, expensive lawsuits, and a negative work environment are just some of the consequences. Think about your attitudes, beliefs, and behaviors. Err on the side of discretion, and avoid being too chummy or touchy or disclosing too

Peak Progress

Team Players

Evaluate the effectiveness of a work team, a study team, or any other team using the following list of skills. Score each item from 1 to 10 (10 = most effective).

Team Function

- Commitment to tasks
- Oral communication skills
- Listening skills
- Writing skills
- Conflict-resolution skills
- Decision-making skills
- Creative problem solving
- Openness to brainstorming and new ideas
- Team spirit and cohesiveness
- Encouragement of critical thinking
- Interest in quality decisions
- Professionalism
- Team integrity and concern for ethics
- Punctuality in starting and ending meetings

When a score is totaled, the team can discuss answers to these questions:

1. How can this team be more effective?

   _____

   _____

   _____

   _____

2. What can individual members do to strengthen the team?

   _____

   _____

   _____

   _____

---

many details about your personal life. If you aren't sure if a remark or joke is appropriate, don't say it.

Organizations are responsible for establishing guidelines. Most colleges and companies employ someone to talk to if you have a complaint or concern. Organizations with more than 25 employees are legally required to have written procedures concerning sexual harassment.

If you feel uncomfortable in a situation or are being sexually harassed, you should

1. **Confront the harasser.** State what you believe the harasser has done, identifying the unwanted behavior, and insist that the harassment stop immediately. (Do not approach the harasser if you fear for your safety.)

2. **Document the harassment.** Keep a log of incidents, including the dates, behavior, witnesses, and the like. Keep copies of any inappropriate e-mails or other correspondence, even if they are anonymous.

3. **Document your performance.** The harasser may be someone who evaluates your work and may retaliate by giving you poor marks. Keep copies of performance evaluations, papers, exams, and correspondence that support the quality of your work.

4. **Read the organization's sexual harassment policy.** All reports of harassment will be followed up on, so you should know the procedures and who may become involved in the investigation.

5. **Contact the appropriate authorities.** At school, this may be the affirmative action or student affairs office, dean of students, or ombudsman. At work, consult with the human resources department.

6. **Mention the harassment to others.** Chances are, others have experienced harassment from the same person and will join your grievance.

7. **Do not make excuses for the harasser.** It is the harasser's behavior that is unwarranted, not your reactions to it.

Everyone's goal should always be to create a supportive, respectful, and productive environment—one that makes all colleagues feel comfortable and valued.

TAKING CHARGE

Summary

In this chapter, I learned to

- **Build rapport with others.** To build rapport, I must first clarify my intention and use corresponding body language. I must be an attentive listener who puts the speaker at ease, contains my criticisms, restates the speaker's point, and declines respectfully if the timing is not good for communicating. I am respectful and considerate, and I use humor when appropriate. I relate to different learning and personality styles, understanding that people differ in how they process and learn information and see the world. I look for the best in others and appreciate the strengths of different styles. I focus on people's strengths, not weaknesses.

- **Be assertive.** I express myself in a direct, above-board, and respectful manner. I can express feelings and opinions calmly, confidently, and authentically without offending others. I do not use sarcasm or criticism to express myself.

- **Communicate with instructors and advisors.** I meet with my instructors often to clarify expectations, get help with homework, consult on drafts of papers or speeches, discuss ways to prepare for tests, get advice about project requirements, and discuss grades or assignments. I attend every class, adapt to my instructor's teaching style, and am positive and open to learning. I take an interest in my instructor's research or area of expertise. Because I have built rapport with my instructor, I feel comfortable asking for a letter of reference.

- **Accept feedback and criticism.** I know that, to grow and learn, I must be open to feedback. I do not take offense when criticism is offered in the spirit of helpfulness. I listen, stay calm, and ask for clarification and suggestions. If I make mistakes, I apologize and try to make amends.

- **Overcome shyness.** When shyness interferes with making friends, speaking in front of groups, working with others, or getting to know my instructors, I must learn to be more confident and outgoing. I use visualization and affirmations to dispute negative self-talk. I use direct eye contact, am warm and friendly, ask questions, and listen. I relax, am able to laugh at myself, and use humor when it is appropriate.

- **Clarify miscommunications.** I do not assume I know what the other person thinks or says. I clear up misunderstandings by asking for clarification and paraphrase what I think I've heard. I focus on listening and seek to understand, rather than to be right. I use "I" statements, apologize for my mistakes, and forgive others.

- **Develop healthy relationships.** I value friendships and take time to get to know others. My relationships are built on honesty, trust, respect, and open communication. I support others' goals and values, and I expect them to respect and support mine. I talk about expectations with friends, both casual and romantic.

- **Communicate with roommates and family.** To improve communication, I clarify and discuss expectations concerning guests, neatness, noise, borrowing, bills, privacy, and other issues that could cause problems. We agree to respect each other's beliefs, views, and private space.

- **Appreciate diversity.** We are diverse by our race, age, ethnicity, gender, learning and physical abilities, and social, economic, and religious backgrounds. I value different cultures and seek to build rapport with diverse people. By sharing different backgrounds, experiences, values, interests, and viewpoints, I can learn new and interesting ways of seeing situations and solving problems. I look for ways to become acquainted with other cultures and opportunities to work with a variety of people.

- **Recognize sexual harassment.** Sexual harassment is behavior that is unwelcome, unwanted, degrading, and detrimental to school and work.

Performance Strategies

Following are the top 10 tips for building supportive, diverse relationships:

- Find common ground.
- Attentively listen to understand.
- Use body language and eye contact.
- Use warmth and humor.
- Communicate in an assertive, clear, calm, and direct yet kind manner.
- Solve conflicts through cooperation.
- Learn to receive and give constructive criticism.
- Make time to develop diverse, supportive, and healthy relationships.
- Clarify relationship expectations.
- Seek interactions with people from various backgrounds.

Tech for Success

Take advantage of the text's website at **www.mhhe.com/ferrett9e** for additional study aids, useful forms, and convenient and applicable resources.

- **Happy virtual birthday.** People love being remembered on their birthdays (even if they are perpetually 29). If you are constantly forgetting or don't have the time to drop a card in the mail, send an e-card instead. Many free e-card sites and apps are available, and many subscription-based sites offer reminder features.

- **Are you oversharing?** Most of us have taken a "selfie" (photo you take of yourself to post to a social media site) now and then. But how much personal information and opinion do you share online? Are you a culprit—or victim—of posting every event that happens in your day, down to what you ate for lunch? Although you might think your escapades are interesting, your acquaintances may not want to join you on every adventure and read every rambling thought you have. A personal journal may be a more effective way to record your thoughts.

Study Team Notes

Kathy Brown
MARINE BIOLOGIST

Related Major: Biological Science

Team Building at Work

Kathy Brown is a marine biologist who manages teams researching saltwater organisms outside Monterey, California. Currently, she is head of a project to gain more knowledge on the navigation techniques of gray whales during migration.

Although Kathy is a top-rate biologist and researcher with a Ph.D., she can accomplish her project goals only by building teams of researchers who work together effectively. To do this, she carefully considers the personalities and leadership styles of each researcher while forming teams. Kathy provides preproject training in communication skills, group decision making, diversity, and conflict resolution. She lets teams brainstorm ideas and come up with solutions for studying wild animals in a controlled experiment. Kathy also has teams rate their effectiveness in several key functions, including creative problem solving and team spirit.

Finally, the teams are sent to sea to set up labs and conduct research from ocean vessels. Kathy travels from vessel to vessel to encourage teamwork, check research procedures, and help solve problems. She ensures that each team knows how to reach her at all times, day and night.

Because teamwork is so important to the overall results, Kathy will not rehire anyone who cannot work as a part of a team. She knows that even the most educated and skillful researchers will fail if they cannot work effectively and cooperatively with a variety of people.

CRITICAL THINKING Why do you think team building is an important part of a science research project?

Peak Performer

PROFILE

Christy Haubegger

At first glance, the glossy magazine looks like many others on the newsstands. The cover offers a snapshot of the current issue: a profile of a famous celebrity, beauty and fashion tips, and a self-help article to improve the inner being. The big, bold letters across the top, however, spell the difference. This is *Latina*, the first bilingual magazine targeted at Hispanic American women and the inspiration of founder Christy Haubegger. More than 2 million bilingual, bicultural women are avid readers of this popular magazine.

Born in Houston, Texas, in 1968, Haubegger has described herself as a "chubby Mexican-American baby adopted by parents who were tall, thin, and blond." As a teenager during the mega-media 1980s, she was especially sensitive to the lack of Hispanic role models in women's magazines. It was a void waiting to be filled. At the age of 20, Haubegger received a bachelor's degree in philosophy from the University of Texas. At 23, she earned her law degree from Stanford, where she joined the editorial staff of the *Law Review,* rising to the position of senior editor: "My experience as senior editor gave me a start in the worlds of journalism and publishing."

Haubegger also took a course in marketing. In that class, she had to write a business plan for a favorite enterprise. *Latina* magazine was born. As one of the best-known publications for Hispanic American women,

Latina covers issues such as health, politics, family, and finance, as well as beauty and entertainment.

Named as one of *Advertising Age*'s "Women to Watch" and *Newsweek*'s "Women of the New Century," Haubegger was tapped by President Obama, along with 27 other distinguished Americans, for the President's Commission on White House Fellowships. Her work through *Latina* and other ventures has definitely given Hispanic women a voice and reminds them that they are part of the American Dream.

PERFORMANCE THINKING If you were assessing the characteristics that make Christy Haubegger a successful entrepreneur, which would you say are the most important?

CHECK IT OUT Go to **www.latina.com** to see the numerous online features the magazine offers of interest to the U.S. Latin community.

Starting Today

At least one strategy I learned in this chapter that I plan to try right away is

_____

_____

_____

What changes must I make in order for this strategy to be most effective?

_____

_____

_____

Review Questions

Based on what you have learned in this chapter, write your answers to the following questions:

1. Describe five strategies for building rapport.

_____

_____

2. How do assertive people communicate?

_____

_____

3. Describe three ways to handle conflict.

_____

_____

4. Name a barrier to effective communication and how to overcome it.

_____

_____

5. List three strategies for creating rapport and improving communication with people you live with.

_____

_____

To test your understanding of the chapter's concepts, complete the chapter quiz at **www.mhhe.com/ferrett9e.**

Successful Teamwork

In the Classroom

Brian Chase is an electronics student who works part-time in an electronics firm. He likes working with his hands and enjoys his technical classes. However, one marketing class is difficult for him. The instructor has formed permanent class teams with weekly case studies to present to the class and a final team project to complete. Brian dislikes relying on others for a final grade and gets frustrated trying to keep the team members focused on their tasks. Some people are late for meetings, others don't do their share of the work, and two team members have a personality conflict.

1. What suggestions do you have for Brian to help him work more effectively with others?

   _____

   _____

2. What strategies in the chapter would increase Brian's listening and team-building skills?

   _____

   _____

In the Workplace

Brian is now a manager of service technicians for a large security company that provides security equipment and alarm systems for banks, hotels, and industrial firms. His department must work closely with salespeople, systems design specialists, clerical staff, and maintenance personnel. Brian is having trouble convincing his technicians that they are part of the team. Sometimes they don't listen to the advice of the salespeople, clerical staff, or each other, which results in miscommunication and frustration.

3. How might Brian build rapport within and among various departments?

   _____

   _____

4. What strategies in this chapter could help create a solid team?

   _____

   _____

Applying the ABC Method of Self-Management

In the Journal Entry on page 371, you were asked to describe a difficult or confrontational situation in which you felt comfortable communicating your needs and ideas assertively, directly, and calmly. What factors helped you be confident and respectful?

_____

_____

_____

Now think of a confrontational situation in which you were passive or aggressive. Apply the ABC Method to explore how you can achieve a positive outcome.

A = Actual event:

_____

_____

_____

B = Beliefs:

_____

_____

_____

C = Challenge:

_____

_____

_____

See yourself calm, centered, and relaxed as you state your needs, ideas, or rights. See yourself talking in a clear, concise, and confident manner. You feel confident because you have learned to communicate in an assertive and direct manner.

PRACTICE SELF-MANAGEMENT

For more examples of learning how to manage difficult situations, see the "Self-Management Workbook" section of the Online Learning Center website at **www.mhhe.com/ferrett9e.**

Study Team Relationships

List some strategies for helping your study team be more organized and effective.

1. **Before the Meeting**

   _____

   _____

   _____

   _____

2. **During the Meeting**

   _____

   _____

   _____

   _____

3. **After the Meeting**

   _____

   _____

   _____

   _____

4. **Think of effective ways to deal with the following list of challenges.**

Challenges	Solutions
Latecomers or no-shows	_____
Passive members	_____
Negative attitudes	_____
Low energy	_____
Arguments	_____
Lack of preparation	_____
Socializing	_____
Members who dominate	_____

Appreciating Diversity

Assess your appreciation for diversity and check Yes or No for each of the following comments.

	Yes	No
1. I am committed to increasing my awareness of and sensitivity to diversity.		
2. I ask questions and don't assume that I know about various groups.		
3. I use critical thinking to question my assumptions and examine my views.		
4. I strive to be sensitive to and respectful of differences in people.		
5. I listen carefully and seek to understand people with different views and perspectives.		
6. I realize I have biases, but I work to overcome prejudices and stereotypes.		
7. I do not use offensive language.		
8. I apologize if I unintentionally offend someone. I do not argue or make excuses.		
9. I celebrate differences and see diversity as positive.		
10. I speak up if I hear others speaking with prejudice.		
11. I try to read about other cultures and customs.		
12. I do not tell offensive jokes.		
13. I encourage members of diverse cultural and social groups to participate in clubs and decision-making groups.		

As you review your responses, think of areas where you can improve. List at least one of those areas and possible strategies you could use:

REVIEW AND APPLICATIONS | CHAPTER 12

Are You Assertive, Aggressive, or Passive?

Next to each statement, write the number that best describes how you usually feel when relating to other people.

3 = mostly true   2 = sometimes true   1 = rarely true

_____ **1.** I often feel resentful because people use me.

_____ **2.** If someone is rude, I have a right to be rude, too.

_____ **3.** I am a confident, interesting person.

_____ **4.** I am shy and don't like speaking in public.

_____ **5.** I use sarcasm if I need to make my point with another person.

_____ **6.** I can ask for a higher grade if I feel I deserve it.

_____ **7.** People interrupt me often, but I prefer not to bring their attention to it.

_____ **8.** I can talk louder than other people and can get them to back down.

_____ **9.** I feel competent with my skills and accomplishments without bragging.

_____ **10.** People take advantage of my good nature and willingness to help.

_____ **11.** I go along with people, so that they will like me or will give me what I want.

_____ **12.** I ask for help when I need it and give honest compliments easily.

_____ **13.** I can't say no when someone wants to borrow something.

_____ **14.** I like to win arguments and control the conversation.

_____ **15.** It is easy for me to express my true feelings directly.

_____ **16.** I don't like to express anger, so I often keep it inside or make a joke.

_____ **17.** People often get angry with me when I give them feedback.

_____ **18.** I respect other people's rights and can stand up for myself.

_____ **19.** I speak in a soft, quiet voice and don't look people in the eyes.

_____ **20.** I speak in a loud voice, make my point forcefully, and can stare someone in the eye.

_____ **21.** I speak clearly and concisely and use direct eye contact.

Scoring

Total your answers to questions 1, 4, 7, 10, 13, 16, 19 (passive): _____

Total your answers to questions 3, 6, 9, 12, 15, 18, 21 (assertive): _____

Total your answers to questions 2, 5, 8, 11, 14, 17, 20 (aggressive): _____

Your highest score indicates your prevalent pattern.

Are you more passive, assertive, or aggressive—or a combination?

Has your tendency towards one behavior helped or hurt you in situations?

What can you do to become more assertive and communicate effectively?

CHAPTER 12

REVIEW AND APPLICATIONS | CHAPTER 12

Assessing Your Relationship Skills

Skills in building diverse and healthy relationships are essential for success in school and throughout your career. Take stock of your relationship skills, and look ahead as you do the following exercises. Add this page to your Career Development Portfolio.

1. **Looking back:** Review your worksheets to find situations in which you learned to build rapport, listen, overcome shyness, resolve conflict, work with diversity, and be assertive. List the situations on the lines provided.

_____

_____

_____

_____

_____

_____

2. **Taking stock:** Describe your people skills. What are your strengths in building relationships? What areas do you want to improve?

_____

_____

_____

_____

_____

_____

3. **Looking forward:** Indicate how you would demonstrate to an employer that you can work well with a variety of people.

_____

_____

_____

_____

_____

4. **Documentation:** Include documentation and examples of team and relationship skills. Ask an advisor, a friend, a supervisor, or an instructor to write a letter of support for you in this area. Keep this letter in your portfolio.

_____

_____

_____

_____

_____

Develop Positive Habits

LEARNING OUTCOMES

In this chapter, you will learn to

13.1 Use the peak performance success formula

13.2 Describe the top 10 habits of peak performers

13.3 Adapt and change by developing positive habits

13.4 Overcome resistors to making changes

SELF-MANAGEMENT

"It's been a soul-searching journey to get to this point, but I now understand I control my destiny. I make choices every day regarding what new things I will learn, how I will interact with others, and where I will focus my energies. I will be successful because I have the power to become a peak performer in everything I do."

Are you ready for the exciting journey ahead of you? Do you know what your greatest assets are and the areas you want to improve? Only you can determine what kind of person—student, employee, family member, and contributor to society—you will be. You have tremendous power to create your own success. Take a few minutes each morning to set the tone for the day. Visualize yourself being focused and positive and successfully completing your projects and goals. Imagine yourself overcoming fear and self-defeating habits. See yourself applying all the strategies you've learned and creating positive, long-lasting habits.

JOURNAL ENTRY In **Worksheet 13.1** on page 426, think of a time when you knew what to do but kept repeating negative habits. How would positive visualization have helped you?

Throughout this text, we have discussed many strategies for doing well in school, your career, and your personal life. You should have a sense of your strengths and areas where you'd like to improve. You have learned how to manage your time, succeed at tests, and develop healthy relationships. Acquiring knowledge and skills is one thing, but actually making these techniques and strategies part of your life is another.

As we've explored, there is no secret to becoming an outstanding athlete or accomplished performer—or to achieving academic excellence. The same principles required to get into Olympic form apply to getting results in school and at work (see **Figure 13.1**). This success formula includes

1. Having a positive attitude that you can succeed (confidence)
2. Setting and focusing on goals (vision)
3. Learning the necessary skills and behaviors (method)
4. Putting all of this into practice—again and again and again (training)

Although steps 1 through 3 are extremely important, practice is what makes the most impact and forms good habits. **Habits** are the behaviors and activities you perform unconsciously as a result of frequent repetition. Thoughts wear a path in the neurons of your brain; the more you think certain thoughts and do certain actions, the deeper the path becomes, until those thoughts and behavior are a habit.

Figure **13.1**

Peak Performance Success Formula

Success takes time, effort, and determination. *Which components of this formula do you need to focus on to accomplish your desired goals?*

1. Confidence is believing in yourself, knowing your worth, and recognizing you have what it takes to do well. Self-confidence is one of the most important mental qualities you can develop for producing results. When you build on the accomplishments of small victories and successes, you realize that you can achieve almost any goal you set.

2. Vision is mental rehearsal of your victory. You must know clearly what you want to achieve. Be realistic about seeing this vision become a reality. Use encouraging self-talk and imagery. Focus internally, listen to your positive voice, and imagine yourself achieving your goal.

3. Method is the process of achieving your goal and knowing the strategies, techniques, tools, and tactics that produce tangible results. Method involves monitoring your actions and techniques, so that you can modify them to excel consistently.

4. Training is the actual practice and consistent effort required to improve your skills and make them into lasting habits. Training requires the capacity to stay with a vigorous program and hours of rehearsal. You must practice relentlessly even if you often see only small improvements. Practice separates the peak performer from the average person.

Knowing how to develop positive thoughts, attitudes, and behaviors will give you the confidence to take risks, grow, contribute, and overcome setbacks. You have what it takes to keep going, even when you feel frustrated and discouraged. This chapter will show you how to turn strategies from this text into lasting habits.

The 10 Habits of Peak Performers

In Chapter 2, we discussed the importance of emotional maturity for school, job, and life success. You may have a high IQ, talent, skills, and experience but, if you lack emotional maturity and such important qualities as responsibility, effort, commitment, a positive attitude, interpersonal skills, and especially character and integrity, you will have difficulty in all areas of life. However, it is not enough to review essential traits and qualities of emotional maturity. You must commit to making them long-lasting habits. You need to find personal meaning and be willing to learn, observe others, reflect, practice, teach, and model. Commit yourself to turning the following 10 essential qualities into long-lasting habits (see **Figure 13.2**).

1. **Be honest.** As we have stressed throughout this book, if you lack integrity, all your positive qualities—from skill and experience to intelligence and productivity—are meaningless. Practice the habit of honesty by being truthful, fair, kind, compassionate, and respectful. Doing the right thing is a decision.

2. **Be positive.** Greet each day and every event as opportunities to focus on your strengths and be your own best friend by working for and supporting yourself. Positive thinking is not wishful thinking; it is rational, hopeful thinking. Develop the habit of being positive and optimistic by looking for ways to create a motivated, resourceful state of mind. Look for the best in others and in every situation. Being enthusiastic about routine but necessary tasks at school and work will get you noticed. Throughout this book, you've had an opportunity to practice the ABC Method of Self-Management. You have discovered that

THE 10 HABITS OF PEAK PERFORMERS

1 Be honest.

2 Be positive.

3 Be responsible.

4 Be resilient.

5 Be engaged.

6 Be willing to learn.

7 Be supportive.

8 Be a creative problem solver.

9 Be disciplined.

10 Be grateful.

Figure 13.2
Peak Habits

Peak performers translate positive qualities into action. *Do you demonstrate these habits consistently?*

your thoughts create your feelings, which can affect how you interpret events. Learn to dispel negative thoughts and replace them with realistic, optimistic, and empowering thoughts and behaviors. This habit of optimism will keep you centered, rational, productive, and peaceful, even in the midst of confusion and turmoil.

3. **Be responsible.** You may not always feel like keeping your commitments to yourself or your instructors, friends, co-workers, or supervisors, but meeting obligations is the mark of a mature, responsible person. For example, a major obligation for many students is the timely repayment of student loans. Develop the habit of responsibility by doing what you say you're going to do, showing up, and keeping your agreements.

4. **Be resilient.** Adversity happens to everyone. Even good students sometimes forget assignments, miss deadlines, and score low on tests. Don't turn one mistake into a recipe for continued failure. You can't always change circumstances, but you always have a choice about how you rebound and prepare to win next time. The key is to make adversity and setbacks work for you. Take control of how you interpret events, as well as how you react to them. You will learn to reframe your setbacks as stepping-stones to your final goal and energize yourself to take positive action.

5. **Be engaged.** Peak performers do not sit back and wait for life to happen. They are engaged, active, and want to contribute. This means shifting a self-centered "what's in it for me?" attitude to a "how can I be more involved and useful?" attitude. One way to sabotage your classes or career is to expect your instructors or supervisor to make your life interesting. All careers are boring or monotonous at times, and some classes are less than spellbinding. Develop the habit of using your imagination and creativity to make any situation challenging and fun.

6. **Be willing to learn.** Employees can wind up at a dead end if they refuse to learn new skills. Shifts in the economy can result in layoffs for even competent, highly educated, and skilled workers. If you are flexible and willing to learn new skills, you can go to plan B if plan A doesn't work.

7. **Be supportive.** School provides an excellent opportunity to develop empathy and to support, cooperate, and collaborate with people with different backgrounds. Your instructors, advisors, classmates, co-workers, friends, family, and supervisors will go the extra mile to help you if you are respectful, kind, and supportive. Listen to what you say and how you say it. Don't interrupt or criticize—people need to be heard and respected. Use a win/win approach to solve problems. Acknowledge and encourage others' accomplishments and goals.

8. **Be a creative problem solver.** Expand your sense of adventure and originality in problem solving, and learn to think critically and creatively. Challenge your beliefs and try new approaches. Critical thinking also helps you distinguish between an inconvenience and a real problem. Some people spend a great deal of time and energy getting

● **Be Willing to Learn**
Many are finding it necessary to further their education after a number of years in the workforce. *What percentage of your fellow students are returning students? What are some of the reasons they are taking classes or pursuing a degree?*

angry at minor annoyances or events they cannot change—such as bad weather, a delayed flight, or a friend who doesn't meet some expectation. A late plane is an inconvenience; a plane crash is a real problem. Critical thinking helps you put events in perspective and "wakes up" your creative mind. Instead of postponing, ignoring, or complaining, you actively engage in exploring solutions.

9. **Be disciplined.** Peak performers do what needs to be done, not simply what they want to do. They keep up on assignments, set goals, and carve out time throughout the day to focus on priorities. Discipline demands mental and physical conditioning, planning, and effort. Using discipline and self-control, you know how to manage your time, stress, money, and emotions, especially anger. As Benjamin Franklin said, "Anger always has its reasons, but seldom good ones." Getting angry rarely solves problems, but it can create big ones. Through discipline and awareness, you can overcome impulsive reactions and learn to use critical thinking before reacting in haste.

10. **Be grateful.** Life often seems like a comparison game, with competition for grades, jobs, relationships, and money. Reflect on your blessings and talents, not on how your life compares with others'. Focus on what you have, not on what you don't have. Learn to listen to, appreciate, and renew your body, mind, and spirit. Appreciating your body means taking time to rest, exercise, and eat healthy foods. Appreciating your mind means spending time reading, visualizing, creatively solving problems, writing, and challenging yourself to learn and be open to new ideas. Appreciating your spirit means finding time for quiet reflection and renewal and making an effort to listen, develop patience, and love others. To develop the habit of gratitude, appreciate what you have in life, and approach each day as an opportunity to serve and grow.

Change Your Habits by Changing Your Attitude

How can you keep a positive attitude when you are discouraged and frustrated? What if some days you have one problem after another? What if your study group or work environment is negative? Is it possible to see life differently?

In Chapter 10, we talked about the tendency to see what we already believe. Whereas we see with our eyes, we perceive with our brain. People have mindsets that filter information. Each of us has attitudes or beliefs about people and events, and these attitudes influence what parts of our perception we allow our brain to interpret and what parts we filter out. Our attitudes shape the way we relate to others and to the world and even how we see ourselves. Go back to the illustration on page 313. Some people see a young woman, and some see an old woman. Of course, both are actually there. Which did you see? The point is that most of us do not see the entire meaning in a situation or have difficulty seeing "the big picture."

Most people resist change. Even when you are aware of a bad habit, it can be difficult to change it. However, the ability to adapt to new situations is not only important in school but also crucial in the workplace. Accountemps, a temporary staffing service for accounting professionals, asked 1,400 executives to rank the characteristics essential for an employee to succeed. From the list, "adapts easily to change" and "motivated to learn new skills" ranked #1 and #2.

WORDS TO SUCCEED

"Notice that the stiffest tree is most easily cracked, while the bamboo or willow survives by bending in the wind."

BRUCE LEE
Actor, martial arts expert

Strategies for Creating Positive Change

Habits are learned and can be unlearned. Adopting new habits requires a desire to change, consistent effort, time, and commitment. Try the following strategies for eliminating old, ineffective habits and acquiring positive new ones.

1. **Be willing to change.** As with all learning, you must see the value of developing positive habits. It's easy to make excuses for keeping everything the same, but you must be willing to find reasons to change. Identify your goals: "I want to be more optimistic and get along with people." "I am determined to see problems as challenges and find creative alternatives." "I will no longer be a victim. I have control over my thoughts and behavior." Lasting change requires desire, effort, and commitment.

Is the glass half empty or half full?

2. **Focus on the positive.** Are you a glass-half-empty or glass-half-full type of person? Practice the ability to see the good qualities in yourself and others and the positive side of situations. Dispute negative thoughts with critical thinking, and use creative problem solving to explore the best alternatives—for example, "I missed my study group meeting. I'll e-mail my test questions to the group, apologize, and offer to do extra summaries for the next meeting. This situation has reminded me how important it is to check my calendar each morning."

3. **Develop specific goals.** Statements such as "I wish I could get better grades" and "I hope I can study more" are too general and only help you continue bad habits. Goals such as "I will study for 40 minutes, two times a day, in my study area" are specific enough to help you measure your achievement.

4. **Change only one habit at a time.** You will become discouraged if you try to change several things about yourself at once. If you have decided to study for 40 minutes, two times a day, in your study area, then do this for a month, then 2 months, then 3, and so on and it will become a habit. After you have made one change, move on to the next. Perhaps you want to exercise more, give better speeches, or get up earlier. When completing **Personal Evaluation Notebook 13.1**, assess your habits, and put a star by the areas you most want to work on.

5. **Start small.** Realize that consistently taking small steps each day will produce major results. Sometimes the smallest changes make the biggest difference. For example, don't put off starting an exercise program because you don't have time for a long workout. Instead, walk to class rather than driving, or take a walk at lunch. Similarly, by being just a little more organized, finding small ways to be kind and supportive, and doing just a little more than what is expected of you are simple steps that can lead to positive change.

6. **Use visualization and affirmations to imagine success.** Imagine yourself progressing through all the steps toward your desired goal. For example, see yourself sitting at your desk in your quiet study area. Affirm, "I am calm and able to concentrate. I enjoy studying and feel good about completing projects." Before you get up in the morning, imagine your day unfolding effortlessly: "I am positive and focused and will accomplish everything on my to-do list."

The talk you give your self

Personal Evaluation Notebook

13.1

Make a Commitment to Learn and Apply Positive Habits

Read the following questions about the habits for success that we have discussed in this text. Answer each question by circling either Yes or No as each statement applies to you. For the statements you circle Yes, answer the follow-up questions to describe how you are making them a habit.

Yes/No   **1.** Have you created a study area that helps you concentrate? If so, where is it?

Yes/No   **2.** Do you make learning physical? How?

Yes/No   **3.** Do you preview each chapter before you read it? What elements do you look at?

Yes/No   **4.** Do you preview other chapters? If so, how has this helped you understand the material?

Yes/No   **5.** Do you rewrite your notes before class? How long does this usually take?

Yes/No   **6.** Do you outline your papers? Which outlining method works best for you?

Yes/No   **7.** Do you proofread your papers several times? What types of mistakes do you usually catch?

Yes/No   **8.** Do you rehearse your speeches until you are confident and well prepared? How many times do you usually practice?

Yes/No   **9.** Do you attend every class? If not, how many classes have you missed in the past 30 days?

Yes/No **10.** Do you sit in the front of the class? If not, where do you normally sit?

Yes/No **11.** Do you listen attentively and take good notes? Which class is the most challenging to follow?

Yes/No **12.** Do you review your notes within 24 hours? Do you usually do it right after class or later in the day?

Yes/No **13.** Do you get help early, if necessary? Who has been the most helpful?

Yes/No **14.** Do you participate in class and ask questions? Are you usually comfortable or uneasy doing this?

Yes/No **15.** Have you developed rapport with each of your instructors? Which instructor(s) do you feel most comfortable asking for additional guidance?

(continued)

Personal Evaluation Notebook

13.1

Make a Commitment to Learn and Apply Positive Habits *(concluded)*

Yes/No   **16.**   Have you joined a study team? For which classes?

Yes/No   **17.**   Do you study and review regularly each day? How many minutes do you usually devote to this task?

Yes/No   **18.**   Do you complete tasks and assignments first and then socialize? Has this ever caused tension with your friends or family?

Yes/No   **19.**   Do you recite and restate to enhance your memory skills? Do you prefer to do so out loud or on paper?

Yes/No   **20.**   Do you take advantage of campus and community activities? Which activities do you enjoy the most?

Yes/No   **21.**   Can you create a motivated, resourceful state of mind? What do you say to yourself or think about to stay motivated?

Yes/No   **22.**   Do you know how to solve problems creatively? What technique(s) seems to work the best for you?

Yes/No   **23.**   Do you use critical thinking in making decisions? Up to which level of Bloom's Taxonomy (knowledge, comprehension, application, analysis, synthesis, or evaluation) do you think you've mastered?

Yes/No   **24.**   Do you exercise daily? Describe your fitness routine.

Yes/No   **25.**   Do you maintain your ideal weight? What is your ideal weight?

Yes/No   **26.**   Do you keep your body free of harmful substances and addictions? What substances are readily available to you that you choose to abstain from?

Yes/No   **27.**   Do you support your body by eating healthy foods? Which healthy foods do you enjoy not simply because they are good for you?

Yes/No   **28.**   Do you practice techniques for managing your stress? What works for you?

Yes/No   **29.**   Have you developed an effective budget? When is it hardest to stay within your budget?

Yes/No   **30.**   Do you take the time for career planning? What are you doing to plan ahead?

If you answered No to many of these questions, don't be alarmed. When old habits are ingrained, it's difficult to change them. Select at least one of the habits you answered No to. Determine what you can do today to turn it into a positive habit.

7. **Observe and model others.** How do successful people think, act, and relate to others? Do students who get good grades have certain habits that contribute to their success? Research indicates that successful students study consistently in a quiet area, regularly attend classes, are punctual, and sit in or near the front row. Model this behavior until it feels comfortable and natural. Form study groups with good students who are motivated and have effective study habits.

8. **Be aware of your thoughts and behaviors.** For example, you may notice that the schoolwork you complete late at night is not as thorough as the work you complete earlier in the day. Awareness of this pattern may prompt you to change your schedule for schoolwork. You may encounter less stress in the morning when you take 10 minutes the night before to decide what to wear and check the next day's events.

9. **Reward yourself.** Increase your motivation with specific payoffs for making a positive change. Suppose you want to reward yourself for studying for a certain length of time in your study area or for completing a project. You might decide, "After I outline this chapter, I'll watch television for 30 minutes." The reward should always come after achieving the results and be limited in duration.

10. **Be patient and persistent.** Lasting change requires a pattern of consistent behavior. With time and patience, the change will begin to feel comfortable. Don't become discouraged and give up if you haven't seen a complete change in your behavior in a few weeks. Give yourself at least a month. If you fall short one day, get back on track the next. Don't expect to get all *A*'s after a few weeks of studying longer hours. Lasting change requires time.

Overcome Resistance to Change

The following are some obstacles that everyone, even peak performers, may encounter. (See **Figure 13.3** on page 416.) Recognize and confront these resistors to create lasting change:

- **Lack of awareness.** Due to daily pressures, you may not recognize the need to make changes until there is a crisis. This concept is best demonstrated by the boiled-frog syndrome. Neurobiologist Robert Ornstein explained that, if you put a frog in a pot of water and heat the water very slowly, the frog remains in the pot. The frog does not detect the gradual change in temperature until it boils to death. Sometimes you may be so preoccupied by daily pressures that you are unaware of the signals your body is giving you. In a sense, you become desensitized to the "pain." Take time each day to reflect about the state of your mind, body, and spirit, and look for signs of gradual pain, such as a deterioration in grades or morale. Don't wait for a crisis to recognize the need for change.

- **Fear of the unknown.** Change creates uncertainty. Some people even choose the certainty of misery over the uncertainty of pleasure. Fear blocks creativity, causes the imagination to run wild, and makes everyday frustrations look catastrophic: "I don't like my living situation and it's affecting my grades, but who knows what kind of roommate I would get if I asked for a change." or "I'd

Take 3 minutes to develop a positive habit:

- What bad habit would you like to change, or what positive habit do you want to adopt?
- What three things do you need to do or change in order to work toward making this a habit?
- Write the new habit and the three things on a sticky note, and put it on your mirror. Realize that making it a habit will take continual practice—and more than just 3 minutes!

What else can you do in 3 minutes?

- Give yourself a mental pep talk by using affirmations and visualization.
- Turn off all unnecessary lights and unused electronics.
- Balance your checkbook.

like to take a computer class, but I don't know if I could do the work." When you face a new and fearful situation, such as a public speaking class or a new roommate, be positive and optimistic.

- **Familiarity and comfort.** Old habits become comfortable, familiar parts of your life, and giving them up leaves you feeling uneasy. For example, you want to get better grades and know you study best in a quiet area. However, you have always read your assignments while watching television. Be open to trying new ideas and methods.

- **Independence.** You may believe that making personal changes means you are giving in to others and losing your independence. Instead, see yourself as part of a team of people working together to achieve a common goal.

- **Security.** You feel secure with your beliefs, and may feel some of the new ideas you are learning may challenge that security. The old saying "knowledge is power" is definitely true and helps you overcome insecurities.

- **Tradition.** There may be expectations for your future based on your experiences at home: "I was always expected to stay home, raise my family, and

Figure 13.3
Courage to Overcome

These peak performers demonstrated discipline, dedication, and a positive attitude to reach their goals despite obstacles. *What stands in your way of realizing your goals? What steps could you take to overcome obstacles?*

Elizabeth Garrett Anderson
Although rejected by medical schools because she was female, she became the first female member of the British Medical Association.

Abraham Lincoln
Although raised in poverty and teased because of his appearance, he was elected president of the United States.

Glen Cunningham
Although doctors believed he would never walk again after he was severely burned at age 3, in 1934 he set the world's record for running a mile in just over 4 minutes.

only to help supplement the family My sister says I'm selfish to go back at this time in my life." If a change in benefits you personally (and possibly sionally), then the important people in ife will also benefit and should support decisions.

barrassment. You may fear that a new iation will embarrass you: "Will I feel mbarrassed being in classes with younger udents? Can I hold up my end of the team projects and class discussions? I haven't had a math course in 20 years, and my study skills are rusty." Remember that learning is all about trial and error.

- **Responsibility.** You may believe the demands on your time are too great to allow for making changes: "I am overwhelmed by the responsibility of working, going to school, and caring for my family. Sometimes it would be easier if someone would just tell me what to do." Use time-management strategies to ensure you are accomplishing what you need to and identifying areas to change.

- **Environment.** You may think your physical environment is too constricting: "My place is not supportive for studying. Our home is noisy, and there is no place where I can create a study area. My husband and children say they are proud of me, but they complain about a messy house and resent the time I spend studying." It's important to negotiate when and where you can get your work done, such as at established quiet times or in the library.

- **Cost.** Your personal finances may limit your ability to make changes: "It's too expensive to go to college. Tuition, textbooks, day care, and supplies all add up. Is it worth it? Maybe I should be saving for my children's education instead." Evaluate all your available resources and make sure you know where your money is going to determine what you can change.

- **Difficulty.** People can and do change. Changing habits is a simple, three-step process:

  1. *Discard what doesn't work.* First, unlearn and discard old ideas, thoughts, and habits in order to learn more positive habits.
  2. *Replace it with what does work.* Replace old habits with new habits.
  3. *Practice! Practice! Practice!* You can learn new habits, but you must consciously apply and practice them. In a sense, you must "freeze" new patterns through consistent repetition.

See **Peak Progress 13.1** on page 418 on applying the Adult Learning Cycle to developing positive habits.

Contract for Change

Most people talk about changing, wishing they could be more positive or organized, but few put their commitment in writing. Many find it useful to take stock of what

Tracy is the most unmotivated person Cameron knows, yet she's been her best friend since first grade. They've done everything together—soccer, summer jobs, and college roommates. With one more year to go, Cameron is looking forward to applying to law school and is focusing on studying for the LSAT exam, while Tracy is focusing on who won last night's celebrity dancing contest.

- How can Tracy's lack of motivation affect Cameron's success?
- Can Tracy become a motivated person? What can Cameron do or say to help her create and focus on important goals?
- If you were Cameron, would you stay best friends with Tracy?

THINK FAST

> "I am always doing that which I cannot do, in order that I may learn how to do it."
>
> PABLO PICASSO
> *Painter*

> "We first make our habits, and then our habits make us."
>
> JOHN DRYDEN
> *Poet and playwright*

Peak Progress

Applying the Adult Learning Cycle to Developing Positive Habits

The Adult Learning Cycle can help you change your behavior and adopt long-lasting positive habits.

1. **RELATE. Why do I want to learn this?** I know that practicing positive habits and creating long-lasting changes will help me succeed in school, work, and life. What are some of my positive habits, and which ones do I need to change or improve? Do I display the 10 habits of a peak performer?

2. **OBSERVE. How does this work?** I can learn a lot about positive habits by watching others and trying new things. I will observe positive, motivated people who know how to manage their lives. What do they do? Are their positive habits obvious? I will also observe people with negative habits to learn from their mistakes.

3. **REFLECT. What does this mean?** I will gather information by going to workshops and taking special classes. I will focus on the 10 habits of a peak performer and create strategies for incorporating them into my routine. I will think about and test

new ways of breaking out of old patterns, negative self-talk, and self-defeating behaviors. I will look for connections and associations with time management, stress and health issues, and addictive behaviors.

4. **DO. What can I do with this?** I will focus on and practice one habit for a month. I will reward myself when I make progress. I will focus on my successes and find simple, practical applications for using my new skills. Each day, I will take small steps. For example, I will spend more of my social time with my friends who like to hike and do other positive things that I enjoy, instead of hanging out with friends who just like to drink.

5. **TEACH. With whom can I share this?** I will share my progress with family and friends and ask if they have noticed a difference.

Something becomes a habit only when it is repeated, just as the Adult Learning Cycle is more effective the more times you go through it.

---

common resistors, or barriers, keep them from meeting their goals. Write a contract with yourself for overcoming your barriers. State the payoffs of meeting your goals. Refer back to your mission statement and goals in Chapter 3, using them to help you determine the positive changes you want to make. Use **Personal Evaluation Notebook 13.2** to begin drafting a personal commitment contract to achieve the "habit" of success.

Personal Evaluation Notebook

13.2

Commitment Contract

Complete the following statements in your own words.

1. I most want to change _____

_____

_____

_____

2. My biggest barrier is _____

_____

_____

_____

3. The resources I will use to be successful are _____

_____

_____

_____

4. I will reward myself by _____

_____

_____

_____

5. The consequences for not achieving the results I want will be _____

_____

_____

_____

Date _____

Signature _____

TAKING CHARGE

Summary

In this chapter, I learned to

- **Live the peak performance success formula.** I know that success comes from having confidence, setting and envisioning my goals, learning skills and behaviors, and practicing.

- **Strive to become a peak performer.** Peak performers are successful because they develop and practice good habits. They are honest, responsible, resilient, engaged, willing to learn, supportive, disciplined, and grateful. They have positive attitudes and creatively solve problems.

- **Develop a positive attitude.** I approach tasks with a can-do attitude. Enthusiasm and a positive attitude help me focus on my strengths and create the thoughts and behaviors that produce the results I want.

- **Embrace change and develop positive habits.** I know that adapting to change is important to my success. I will create positive habits by developing specific goals, focusing on one habit at a time, taking small steps each day, and remaining positive and persistent. I know that developing positive habits takes time.

- **Avoid and overcome resistors and fears.** Fear of the unknown, insecurities, embarrassment, and overwhelming responsibilities are just some of the obstacles to my progress if I don't focus on positive outcomes.

- **Make a commitment.** I have made a commitment to turn the strategies I have learned into lasting habits. I have put my commitment in writing by developing a commitment contract.

Performance Strategies

Following are the top 10 tips for developing good habits:

- Commit to changing self-defeating behaviors.
- Set realistic goals and specify behaviors you want to change.
- Be flexible and open to new things.
- Dispute irrational thoughts and describe events objectively.

- Work on one habit at a time, focusing on success.
- Be resilient and get back on track after setbacks.
- Use affirmations and visualization to stay focused.
- Reward yourself for making improvements.
- Observe your progress and make appropriate changes until you achieve the results you want.
- Surround yourself with support and positive influences.

Tech for Success

Take advantage of the text's website at **www.mhhe.com/ferrett9e** for additional study aids, useful forms, and convenient and applicable resources.

- **Inspiration.** In this text, you have read about many peak performers who have overcome major obstacles to get where they are today. Who truly represents a peak performer to you? If the person is even relatively well known chances are you will find his or her story online.

Spend at least a few minutes searching and reading about what makes this person stand out. Do you recognize any of the 10 habits?

- **A log of positive habits.** Record every time you use 1 of the 10 habits of peak performers. Eventually, this will create an ideal list of personal examples, which you can relay to a future employer. Keep a copy in your Career Development Portfolio.

Study Team Notes

Career*in* focus

Rick Torres
CARPENTER

Related Majors: Carpentry, Construction Management, Business, Computer Drafting and Design

Good Habits in the Workplace

Rick Torres is a carpenter who, like one-third of the carpenters in the United States, works as an independent contractor. This means Rick is self-employed and does a variety of carpentry jobs for homeowners, from building decks to completing remodeling jobs.

Rick starts by figuring out how to accomplish each task. Then he gives the customer a written time and cost estimate, purchases materials, completes the work, and hauls away construction debris. He needs basic math skills to provide an accurate estimate and calculate the amount of materials required for the job. Bookkeeping skills also help Rick keep track of his earnings and prepare to pay quarterly taxes. Carpentry work is often strenuous and requires expertise with large tools, such as power saws and sanders; the handling of heavy materials; and prolonged standing, climbing, bending, and kneeling. Rick often works outdoors and enjoys the flexibility and physical activity of his work.

Through the years, Rick has learned that good habits are essential to his future. Rick gains new customers through word of mouth. Customers pass his name on to others because he is reliable and has excellent skills. Rick's business has been successful because he cultivates positive attitudes and is committed to providing quality service. He shows up on time for appointments, is courteous, and follows through with his commitments. Occasionally, Rick works on neighborhood low-income projects. He sometimes hires younger carpenters to work with him and enjoys teaching them old tricks and new methods of construction.

CRITICAL THINKING What might be the result of poor work habits for a carpenter working as an independent contractor?

Peak Performer

PROFILE

Ben Carson, M.D.

Ben Carson's life is a testament to having a positive attitude, motivation, and integrity. Despite major obstacles, he has become a world-renowned neurosurgeon and author who has touched many lives.

Overcoming the disadvantages of growing up in an economically depressed neighborhood in Detroit, Carson has lived by the words "no excuses." As a child, when difficult situations would confront him or his brother, his mother would ask, "Do you have a brain? Then you can think your way out of it." Carson did just that.

During the 1950s, Carson's mother worked multiple domestic jobs to keep the family afloat. Though life at home was challenging, days at school were even more so. Carson recalls, "There was an unspoken decree that the black kids were dumb." His mother knew better. When the two brothers brought home failing grades, she turned off the TV and required the boys to read two books a week and write reports. Eventually, Carson rose to the top of his class and went on to graduate from Yale University and the University of Michigan School of Medicine.

However, one biographer wrote that, during Carson's youth, his temper made him seem "most qualified for putting someone else in the hospital." It was only after a life-threatening confrontation that Carson realized his choices were "jail, reform school—or the grave."

Eventually becoming a neurosurgeon and director of pediatric neurosurgery at Johns Hopkins Medical

Institutions, Carson succeeded against the odds in 1987 when he separated 11-month-old twins who were joined at the head. A recipient of the Presidential Medal of Freedom, the man who was tagged "dummy" has saved the lives of children whom others label as hopeless.

PERFORMANCE THINKING Explain how attitude played a part in Ben Carson's success. What are some of the habits he established in his childhood that contributed to his future achievements?

CHECK IT OUT Ben Carson continues his service of helping others through the Carson Scholars Fund (**www.carsonscholars .org**). The foundation's mission is to promote the joy of reading and to recognize and reward students in grades 4–11 who strive for academic excellence and demonstrate a strong commitment to their community. "THINK BIG" is Carson's philosophy, which promotes outstanding academic achievement and dedication to helping others.

Starting Today

At least one strategy I learned in this chapter that I plan to try right away is

_____

_____

_____

What changes must I make in order for this strategy to be most effective?

_____

_____

_____

Review Questions

Based on what you have learned in this chapter, write your answers to the following questions:

1. Name the 10 habits of a peak performer.

_____

_____

2. What are three strategies for creating positive change in your life?

_____

_____

3. Why is adapting to change so critical to job success?

_____

_____

4. Describe one resistor to change you have experienced and how you overcame it.

_____

_____

5. Why is practice important to changing a habit?

_____

_____

To test your understanding of the chapter's concepts, complete the chapter quiz at **www.mhhe.com/ferrett9e.**

Spreading Good Habits

In the Classroom

Craig Bradley is a welding student. He never liked high school, but his mechanical ability helped him get into a trade school. He wants to be successful and knows this is a chance for him to get a good job. Both of Craig's parents worked, so he and his sister had to get themselves off to school and prepare many of their own meals. Money has always been tight, and he hardly ever receives encouragement for positive behavior. He has never learned positive study or work habits.

1. What kind of study plan can you suggest to Craig to build his confidence and help him succeed?

   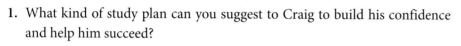
   _____

   _____

2. What strategies in this chapter can help him develop positive, lasting habits?

   _____

   _____

In the Workplace

Craig is now working in a large farm equipment manufacturing plant. He has just been promoted to general supervisor in charge of welding and plumbing. He is a valued employee and has worked hard for several years for this promotion. Craig wants to ensure his success in his new job by getting training in motivation, team building, quality customer service, and communication skills.

3. What suggestions do you have for Craig to help him train his staff in good habits?

   _____

   _____

4. What strategies in this chapter can help him be more successful?

   _____

   _____

Applying the ABC Method of Self-Management

In the Journal Entry on page 407, you were asked to think of a time when you knew what to do but kept repeating negative habits. How would positive visualization have helped you?

_____

_____

_____

Now apply the ABC Method of Self-Management. How is the outcome different?

A = Actual event:

_____

_____

_____

B = Beliefs:

_____

_____

_____

C = Challenge:

_____

_____

_____

PRACTICE SELF-MANAGEMENT

For more examples of learning how to manage difficult situations, see the "Self-Management Workbook" section of the Online Learning Center website at **www.mhhe.com/ferrett9e.**

Developing Positive Habits

On the following lines, list five habits you would like to change into positive behavior. Focus on changing one habit at a time for a successful transition. Then, in the following chart, list the steps you will need to take, the barriers standing in your way, and the methods by which you can overcome these barriers to reach your goal.

POSITIVE HABITS YOU WANT TO DEVELOP

1. _____

2. _____

3. _____

4. _____

5. _____

Steps	Barriers	Methods to Overcome Barriers
1.		
2.		
3.		
4.		
5.		

Overcoming Resistance to Change

Complete the following statements in your own words.

1. I resist _____

2. I resist _____

3. I resist _____

4. I resist _____

5. I resist _____

6. I resist _____

7. I resist _____

8. I resist _____

9. I resist _____

10. I resist _____

For each item you listed, write a strategy for overcoming your resistance to change.

1. _____

2. _____

3. _____

4. _____

5. _____

6. _____

7. _____

8. _____

9. _____

10. _____

Planning Your Career

Developing good planning habits will benefit your career. Use the following form to create a career action plan. Add multiple companies and contacts, or develop a page for each company. Add this page to your Career Development Portfolio.

Career objective:_____

What type of job?_____

When do you plan to apply? _____

Company: _____ City/State: _____

Whom should you contact?_____

How should you contact? Letter, e-mail, phone, or walk-in?_____

- Phone number: _____ E-mail: _____

- Address: _____

Why do you want this job?_____

_____

Skills applicable to this job:_____

_____

Education: _____

- Internship/co-op: _____

- Courses taken:_____

- Grade point average: _____

References:

1. _____

2. _____

3. _____

REVIEW AND APPLICATIONS | CHAPTER 13

Explore Majors and Careers

LEARNING OUTCOMES

In this chapter, you will learn to

14.1 Explore majors and careers

14.2 Determine your values, interests, abilities, and skills

14.3 Assemble a Career Development Portfolio

14.4 Prepare for the job-hunting process

14.5 Take charge of your career development

SELF-MANAGEMENT

I'm not certain if the major I chose will lead to the job I want. One of my biggest fears is that I'll be stuck in a dead-end job and won't have an interesting career. What if I spent all this time and money and still can't get a good job?

Have you ever wondered if you're learning the skills and developing the qualities that will help you get and keep the job you want? Sometimes it's difficult to see the connection between college and the world of work. Have you ever taken a class and wondered how it relates to real life and if it will help you be more successful? How do you integrate all you are learning to make it meaningful and personal? In this chapter, you will learn steps for exploring college majors and careers. You will see that career planning is an exciting, lifelong process. You will also learn how to translate the information, experiences, and skills you are acquiring in school into a useful Career Development Portfolio.

JOURNAL ENTRY In **Worksheet 14.1** on page 464, write down one of the classes you are currently taking, and list at least three skills you will acquire in this class that will benefit you in your career.

Early Roman philosopher Plotinus of Delphi (AD 205–270) recognized three main universal career concerns:

- Who am I?
- What shall I do?
- What shall become of me?

You will be continually challenged to understand who you are and what you want in life. In this rapidly changing world, you may have a chance to do many kinds of work. The average working American will have 3 to 5 careers and 10 to 12 jobs during his or her lifetime. Many of the career opportunities that will be available in 10 years don't even exist today. Thus, career planning is more than just picking a profession. It involves learning about yourself and what you want out of life.

In this chapter, we will examine ways to choose a college major and explore careers. The strategies in this chapter, including step-by-step instructions on how to assemble a Career Development Portfolio, will help you create new career opportunities in response to your ever-changing needs, desires, and interests.

Connecting School and Job Success

The path to career success began the day you started classes. As you have read in this text, the same habits, attitudes, and personal qualities required for school success are also required for job success. The same strategies—assessing yourself, knowing your learning style, thinking critically, creatively solving problems, effectively communicating, and establishing healthy relationships—apply to career exploration and planning, no matter what your college major is.

Exploring and Choosing a Major

In our society, people are identified by their profession: "What do you do for a living?" In college, the question is "What is your major?" A college major helps define who you will become professionally. It is a declaration of academic purpose and gives many students structure and goals. It provides entry into an academic department and fellowship with instructors and other students.

Some students know from an early age what their major will be. They may have known for years that they want to be an engineer, a writer, a business owner, a nurse, or a computer programmer. For many students, choosing a college major is daunting. Some students

- Have many interests, so it is difficult to narrow them to one major
- Have not assessed their interests, values, or goals
- Have not explored the wide range of majors at their school
- Have difficulty making decisions

- Fear they will get stuck with a major they won't like
- Fear a major will lead to a career they dislike
- Are influenced by family expectations
- Are unsure of the job market
- Know they like a specific subject area but don't know what they can do with it

If you are unsure of your college major, you're not alone. On some campuses, "undeclared" is the largest major. The average student changes majors three times. Community colleges are experiencing a growth in students who want to change careers or learn new skills. Many students already have a 4-year degree but now want to learn cooking, woodworking, real estate, nursing, firefighting, or fashion design. What you want to do at 18 may be very different from what you want to do at 40, 50, or 60. The strategies for choosing a major are similar to those for choosing a career:

1. **Assess yourself.** Because major and career planning begins with self-assessment, return to Chapter 1 and review the assessment tools. People are happiest when they do work that is consistent with their values, interests, abilities, and skills (which we will discuss further in this chapter). When your job is an extension and expression of who you are, you experience joy and fulfillment.

2. **Meet with a career counselor at your school.** Counselors are trained to offer and interpret self-assessment tools and interest inventories. They can help you clarify values, talents, and skills; offer insight into your interests, personality type, and goals; and help you link majors with careers.

3. **Talk with your support system.** Discuss possible majors with family, friends, instructors, other students, and advisors. People who know you best may shed light on your unique abilities and talents.

4. **Explore through college classes.** Taking general education classes is a great way to experience various disciplines, get to know instructors and students, and still meet college requirements.

5. **Explore through the course listings.** Check out departments and courses to find a major you didn't know existed. Pick at least two majors you'd like to research further.

6. **Go to the academic department.** Go to the departments of majors you are interested in, and gather more information, such as the requirements, the job outlook, and possible careers.

7. **Take classes or workshops.** Many schools provide assessments to determine interests, traits, and self-understanding. Sometimes alumni are invited to speak at campus events.

8. **Gain experience.** Get involved through internships, co-ops, volunteer work, part-time jobs, and service learning activities offering hands-on experience (see **Peak Progress 14.1** on page 434). On- and off-campus jobs help you explore possible major and career interests. Also join clubs, participate in extracurricular activities, seek out leadership opportunities, and travel with educational tours.

9. **Be creative with your major.** Your school may have an interdisciplinary major, a self-designed major, or a broad liberal arts major that allows you

Service Learning

As we discussed in Chapter 4, service learning enables you to use what you are learning in the classroom to solve real-life problems. The service reinforces and strengthens the learning, and the learning reinforces and strengthens the service. You learn about democracy and citizenship while becoming an actively contributing citizen and community member.

Many colleges offer courses that provide service learning opportunities. These courses include structured time for you to reflect on your service and learning experiences through a mix of writing, reading, speaking, listening, and creating in groups and individual work. This fosters the development of personal qualities—empathy, personal values, beliefs, awareness, self-esteem, self-confidence, and social responsibility. Credit is awarded for learning, not for a required number of service hours.

Service learning has many benefits:

- It gives you opportunities to use newly acquired skills and knowledge in real-life situations.
- It fills a need for volunteer support in the community and uses that need as a foundation for participants

to examine themselves, their society, and their future.

- It tracks progress toward preset learning objectives and goals (as well as the intangible ones).
- The service performed is valuable and significant for the community.
- You feel empowered by contributing to your community.

Service learning experiences can be personally rewarding and enriching, and they are important points in a portfolio or resumé. As employers assess equally qualified job applicants, they look for experiences, skills, or qualities that make one candidate stand out. Service learning opportunities may also allow you to work with administrators and community members you might not have otherwise met, giving you job contacts and mentors who may open doors for you in the future.

Source: Adapted from "What Is Service-Learning?" Corporation for National and Community Service, www.learnandserve.gov; "Four Things Faculty Want to Know About!" Mark Cooper, Florida International University, www.fiu.edu/~time4chg/Library/fourthings.html.

to take a wide range of courses in areas that interest you. Many employers look for liberal arts graduates who are skilled in writing, critical thinking, reasoning, and creative problem solving and can work well with diverse groups.

10. **Relax and reflect.** Be proactive about exploring various majors, but also listen to your inner wisdom and what makes you happy and fulfilled. In Chapter 2, we reviewed Maslow's hierarchy of needs, which identifies what motivates people and gives their actions meaning. Self-actualization is the process of fulfilling your potential, becoming everything you are capable of, and experiencing satisfaction and joy. Achieving self-actualization requires listening to your inner voice.

Consult with your advisor to determine an optimal time line. If you delay too long, you may discover that some of your courses won't count toward your selected major and other courses still need to be taken. You may also find that your GPA isn't high enough to get into a preferred program and courses you "tried out" but struggled with have pulled down your average.

Finally, remind yourself that getting a college degree in anything will help launch your career. There are no guarantees, but a college degree—plus hard work, additional experience and skills, and positive habits and qualities—go a long way toward creating opportunities.

Values, Interests, Abilities, and Skills

As we discussed in relation to self-assessment, it's important to determine your values, interests, innate abilities, and already acquired skills to help you decide which career direction you want to take and thus which major course of study you should pursue.

VALUES

Values are the worth or importance you attach to various factors in your life. They are formed in early childhood and are influenced by parents, teachers, the environment, and your culture. Your values can reflect your self-esteem, optimism, self-control, and ability to get along with others. You will be much happier if your career reflects your values. Complete **Personal Evaluation Notebook 14.1** on page 436 to determine your personal values and the values important to your career.

INTERESTS

Interests are the activities and subjects that draw you in and cause you to feel comfortable, enthusiastic, or passionate. Psychologist John L. Holland explored interests and their relation to college major and career choice. His theory suggests that career choice often reflects personality type and that most people fit into one of six occupational personality types, which are largely determined by their interests. Revisit Chapter 1 and review your personality assessments. Then read Holland's types and see if you fall into one or two of the categories:

- *Realistic.* Realistic people have athletic or mechanical ability and prefer to work with objects, machines, tools, plants, or animals or to be outdoors. They like to work with their hands. Possible careers include architect, optician, surveyor, laboratory technician, automotive mechanic, zoologist, engineer, chef, and bus or truck driver.

- *Investigative.* Investigative people like to observe, learn, investigate, analyze, evaluate, or solve problems. They enjoy academic and scientific challenges. Possible careers include computer programmer, pilot, mathematics teacher, surgical technician, doctor, economist, and chemist.

- *Artistic.* Artistic people have creative, innovative, or intuitive abilities and like to work in unstructured situations. Possible careers include actor, commercial artist, public relations representative, editor, decorator, fashion designer, and photojournalist.

- *Social.* Social people like to work with people—to inform, enlighten, help, train, develop, or cure. They have strong verbal and written skills. Possible careers include social worker, minister, psychologist, parole officer, teacher, rehabilitation therapist, and hair stylist.

- *Enterprising.* Enterprising people enjoy leading—influencing, persuading, performing, or managing to meet organizational goals or achieve economic

> **"** Mostly I just followed my inner feelings and passions . . . and kept going to where it got warmer and warmer, until it finally got hot . . . Everybody has talent. It's just a matter of moving around until you've discovered what it is. **"**
>
> GEORGE LUCAS
> *Director*

WORDS TO SUCCEED

Personal Evaluation Notebook

Your Values

Your values influence what will satisfy you in a career. By each value, rank them as

1 = Not that important   2 = Somewhat important   3 = Most important

Overall Values	**Rank**
Security	_____
Helping others	_____
Recognition	_____
Collaborating with others	_____
Religious or spiritual beliefs	_____
Adventure	_____
Variety	_____
Serving community/national/international concerns	_____
Artistic/creative expression	_____
Personal growth and learning	_____
Focusing on family	_____
Others	_____

Specific Factors You Value in a Career	**Rank**
High salary	_____
Great deal of freedom/autonomy	_____
Flexible working hours	_____
Opportunities for advancement	_____
Good vacation/benefits	_____
Supportive co-workers	_____
Working with others	_____
Working alone	_____
Telecommuting/working at home	_____
Working outdoors	_____
Social environment	_____
Job status	_____
Clean and comfortable working environment	_____
Others	_____

Take note of the factors you rated "3," as these values are most important to you.

gain. Possible careers include small business owner, communications consultant, stockbroker, sales representative, restaurant manager, and motivational speaker.

- *Conventional.* Conventional people like to work with data, have clerical or numerical abilities, are detail-oriented, and follow directions well. They like working with numbers and facts and enjoy bringing situations to closure. Possible careers include accountant, court reporter, credit manager, military officer, and title examiner.

ABILITIES

Abilities are the qualities that are an intrinsic part of who you are. They are innate talents or gifts, which can be developed to their maximum potential through study and practice. You may have the ability to understand mathematics, play many musical instruments, resolve conflict, or handle a crisis calmly.

SKILLS

Skills are capabilities you have learned and developed. They often have a more technical connotation than abilities. Some skills are job-specific, such as operating a bulldozer, conducting lab tests, or editing manuscripts. **Transferable skills** are those that can be used in a variety of careers, such as negotiating, analyzing data, preparing presentations, effectively managing people or resources, and using technology.

It's important to identify your skills to see how they can be developed throughout your career. Read the following broad list of skills, and determine the areas in which you excel. What careers using these skills might you like to explore?

People	Data	Mechanical
Instructing	Analyzing	Handling
Supervising	Coordinating	Setting up
Negotiating	Comparing	Driving
Entertaining	Computing	Operating
Persuading	Compiling	Selecting

Exploring Careers

After assessing your personal values and what you are looking for in a career, you can determine what opportunities lie ahead. You may be starting out at the bottom or taking courses to prepare for a promotion or new responsibilities. As mentioned earlier, the strategies for choosing a major also apply to determining a career path. Also investigate these resources:

- *Career center.* Career center personnel can give you information about career trends, opportunities, salaries, and job availability.
- *Library.* Your school or local library has many resources, such as the *Dictionary of Occupational Titles, The New Guide for Occupational Exploration,* and the classic *What Color Is Your Parachute?* by Richard Bowles.

- *Professional organizations.* Visit the websites of professional organizations in your field of interest and consider joining. Students often can join at a discount. Find out what you would receive with a membership, such as access to journals and job listings. At the website or in journals, look for individuals who have received promotions or contributed to the field. See if any are local or provide contact information. Most professionals enjoy talking to young people who are entering their field and are happy to offer advice.

- *Your network.* Personal contacts are excellent ways to explore careers and find a job. As we discussed in Chapter 4, networking provides access to people who can serve as mentors and connect you to jobs and opportunities. Create and cultivate personal and professional contacts. Talk with instructors, advisors, counselors, and other students. Collect business cards and e-mail addresses. (See **Worksheets 14.4** and **14.5** on potential questions to ask during informational interviews with professionals and hiring managers.)

- *Government organizations.* Several organizations, such as the U.S. Department of Labor, track job statistics, predict future opportunities, and provide employment guidance, such as SCANS. The *Occupational Outlook Handbook* (go to the Bureau of Labor Statistics website at **www.bls.gov/oco**) lists the outlook for hundreds of types of jobs and provides employment guidance, such as job search and application methods, places to learn about job openings, and resumé and job interview tips. See **Peak Progress 14.2** on using the Adult Learning Cycle when exploring majors and careers.

Peak Progress   14.2

Applying the Adult Learning Cycle to Exploring Majors and Careers

1. **RELATE. Why do I want to learn this?** Write down the top three things that are important to you in a career, such as independence, high visibility, flexible hours, ability to work from home, and management opportunities. Compare those wishes with your personality type. Which careers that fit your personality offer these features?

2. **OBSERVE. How does this work?** Explore three potential opportunities for learning more about this career, such as acquaintances in the field, instructors, professional organizations, and introductory courses.

3. **REFLECT. What does this mean?** Based on your research, does this career still appeal to you? What are the drawbacks? Are they significant enough to outweigh the positives? Did any related professions come to light?

4. **DO. What can I do with this?** If the career choice still looks promising, identify three ways you can gain experience or related skills required for the profession, such as joining a club or securing an internship. Construct a time line for accomplishing those tasks.

5. **TEACH. Whom can I share this with?** Relay your impressions and reservations to your family, friends, or fellow students who are also career searching. Some will ask you questions that will make you think about where you are in selecting a major and what your next steps should be. You will also enlighten others by sharing the resources you are using.

If you conclude that you are still undecided, explore other career options and retry some or all of the steps. Practice visualization when you need help focusing. Eventually, you will find a career path that suits your personality and interests.

Building a Career Development Portfolio

A Career Development Portfolio is a collection of documents that highlights your strengths, skills, and competencies. It includes grades, summaries of classes, certificates, letters of recommendation, awards, lists of activities, inventories you've taken, and samples of written work. A portfolio can help you connect what you have learned in school to your current or future work, and it demonstrates you have the necessary education, skills, competencies, and personal qualities to perform a job.

Even if you have little work experience, this documentation can give you an edge when applying for a job. For example, Janet convinced an employer to hire her based on her portfolio: She showed the manager samples of her work and the certificates she had earned. Jake used his portfolio to receive a promotion based on documentation of his skills and experiences.

Your Career Development Portfolio helps you

- Plan and design your educational program and postgraduate learning
- Describe how your experiences have helped you grow professionally
- Document skills and accomplishments in and out of the classroom
- Link what you can do with what an employer is looking for
- Identify areas you want to augment or improve
- Record and organize experiences for your resumé and job interviews
- Express talents creatively and artistically
- Justify college credit for prior learning and military, internship, or life experiences
- Prepare for a job change

When Should You Start Your Portfolio?

You can start your portfolio at any time—the sooner the better. If you completed assessments, journal entries, and worksheets at the end of each chapter in this text, then you've already started your portfolio. Ideally, you will begin your portfolio during your first term or year in school. During each term, add papers or other coursework to your portfolio. Make note of courses related to your career interests. If you have a work-study job or an internship related to your career goal, include records of your experiences, any written work, and letters of recommendation. By the time you graduate, you will have a portfolio that is distinctly personal and persuasive.

A sample planning guide appears in **Figure 14.1** on page 440. Students in both 2- and 4-year schools can use this guide. Students in a 2-year school can use freshman and sophomore years for the first year, junior and senior years for the second year. Modify the planning guide to fit your needs.

How to Organize and Assemble Your Portfolio

The steps for organizing and assembling your portfolio will vary, depending on your purpose and your school's guidelines. You may be developing your portfolio as a general documented system of achievements and professional growth, as a graduation requirement for your major, or for a more specific reason, such as obtaining credit for prior learning experiences.

> **"**I am learning all the time. The tombstone will be my diploma.**"**
>
> EARTHA KITT
> *Entertainer; passed away*
> *December 25, 2008*

WORDS TO SUCCEED

Figure 14.1

Career Development Portfolio Planning Guide

This planning guide will help you review your skills and maintain your Career Development Portfolio as you move toward your career goal. This and a modified plan for a 2-year degree can be found at the book's website at **www.mhhe.com/ferrett9e.** *What other strategies can you use to prepare for your career?*

Freshman Year

- Begin your Career Development Portfolio.
- Explore and join clubs, and get involved on campus.
- Assess your interests, skills, values, goals, and personality.
- Go to the career center at your school, and explore majors and careers.
- Set goals for your first year.
- Explore college majors and minors.
- Explore the community.
- Network with professors and students. Get good grades.
- Keep a journal. Label the first section "Self-Assessment." Begin to write your autobiography.
- Label another section "Exploring Careers."

Sophomore Year

- Add to your Career Development Portfolio.
- Start a file about careers and majors.
- Choose a major.
- Review general education requirements.
- Continue to explore resources in the community.
- Build your network.
- Join clubs and take a leadership role.
- Read articles and books about your major area.
- Find a part-time job or volunteer your time.
- Start or update your resumé.
- Explore internships and co-op programs.
- Add a section to your journal called "Job Skills and Qualities."

Junior Year

- Update and expand your Career Development Portfolio.
- Gain more job experience.
- Write and submit a major contract, outline your program, and apply for graduation.
- Join student organizations and professional organizations, and add to your network.
- Develop relationships with faculty, administrators, and other students.
- Identify a mentor or someone you can model to achieve your goals.
- Start to read the journal of your profession.
- Obtain an internship, or gain additional job experience.
- Update your journal with job tips and articles about your field.
- Update your resumé.
- Visit the career center on campus for help with your resumé, internships, and job opportunities.

Senior Year

- Refine your Career Development Portfolio.
- Put your job search into high gear. Go to the career center for advice.
- Read recruitment materials. Schedule interviews with companies.
- Update and polish your resumé and print copies. Write cover letters.
- Actively network! Keep a list of contacts and their telephone numbers, e-mails, etc.
- Join professional organizations and attend conferences.
- Start sending out resumés and attending job fairs.
- Find a mentor to help you with your job search and career planning.
- Meet with an evaluator or advisor to review graduation requirements.
- Log interviews in your journal or notebook.

After you have identified your purpose, determine the best way to show your portfolio to others. This, too, may depend on your school's or profession's expectations. You may be required to develop a digital portfolio rather than a physical one—or both. When developing a physical copy of your portfolio, make sure to print copies on high-quality, durable paper.

Elements of Your Portfolio

As mentioned, if you need to submit your portfolio to your school for review or evaluation, you probably have to follow established guidelines. If not, the following sections describe elements that apply to most portfolios.

TITLE, OR COVER, PAGE

You may need to include a title page with the title of your document, your name, the name of the college, and the date. See **Figure 14.2** for an example. You can also put your own logo or artwork on the cover to make it unique.

CONTENTS PAGE

On the contents page, list the sections of the portfolio. You can make a draft when you start your portfolio, but it will be the last item you finish, so that the page numbers and titles are correct. See **Figure 14.2** for an example of a contents page.

INTRODUCTION

In the introduction, discuss the purpose of your portfolio and the goals you are trying to achieve with its development. See **Figure 14.3** for an example of an introduction page.

Sample Title Page	Sample Contents Page
CAREER DEVELOPMENT PORTFOLIO Kim Anderson Louis College April 30, 2014	**CONTENTS** Introduction — 1 List of Significant Life Experiences — 2 Analysis of Accomplishments — 3 Inventory of Skills and Competencies — 5 Inventory of Personal Qualities — 6 Documentation — 7 Work Philosophy and Goals — 9 Resumé — 11 Samples of Work — 13 Summary of Transcripts — 17 Credentials, Certificates, Workshops — 18 Experience — 25 Bibliography — 27

Figure 14.2

Career Development Portfolio Elements

The presentation of your Career Development Portfolio reflects your personality and makes a valuable first impression. *What elements could be modified to better reflect your field of study?*

No #'s

Figure 14.3
Sample Introduction Page

The introduction highlights the goals of the portfolio. *How might this person use her portfolio during her job hunt?*

> ### INTRODUCTION
>
> My Career Development Portfolio reflects many hours of introspection and documentation. I recently made a career change and would like to pursue further opportunities in the marketing field. Thus, I plan to obtain my Bachelor's degree in Business Administration at Louis College. My career goal is to eventually become a store manager or a regional marketing director for a large retail department store. *the purpose for this portfolio is to get a job.*

LIST OF SIGNIFICANT LIFE EXPERIENCES

The next section of your portfolio is a year-by-year account of your significant life experiences (turning points). It is a chronological record, or time line. Resources to consult include family members, friends, photo albums, and journals. Include experiences that are important because you

- Found the experience enjoyable (or painful)
- Learned something new about yourself
- Achieved something you value
- Received recognition
- Expended considerable time, energy, or money

This section can also be written as an autobiography. It can include

- Graduation and formal education
- Jobs/promotions
- Marriage/divorce and other events in your family
- Special projects
- Volunteer work
- Training and workshops
- Self-study or reentry into college
- Extensive travel
- Hobbies and crafts
- Military service

ANALYSIS OF ACCOMPLISHMENTS

Once you have completed your list of significant life experiences, you are ready to identify and describe what you learned and how you learned it. Specifically, what have you learned in terms of knowledge, skills, competencies, and values and how can you demonstrate the learning? When possible, include evidence or a measurement of the learning. Review your list of significant experiences, looking for patterns, themes, or trends. Did these experiences

- Help you make decisions?
- Help you clarify and set goals?
- Help you learn something new?

> "When your work speaks for itself, don't interrupt."
>
> **HENRY KAISER**
> *Industrialist*

- Broaden your view of life?
- Accept diversity in people?
- Help you take responsibility?
- Increase your confidence and self-esteem?
- Result in self-understanding?
- Change your attitude? Your values?

INVENTORY OF SKILLS AND COMPETENCIES

Use your completed Career Development Portfolio worksheets, inventories from the career center, and activities in this text to record your skills and competencies. Your college may also provide a list of specific courses, competencies, or categories. You can also use SCANS as a guide. (See **Figure 14.4**.) Complete **Personal Evaluation Notebook 14.2** on page 444 to determine your transferable skills.

Also, as you take each college course, determine which skills you are learning in the classroom may translate to job skills. For example, long-term budgeting goals learned in a personal finance course can be helpful in managing project budgets on the job. Keep a list of these courses and skills.

INVENTORY OF PERSONAL QUALITIES

SCANS lists important personal qualities for success in the workplace: responsibility, a positive attitude, dependability, self-esteem, sociability, integrity, and self-control. Your personal qualities will set you apart from others in the workplace. In **Personal Evaluation Notebook 14.3** on page 445, use critical thinking to explore ways you've demonstrated your personal qualities.

DOCUMENTATION

For your Career Development Portfolio, document each of the SCANS skills, competencies, and personal qualities. Indicate how and when you learned each. Write the names of people who can vouch that you have these skills, competencies, and personal qualities. Include letters of support and recommendation. These letters can be from your employer, co-workers and community members, and clients or customers expressing their appreciation. Your skills and competencies may have been learned in college, vocational training programs, community service, on-the-job training, or travel.

Basic Skills: reading, writing, listening, speaking, and math

Thinking Skills: critical thinking, creative problem solving, knowing how to learn, reasoning, and mental visualization

Personal Qualities: responsibility, positive attitude, dependability, self-esteem, sociability, integrity, and self-management

Interpersonal Skills: teaches others, team member, leadership, works well with diverse groups, and serves clients and customers

Information: acquires, evaluates, organizes, maintains, and uses technology

Systems: understands, monitors, corrects, designs, and improves systems

Resources: allocates time, money, material, people, and space

Technology: selects, applies, maintains, and troubleshoots

Figure 14.4
SCANS Skills

Acquiring these skills and competencies will help you succeed throughout your career. *Which of these skills do you need to develop?*

Personal Evaluation Notebook

14.2

Transferable Skills

1. What transferable skills do you have? (See page 437 for ideas.)

   _____

   _____

2. What specific content skills do you have that indicate a specialized knowledge or ability, such as plumbing, computer programming, or cooking?

   _____

   _____

3. List your daily activities and determine the skills involved in each. Then consider what you like about the activities, such as the environment, interactions with others, or a certain emotional reaction—for example, "I like bike riding because I am outdoors with friends, and the exercise feels great."

Activity	Skills Involved	Factors
Bike riding	Balance, stamina, discipline	Being outdoors
_____	_____	_____
_____	_____	_____
_____	_____	_____
_____	_____	_____

WORK PHILOSOPHY AND GOALS

Your work philosophy is a statement about how you approach work. It can also include changes you believe are important in your career field. For example, the following statement defines one student's educational goals: "My immediate educational goal is to graduate with a certificate in fashion design. In 5 years, I plan to earn a college degree in business with an emphasis in marketing." The following examples illustrate career goals:

- To hold a leadership role in fashion design
- To upgrade my skills
- To belong to at least one professional organization

Expand on your short-term, medium-range, and long-term goals. Include a mission statement and career objectives. (Recall the discussion of creating a mission statement in Chapter 1. See also **Figure 14.5** on page 446.) You may also write your goals according to the roles you perform. What do you hope to accomplish in each area of your life? Consider the following questions:

- Do I want to improve my skills?
- Do I want to change careers or jobs?
- Do I want to become more competent in my present job or earn a promotion?

Personal Evaluation Notebook

Inventory of Personal Qualities

Indicate how you have learned and demonstrated each of the SCANS qualities. Next indicate how you would demonstrate them to an employer. Add personal qualities you think are important. Use additional pages if needed.

1. Responsibility: _____

   _____

   _____

2. Positive attitude: _____

   _____

   _____

3. Dependability: _____

   _____

   _____

4. Self-esteem: _____

   _____

   _____

5. Sociability: _____

   _____

   _____

6. Integrity: _____

   _____

   _____

7. Self-control: _____

   _____

   _____

- Do I want to spend more time in one or more areas of my life?
- Do I want to learn a new hobby or explore areas of interest?
- Do I want to become more involved in community service?
- Do I want to improve my personal qualities?
- Do I want to improve my human relations skills?
- Do I want to spend more time with my family?

Return to Chapter 3 and review Personal Evaluation Notebook 3.3: Looking Ahead. Reflect on what you wrote, and update it. How has it changed in just a few

Figure 14.5

Sample Mission Statement

As discussed in Chapter 1, a mission statement reveals your aspirations, states your philosophy on work and life, and reflects your highest values. *What other types of information can your mission statement reveal?*

Mission Statement: Anna Marcos

My mission is to use my talent in fashion design to create beauty and art. As a women's clothing designer, I want to influence the future development of fashion for women of all ages. I seek opportunities to learn more about how fashion affects confidence and self-esteem and how that can be reflected in affordable clothing lines. I strive to enjoy healthy and supportive personal relationships, collaborative and creative teams at work, and community involvement that promotes empowerment and success for women of all socioeconomic classes.

Long-Term Goals
Career goals: I want to own my own fashion design company.
Educational goals: I want to teach and lead workshops.
Family goals: I want to be a supportive parent.
Community goals: I want to belong to different community organizations.
Financial goals: I want to earn enough money to live comfortably and provide my family with the basic needs and more.

Medium-Range Goals
Career goals: I want to be a manager of a fashion company.
Educational goals: I want to earn a college degree in business and marketing.

Short-Term Goals
Career goals: I want to obtain an entry-level job in fashion design.
Educational goals: I want to earn a certificate in fashion design.

---

weeks? Make it a habit to reflect on what you are learning in class and connect it to work and life. How are these experiences changing the way you see yourself, others, and the world? How are they changing your values, interests, and goals? When you finish college, record these questions in your portfolio and update it often.

RESUMÉ

The purpose of a resumé is to show your strengths, accomplishments, and skills and their connections to an employer's needs. Your resumé is almost always the first contact an employer will have with you because most companies initially screen potential candidates through online applications. You want it to stand out, highlight your skills and competencies, look professional, and, ideally, fit on one page. Several online services can help you format your resumé, design it to fit the needs of specific professions, link it to hiring companies, and allow you to create your own home page. Also, resumé classes may be offered in the career center. See **Figure 14.6** on page 447 for a sample resumé.

Even if you aren't actively looking for a job right now, it's good practice to have at least a draft resumé in your portfolio to build on. This will make creating a polished version an easier task. Although your resumé's final format and content may depend on the preferences of your prospective employers or career field, you will most likely include the following components:

1. **Personal information.** Include your name, address, phone number, and e-mail address. If you have a temporary or school address, also include a permanent address. Don't include marital status, height, weight, health, interests, a picture, or hobbies unless they are relevant to the job. Keep your resumé simple.

CAITLYN J. JENSEN

1423 10th Street
Arlin, Minnesota 52561
(320) 555-2896
cjjensen@att.net

JOB OBJECTIVE: To obtain an entry-level position as a travel agent

WORK EXPERIENCE
University Travel Agency, Arlin, Minnesota
Tour Guide, August 2012–present
- Arrange tours to historic sites in a four-state area. Responsibilities include contacting rail and bus carriers, arranging for local guides at each site, making hotel and restaurant reservations, and providing historical information about points of interest.

- Develop tours for holidays and special events. Responsibilities include event planning, ticketing, and coordination of travel and event schedules.

- Specialized tour planning resulted in 24 percent increase in tour revenues over the preceding year.

Arlin Area Convention Center
Intern Tourist Coordinator, December 2008–June 2012
- Established initial contact with prospective speakers, coordinated schedules, and finalized all arrangements. Set up database of tours.

- Organized receptions for groups up to 250, including reserving meeting rooms, contacting caterers, finalizing menus, and preparing seating charts.

EDUCATION
Arlin Community College, Arlin, Minnesota
    Associate of Arts in Business, June 2013
    Magna Cum Laude graduate

Cross Pointe Career School, Arlin, Minnesota
    Certificate in Tourism, June 2011

HONORS AND AWARDS
Academic Dean's List
Recipient of Arlin Rotary Scholarship, 2011

COLLEGE AND COMMUNITY ACTIVITIES
Vice President, Tourist Club, 2012–2013
Co-chaired 2012 home-tour fundraising event for Big Sisters

PROFESSIONAL MEMBERSHIP
Arlin Area Convention and Visitors Bureau

REFERENCES
Available upon request.

Figure 14.6
Sample Resumé

An effective resumé should be clear, concise, and eye-catching to create the best possible first impression. *What is the most important element of your resumé?*

2. **Job objective.** Include a job objective if you will accept only a specific job. You may be willing to accept various jobs in a company, especially if you're a new graduate with little experience. If you decide not to list a job objective, use your cover letter to relate your resumé to the specific job for which you are applying.

3. **Work experience.** List the title of your last job first, dates worked, and a brief description of your duties. Don't clutter your resumé with needless detail or irrelevant jobs. You can elaborate on specific duties in your cover letter and in the interview.

4. **Educational background.** List your highest degree first, school attended, dates, and major field of study. Include educational experience that may be relevant to the job, such as certification, licensing, advanced training, intensive seminars, and summer study programs. Don't list individual classes on your resumé. Your cover letter can mention any classes that relate directly to the job you are applying for.

5. **Honors and awards.** List honors and awards that are related to the job or indicate excellence. In addition, you may want to list other qualifications related to the job, such as fluency in another language.

6. **College and community activities.** List activities that show leadership abilities and willingness to contribute.

7. **Professional memberships and activities.** List professional memberships, speeches, or research projects connected with your profession.

8. **References.** Gather three to five references, including employment, academic, and character references. Ask instructors for a general letter before you leave their last class or soon after. (If you receive an actual letter versus an e-mail attachment, scan the letter and create a digital file to submit to future employers.) Fellow members of professional associations, club advisors, a coach, and students who have worked with you on projects can also provide good character references. See **Figure 14.7** for a sample request for a recommendation. Ask your supervisor for a letter before you leave a job. Be sure to ask your references for permission to use their names and contact

Figure 14.7
Request for a Letter of Recommendation

Instructors, advisors, coaches, and previous employers are ideal candidates to ask for a letter of recommendation. *Whom might you ask to write a letter of recommendation?*

May 2, 2014

Eva Atkins
Chair of the Fashion Department
Green Briar Business Institute
100 North Bank Street
Glenwood, New Hampshire 03827

Dear Professor Atkins:

I was a student of yours last term in Fashion Design and earned an A in your class. I am currently assembling my Career Development Portfolio so I can apply for summer positions in the fashion business. Would you please write a letter of recommendation addressing the following skills and competencies?

- My positive attitude and enthusiasm
- My ability to work with diverse people in teams
- My computer and technical skills
- My skills in design and art

I have also included my resumé, which highlights my experience, my GPA, and selected classes. If it is convenient, I would like to stop by your office next week and pick up your signed letter of recommendation or please feel free to send a file to my e-mail address provided below. Your advice and counsel have meant so much to me over the last three years. You have served as an instructor, an advisor, and a mentor. Thank you again for all your help and support. Please call or e-mail me if you have questions.

Sincerely,
Susan Sanchos
Susan Sanchos
242 Cherry Lane
Glenwood, New Hampshire 03827
Home phone: (304) 555-8293
e-mail: susans@edu.glow.com

information. Don't print your references on the bottom of your resumé. It's best to include "References available upon request" and list them on a separate sheet of paper. Provide that list only if asked to do so. You may not want your references to be called until you have an interview. Include letters of recommendation in your Career Development Portfolio.

SAMPLES OF WORK

Think of how you can visually demonstrate your expertise in your field. Work samples can include articles, portions of a book, artwork, fashion sketches, drawings, photos of work, poetry, pictures, food demonstrations, brochures, job descriptions, and performance reviews. Include samples of flyers or digital samples of music or media projects on DVD.

SUMMARY OF TRANSCRIPTS

Include a copy of all transcripts of college work.

CREDENTIALS, CERTIFICATES, AND WORKSHOPS

Include a copy of credentials and certificates. List workshops, seminars, training sessions, conferences, continuing education courses, and other examples of lifelong learning.

EXPERIENCE

Include internships, leadership experiences in clubs and sports, volunteer work, service to the community, and travel experiences related to your goals. You can also include awards, honors, and certificates of recognition.

BIBLIOGRAPHY

Include a bibliography of books you have read that pertain to your major, career goals, or occupation. Consider annotating those that you found most helpful and why.

PORTFOLIO COVER LETTER

If you are submitting your portfolio for review, include a cover letter that indicates the purpose of the submission (such as to prove previous experiences or college credit), a list of the documents enclosed, a brief review, and a request for a response (such as an interview or acceptance). See **Figure 14.8** on page 450 for an example of a portfolio cover letter.

Overcome the Barriers to Portfolio Development

The biggest barrier to portfolio development is procrastination. The idea of a portfolio may sound good, but you also think of these excuses:

- It's a lot of work and I don't have the time.
- I wouldn't know where to start.
- I'll do it when I'm ready for a job.
- I don't have enough work samples.

Take 3 minutes to draft (or update) your resumé:
- What employment experiences and responsibilities should you list?
- List your education history and GPA (if exemplary).
- Which honors and related activities should you include? Every few weeks, return to your resumé and flesh it out further, updating it with new experiences.

What else can you do in 3 minutes?
- Call the career center to find out what resources it offers in your field of study.
- Contact local businesses to see if they offer internship opportunities.
- Make a list of people who could give you a letter of recommendation.

Take 3

Figure 14.8
Portfolio Cover Letter

Because your portfolio showcases your variety of experiences, your cover letter should pinpoint the reason you are presenting it for review at this time. *What are some possible reasons for submitting your portfolio for review?*

737 Grandview Avenue
Euclid, Ohio 43322

October 2, 2014

Dr. Kathryn Keys
Director of Assessment of Prior Learning
Louis College
333 West Street
Columbus, Ohio 43082

Dear Dr. Keys:

I am submitting my portfolio for credit for prior learning. I am applying for credit for the following courses:

Marketing 201   Retail Marketing
Management 180   Introduction to Management
Business Writing 100   Introduction to Business Writing

I completed my portfolio while taking the course Special Topics 350. My experiences are detailed in the portfolio and I believe they qualify me for six units of college credit. I look forward to meeting you to discuss this further. I will call your office next week to arrange an appointment. If you have questions, please contact me at (202) 555-5556 or kanderson@att.net.

Sincerely,
Kim Anderson
Kim Anderson

A Career Development Portfolio is an ongoing process. It takes time to develop your work philosophy, goals, documentation of skills and competencies, and work samples. If you are resisting or procrastinating, work with a partner or study group. Together you can organize supplies, brainstorm ideas, review each other's philosophies and goals, and assemble the contents.

Planning the Job Hunt

As discussed earlier in this chapter, many resources are available when you begin your search for a job: the career center and career counselor, instructors, mentors, and alumni. Also, numerous Internet sites match employers with future employees. Most major employers list their job openings on their websites. Review job descriptions posted by potential employers to see what types of jobs they often have available and what types of qualifications they are looking for. This can also help you determine if you need to redesign or enhance your portfolio to fulfill certain requirements.

There is no set time to do certain activities. Even so, whether you are a 2-year, 4-year, or transfer student, you will want to put your job search in high gear during your senior or final year.

Submitting a Cover Letter

A cover letter is a written introduction; it should state what job you are applying for and what you can contribute to the company. Find out to whom you should address your cover letter. Often, a call to the personnel office will yield the correct name and title. Express enthusiasm, and highlight how your education, skills, and experience relate to the job and will benefit the company.

Submit your cover letter along with your resumé and, if applicable, parts of your portfolio. (Because most job applications or letters of inquiry are submitted via company websites, follow their guidelines regarding submission of your application, resumé, or sample materials.) Follow up with a phone call in a week or two to verify that your resumé was received. Ask if additional information is needed and when a decision will be made.

As you develop your portfolio, include good examples of helpful cover letters. See **Figure 14.9** for a sample cover letter.

Interviewing

The resumé and cover letter open the door, but the job interview is when you can clearly articulate why you are the best person for the job. Many of the tips discussed in this text about verbal and nonverbal communication skills will be extremely important during your job interview. Here are some interview strategies for making full use of these and other skills:

1. **Be punctual.** A good first impression is important and can be lasting. If you arrive late, you have already said a great deal about yourself. Be sure you know the interview's time and location. Allow time for traffic and parking.

July 1, 2014

Dr. Sonia Murphy
North Clinic Health Care
2331 Terrace Street
Chicago, Illinois 69691

Dear Dr. Murphy:

Mr. David Leeland, Director of Internships for Bakers College, informed me of your advertisement for a medical assistant. I am interested in being considered for the position.

Your medical office has an excellent reputation, especially regarding health care for women. I have taken several courses in women's health and volunteer at the hospital in a women's health support group. I believe I can make a significant contribution to your office.

My work experiences and internship have provided valuable hands-on experience. I set up a new computer program for payroll in my internship position. In addition to excellent office skills, I also have clinical experience and people skills. I speak Spanish and have used it often in my volunteer work in hospitals.

I have paid for most of my college education through scholarships and work-study. My grades are excellent, and I have been on the dean's list in my medical and health classes. I have also completed advanced computer and office procedures classes.

I will call you on Tuesday, July 22, to make sure you received this letter and to find out when you might be able to arrange an interview. Thank you for your consideration.

Sincerely,

Julia Andrews

Julia Andrews
242 Cherry Lane
Chicago, Illinois 69692
Home phone: (304) 555-5593
e-mail: juliaa@edu.BakersC.com

Figure 14.9
Sample Cover Letter

A good cover letter captures the employer's attention (in a positive way) and shows how your qualifications connect to what is being sought for the position. *Whom might you ask to review your cover letter before you send it?*

The Hand Shake
In most cultures, a hand shake at the beginning and end of an interview is considered a sign of respect, enthusiasm, and confidence. Some people are not comfortable shaking hands because of shyness or hygiene concerns. However, career counselors say to initiate a firm hand shake (discreetly wiping sweaty palms beforehand if necessary). *Do you routinely shake hands with instructors or other acquaintances?*

2. **Be professional.** Know the interviewer's name and title, including the pronunciation of the interviewer's name. Don't sit down until the interviewer does. Never call anyone by his or her first name unless you are asked to.

3. **Dress appropriately.** In most situations, you will be safe if you wear clean, pressed, conservative business clothes in a neutral color. Your nails and hair should be clean, trimmed, and neat. Keep makeup light and wear little jewelry. Don't carry a large purse, a backpack, books, or a coat. Leave extra clothing in an outside office, and simply carry a pen, a pad of paper, and a small folder with extra copies of your resumé and references.

4. **Learn about the company.** The Internet makes researching employers easy, as most companies have a website, even if just for informational purposes. Be prepared and show that you know about the company. What product(s) does it make? How is it doing? What is the competition? Refer to the company when you give examples.

5. **Learn about the position.** Before you interview, request a job description from the personnel office. What kind of employee—and with what skills—is the company looking for? You will likely be asked why you are interested in the job. Be prepared to answer with a reference to the company.

6. **Relate your experience to the job.** Use every question as an opportunity to show how your skills relate to the job. Use examples from school, previous jobs, internships, volunteer work, leadership in clubs, and experiences growing up to indicate that you have the personal qualities, aptitudes, and skills needed at the new job.

7. **Be honest.** Although it is important to be confident and stress your strengths, honesty is equally important. Someone will verify your background, so do not exaggerate your accomplishments, grade point average, or experience.

8. **Focus on how you can benefit the company.** Don't ask about benefits, salary, or vacations until you are offered the job. During a first interview, try to show how you can contribute to the organization. Don't appear too eager to move up through the company or suggest you are more interested in gaining experience than in contributing to the company.

9. **Be poised and relaxed.** Avoid nervous habits, such as tapping your pencil, playing with your hair, or covering your mouth with your hand. Watch language such as *you know, ah,* and *stuff like that.* Don't smoke, chew gum, fidget, or bite your nails.

10. **Maintain comfortable eye contact.** Look the hiring manager in the eye and speak with confidence, interest, and sincerity.

11. **Turn off electronic devices.** Even if the interviewer needs to take a call during your interview, never answer your phone or read or respond to a text during your interview. Your focus should be on establishing a rapport with your interviewer.

12. **Practice interviewing.** Consider videotaping a mock interview. Most colleges offer this service through the career center or media department. Rehearse questions and be prepared to answer directly.

13. **Anticipate question types.** Expect open-ended questions, such as "What are your strengths?" "What are your weaknesses?" "Tell me about your best

Marketing "Me"

Practice for an interview by completing the following:

- My traits that help me be successful are

- I'm experienced in

- I'm knowledgeable about

- I'm capable of operating the following

- I can contribute to this company because

work experience," and "What are your career goals?" Decide in advance what information is pertinent and reveals your strengths—for example, "I learned to get along with a diverse group of people when I worked for the park service."

14. **Close the interview on a positive note.** Thank the interviewer for his or her time, shake hands, and say you are looking forward to hearing from him or her.

15. **Send a thank-you.** A follow-up thank-you is especially important. Surprisingly, few jobseekers actually send one. A thank-you note shows gratitude, and most employers think a person who appreciates an opportunity will appreciate the job. It reminds the interviewer about you and gives you a chance to reiterate your interest in the position and company and to add anything you forgot to mention previously. Send thank-you notes to every person involved in the interview: the hiring manager, administrative assistant, human resources personnel, and others who were especially helpful. If you are hand writing the letter, use nice stationery or a card and write neatly. If typing the note, include a legible signature at the bottom. If sending via e-mail, make sure your note stands out in some way, either by specifically mentioning a topic you discussed or by providing further research you have done since the conversation. Send the thank-you note no later than 1 day after your interview. See **Figure 14.10** on page 454 for a sample follow-up letter.

16. **Determine what's next.** Although you may be eager for a response, do not bombard the employer with e-mails and phone calls. Ask the human resources manager (or the hiring manager during the interview) how the company notifies candidates about the hiring process. Some organizations send a letter or e-mail that declines further interest, or others have so many interviews that, unfortunately, they do not call unless you are a selected candidate. The interview process can be lengthy, so it's wise to explore many potential opportunities.

● **If You Post It, It Will Come . . . Back to Haunt You**
Sites such as Facebook, Twitter, and LinkedIn are often reviewed by companies as they check the background of job candidates. What may seem as a harmless, humorous video on YouTube today may be the reason you are turned down for a job tomorrow. *Have you posted anything online that you would not want a potential employer to see?*

Figure 14.10
Sample Follow-Up Letter

A follow-up letter is another opportunity to set yourself apart from other job candidates. *What should you include in your follow-up letter?*

May 29, 2014

Mr. Henry Sanders
The Mountain View Store
10 Rock Lane
Alpine, Montana 79442

Dear Mr. Sanders:

Thank you for taking the time yesterday to meet with me concerning the position of sales representative. I enjoyed meeting you and your employees, learning more about your growing company, and touring your facilities. I was especially impressed with your new line of outdoor wear. It is easy to see why you lead the industry in sales.

I am even more excited about joining your sales team now that I have visited with you. I have the education, training, enthusiasm, and personal qualities necessary to succeed in business. I am confident I would fit in with your staff and make a real contribution to the sales team.

Thank you again for the interview and an enjoyable morning.

Sincerely,

John A. Bennett

John A. Bennett
124 East Buttermilk Lane
LaCrosse, Wisconsin 54601
Home phone: (608) 555-4958
e-mail: johnb@shast.edu

Take Charge of Your Career

If we learned anything from the economic downturn that hit the past decade, it's that few (if any) jobs are guaranteed. At some time in your career, possibly even now, you may find yourself suddenly out of work and needing new skills or experiences to make you an attractive job candidate. Also, when jobs are eliminated, the remaining employees must take on more work, along with responsibility for managing themselves and their work progress. Salary increases and advancement are based on performance and production, rather than seniority.

However, there are steps you can take concerning your education, planning, and assessment and documentation of skills that can keep you marketable and prepare you for whatever career opportunities come your way:

1. **Conduct a personal performance review.** Don't wait for your annual review to assess how you are achieving your goals, whether established by your boss or self-imposed. Map your performance and productivity each month. Continually ask yourself, "How have I added value to the company? What can I do to contribute?"

2. **Keep your portfolio and resumé up to date.** Add examples of successful assignments and team projects that you can use to demonstrate your skills and performance to your current or a potential employer. Every few months, check your resumé and update it with new personal information, education, and responsibilities. You never know when a good opportunity will arise and your resumé needs to be in someone's in-box immediately.

3. **Watch job trends.** Technology has affected and will continue to shape future job opportunities. How will it affect the field you are pursuing? Will you need more training? Is it opening up new kinds of jobs? Watch related

fields where growth is predicted. For example, government actions and the focus on clean energy and global environmental issues are expected to fuel the creation of "green" jobs (also known as green-collar jobs) in various industries. According to the Clean Edge research firm, by 2019, the global biofuels market, wind power, and solar energy will have expanded and may hit more than $100 billion in revenues in each area. Other trends in employment will result from demographic changes, such as growth in the elderly and very young populations (In 2007, the United States experienced the greatest baby boom to date.) Read the business section of the newspaper or the local business journal to see what trends and opportunities your community is experiencing.

After 10 years on the job, Christina just got laid off from her IT position, because her company decided to outsource the work overseas. She wouldn't say she "loved" the job, but it paid the bills and gave her flexible hours, which was important to her as a single mom of two young boys. Her sister, an instructor at a local university, is pushing her to go back to school at night to get an advanced degree, even though Christina just finished repaying her student loans.

- What pros and cons should she consider when making this decision?
- If she enrolls in school, should she get an advanced degree or pursue other careers she is interested in?
- How can she find out if her skills would transfer to other types of jobs?

THINK FAST

4. **Look over the horizon.** As the global economy grows and companies expand overseas, you may find exciting opportunities in other countries. If relocation is an option for you, consider what additional skills would be useful, such as the ability to speak and write in other languages and knowledge of other customs and cultures.

5. **Further your education.** See if your employer offers additional training in job skills or related topics, such as conflict resolution, diversity, team building, communication, or motivation. Does your employer provide tuition reimbursement if you take academic courses online or from a local college? Must the courses be directly tied to the job or advanced certification? Determine which degrees or certifications would make you a more knowledgeable professional and more valuable to an employer. See if related workshops or seminars are available locally or online.

An employee who learns new skills, cross-trains in various positions, and has excellent human relations skills will be sought after and promoted. Complete **Personal Evaluation Notebook 14.4** pages 456 and 457 to assess how your skills have improved during just the past few months.

6. **Keep networking.** Not only does networking help you land your first job, but also you'll attain many subsequent jobs based on whom you know. It is rare today for someone to spend 30 years at one company, which was commonplace just a few decades ago. As people change employers, they build substantial contacts at related companies. Your colleague who is leaving today for a higher position at another company may hire you away tomorrow. Get involved in professional organizations, and join online business sites that link you with other professionals in your field.

7. **Be your own "career coach."** The most important person you report to is the one you see in the mirror. Only you know what type of work keeps you motivated and makes you passionate about contributing day after day. This is *your* career and *your* life—only you can make the best of it by learning to endure the challenging times, overcoming setbacks, gaining valuable

> "It's easy to make a buck. It's a lot tougher to make a difference."
> TOM BROKAW
> *Journalist*

WORDS TO SUCCEED

Personal Evaluation Notebook

Assessment Is Lifelong

Read the following skills. Then rate your skill level on a scale of 1 to 5 (1 being poor and 5 being excellent). Refer back to **Personal Evaluation Notebook 1.2** in Chapter 1, and compare it with your answers here. Have you improved your skills and competencies?

Skills	Excellent		Satisfactory		Poor
	5	4	3	2	1
1. Reading			_____		
2. Writing			_____		
3. Speaking			_____		
4. Mathematics			_____		
5. Listening and note taking			_____		
6. Critical thinking and reasoning			_____		
7. Creative problem solving			_____		
8. Positive visualization			_____		
9. Knowing how you learn			_____		
10. Honesty and integrity			_____		
11. Positive attitude and motivation			_____		
12. Responsibility			_____		
13. Flexibility/ability to adapt to change			_____		
14. Self-management and emotional-control			_____		
15. Self-esteem and confidence			_____		
16. Time management			_____		
17. Money management			_____		
18. Management and leadership of people			_____		
19. Interpersonal and communication skills			_____		
20. Ability to work well with cultural diversity			_____		
21. Organization and evaluation of information			_____		
22. Understanding technology			_____		
23. Commitment and effort			_____		

(continued)

Personal Evaluation Notebook

Assessment Is Lifelong (*concluded*)

Assess your results. What are your strongest skills? What skills need the most improvement?

Do you have a better understanding of how you learned these skills and competencies? Do you know how to document and demonstrate them?

Following are six broad skill areas that can be transferred to many situations or jobs:

- Communication skills
- Human relations skills
- Organization, management, and leadership skills
- Technical and mechanical skills
- Innovation and creativity skills
- Research and planning skills

How would each of these skill areas relate to your major or career choice? What other skill areas might your major or career choice include?

knowledge, and being a better person from the experience. What Hsi-Tang Chih Tsang, renowned Zen master, said 1,200 years ago is still true: "Although gold dust is precious, when it gets in your eyes it obstructs your vision." If you focus on your values, positive personal qualities, and mission in life, you will attain whatever you deem precious—and will become a true peak performer.

TAKING CHARGE

Summary

In this chapter, I learned to

- **Explore potential majors and career paths.** To determine my major course of study, I consult with available resources, such as a career counselor, family, and friends; explore the college catalog; visit academic departments; and participate in classes, workshops, internships, and service learning opportunities.

- **Assess my values, interests, abilities, and skills.** Knowing my values helps me identify what I will value in a future career. I have certain interests that may lead me in one occupational direction. I have innate abilities that help me succeed in certain areas. I also have acquired transferable skills that apply to many different fields.

- **See the value of Career Development Portfolios.** My portfolio helps me assess, highlight, and demonstrate my strengths, skills, and competencies. Starting my portfolio early helps me get organized and gives me a chance to update, edit, and add to it throughout my college experience and into my career.

- **Organize essential elements.** Assembling my portfolio helps me collect and organize work samples, information, lists, examples, transcripts, credentials, certificates, workshop experiences, and documentation of personal qualities.

- **List significant life experiences and accomplishments.** I include such experiences as formal education, special classes and projects, volunteer work and service learning, jobs, travel, hobbies, military service, special recognition, and accomplishments and events that helped me learn new skills or something about myself or others. I list books I have read that pertain to my major or career or that have helped me develop a certain philosophy.

- **Document skills and competencies.** I connect essential skills to school and work, and I look for transferable skills. I document critical thinking, interpersonal, technology, financial, and basic skills related to school and job success. When appropriate, I include samples of my work.

- **Create an effective resumé.** My resumé is an essential document that helps me highlight my education, work experience, awards, professional memberships, and college and community activities.

- **Write a cover letter, and prepare for an interview.** My cover letter succinctly communicates my interest in and qualifications for a specific job. I prepare for an interview by researching the company and the job requirements and practicing responses to anticipated questions. I am on time for the interview, well groomed, and dressed appropriately. I focus on how I can contribute to the company, using personal examples and positive body language. I end the interview on a positive note, ask about follow up, and thank the hiring manager immediately in a letter.

- **Take charge of my career.** I realize that job opportunities are constantly changing, and I must be proactive by continually assessing my performance and abilities, keeping my portfolio and resumé up to date, and watching job trends for new opportunities and ways to improve my skills. I continue to cultivate personal contacts that benefit me personally and professionally, and I know only I can determine what's important to me in a career and life. I take the time to learn more about career opportunities, and I observe workplace trends, especially needs for additional education and training.

Performance Strategies

Following are the top 10 tips for planning a career:

- Determine what you value in life and a career.
- Know how to connect essential work skills and competencies to school and life and how to transfer skills.
- Assemble your portfolio, and frequently review, assess, and update it.
- Document skills, competencies, and personal qualities in your portfolio.
- Include essential elements in your portfolio, such as a resumé, transcripts, and a list of accomplishments.

- Value, document, and demonstrate service learning and volunteer work on campus and in the community.
- Use your portfolio to reflect on your work philosophy and life mission, as well as to set goals and priorities.
- Prepare for the job-hunting and interview process early.
- Be prepared for changes in job opportunities and expectations.
- Take personal responsibility for directing your career.

Tech for Success

Take advantage of the text's website at **www.mhhe.com/ferrett9e** for additional study aids, useful forms, and convenient and applicable resources.

- **Your resumé online.** Most potential employers prefer to receive your resumé and supporting documents by e-mail or online either via the company's website or an employment service. Programs and services are available to help you develop your portfolio online. Some include virtual space for storing digital files, such as graphic images, video, and PowerPoint presentations. Your school

may use its preferred source for developing a portfolio, so consult your advisor as you get started.

- **Job search websites.** Job search sites, such as monster.com, allow you to upload your resumé or create one using their format, which then feeds into their search engine. When you start your job hunt, it's worth investigating these and more specialized sites that cater to the field you are pursuing. Also, check out any professional organizations in the field, as they may also provide job listings online.

Study Team Notes

Career *in* focus

Steven Price
SOCIAL STUDIES TEACHER/LEGISLATOR

Related Majors: Education, Social Studies, Political Science

Career Planning Is Lifelong

Steven Price taught social studies at a high school. With an avid interest in politics, Steven soon developed a strong curriculum for teaching government and current affairs. He was well known in the district for his innovative classes in which students researched and debated local issues and then voted on them.

Throughout the years, Steven remained active in a local political party. Each year, he could be counted on to help hand out flyers and canvass neighborhoods before the September primaries and November elections. One year, a party member suggested that Steven run for state legislator.

Steven took the offer seriously. After 21 years of teaching, he felt ready for a change. He had enjoyed being in the classroom, especially when his students shared his passion for politics. However, he felt that, as a state legislator, he could more directly bring about changes in his community. He took a leave of absence from his teaching job. He filed the appropriate papers and worked hard with a campaign manager to get his name out to the voters in his district. Because Steven had maintained a Career Development Portfolio over the years, the manager was able to use the collected information to promote Steven.

Using his years of experience teaching government and current affairs, Steven felt rejuvenated and excited as he worked on his political campaign. His lifelong commitment to politics paid off when he won the election! He was glad he had taken the risk. The career change was a positive move for both Steven and his community.

CRITICAL THINKING What might have happened to Steven if he had not taken the risks of moving to a different career?

Peak Performer

PROFILE

Ursula Burns

As you contemplate any future career, it's important to consider what you value, what you enjoy doing, and how those important factors should play a role in your decisions. Ursula Burns, CEO of Xerox and the first African American woman to be named CEO of a Fortune 500 company, exemplifies someone who worked through that process to determine what career area to pursue.

Burns grew up on the Lower East Side of Manhattan in a low-income housing project where crime and poverty were rampant. Burns claims that, when she was a child, her mother's constant hard work and attitude kept her unaware of her family's poverty. Her mother, Olga, ran an at-home day care, took in ironing, and raised three children alone. As Burns says, "She gave us courage. She gave us will and love. I can still hear her telling me that where you are is not who you are."

This advice followed Burns throughout her long career. From a young age, she excelled in mathematics. When it came time for college, she went to the library to research top-paying jobs for people with math or science degrees. Acknowledging her strengths and interests, Burns ultimately decided to pursue a degree in mechanical engineering instead of other degrees her teachers thought she should consider. She attended the Polytechnic Institute of New York and earned her graduate degree from Columbia University.

Burns quickly worked her way up the corporate ladder, beginning as an engineering intern for Xerox

in 1980. Her work ethic and straightforward approach to business earned her respect in the company. In 2009, she was named CEO of the $17 billion corporation. *Forbes* magazine ranked her the 14th most powerful woman in the world, and she was named among *BusinessWeek*'s Top 20 Inspirational Leaders, placing her amid the likes of Bill Gates and former president Bill Clinton. She was chosen by President Barack Obama to help direct the national STEM program, which focuses on providing equal science, technology, engineering, and mathematics education to all students. Ultimately, Burns will not only make a tremendous impact on the performance of a multibillion-dollar company but also help shape the nation's curriculum and global leadership position in the fields of science and technology.

PERFORMANCE THINKING Which values and interests are important to you? How are they reflected in the job or career you are studying for? Do your strengths and personal qualities coincide with the skills and abilities needed for success in this career? Are there alternate career areas you should also explore? How does Ursula Burns's mother's advice, "Where you are is not who you are," apply to your life?

CHECK IT OUT Read *Bloomberg Businessweek*'s list of qualities possessed by inspirational leaders (**www.businessweek.com/managing/content/dec2009/ca20091217_472500.htm**). Keep track of your score as indicated in the directions. Are you acting as an inspirational leader? In what ways could you become more of a leader in your classes or school organizations?

Starting Today

At least one strategy I learned in this chapter that I plan to try right away is

_____

_____

_____

What changes must I make in order for this strategy to be most effective?

_____

_____

_____

_____

Review Questions

Based on what you have learned in this chapter, write your answers to the following questions:

1. Why is it important to determine your values during career planning?

_____

_____

2. Define *transferable skill* and give an example.

_____

_____

3. What is a purpose of a Career Development Portfolio?

_____

_____

4. Name at least four elements that should be included in a portfolio.

_____

_____

5. What information should be included in a resumé?

_____

_____

To test your understanding of the chapter's concepts, complete the chapter quiz at **www.mhhe.com/ferrett9e.**

Exploring Careers

In the Classroom

Maria Lewis likes making presentations, enjoys working with children, and is a crusader for equality and the environment. She also values family, home, and community. Making a lot of money is less important to her than making a difference and enjoying what she does. Now that her children are grown, she wants to complete a college degree. However, she is hesitant because she has been out of school for many years.

1. How would you help Maria with her decision?

_____

_____

2. What careers would you have Maria explore?

_____

_____

In the Workplace

Maria completed a degree in childhood development. She has been a caregiver at a children's day care center for 2 years. She enjoys her job but feels it is time for a change. If she wants to advance in her field, she has to travel and go into management. She wants more time off to spend with her family, write, and become more involved in community action groups. Maria would like to stay in a related field. She likes working with children but also enjoys giving presentations and workshops and writing. She has thought about consulting, writing, or starting her own small business.

3. What strategies in this chapter would help Maria with her career change?

_____

_____

4. What one habit would you recommend to Maria to help her plan her career?

_____

_____

Applying the ABC Method of Self-Management

In the Journal Entry on page 431, you were asked to write down one of the classes you are currently taking and list at least three skills you will acquire in this class that will benefit you in your career:

_____

_____

_____

Now think about a class you are taking that doesn't seem to relate directly to your career plans. Use the ABC Method to analyze what you are learning in that class and how it benefits you, either today or later on.

A = Actual event:

_____

_____

_____

B = Beliefs:

_____

_____

_____

C = Challenge:

_____

_____

_____

Use visualization to help you achieve the results you want. See yourself creating a portfolio that helps you organize the information you're learning and relate it to job success. Think of the confidence you'll have when you've developed a resumé and practiced for job interviews. See yourself focused with a vision and purpose and working in a job you love.

PRACTICE SELF-MANAGEMENT

For more examples of learning how to manage difficult situations, see the "Self-Management Workbook" section of the Online Learning Center website at **www.mhhe.com/ferrett9e.**

Checklist for Choosing a Major

Use the Adult Learning Cycle to explore majors and career opportunities.

RELATE

- What are the most important criteria for my future career, such as independence, high visibility, flexible hours, ability to work from home, and management opportunities?
- What is my personality type and/or temperament?
- Do the careers that fit my personality offer these features?
- What skills do I already have that would be useful or necessary?

OBSERVE

- Do I know anyone currently working in this field whom I could interview or talk to?
- Which instructors at my school would be most knowledgeable about the field? Who are the most approachable and available to advise me?
- What are the major professional organizations in this field? Have I explored their websites for additional information? Can I join these organizations as a student? Would it be worth the investment?
- Which courses should I be enrolled in now or next semester that will further introduce me to this area?
- I've visited the career center at my school and have talked with my advisor and/or a career counselor about:

REFLECT

- What positives am I hearing?
- What drawbacks am I hearing?
- What education and skills will be necessary for me to pursue this major and career?
- Are there related professions that seem appealing?

DO

- I've constructed a time line for gaining experience in this area that includes tasks such as
  1. Securing an internship; to be secured by
  2. Joining a student club; to be involved by
  3. Participating in related volunteer activities; to be accomplished by
  4. Getting a related part-time job; to be hired by
  5. Other:

TEACH

- I have relayed my impressions to my family and/or friends. Some of their questions/responses are
- I have talked with fellow students about their major and career search. Some tips I have learned from them are
- The most important resources I have found that I would recommend to others are

As of now, the major/career I would like to continue exploring is

REVIEW AND APPLICATIONS | CHAPTER 14

Preparing Your Resumé

To prepare for writing your resumé, start thinking about the information you will include. On the following lines, summarize your skills and qualifications, and match them to the requirements of the job you are seeking. Use proactive words and verbs. Here are some examples:

- *Organized* a group of after-school tutors for math and accounting courses
- *Wrote* and *published* articles for the school newspaper
- *Participated* in a student academic advisory board
- *Developed* a new accounting system
- *Managed* the petty cash accounts for the PTA
- *Created* PowerPoint presentations for a charity benefit

You should not be discouraged if you have only a few action phrases to write at this time. Add to your list as you continue your studies and become an active participant in school activities and with your courses of study.

SKILLS AND QUALIFICATIONS

1. _____

2. _____

3. _____

4. _____

5. _____

6. _____

7. _____

8. _____

9. _____

10. _____

REVIEW AND APPLICATIONS | CHAPTER 14

Informational Interview: What's the Job Like?

List the types of jobs you think you would like. Then list people you know in those types of jobs. Ask family, friends, neighbors, or instructors, or contact the alumni office or local Rotary or chamber of commerce to see if they can arrange an interview. The purpose of each interview is to find out about the person's career and what the job is really like. You will also be establishing a contact for the future. Remember to send a thank-you note after each interview.

Following is a list of potential questions to ask.

Person interviewed _____ Date _____

Job title _____ Contact e-mail _____

1. Why did you choose your career? _____

   _____

   _____

2. What do you do on a typical day? _____

   _____

   _____

3. What do you like best about your job? _____

   _____

   _____

4. What do you like least? _____

   _____

   _____

5. What classes, internships, jobs, certifications, or experiences do you wish you had explored when you were in college? _____

   _____

   _____

6. If you had to do it again, would you choose the same job? If not, what would you do differently? _____

   _____

   _____

7. What advice can you give me for planning my career? _____

   _____

   _____

REVIEW AND APPLICATIONS | CHAPTER 14

Informational Interview: Who Are You Looking For?

Make a list of the types of jobs you think you would like. Then list local companies that may hire for those kinds of positions. Check out their websites to see what types of positions are available and job descriptions, so that you understand their general responsibilities and qualifications. Find out who the hiring managers are (or if they have a human resources department). Contact this person to request an informational interview. Following is a list of potential questions to ask. (Remember to send a thank-you note after each interview.)

Person interviewed _____ Date _____

Job title _____ Contact e-mail _____

1. What specific skills and education do you want in a candidate for this position?

   _____

   _____

2. What two or three traits or qualities are very important in this position?

   _____

   _____

3. What are the difficult aspects of this position?

   _____

   _____

4. Are there areas of professional development in this position?

   _____

   _____

5. What is generally the beginning salary for this position?

   _____

   _____

6. What could I be doing right now that would make me more marketable for your company?

   _____

   _____

Exploring Careers

Go to the library or career center and find careers you've never heard of or are interested in exploring. Do the following exercises. Then add this page to your Career Development Portfolio.

1. Use the Internet to explore at least one career. List the career and skills, education, and abilities needed to be successful.

   _____

   _____

   _____

2. What is the long-term outlook for this career? Is it a growing field? How does technology impact it?

   _____

   _____

   _____

3. List your skills and interests. Then list the careers that match these skills and interests. Create names for careers if they are unusual.

Skills/Interests	Possible Careers
_____	_____
_____	_____
_____	_____

4. Review your list of skills and interests. What stands out? Do you like working with people or accomplishing tasks? Think of as many jobs as you can that relate to your skills and interests. Your skills and interests are valuable clues about your future career.

   _____

   _____

   _____

5. Describe an ideal career that involves the skills you most enjoy using. Include the location of this ideal career and the kinds of co-workers, customers, and employees you would encounter.

   _____

   _____

   _____

REVIEW AND APPLICATIONS | CHAPTER 14

Glossary

A

abilities Innate talents or gifts that can be enhanced through study and practice.

academic advisor An educational advisor who assists students in the development of meaningful educational plans compatible with the attainment of their life goals.

acronym A word formed from the first letter of a series of other words.

acrostic A made-up sentence in which the first letter of each word stands for something.

affirmation Positive self-talk or an internal thought that counters self-defeating thought patterns with positive, hopeful, or realistic thoughts.

anorexia nervosa An eating disorder that involves a pathological fear of weight gain leading to faulty eating patterns, malnutrition, and usually excessive weight loss.

assertive communication Expressing oneself in a direct and civil manner.

attentive listening A decision to be fully focused with the intent of understanding the speaker.

B

binge drinking Excessive consumption of alcohol within a short duration of time.

blogging Writing personal reflections and commentary on a website, often in a journal format and including hyperlinks to other sources.

body smart People who have physical and kinesthetic intelligence; have the ability to understand and control their bodies; and have tactical sensitivity, like movement, and handle objects skillfully.

bulimia nervosa An eating disorder that involves binge eating and purging through forced vomiting and/or the use of laxatives.

C

character Attributes or features that make up and distinguish an individual and are considered constant and relatively noncontroversial by most people.

cheating Using or providing unauthorized help.

chunking Breaking up long lists of information or numbers to make them easier to remember.

civility Interacting with others with respect, kindness, and good manners.

codependency A psychological condition or a relationship in which a person is controlled or manipulated by another who is affected by an addictive condition.

common ground

common ground A basis of mutual interest or similarities of core values.

communication Giving and receiving ideas, feelings, and information.

comprehension Understanding main ideas and details.

convergent thinking The ability to look at several unrelated items and bring order to them.

creators People who tend to be innovative, flexible, spontaneous, creative, and idealistic.

critical thinking A logical, rational, systematic thought process that is necessary to understand, analyze, and evaluate information in order to solve a problem or situation.

D

decision making Determining or selecting the best or most effective answer or solution.

decoding The process of breaking words into individual sounds.

deductive reasoning Drawing conclusions based on, going from the general to the specific.

depression An emotional state marked especially by sadness, inactivity, difficulty in thinking and concentration, a significant increase or decrease in appetite and time spent sleeping, feelings of dejection and hopelessness, and sometimes suicidal tendencies.

directors People who are dependable, self-directed, conscientious, efficient, decisive, and results-orientated.

discrimination Treating someone differently based on a characteristic.

divergent thinking The ability to break apart an idea into many different ideas.

diversity Differences in gender, race, age, ethnicity, sexual orientation, physical ability, learning styles and learning abilities, social and economic background, and religion.

E

emotional intelligence The ability to understand and manage oneself and relate effectively to others.

empathy Understanding and having compassion for others.

ethics The principles of conduct that govern a group or society.

evaluator A person in an advising center who performs degree checks and reviews transcripts and major contracts.

external locus of control The belief that success or failure is due to outside influences, such as fate, luck, or other people.

extrovert A person who is outgoing, social, optimistic, and often uncomfortable with being alone.

feeler A person who is sensitive to the concerns and feelings of others, values harmony, and dislikes creating conflict.

forgiveness Accepting that circumstances cannot be changed and letting go of resentment and anger for another person's actions or words.

formal outline A traditional outline that uses Roman numerals and capital letters to highlight main points.

habits Behaviors performed as a result of frequent repetition.

hardiness A personal characteristic that combines commitment, control, and challenge, giving one the courage and motivation to turn rough patches into opportunities for personal growth.

homophobia An irrational fear of gays and lesbians.

important priorities Essential tasks or activities that support a person's goals and that can be scheduled with some flexibility.

inductive reasoning Generalizing from specific concepts to broad principles.

inference Passing from one statement, judgment, or datum considered as true to another whose truth is based on that of the former.

informal outline A free form of outline that uses dashes and indenting to highlight main points.

integrity Firm adherence to a code of moral values.

interests Activities and subjects that cause you to feel comfortable, excited, enthusiastic, or passionate.

internal locus of control The belief that control over life is due to behavior choices, character, and effort.

Internet A vast network of computers connecting people and resources worldwide.

internship An advanced student or graduate program, usually in a professional field, that provides students with supervised practical experience.

interpreting Developing ideas and summarizing the material.

introvert A person who tends to like time alone, solitude, and reflection and prefers the world of ideas and thoughts.

intuitive People who are more comfortable with theories, abstraction, imagination, and speculation.

judgers People who prefer orderly, planned, and structured learning and working environments.

Learning and Study Strategies Inventory (LASSI) A self-assessment system that looks at attitude, interest, motivation, self-discipline, willingness to work hard, time management, anxiety, concentration, test strategies, and other study skills to gather information about learning and studying attitudes and practices.

logic smart People who have logical/mathematical intelligence; like numbers, puzzles, and logic; and have the ability to reason, solve problems, create hypotheses, and think in terms of cause and effect.

maturity The ability to control impulses, to think beyond the moment, and to consider how words and actions affect others.

memorization The transfer of information from short-term memory into long-term memory.

mentor A role model who takes a special interest in another's goals and personal and professional development.

mind map A visual, holistic form of note taking that starts with the main idea placed in the center of a page and branches out with subtopics through associations and patterns.

mindfulness The state of being totally in the moment and part of the process.

mission statement A written statement focusing on desired values, philosophies, and principles.

mnemonic A memory trick.

motivation An inner drive that moves a person to action.

multitasking Performing many tasks, jobs, or responsibilities simultaneously.

music smart People who have rhythm and melody intelligence; the ability to appreciate, perceive, and produce rhythms.

networking Exchanging information or services for the purpose of enriching individuals, groups, or institutions.

nontraditional students Students who do not go directly from high school to college, but return later in life.

note taking A method of creating order and arranging thoughts and materials to help a person retain information.

ongoing activities Necessary "maintenance" tasks that should be managed carefully, so that they don't take up too much time.

outdoor smart People who have environmental intelligence and are good at measuring, charting, and observing animals and plants.

paraphrase To restate another's ideas in your own words.

peak performer A person who is successful and desires to pursue a lifetime of learning.

people smart People who have interpersonal intelligence; like to talk and work with people, join groups, and solve problems as part of a team; and have the ability to work with and understand people, as well as to perceive and be responsive to the moods, intentions, and desires of other people.

perceiver A person who prefers flexibility and spontaneity and likes to allow life to unfold.

picture smart People who have spatial intelligence; like to draw, sketch, and visualize information; and have the ability to perceive in three-dimensional space and re-create various aspects of the visual world.

plagiarism To steal and pass off the ideas or words of another as one's own.

problem solving Creating or identifying potential answers or solutions to a question or problem.

procrastination Deliberately putting off tasks.

professional advisors Professional and peer staff who answer questions, help students register, and instruct students about deadlines and other important information.

R

racial profiling Using racial or ethnic characteristics to determine whether a person is likely to commit a particular type of crime or illegal act.

rapport The ability to find common ground with another person based on respect, empathy, and trust.

recall The transfer of information from long-term memory into short-term memory.

reflect To think about something in a purposeful way with the intention of creating new meaning.

reframing Choosing to see a situation in a new way.

resilient Able to recover from or adjust easily to misfortune or change.

retention The process of storing information.

S

self smart People who have interpersonal and inner intelligence and the ability to be contemplative, self-disciplined, and introspective.

self-assessment Recognition of the need to learn new tasks and subjects, relate more effectively with others, set goals, manage time and stress, and create a balanced and productive life.

self-esteem How you feel about yourself; sense of self worth.

self-management A thought process that involves techniques you can use to help you manage your thoughts and behaviors, remain focused, overcome obstacles, and succeed.

sensors People who learn best from their senses and feel comfortable with facts and concrete data.

sexism A belief or an attitude that one gender is inferior or less valuable.

sexting Exchanging sexually explicit material, often via cell phone.

skills Capabilities that have been learned and developed.

supporter A person who tends to be cooperative, honest, sensitive, warm, and understanding.

T

thinker A person who likes to analyze problems using facts and rational logic.

traditional student A student 18 to 25 years old, usually going from high school directly to college.

transferable skills Skills that can be used in a variety of careers.

trivial activities Nonessential activities that are completely discretionary and do not directly support a person's goals.

U–W

urgent priorities Tasks or activities that support a person's goals and must be accomplished by a specified date or time to avoid negative consequences.

values Worth or importance you attach to various factors in your life.

visualization The use of imagery to see goals clearly and envision engaging successfully in new, positive behavior.

website A collection of mechanisms used to locate, display, and access information available on the Internet.

wellness To live life fully with purpose, meaning, and vitality.

word smart People who have verbal/linguistic intelligence; like to read, talk, and write about information; and have the ability to argue, persuade, entertain, and teach with words.

Additional Credits

Credits

Image Researcher: Nancy Null

Interior Designer: Matthew Baldwin

Cover Designer: Matthew Baldwin

Photo Credits

Front Matter Page xxiii, © Sam Edwards/AGE Fotostock.

Chapter 1 Page 1: © Paul Bradbury/AGE Fotostock; p. 3: © Jon Feingersh/Blend Images LLC RF; p. 13(top): © Rubberball Productions RF; p. 13(bottom): © PhotoDisc/Getty Images RF; p. 16: © Getty Images/Digital Vision RF; p. 19(top): © BananaStock/Jupiter Images RF; p.19 (bottom): © Digital Vision/SuperStock RF; p.31: © Comstock/Getty Images RF; p. 34: © Royalty-Free/Corbis; p. 35: © Wire Image/Getty Images; p. 37: © Digital Vision RF.

Chapter 2 Page 43: © Fancy Photography/Veer RF; p. 45: © Roy McMahon/Corbis RF; p. 48: © Rubberball Productions RF; p. 51(both): © Rubberball Productions RF; p. 60: © Brian Snyder/Reuters/Corbis; p. 61: © Stockbyte/PunchStock RF; p. 66: © Jacobs Stock Photography/Getty Images RF; p. 67: © Kate Brooks; p. 69: © Ronnie Kaufman/Corbis.

Chapter 3 Page 75: © Eternity in an Instant/Getty Images RF; p. 77: © CORBIS – All Rights Reserved; p. 85: © McGraw-Hill Education RF; p. 86: © Getty Images/Digital Vision RF; p. 89: © Ingram Publishing/AGE Fotostock RF; p. 95: © E. Dygas/Getty Images RF; p. 100: © Ryan McVay/Getty Images RF; p. 101: © FilmMagic/Getty Images; p. 103: © Keith Brofsky/Getty Images RF.

Chapter 4 Page 113: © Goodshoot/Punchstock RF; p. 114: © BananaStock/Jupiter Images RF; p. 115: © Rubberball Productions RF; p. 119: © Digital Vision RF; p. 120: © Blend Images LLC/Ariel Skelley/Getty Images RF; p. 121: © Frederick Bass/Getty Images RF; p. 125: © PhotoAlto/SuperStock RF; p. 128: © Ryan McVay/Getty Images RF; p. 128: © McGraw-Hill Education. Mark A. Dierker, photographer; p. 133: © Rubberball/Getty Images RF; p. 135: © Ryan McVay/Getty Images RF; p. 138: © Royalty-Free/Corbis; p. 139: © JC Olivera/Getty Images Entertainment; p. 141: © Fancy/Alamy RF.

Chapter 5 Page 147: © Image Source/Getty Images RF; p. 161(top): © Valueline/PunchStock RF; p. 161(bottom): © Royalty-Free/Corbis; p. 166: © Ryan McVay/Getty Images RF; p. 167: © Steve Azzara/Corbis; p. 169: © Ryan McVay/Getty Images RF.

Chapter 6 Page 175: © Alejandro Rivera/Getty Images RF; p. 176: © Andersen Ross/Getty Images RF; p. 179: © BananaStock/Jupiter Images; p. 185: © PhotoDisc RF; p. 192: © Image Source/Getty Images RF; p. 195: © Hill Street Studios/Getty Images RF; p. 196: © Steve Cole/Getty Images RF; p. 200: © Blend Images LLC/Getty Images RF; p. 201: © Gary Fabiano/Pool/Corbis; p. 203: © Andrew Ward/Life File/Getty Images RF.

Chapter 7 Page 213: Glow Images RF; p. 217(left): © McGraw-Hill Education. Mark Dierker, photographer; p. 217(middle): © Gregor Schuster/Getty Images RF; p. 217(right): © McGraw-Hill Education. Gary He, photographer RF; p. 221: © image 100 Ltd RF; p. 224: © McGraw-Hill Education. Ken Cavanagh, photographer RF; p. 229: © Rubberball/Getty Images RF; p. 232: © Dex Image/Getty Images RF; p. 233: © Sonya Sones; p. 235: © Antonio Mo/Getty Images RF.

Chapter 8 Page 241: © Fancy Photography/Veer RF; p. 242: © PhotoDisc/PunchStock RF; p. 255: © image 100 Ltd RF; p. 258: © Digital Vision RF; p. 262: © Keith Brofsky/Getty Images RF; p. 263: © Corbis; p. 265: © PhotoDisc/Getty Images RF.

Chapter 9 Page 271: © Fancy/Photolibrary RF; p. 278: © Brand X Pictures/Jupiter Images/Getty Images RF; p. 285: © Jeff Maloney/Getty Images RF; p. 287: © BananaStock/PictureQuest RF; p. 294: © Ryan McVay/Getty Images RF; p. 295: © Marc Brasz/Corbis; p. 297: © Nasi Sakura/Purestock/SuperStock RF.

Chapter 10 Page 301: © Noel Hendrickson/Digital Vision/Getty Images RF; p. 306: © PhotoAlto/PunchStock RF; p. 311: © McGraw-Hill Education. Mark A. Dierker, photographer; p. 320: © image 100 Ltd RF; p. 324: © Chuck Savage/Corbis; p. 325: © Ben Margot/AP Photo; p. 327: © Keith Brofsky/Getty Images RF.

Chapter 11 Page 335: © Purestock/SuperStock RF; p. 337: © McGraw-Hill Education. Jill Braaten, photographer; p. 338: © PhotoDisc/Getty Images RF; p. 341: © Digital Vision RF; p. 344: © Royalty-Free/Corbis; p. 345: © Ingram Publishing/AGE Fotostock RF; p. 346: © PhotoDisc/PunchStock RF; p. 348: © Ingram Publishing RF; p. 350: © Digital Vision/Getty Images RF; p. 351: © Michael

474

Bodmann/Getty Images; p. 351: © Courtesy of the Heit Family, Boulder, CO; p. 353: © Thinkstock/Masterfile RF; p. 354: © BananaStock/PunchStock RF; p. 362: © Royalty-Free/Corbis; p. 363: © Doug Benc/Getty Images; p. 365: © Brand X Pictures/Getty Images RF.

Chapter 12 Page 371: © Fuse/Getty Images RF; p. 373: © Kristy-Anne Glubish/Design Pics; p. 375: © McGraw-Hill Education. Ken Karp, photographer; p. 377: © Blend Images LLC/Corbis RF; p. 385: © Darren Greenwood/Design Pics; p. 388: © Larry Williams/Corbis RF; p. 392: © Ingram Publishing RF; p. 398: © Tony Freeman/Photo Edit; p. 399: © James Leynse/Corbis; p. 401: © Jon Feingersh/Blend Images LLC RF.

Chapter 13 Page 407: © Ingram Publishing /AGE Fotostock RF; p. 409: © Image Source/Getty Images; p. 410: © DynamicGraphics/Jupiter Images RF; p. 412: © Brand X Pictures/PunchStock RF; p. 416: © Image Source/Javier Perini CM; p. 422: © Skip Nall/Getty Images RF; p. 423: © Courtesy Carson's Scholars Fund; p. 425: © Adam Crowley/Getty Images RF.

Chapter 14 Page 431: ©Jose Luis Pelaez Inc/Blend Images LLC RF; p. 452: © McGraw-Hill Education. Mark Dierker, photographer; p. 453(top): © Jack Hollingsworth/Getty Images RF; p. 453(bottom): © Getty Images/PhotoDisc RF; p. 460: © Doug Menuez/Getty Images RF; p. 461: © Ramin Talaie/Corbis; p. 463: © Royalty-Free/Corbis.

Features Guide

Index

Your School's Resources

Check your school's Web site, look through the catalog, or go to student services to determine which resources are available, especially those that are of particular interest to you and your needs. In the "Notes" section, include information such as location, office hours, fees, and so on. *These services are for you, so use them!*

Resource	Notes	Contact/phone/e-mail
Activities/Clubs Office		
Adult and Re-entry Center		
Advising Center		
Alumni Office		
Art Gallery/Museum		
Bookstore		
Career Center/Employment Services		
Chaplain/Religious Services		
Child Care Center		
Cinema/Theater		
Computer Lab(s)		
Continuing Education		
Disability Center (learning or physical disabilities)		
Distance Learning		
Financial Aid		
Health Clinic		
Honors Program		
Housing Center		
Information Center		
Intramural Sports		
Language Lab		

(continued)

Resource	Notes	Contact/phone/e-mail
Learning Center		
Library Services		
Lost and Found		
Math Lab		
Multicultural Center		
Off-Campus Housing and Services		
Ombudsman/Conflict Resolution		
Performing Arts Center		
Photography Lab		
Police/Campus Security		
Post Office/Delivery Services		
Printing/Copying Center		
Registration Office		
School Newspaper		
Student Government Office		
Study Abroad/Exchange		
Testing Center		
Tutorial Services		
Volunteer Services		
Wellness and Recreation Center/Gymnasium		
Work-Study Center		
Writing Lab		
Other:		
Other:		
Other:		